THE ART OF THE DESSERT

THE ART OF THE DESSERT

ANN AMERNICK *with* MARGIE LITMAN

PHOTOGRAPHY BY TARAN Z

BICENTENNIAL
1807
WILEY
2007
BICENTENNIAL

JOHN WILEY & SONS, INC.

Copyright © 2007 by Ann Amernick. All rights reserved
Photography © 2007 by Taran Z
Published by John Wiley & Sons, Inc., Hoboken, New Jersey
Published simultaneously in Canada
Wiley Bicentennial Logo: Richard J. Pacifico

Limit of Liability/Disclaimer of Warranty: While the publisher and the author have used their
best efforts in preparing this book, they make no representations or warranties with respect to
the accuracy or completeness of the contents of this book and specifically disclaim any implied
warranties of merchantability or fitness for a particular purpose. No warranty may be created or
extended by sales representatives or written sales materials. The advice and strategies contained
herein may not be suitable for your situation. You should consult with a professional where
appropriate. Neither the publisher nor the author shall be liable for any loss of profit or any
other commercial damages, including but not limited to special, incidental, consequential, or
other damages.

For general information about our other products and services, please contact our Customer
Care Department within the United States at (800) 762-2974, outside the United States at
(317) 572-3993 or fax (317) 572-4002.

Wiley also publishes its books in a variety of electronic formats. Some content that appears in
print may not be available in electronic books. For more information about Wiley products,
visit our web site at www.wiley.com.

INTERIOR AND COVER DESIGN BY DEBORAH KERNER DESIGN

Library of Congress Cataloging-in-Publication Data:

Amernick, Ann.
    The art of the dessert / Ann Amernick.
        p. cm.
    Includes index.
    ISBN 978-0-471-44381-0 (cloth)
    1. Desserts. I. Title.
    TX773.A417 2007
    641.8'6--dc22

                                    2005021359

Printed in the United States of America

10 9 8 7 6 5 4 3 2 1

For Jay

and Dan Amernick

CONTENTS

COLD DESSERTS 144

WARM DESSERTS 216

DESSERT SANDWICHES 278

ACKNOWLEDGMENTS

It's been said before and it still holds true, a book doesn't get written by itself. In the bakery, both at Wheaton and at Cleveland Park, where would I have been without Irene Borjas, Noris Pineda, Mal Krinn, Margie Litman, Noel Sanchez, Robert De Lapeyrouse, Julia Hastings-Black, Ariel Kennedy, Jarla and Bill Ulman, and Lydia Schlosser? To all working so hard and some without pay, my heartfelt thanks. An added thanks to Lydia Schlosser and Margie Litman, for their invaluable help with this book.

My gratitude to the upstairs staff at Palena—Denis Loli, Kelli Walbourne, Frederic Cabocel, and "Elvis"–Oudom Doumtakoum, and in the kitchen, Jonathan Copeland, Eric McKamey, Neil Wilson, Sarah McCarty, and Wilbur Barona. To Frank and Anne Ruta, my appreciation for giving me the experience of being part of Palena.

To the staff at Wiley: Pamela Chirls, my editor, and Ava Wilder, Rachel Bartlett, Christine DiComo, Christina Solazzo, and Jacqueline Beach. I will be eternally grateful for your patience and help on a long-overdue manuscript. To Deborah Kerner, the book's designer. To Deborah Krasner, my agent, and to Lisa Ekus, for their extended support and stamina for what seemed a never-ending project. To Taran Z, photographer of the gods, for her art.

To Marion and Harvey Mudd (my guardian angels), Leo and Beverly Bernstein, Norman and Diane Bernstein, Josh and Lisa Bernstein, Joel and Goldie Berg, Patrick Musel, the late Jean-Louis Palladin, Gerard Cabrol, George Lang, Richard Chirol, Diane Brounstein, Crystal Marcus August, Michael D. Rubin, Lilly Rubin, Susan Limb, Roland Mesnier, Berle Cherney, Phyllis Richman, Joan Nathan, Marian Burros, Lisa Yockelson, Cathy Sulzberger, Jonathan Schiller, Alice Medrich, Audrey Freed, Gale Gand, Geri Elias, Daniel Sriqui, Tony Cola, Debbie Benedek, Bethany Hitzelberger, and Shane Long, for help, support, and a guiding hand or a point in the right direction. I thank you.

And my gratitude to my family, for the loyalty and support of my mother and father, Helen Silverberg and the late Morris Silverberg, to Abby and Steve Lazinsky, David and Linda Silverberg, Alan and Sherry Silverberg, the late Beatrice Goldberg, and of course my sons, Jay and Dan Amernick.

INTRODUCTION

I have been fascinated by desserts, cakes, and pastries for as long as I can remember. My favorite childhood books were always the ones that had some mention of food, and the specific mention of a dessert in some of them still stands out in my memory. One of the very first jobs I had was working in a diner that my father had somehow inherited from a customer who had a business arrangement with him. It was the summer before I graduated from college, and I was supposed to be a waitress. Instead I gravitated toward the kitchen, where Maggie, a woman who had helped my mother around the house, was ensconced. She was a wonderful cook, and I loved watching her work and helping her, in between waiting on the counter.

Food and cooking continued to shape my adult life. In the spring of 1992, Clarkson Potter published my second book, *Special Desserts*. The first line of the introduction states, "In 1970, as the mother of two young sons, I went to Europe for the first time. And Paris changed my life." It really did. It drew me into the world of fine dining and, more specifically, desserts. In 1976, after having dabbled in private catering at home while the boys were little, I ended up working in the kitchen of the restaurant The Big Cheese, a wonderfully innovative eatery in Washington, D.C.'s Georgetown. I had actually planned to go back into the workforce via the educator route, having a bachelor of science degree in elementary education. But, instead, I chose the culinary path. I started out as a "salad girl" (what we were called then), working the 4:00 P.M.–to-midnight shift. I plated desserts as well as all the garde manger dishes, and it was a hoot! I loved the work, I was absolutely entranced by the restaurant scene, and I have never been able to stray from it for very long. The Cheese, as it was called, was a unique place—original, high quality, and known for years among young people starting out in the business as *the* place to work in D.C. After a year of plating salads and appetizers and making the desserts, I stepped back and made only desserts. The origins of some of the desserts in this book trace back to those early years. From then on through the 1980s, I worked in many restaurants. In 1988, I began working on my own, making wedding cakes, then stopping to co-author my first book, *Soufflés*, with Richard Chirol, who was the pastry chef after me at Jean-Louis at The Watergate. In 1992 *Special Desserts* was realized. The recipes were the culmination of my years as a pastry chef in the restaurants, bakeries, and catering companies where I had worked. That edition had problems, however, as it was illustrated with sweetly homey and quite lovely drawings that didn't convey the seriousness or intricacy of the recipes. Another issue was that the book was difficult to use, with readers having to go back and forth between cross-referenced recipes to assemble a cake. This book minimizes that problem, as all of the recipes needed for each master recipe appear together. This way, even though it might seem repetitious, it makes following a recipe so much easier. It has been a goal of mine for so long to make right what I felt was lacking in that second book.

From the time that I tried to make this book happen until it became a reality, years passed, and my life changed drastically, leading me back into the restaurant

world that I had left twelve years before. By 1996 it was a whole new generation of pastry "cheffing," and I stayed in restaurant kitchens for three years, until I had the opportunity to take over a small bakery in the suburbs of Maryland in 1999. Then, in the fall of 2000, my old friend Frank Ruta (from the days when we both worked at the White House) and I opened a new restaurant, Palena. Frank is the artist, and Palena is his canvas. The restaurant is the food of Frank's soul. That is the only way I can aptly describe it. I think that the restaurant is one of the best in the country. When the lease at the bakery in Maryland was up, we moved the bakery one and one half blocks down the street from Palena. It opened in February of 2001, just four months after the opening of Palena. The bakery supplied the desserts to the restaurant and sold cakes and cookies as well. I tried to make Palena's desserts follow Frank's cooking with grace and little fanfare. They reflected the simplicity and spirit that I felt defined Frank's art.

The bakery was an integral part of the restaurant's persona, being owned, as well, by Frank and me. We closed the bakery, gracefully but sadly, in December of 2004, a little more than five and a half years since its inception in the suburbs of Maryland. The bakery is well missed by all of us.

And it's because of this sense of wanting to keep the spirit of Palena and Amernick Bakery intact that I found myself with a much greater task in writing this book than I would have imagined. I have taken *Special Desserts* and *Soufflés,* many of the bakery desserts, restaurant desserts of the past, pastries and sweets created for catering, as well as their dressed-up counterparts at Palena and expanded the "repaired" *Special Desserts.* The desserts in this book have traveled far and have had many different transformations, starting at the diner where Maggie made her famous rice pudding.

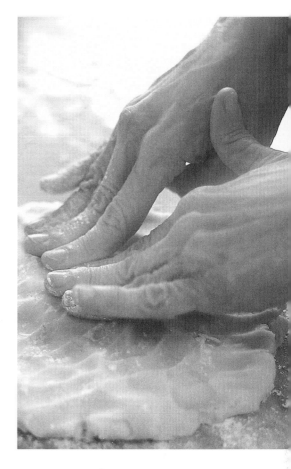

I have spent my life's career learning what I regard as the art of the pastry chef. And now I think my greatest challenge is to try to pass on what I have learned to people who love to bake, as well as to people who are new to this form of cooking. It would be the greatest thrill to know that someone has gleaned insights, techniques, and a novel way of creating pastry from something they read here. Let me help you use this book to make that happen.

THE ART OF THE DESSERT

MY TRUCS
OF THE TRADE

I N THIS CHAPTER, I HAVE TRIED TO IMPART FACTS, AS I KNOW THEM, ALONG
WITH MY OPINIONS, IN ORDER TO GIVE THE READER THE BENEFIT OF MY EXPE-
RIENCE OF OVER THIRTY-FOUR YEARS OF BAKING ON EVERY LEVEL. I HAVE BAKED
AT HOME, IN BAKERIES, HOTELS, RESTAURANTS, AND IN CATERING KITCHENS.
AND IN ALL THESE SETTINGS, THERE ARE BASIC SENSIBILITIES UPON WHICH THE
SUCCESS OF A RECIPE RESTS.

METHODS

MEASUREMENTS MY WAY

W ithout a doubt, in baking, the exact measurements of certain basic
ingredients, such as flour, eggs, sugar, butter, and leavening, are
crucial to the success of a recipe. My first ten years of baking were filled
with cup and tablespoon measurements. For the last twenty-five years,
however, I have mixed and matched ounces and grams with the occasional
cup measure. I understand that Americans don't like working in grams,
therefore I offer other choices here. But I would give anything if I could
persuade you to just try measuring your shelled eggs in grams! It will
require a gram-and-ounce scale, which is available in specialty kitchen-
ware stores and now even department stores, hardware stores, and, of
course, online. It wasn't until I started measuring this way that I was able
to achieve the same perfect results with my génoise on a continuing basis.

The size of eggs is so varied. Forget medium, large, and jumbo, the variation in a grade-A large egg is amazing. The standard of a large egg is 50 grams shelled. I have found eggs graded large that weighed 62 grams!

With some recipes, the difference won't hurt the taste, just change the texture. But with sponge cakes, it can make a huge difference in the quality of the dessert.

This is why I have included gram weights for eggs in the recipes. That said, you will note that I have included cup measures for eggs, as well as the approximate number of whole eggs you will need. The weight is the most important element here, not the quantity.

In my recipes, I always call for a weighed amount of chocolate, never a cup amount. And even though some chocolate comes in 1-ounce squares, high-quality chocolates are available in bulk, so the amount you use will need to be weighed out. A scale that calibrates in ounces as well as grams is essential.

Now, let's tackle the issue of dry measures versus wet measures. Use graduated nested sets of ¼, ⅓, ½, and 1 cup for measuring dry ingredients such as flour and sugar, or solids such as vegetable shortening. When measuring flour and other dry ingredients, I use the dip-and-level technique. I scoop the cup measure into the container of flour or sugar, and then level it off with the straight edge of a knife. Use this method for all the recipes in this book. Measure liquids in glass measuring cups with spouts and lines delineating the various quantities on the outside. Pour the liquid into the cup on a level work surface, then bend down and check the amount at eye level. You may also measure liquids in clear plastic cups that have measurement levels visible inside, making it unnecessary to check at eye level.

I like to use a large half-sheet or jelly-roll pan (18 X 13 inches) to collect my weighed and measured ingredients *mise en place* (which means "put in place" in French) before I prepare a recipe. But before I gather anything, the very first thing I do is preheat my oven (but only if I will be baking immediately or within an hour or two). Or if the oven is already on, I make sure the temperature is the one I want. (See Knowing Your Oven, pages 7–9, for more about ovens.) I keep in mind the temperature of the ingredients as I prepare the mise en place. In these recipes all the ingredients should be at room temperature unless specified otherwise. If an ingredient requires chilling, last-minute melting, or very hot water, I put a piece of paper in its place on the half-sheet or jelly-roll pan so there's no chance of omitting it because it's out of sight. You'd be surprised at how easy it is to leave something out of a recipe.

INGREDIENTS

I have always recommended using the best ingredients. Butter, chocolate, heavy cream, liqueurs—anything that you put in your baked goods should be top grade.

BUTTER. I always use 83 percent–milkfat butter. And I have worked hard to find it. It is fabulous butter that contains less water than other butters, ensuring a flakier puff pastry and more tender pastry dough. I have recently gone back to using a bit of vegetable shortening along with the butter in my pâte brisée, which has resulted in a much flakier pastry. I had gotten away from using shortening for many years and was amazed at the difference a bit of it makes.

CHOCOLATE. I have always used Callebaut and Valrhona chocolates and have just been reintroduced to Scharffen Berger chocolate, which is made in San Francisco. I was lucky enough to be given an in-depth tour of the factory, by Alice Medrich, who spent a day with me when I went to San Francisco. I felt lucky to have her expertise and guidance, and I learned so much from her in that one day. My Amernick Bakery used 60 to 70 percent chocolate. You won't find very many white chocolate recipes in this book because I've never really liked white chocolate the way I like milk and dark. I do, however, brush my baked pâte sucrée tartlet shells with white chocolate to keep them from becoming soggy once they have been filled. For this, I use Valrhona Ivoire.

COCOA. I use only unsweetened cocoa, either natural cocoa or, for certain recipes, Dutch-processed. Scharffen Berger's natural cocoa is excellent, especially in recipes that call for baking powder and baking soda. The chocolate flavor is so much better with natural cocoa—another tip from Alice Medrich. I have also found that the lower the fat content in cocoa, the higher a génoise will rise. For a chocolate génoise, I would use Droste cocoa, which is Dutch-processed, meaning that it is treated with a chemical alkali to make it less acidic, but it also has a lower fat content.

COCONUT. I use only dried unsweetened shredded or flaked coconut. I get great results by soaking dried coconut in whole milk, then wringing it out and adding confectioners' sugar to taste. I then spread it on a parchment-lined sheet pan and bake at 275°F for as long as it takes to toast to a golden brown. I set the timer for 5-minute intervals and mix the coconut with a spatula to ensure an even color. And the flavor of the milk is heavy with the essense of coconut, which is then used to flavor the coconut cup custards (see page 175).

COFFEE. My favorite is freshly ground beans, our Palena blend from Santa Lucia, freshly brewed for any recipe that calls for coffee. To make coffee extract, I use Medaglia d'Oro instant espresso with just a touch of Myers's dark rum. This makes a deeply flavorful extract that is pure coffee.

CREAM. I recommend using 40 percent–milkfat heavy cream. When a recipe calls for buttermilk, such as in the DeMayo Chocolate Cake recipe (page 70), use low-fat buttermilk.

EGGS. Use grade-A large. See Measurements My Way (page 1) for more information.

FLOUR. Bleached all-purpose and cake flours are used in the recipes. I have always liked Gold Medal All Purpose, Pillsbury 4X, and Swans Down Cake Flour, and use high-gluten flour for bread recipes. If given a choice, I like to use half Sir Lancelot (from King Arthur) and half All Trumps (from Gold Medal) for croissants.

FRUITS. I love fresh fruit almost more than anything, but I feel that if the quality of the fruit is iffy, the end result will be less than wonderful.

Whenever possible, and especially in the summer, I try to use only fresh fruits, particularly in my sorbets. But during the winter, when flavorful fruit is scarce in Washington, D.C., there doesn't seem to be much point in making sorbets with substandard fruit. And in spite of the influx of fruit from warmer climates, I haven't been happy. So I have come to depend on high-quality frozen purees consisting of 90 percent fruit and 10 percent sugar. But to tell you the truth, in the summer, when I go to the fruit stand to buy the most glorious fruit, it seems a sacrilege to crush the most fragrant red raspberries—I prefer to pile them on a memorable fruit plate with some cookies set to the side. And fresh fruit tarts are so beautiful and delectable when the fruit is perfect. Bananas, grapefruit, figs, melons, limes, lemons, oranges, tangerines, mangos, nectarines, apples, pears, cherries (my favorites are the Mount Rainier), raspberries, blueberries, blackberries, apricots, strawberries, pineapples, peaches, plums, grapes—

all of these fruits can be used as garnishes for the desserts here or substituted for the fruits listed in the recipes.

LIQUEURS. I use Grand Marnier, Myers's dark rum, Harvey's Bristol Cream sherry, Amaretto di Saronno liqueur, Hidalgo sherry, eau-de-vie framboise, eau-de-vie Pear William, Kirschwasser (kirsch), almond grappa, Armagnac, Mirabelle, and Calvados. I suggest using the best-quality liqueurs you can afford, as they will make all the difference.

NUTS. Purchase nuts raw and store them in the freezer in plastic freezer bags or in airtight containers to maintain their freshness. Nuts, especially hazelnuts, become rancid very quickly. Toast them as you need them.

SPICES. Use only the freshest spices, stored in a cool spot, and discard them after six months to one year, being vigilant especially in the warmer months. If a spice doesn't smell fragrant, it won't impart a good flavor to your baked product. Spices can also be purchased whole, and then ground with a Microplane grater when needed. I like to use whole nutmeg and grate it as needed.

VANILLA. I have tried them all, and I still prefer the bourbon bean from Madagascar. I find Tahitian vanilla just a little too flowery for my taste. I suggest that you try several kinds and decide which one you like best. I use vanilla beans and pure vanilla extract. Make sure it says "pure" on the label, as artificial vanilla is out of the question.

WATER. I use any kind of bottled water, either distilled, filtered, or spring water. In different parts of the country, water can have a lot of minerals that can impart an unpleasant taste to your creation.

In the end, go for the very best ingredients you can. It makes all the difference in the world!

KNOWING YOUR OVEN

When I began working at the White House, the very first words I heard were "Know your oven." The most basic tenet in baking is to know how your oven bakes, meaning whether it bakes fast or slow, if there are any hot spots, and how true the oven's temperature is. This means having a good oven thermometer. And always preheat your oven, which takes approximately fifteen minutes, when the recipe indicates. You will see that in all of the recipes, the "preheat the oven" wording is placed in the method in just the right place, so your oven will have enough time to heat to temperature. Incidentally, I have found that the longer the oven has been on, the faster something will bake. The difference in bake time at our bakery between morning baking, when the ovens were only on for an hour or so, and the afternoon or evening baking times was measurable. All the baking times in this book are an estimate. Your oven may bake a little more quickly or a little more slowly. And that is why

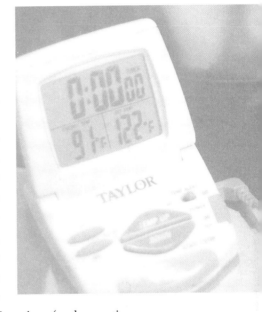

I have included not only the approximate baking time (and sometimes a range) but a visual doneness description as well. I suggest setting your timer for about five minutes less than the minimum suggested doneness time, then begin checking every five minutes or so after that until the item is done.

Here is an oven fact that seems to amaze a lot of the people. You will notice that in the book some cookies are baked at only 275°F, no higher. I use the same temperature for my sweet dough and pâte sucrée. It took me many years of baking to find that by lowering the oven temperature for these cookie and tart doughs, they turned out very tender and perfectly even-colored. Plus, they are far less likely to burn! I do not use this method for puff pastry, croissants, and Danish doughs, as these doughs require a full burst of heat in order to give them that big rise we look for, at least for the first fifteen minutes or so of baking. I then reduce the oven temperature to finish the baking. When baking puff pastry, I never weight down my puff. I feel that the reason it's called puff pastry is because it puffs! It

does this because of the many layers of butter folded into the flour that expand from the high heat of the oven. When puff has been properly rolled and folded, the lightness and crispness achieved is unmatched. I love to cut into it and hear the crisp shattering of the mille-feuille, which I do so prefer to the very compressed cardboard quality of some puff pastry.

I suppose here would be the place to mention kitchen timers. Any kind will do as long as it works. I have found the type you wear around your neck to be invaluable. If you have a tendency to wander a distance from a stationary timer, like I do, these rope timers are the best. You will always be able to hear the timer going off. Of course, you must remember to set the timer again for the second go-round, if required. An easily forgotten task!

I will never forget the heart-racing moment when I was making a dessert with puff pastry at the James Beard House in New York City. I had placed puff for about ninety people in the oven to warm it and forgot to reset the timer. When I realized that the puff was still in the oven and could have burned to a crisp, I literally jumped about a foot, scaring everyone in the kitchen. I raced over to the ovens and, luckily, because the temperature was so low, the puff was still perfect. A great example of why a lower temperature works so well and also why you want to use a timer!

Something else that I have found makes a difference is the rotation of baking pans in the oven. When recipes in this book instruct you to rotate the pans, it should be done both front to back and upper shelf to lower shelf. The ideal, of course, is to bake on only one shelf and not have two trays going at once. I find that two trays compete with each other for the heat. There are times, however, when it is simply easier to bake more than one pan at a time, so it is especially important that the pans be rotated.

I always wait, however, until cakes have set or "domed," meaning risen and rounded, and are well on the way to being browned, before opening the oven door, in order to prevent the cakes from collapsing.

INCORPORATING THE INGREDIENTS

The second thing that I remember being drummed into me when I worked at the White House was using the *lowest speed* for incorporating ingredients into cookie and pastry doughs. I never went above speed one on the mixer. The rationale is that beating at too high a speed creates air in the dough, causing it to rise and then deflate, making a tougher cookie or pastry. And I have found this to be true over and over again.

The other rule was always to finish mixing dough by hand. When a dough is mostly mixed, there is usually some unmixed ingredient at the bottom of the bowl of the electric mixer. Slow mixing in the mixer, then finishing the dough by hand using a plastic bowl scraper, allows you to get to the bottom of the bowl and mix everything together thoroughly without overbeating and toughening the dough.

Something that has come full circle for me is making pâte brisée completely by hand. I started out making it by hand, but with the acquisition of my KitchenAid mixer, I began to make the dough in the machine. Now I no longer use the electric mixer for this task, beloved though my KitchenAid and Hobart mixers are to me. I use an old-fashioned pastry blender to cut my butter and shortening into the flour, then mix the water in a little at a time. The dough, very crumbly and not seemingly mixed at all, is then spread with the heel of my hand across the table in the method known as *fraisage*. This helps to keep the dough tender, and I remain more in control of the process. Very satisfying!

Another tip I'd like to suggest is that you use heavy-duty gloves and wear long-sleeved clothing when making caramel sauce. I do this so that every part of my arm is covered, to protect me from the steam and spattering caramel.

I'd also like to share my method of preventing an ice-cream base from curdling: After I temper the eggs with the milk and cream, I do not give the mixture any more heat. I always make sure the milk-and-cream mixture has come to a boil and risen in the pot; it will then be hot enough to cook the eggs without adding more heat.

RECIPE YIELDS

Some of the subrecipes in the book make more than is needed for the dessert, so in many cases I have noted this in the recipe headnote. These recipes freeze beautifully, so you will find having a bit extra to be more than welcome for a last-minute dessert or cake. My recipes for tartlet shells also yield more shells than you will need, but I feel that it's always better to have a few more in case of breakage. Plus, it seems easier while you are in the middle of the task to make a few extra rather than having to start from scratch again the next time you need them. The baked shells freeze well, wrapped in plastic wrap or unbaked, still in their pans.

FREEZING

Where would we be without the freezer? When I worked at the White House, I learned that the freezer was our best resource. We produced thousands of mini pastries and petits fours for countless receptions. To keep them fresh, we would prepare them in advance and store them in huge walk-in freezers.

For President Reagan's seventieth birthday party, we prepared hundreds of sorbet scoops that had to be attached to ice sculptures fitted with batteries, so colored lights would be visible through the ice. It was my job on the day of the reception to affix the scoops of sorbet to the sculptures while working in the big blast freezer. On a rack next to the freezer were enormous coats that you had to put on before entering the twenty-degrees-below-zero freezer. Since I am only five feet one inch, the coat reached the floor. I think I must have been a sight to behold because people kept coming in to look and then leaving very quickly!

In the White House, we stored everything from prepared doughs to finished cookies in the freezer, to have on hand at a moment's notice. While at my bakery, we had very limited freezer space. But we held many of our tiny cookies there, placed in plastic bins and then wrapped in plastic. The key to successful freezing is wrapping items to be frozen very well, preferably in several layers of plastic wrap, which keeps freezer odors out. This odor occurs when an uncovered object comes in contact with the air in the freezer. At the bakery, I preferred to store freshly baked butter and almond cookies in the freezer because we baked in very large quantities. If the cookies had been left out at room temperature until the next day, much of their flavor would have been gone. When frozen and wrapped well until ready to be eaten, the cookies always tasted fresh and flavorful. We sold the cookies at room temperature, but I liked to wrap the filled boxes for our customers with plastic wrap and let them know that freezing the cookies was perfectly fine . . . if they had any left.

Many of the recipes in this book, with the exception of those containing gelatin, can be frozen, to be used at another time. Having extra components such as ganache and buttercream in the freezer can really come in handy when you need to put together a last-minute dessert. To be able to whip up a lemon buttercream torte with little advance notice is a breeze when your freezer holds the answer.

EQUIPMENT

MAINTAINING BAKING TOOLS

I have made a list of the tools that I think most home bakers will find useful. But before I go into the list, I would like to discuss one of the most important aspects of owning tools: their proper care and maintenance. Anyone who has worked in a commercial kitchen will tell you that the best way to hold onto your tools is to wash them yourself. If you send your things to the pot-washing station, they could be misplaced or—worse—thrown out. I always wash anything that I use, which includes all my spatulas, measuring devices, pastry tips, pastry cutters, or anything that has become part of my daily routine. Pastry tips, especially, can become bent and irreparably damaged if heavier objects are placed on top of them in the sink. I am also always careful of where I place the wire whisk attachment of my electric mixer. When I am finished with it, I make sure to set it on the side of the sink, not *in* the sink, where it can get damaged by a heavy pot. Since I started doing this, I have never had to replace a whisk because one of the wires broke off from the top. I've lost count of the times in the past when a loud clacking from the electric mixer let me know that yet another wire whisk had broken. The list that follows includes the tools that I've found essential.

BAIN-MARIE. See Double Boiler.

BLENDER. Invaluable for pureeing fruits in a finer manner than a food processor can. And great for that healthful early-morning smoothie!

BOWLS. Graduated sizes from 4 cups to 2 gallons in stainless steel and plastic. The larger bowls give you plenty of space to mix quantities that seem to outgrow a smaller bowl. I especially love a 2-gallon bowl for making my pâte brisée for tartlet shells. I also make copious use of plastic bowls of varying sizes for microwaving.

CAKE-DECORATING TURNTABLE. I like the very heavy-bottomed one by Ateco, which is available at cake-decorating stores and other specialty suppliers.

CAKE PANS. I use round aluminum cake pans in graduated sizes of 8 inches to 10 inches in diameter, with depths of 2 and 3 inches. For cakes such as the DeMayo and certain very fragile cakes, which do not lend themselves to being split horizontally, I always use shallower pans and bake each layer separately. Heavier cakes that will be layered or cakes that contain baking soda or baking powder—such as the Banana Cake (page 27), the Chocolate Marble Cake (page 50), or the DeMayo Chocolate Cake (page 70)—bake best in shallow pans. If all of the batter is baked in one deep pan instead of being spread out in several shallower ones, the cake will never finish baking in the center before it burns on the outside. The Almond Génoise (page 22) and the Chocolate Toffee Torte (page 57), however, fare well in one 3-inch-deep pan. I use 8-inch, 10-inch, and 12-

inch square pans, 13 X 9–inch pans, 8 X 4–inch and 9 X 5–inch loaf pans, and 18 X 13–inch half-sheet or jelly-roll pans. Half-sheet pans and jelly-roll pans can be used interchangeably in most cases.

COOLING RACKS. These are essential for resting hot cake pans and half-sheet or jelly-roll pans on, as they allow air to reach the bottoms of the pans. They come in various sizes and shapes, from a 9-inch round up to a 24 X 18–inch rectangle. I also use the racks, set inside or across the top of a half-sheet or jelly-roll pan, when glazing cakes. The cake sits on the rack, the glaze is poured over, and the extra glaze is caught in the pan below.

DOUBLE BOILER. I use a pot filled with hot water with a bowl set over it to warm something or to melt very large quantities of chocolate. To cool something down quickly, I nest two bowls and fill the slightly larger bottom one with ice. I call both of these techniques using a bain-marie, even though this is not exactly accurate, as a true bain-marie is a hot water bath.

ELECTRIC MIXER. I have always loved my KitchenAid mixers, from the seventies version to the new Artisan mixer. And it goes without saying that I cherish my 20- and 30-quart Hobarts from yesteryear. (Hobart manufactured KitchenAid mixers until a few years ago, when they were bought out.) These mixers come with paddle, whisk, and dough hook attachments. I also have a pastry blender that came with the 20-quart Hobart. The pastry blender is fashioned in such a way that it cuts the butter or shortening into the flour in half the time of the paddle attachment, which it resembles. If you have the opportunity to purchase one of these older models, jump on it. Early Hobarts are sought after on eBay and elsewhere because of their quality and longevity. They are workhorses without peer. These larger-size machines can mix doughs in ways that can cause the 5- and 6-quart machines to gasp. If you work in large quantity, they are invaluable. Commercial Hobarts are indestructible.

FOOD PROCESSOR. I find that the first Robot Coupe (I still have it!) ever made, the KitchenAid, Cuisinart, and Black and Decker food processors all work well. I have, in addition, a Sunbeam Oskar, which was the precursor of the small-size food processors, which grinds nuts beautifully.

MICROWAVE. For years, I resisted a microwave. Didn't have one, didn't want one. Now I wouldn't be without it. But it's important to use the microwave judiciously. You will need to "know your microwave" also. For melting chocolate and butter, as well as for soft-ening butter, buttercreams, ganaches, and glazes, the microwave has no peer. Some microwaves, however, are more powerful than others, so you can make costly errors if not careful. I always microwave for 10 seconds, stir, then microwave for 10 more seconds, and keep adjusting the time until my item is perfectly done. At the restaurant, I use the microwave to warm our fudge brownie and to heat Toll House cookies for a few seconds to soften the chocolate.

PAINT EDGERS AND TROWELS. I have a field day in hardware stores because I can find the greatest tools for various baking tasks. I use different-size trowels as templates for cutting puff pastry, Danish, pain au chocolate, and even for cutting uniform-size croissants. A 24-inch paint edger allows me to cut thinly rolled marzipan straight to use as plaques on birthday cakes. It's really like an enormous pastry scraper.

PARCHMENT PAPER. I like to use 24 X 18–inch sheets of parchment paper, but you can also use rolls, which are available at specialty kitchen-ware stores. The paper is treated so baked items won't stick and can be eas-ily removed.

PASTRY AND BOWL SCRAPERS. A pastry (bench) scraper is perfect for releasing a sticky dough from the work surface and for cleaning your work area of any residue. I like to use scrapers with the thinnest blades

I can find, but they are becoming harder to come by. For scraping bowls, I love the Matfer plastic scraper. It is super thin and slightly flexible, so you can really scrape every last bit of a batter and dough from the sides of bowls. They are available at J.B. Prince and some specialty kitchen supply stores.

PASTRY BAGS AND TIPS. I like 10-, 12-, and 16-inch bags made by Matfer. When using a pastry bag, it is best to fill it no more than two-thirds, because the fuller the bag is, the more difficult it is to pipe a mixture. I like the pastry tips from Ateco, either purchased separately to include ⅛-inch and up to ⅔-inch (4-mm to 15-mm) tips. There are also

handsome sets of plain and fluted tips at kitchen specialty stores. The recipes in the book give both the numbered sizes as well as the inch measurement. Wilton online offers a wonderful array of pastry and decorating tips (see Sources, page 333).

PASTRY BRUSHES. I use bristle brushes in various sizes. The largest-size brush, which measures 4 inches across, can be used to brush excess flour from dough and confectioners' sugar from rolled fondant. The thinner brushes are for brushing on an egg wash. When brushing pans with melted butter, I also like plastic brushes that have hooks at the top, so they can be hung on the edge of my bowl of melted butter.

PASTRY CUTTERS. I have a vast collection of cutters, but the most used are the graduated plain round ones, which range in size from ½ inch to 5 inches. I cut all my round tartlet doughs with these cutters, cutting the circles about ¼ inch larger than the pan diameter. I always wipe them off with a damp cloth and store them in the box they came in. No kitchen should be without these. They are available at most kitchenware stores.

PIZZA WHEEL CUTTER. A pizza wheel cutter is great for cutting puff pastry cleanly and sharply, as the sharper the cut, the higher the rise. If you use a dull knife to cut puff pastry, the sides of the puff get pressed together, which prevents the dough from achieving its full height.

POTS. I use *very* heavy stainless-steel pots with very thick bases for caramel, pâtes des fruits, custards, pastry cream, and the like. I have three or four Dansk pots, which I bought years ago, that range in size from 5½ quarts to 14 quarts and that I use for caramel and larger quantities of ganache. This brand can still be found, but I have noticed that they aren't as heavy duty as the early ones. Nonetheless, there are a number of very good, heavy-duty pots and other pieces of cookware available today. Most kitchenware stores have a sizeable array to choose from. As a rule of thumb, it's best to buy a pot that will hold at least three times the quantity you will be using it for, as you need to account for the possible boiling up of cream in various recipes.

ROLLING PIN. My preference is a big heavy, wooden ball-bearing pin with handles.

SCALE. As I mention in Measurements My Way (page 1), I highly recommend a digital scale that calibrates in ounces and grams. Terraillon, Salter, and Polder are all excellent.

SCISSORS. A large pair of scissors is great for cutting parchment paper, the ribbons that edge my fondant-cloaked cakes, and for cookie boxes that are wrapped as gifts. I even use scissors to trim the edge of a piecrust with ease. And I love a tiny sharp pair of scissors for cutting off the tip of a paper decorating cone (cornet).

STRAINERS. I like a stainless-steel metal China cap, which is conical shaped and medium size, with holes that are not too fine, as opposed to a chinois, which has a flexible mesh area for the strainer. I always use plastic-edged stainless-steel strainers for straining citrus. Remember that acids react with aluminum and produce a metallic aftertaste. Most China caps are stainless, but many chinois are aluminum mesh, so be careful. I especially like to use these for straining crème anglaise, pastry cream, and ice-cream bases.

TART AND TARTLET PANS. I use shiny metal 4-inch plain-edged tartlet pans for sweet dough tartlets and flute-edged pans for the desserts that use pâte brisée. I call for a 10-inch-round, 1-inch-high fluted tart pan with a removable bottom for the Orange Frangipane Tart (page 119). When baking some types of doughs in tart pans, I use a technique called blind baking. To do this, I lay a piece of aluminum foil over the dough, dull side up, pressing it in gently to conform to the pan shape, then fill it with uncooked rice or dried beans. The rice and beans can be reused, so store them in an airtight container and label the container. The weight of the rice or beans keeps the dough in place in the tart shell and prevents it from puffing up or sagging. The dough is baked for most of the oven baking time, then the rice or beans are removed for the last 2 minutes, or until the shells brown. Sweet pastry dough does not need to be blind baked. The egg and yolk in the dough seem to give it stability that helps it hold its shape. Chilling dough-lined tart (or tartlet) pans for at least 1 hour before being baked is critical because it helps the dough keep its shape. Twenty-four hours is even better. I have frozen unbaked dough-lined tart pans for one week or longer.

TIMER. It's crucial to set a timer when something is in the oven. I've even taken to setting a timer when I'm cooking something on the stovetop for very long periods, such as candied grapefruit peel, 25-minute intervals then 15-minute intervals, just to keep what I'm doing in mind. See more discussion of the timer on page 8.

THERMOMETER. For stovetop cooking, I like to use a probe thermometer, which is a combination timer-thermometer with a probe that can be put into a pot. Polder is my favorite brand, as it even has a magnet that can be attached to a metal surface near the stove. A beeper goes off when the desired temperature, which can range from 32°F to 392°F, is reached. I especially like it for custards and sugar syrups. A candy thermometer can also be used. For oven-temperature accuracy, an oven thermometer is critical. Thermometers are available at specialty cookware stores and even good hardware stores.

TORCH. I use a butane-heated torch to heat bowls on my electric mixer. When butter is being mixed with sugar, but it feels a little too cold to beat properly, a little heat from a torch along the base of the outside of the bowl warms the butter just enough to soften it, so it can be creamed nicely.

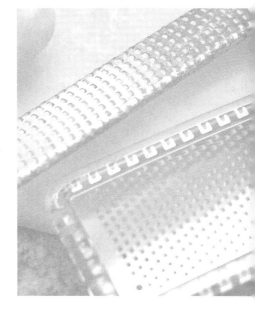

VEGETABLE PEELER. I still like the old-fashioned swivel peeler, but I prefer the ones I bought years ago. Somehow they seem sharper and hold their edge better. Estate sales are a good source for them. If you are buying a new one, the U-shaped peeler works well. I use this to peel apples, pears, and oranges.

ZESTER. What more can be said about the Microplane zesters that have cropped up in recent years? The citrus zester is scraped across the fruit in one direction, making it a cinch to get the essence of the peel without the bitter pith. What once was a tedious task has been transformed into a kitchen job that is almost fun. The graters come in various shapes, and the size of the grate ranges from large to very fine, making it ideal for citrus and hard cheeses. A box grater comes in handy for grating almond paste.

CAKES AND TORTES

f all the desserts I make, cakes and tortes are the nearest and dearest to my heart. When I was a child, these were the dessert sweets that fascinated me the most. I still have books from my childhood that contain pictures of cakes, as well as descriptions of fudge cakes, cream cakes, and layer cakes that thrilled me beyond words. When I started in the food business, I made cakes for weddings and other special occasions. I loved filling and decorating them, and when I look over this chapter, I can still picture those cherished images from my childhood books.

This chapter is chock-full of the cakes that were influenced by ones I read about as a child, and many reflect changes that have been made over time. Here you will also find new cakes I have always thought about making—Chocolate Viennese Cake, Chocolate Marble Cake, Banana Cake, Lemon Buttercream Torte—all cakes that make me happy, and I hope they will inspire you as well.

APRICOT ORANGE TORTE

SERVES 10 TO 12

Hints of Grand Marnier and fresh orange permeate the delicate, airy layers of this sponge cake. My inspiration for infusing a classic egg-yolk buttercream with orange marmalade, apricots, and Grand Marnier comes from the late and much-revered Julia Child. Her method of cooking down dried apricots with wine into a delicious paste is one that I love, as the paste adds a wonderfully intense flavor to the buttercream. In the génoise recipe, you can always substitute a plain génoise for the almond génoise, if you like, in order to make this cake nut free. For the apricot glaze, choose apricot preserves where apricots—not sugar— are listed as the first ingredient, which indicates good quality.

SPECIAL EQUIPMENT: CANDY THERMOMETER • PASTRY BAG FITTED WITH A STAR TIP (ATECO #24)

ALMOND GÉNOISE

YIELD: THREE 8 X 2-INCH ROUND CAKE
LAYERS

1½ cups (180 grams) cake flour

7 large eggs (350 grams or 1½ cups)

1¼ cups sugar

½ cup (4 ounces) almond paste, grated on the largest holes of a box grater

PREPARATION. Position racks in the middle and lower third of the oven and preheat the oven to 350°F. Butter three 8 X 2–inch round cake pans.

MAKE THE GÉNOISE. Sift the flour onto parchment or waxed paper; set aside. Place the eggs and sugar in the bowl of an electric mixer. Place the bowl containing the egg mixture over a larger bowl that contains enough hot water to come at least 2 inches up the side of the bowl. Whisk the mixture by hand until the sugar has dissolved and the eggs are warm and dark yellow, about 3 minutes.

Place the bowl with the egg mixture in the mixer fitted with the whisk attachment and beat on high speed until the mixture triples in volume and the bowl feels cool to the touch, about 5 minutes. Reduce the mixer speed to low and add the almond paste 1 tablespoon at a time. The batter will deflate, but that's okay. Beat on low for an additional minute. Don't worry if the batter doesn't look smooth. The almond paste will remain in clumps and not become fully incorporated into the batter.

With the mixer still on low, add the flour to the egg mixture in a quick and steady stream, using the parchment paper to funnel it in and turning off the mixer while the flour is still visible. Remove the bowl from the mixer and use a rubber spatula to finish folding in the flour, being

22 | THE ART OF THE DESSERT

sure to scrape the batter from the bottom of the bowl and fold over the top.

Divide the batter evenly among the prepared pans. Bake for 15 to 20 minutes, or until the tops are light brown and the cakes pull away slightly from the sides of the pans. Let the cakes cool in their pans on cooling racks for 10 minutes, then invert onto racks to cool completely. Wrap the cakes in plastic wrap and refrigerate for several hours, up to 24, before assembling. They can also be frozen. To defrost, keep them at room temperature for 2 hours.

MAKE THE MARMALADE. Proceed to the apricot paste recipe if using store-bought orange marmalade. Otherwise, use a vegetable peeler to remove the colorful outer skin of the oranges, leaving the bitter white pith. Then use a small paring knife to cut away the pith, and discard. Chop the orange flesh and thinly slice the peel. Combine the sugar, orange flesh and peel, and lemon juice in a nonreactive large saucepan and bring to a boil, stirring constantly. Reduce the heat to very low and simmer, stirring frequently and skimming off the scum as it accumulates, until the juices have thickened and the marmalade is clear, at least 1 hour. Spoon the marmalade into a bowl and refrigerate until cold. The marmalade will keep for at least 1 month in the refrigerator.

MAKE THE APRICOT PASTE. Place the apricots in a medium saucepan with the wine. Bring to a boil over medium heat, then lower heat, cover, and cook 5 minutes. Set aside for about 15 minutes, then add the marmalade, orange zest, lemon juice, and cinnamon to the saucepan. Cook the mixture over low heat, stirring constantly, until it forms a thick paste, about 5 minutes. Spoon into a bowl and cool, then cover and refrigerate until ready to use.

ORANGE MARMALADE

YIELD: ABOUT 3 CUPS

3¾ pounds navel oranges, peeled and chopped (about 6 cups); approximately 12 oranges

1½ cups sugar

1 lemon, quartered and juiced

or

1 (12-ounce) jar orange marmalade

◆ TO ENHANCE THE FLAVOR, I LIKE TO FILL A CHEESECLOTH BAG WITH JASMINE TEA LEAVES AND ADD IT TO THE ORANGE MARMALADE AS IT SIMMERS.

APRICOT PASTE

YIELD: 2 CUPS

12 ounces dried apricots, chopped

1 cup dry white wine or vermouth

½ cup Orange Marmalade

1 teaspoon finely grated orange zest

3 tablespoons freshly squeezed lemon juice

½ teaspoon ground cinnamon

EGG-YOLK BUTTERCREAM

YIELD: 4 CUPS

½ cup sugar

¼ cup water

12 large egg yolks (240 grams or 1 cup)

1 pound (4 sticks) unsalted butter,
  at room temperature

PREPARATION. Have ready a pastry brush
  and cup of cold water.

◆ IF A BUTTERCREAM APPEARS
BROKEN (ROUGH LOOKING OR WITH
DROPS OF MOISTURE SHOWING),
PLACE THE BOWL IN A LARGER BOWL
OF HOT WATER FOR 10 SECONDS AND
THEN WHIP WITH A WHISK. USUALLY
A BUTTERCREAM BREAKS BECAUSE
THERE IS EITHER TOO MUCH LIQUID
TO BUTTER OR IT'S TOO COLD.
HEATING IT BRIEFLY MAY BE ALL IT
NEEDS. IF IT STILL APPEARS BROKEN,
WHISK IN SOME ROOM-TEMPERATURE
BUTTER (USUALLY ONLY 2 TO 3
TABLESPOONS ARE NEEDED), 1
TABLESPOON AT A TIME, UNTIL THE
BUTTERCREAM COMES TOGETHER
AND BECOMES SMOOTH AND SILKY.

MAKE THE EGG-YOLK BUTTERCREAM. Combine the sugar and water in a small saucepan and stir to mix well. Place the saucepan over high heat and bring to a boil, stirring to dissolve the sugar. Wash away any sugar from the sides of the pan with the pastry brush dipped in water. Do not stir the syrup after it boils.

Meanwhile, beat the egg yolks on low speed in the bowl of an electric mixer fitted with the whisk attachment until light and pale yellow, about 5 minutes. The yolks should reach this point at the same time that the sugar syrup reaches the firm-ball stage (242°F on a candy thermometer). Immediately pour the syrup into the egg yolks in a thin, steady stream down the inside of the bowl to prevent spattering. Increase the speed to medium high and continue to beat until the yolks are at room temperature, about 15 minutes. If the outside of the bowl has cooled to room temperature, the yolks are done. Reduce the speed to medium low and add the butter several tablespoons at a time, beating until all the butter has been incorporated and scraping down the side of the bowl if necessary.

ORANGE APRICOT BUTTERCREAM

YIELD: 4½ CUPS

3 cups Egg-Yolk Buttercream

1 cup Apricot Paste

1 cup Orange Marmalade

¼ cup Grand Marnier

1 tablespoon finely grated orange zest
  (from about 1 large orange)

MAKE THE ORANGE APRICOT BUTTERCREAM. Combine the buttercream, apricot paste, orange marmalade, Grand Marnier, and orange zest in a large bowl and whisk until combined.

MAKE THE APRICOT GLAZE. Use the back of a spoon or a rubber spatula to press the preserves through a strainer set over a small saucepan. Add the Grand Marnier and cook over medium heat, stirring often, until slightly thickened, about 2 minutes. The glaze can be kept warm over low heat, stirring occasionally, for up to 30 minutes. Or cool the glaze to room temperature and store covered in the refrigerator for up to 3 weeks. When ready to use, reheat to boiling and use immediately.

APRICOT GLAZE

YIELD: 1 CUP

1 (12-ounce) jar apricot preserves
¼ cup Grand Marnier

ASSEMBLE THE CAKE. Combine the orange juice and Grand Marnier in a small bowl. Set aside.

Place 1 génoise layer on a cake plate or cardboard cake round. Brush with about one-third of the orange juice mixture. Use an offset metal spatula to spread about ¾ cup marmalade over the layer, then top with ⅔ cup buttercream. Place the second génoise layer on top of the buttercream, pressing down gently. Repeat with the orange juice mixture, marmalade, and buttercream. Top with the last génoise layer and brush with the remaining juice mixture. Use the spatula to smooth out the filling around the side of the cake. Refrigerate the cake for 20 minutes to set the buttercream.

Spread the remaining buttercream over the top and side of the cake. For a final decoration, swirl the buttercream, using a pastry bag fitted with a star tip (Ateco #24) to create a slightly raised scalloped edge. Refrigerate the cake for at least 3 hours or up to 24 hours, well covered.

Warm the apricot glaze and pour it into the center of the cake, allowing it to run up to the scalloped edge. Make sure the glaze is just tepid—not hot—or it will melt the buttercream.

ASSEMBLY

1 cup freshly squeezed orange juice
2 tablespoons Grand Marnier
3 Almond Génoise layers
1½ cups Orange Marmalade
4½ cups Orange Apricot Buttercream
1 cup Apricot Glaze

CITRUS SORBET

YIELD: 1 QUART

2 cups freshly squeezed and strained
Valencia or navel orange juice

2 cups freshly squeezed and strained
grapefruit juice

2 tablespoons Grand Marnier

1½ cups sugar, or more to taste

This very rich cake is perfect served as is. But for a special presentation, I like to serve each slice along with a scoop of simple, refreshing citrus sorbet.

SPECIAL EQUIPMENT: ICE-CREAM MAKER

MAKE THE SORBET. Combine all the ingredients in a large bowl. Taste the mixture to ensure that it is sweet enough. If the fruit is not very sweet, more sugar may need to be added. Too little sugar will cause the sorbet to harden and not have the proper consistency. Keep in mind that some of the sweetness will be lost during freezing, so make the sorbet a little sweeter than you think necessary. Make sure the sugar is dissolved, then transfer the mixture to an ice-cream maker and freeze according to manufacturer's instructions.

BANANA CAKE
WITH BANANA ICE CREAM

SERVES 8

I have experimented with many banana-cake and banana-bread recipes, but I particularly like this one for its intense banana flavor and subtle sweetness. I developed it after researching recipes in several vintage cookbooks, then altered the ingredients a bit to get a lighter cake. It's a wonderfully versatile cake. Instead of preparing it in loaf pans, you can bake it in individual muffin cups, then split them and fill with fruit and pastry cream for delightful individual banana trifles. Or try what we have done here and sandwich banana ice cream between cake slices for a lovely, satisfying dessert.

SPECIAL EQUIPMENT: ICE-CREAM MAKER

MAKE THE ICE-CREAM BASE. Combine the milk and cream in a heavy nonreactive medium saucepan. Use the back of a knife to scrape the seeds from the vanilla bean and add the seeds and pod to the saucepan. Bring to a rolling boil over medium-high heat. Let the mixture rise up the side of the pan, then immediately remove from the heat.

Meanwhile, beat the egg yolks with the sugar on high speed in the bowl of an electric mixer fitted with the whisk attachment until very thick and pale, about 5 minutes. The mixture will triple in volume and hold its shape when dropped from the whisk. It should be very stiff.

Bring the bowl over to the saucepan. Whisk about 1 cup of the hot cream mixture into the yolk mixture to temper it, then pour the mixture back into the saucepan and whisk until thoroughly combined. The mixture should be thick enough to coat a wooden spoon. (Run your finger through the custard on the back of the spoon. The custard is thick enough if the line remains.) Pour the custard through a fine-mesh strainer or China cap into a large bowl. Place in an ice bath or refrigerate until chilled, stirring occasionally.

ICE-CREAM BASE
YIELD: 1 QUART

2 cups milk

2 cups heavy cream

1 vanilla bean, split lengthwise

11 to 12 large egg yolks
    (225 grams or 1 cup)

1¼ cups sugar

BANANA ICE CREAM

YIELD: 1 QUART

1 quart Ice-Cream Base

1¾ cups mashed very ripe bananas

½ cup sour cream

1 tablespoon dark rum, such as Myers's

½ cup sugar, or to taste

MAKE THE BANANA ICE CREAM. Place the ice-cream base, bananas, sour cream, and rum in a large bowl. Mix well. Add enough sugar to sweeten the mixture, depending on the sweetness of the bananas. Add more sugar than seems necessary, as some of the sweetness will be lost during freezing. Transfer the mixture to an ice-cream maker and freeze according to manufacturer's instructions.

BANANA CAKE

YIELD: TWO 8½ x 4½-INCH LOAVES. YOU WILL NEED ONLY ONE LOAF FOR THE SANDWICHES, BUT THE CAKE IS SO EASY TO MAKE AND SO DELICIOUS THAT IT MAKES SENSE TO MAKE TWO LOAVES AND THEN FREEZE ONE FOR LATER USE.

2 cups (240 grams) cake flour

2 teaspoons baking soda

4 ounces (1 stick) unsalted butter,
   at room temperature

⅔ cup sugar

2 large eggs (100 grams or
   ½ liquid cup)

2 teaspoons vanilla extract

1½ cups mashed ripe bananas

¼ cup sour cream

¼ cup dark rum, such as Myers's

PREPARATION. Preheat the oven to 350°F. Butter two 8½ x 4½-inch loaf pans and line all sides of the pans with parchment paper.

MAKE THE CAKE. Sift the flour and baking soda into a bowl and set aside.

Cream the butter and sugar in the bowl of an electric mixer fitted with the paddle attachment until light and fluffy. Add the eggs one at a time and mix well. Beat in the vanilla. Add the flour mixture alternately with the bananas and sour cream, beginning and ending with the flour mixture, and blending after each addition.

Pour into the prepared pans and spread evenly. Bake for 20 minutes, rotate the pans from front to back, and bake for another 5 minutes, or until the cakes pull away slightly from the sides of their pans, are firm to the touch, and are deep brown in color. Cool the cakes in their pans on cooling racks for 25 minutes, then invert onto racks and place right side up. While the cakes are still warm, brush with the rum. The cakes can be stored at room temperature for up to 2 days or frozen for up to 1 month.

◆ I ALWAYS SIFT THE DRY INGREDIENTS THROUGH A LARGE SIEVE SET OVER PARCHMENT PAPER. THEN WHEN I AM READY TO ADD THE FLOUR TO MY BATTER, I LIFT THE TWO SIDES OF THE PAPER AND HOLD THEM TOGETHER TO FORM A CRADLE AND POUR IT IN.

MAKE THE CRÈME ANGLAISE. Place the milk in a heavy nonreactive medium saucepan, scrape the half vanilla bean seeds in, and bring to a boil over medium-high heat. Let the mixture rise up the side of the pan, then immediately remove from the heat.

Meanwhile, in the bowl of an electric mixer fitted with the whisk attachment, beat the egg yolks with the sugar on high speed until very thick and pale, about 3 to 4 minutes. The mixture will triple in volume and form a ribbon when dropped from the whisk.

Bring the bowl over to the saucepan. Whisk about 1 cup of the hot milk into the yolk mixture to temper it, then pour the mixture back into the saucepan. Off heat, stir until the custard is thick enough to coat a wooden spoon. (Run your finger through the custard on the back of the spoon. The custard is thick enough when the line remains.) Immediately pour the crème anglaise through a China cap or fine-mesh strainer into a bowl and whisk until cool. Refrigerate for up to 3 days. Cover after completely cool.

CRÈME ANGLAISE

YIELD: 2 CUPS

2 cups milk

½ vanilla bean, split lengthwise

5 large egg yolks (100 grams or scant ½ cup)

½ cup sugar

ASSEMBLE THE SANDWICHES. Cut the cake into sixteen ½-inch slices. Place a cake slice on each plate, top with a scoop of ice cream, and gently press a second cake slice on top. Drizzle with the crème anglaise and serve.

ASSEMBLY

Banana Cake

Banana Ice Cream

2 cups Crème Anglaise

I sometimes like to garnish the plates with either fresh baby bananas, when in season, or sautéed bananas.

Melt the butter in a skillet until very hot, add the bananas and sugar, and sauté until warm and until the sugar has dissolved. Serve immediately.

SAUTÉED BANANAS

2 tablespoons unsalted butter

2 large bananas, sliced in rounds

2 tablespoons sugar

BANANA CHOCOLATE
FUDGE SPLIT

The chocolate fudge cake for this dessert is devilishly rich, moist, and intensely chocolatey due to two layers of chocolate flavor: unsweetened chocolate plus dark cocoa. My preference is to use Valrhona cocoa for the best results. Going on the assumption that you can never have too many recipes for what is in essence a great brownie, here is our version. This cake is always a great hit at children's birthday parties, especially when slathered with the Chocolate Fudge Frosting on page 45. Here brownies and silky vanilla ice cream are topped with banana chunks and smothered with a warm fudge sauce.

SPECIAL EQUIPMENT: 12-INCH SQUARE CAKE PAN ● ICE-CREAM MAKER

FUDGE CAKE

YIELD: ONE 12-INCH SQUARE CAKE

10 ounces unsweetened chocolate,
    chopped

1 pound (4 sticks) unsalted butter

¼ cup Dutch-processed cocoa

8 large eggs (396 grams or 1¾ cups)

3¼ cups sugar

2 teaspoons vanilla extract

2 cups (280 grams) all-purpose flour,
    sifted

PREPARATION. Preheat the oven to 350°F. Butter a 12-inch square cake pan.

MAKE THE CAKE. Combine the chocolate, butter, and cocoa in a large bowl set over a large saucepan of simmering water. Heat, stirring frequently, until the chocolate and butter melt and the mixture is well blended. Remove from the heat. (Or use a microwave to heat the mixture on high power in 20-second then 10-second intervals, stirring frequently, until melted.)

Beat the eggs and sugar on high speed in the bowl of an electric mixer fitted with the whisk attachment until thick and pale yellow. Don't worry if the batter looks grainy; the addition of the warm chocolate will melt the sugar. Reduce the speed to low and add the warm chocolate mixture; beat until well combined. Add the vanilla. Add the flour one-fourth at a time, mixing well after each addition.

Pour the batter into the prepared pan and bake for 15 minutes. Rotate the pan from front to back and bake for 15 minutes more, or until the top of the brownie cracks and a cake tester inserted in the center comes out with a few crumbs clinging. The cake should be soft and a bit gooey in the center. To maintain the soft center, immediately place the pan in the refrigerator and leave it for 1 hour. Invert the brownie onto a parchment-covered cutting board. When completely cool, trim the edges of all four sides of the brownie and cut into 2½-inch squares.

◆ I HAVE A STOCK OF STURDY PLASTIC CUTTING BOARDS IN VARIOUS SIZES THAT I LIKE TO USE FOR INVERTING AND EASILY SLICING RECTANGULAR CAKES AND BROWNIES. THEY COME IN VERY HANDY AND ARE FAIRLY INEXPENSIVE.

MAKE THE ICE-CREAM BASE. Combine the milk and cream in a heavy nonreactive medium saucepan. Use the back of a knife to scrape out the seeds from the bean and add the seeds and pod to the saucepan. Bring to a rolling boil over medium-high heat. Let the mixture rise up the side of the pan, then immediately remove from the heat.

Meanwhile, beat the egg yolks with the sugar on highest speed in the bowl of an electric mixer fitted with the whisk attachment until very thick and pale, about 5 minutes. The mixture will triple in volume and hold its shape when dropped from the whisk. It should be very stiff.

Bring the bowl over to the saucepan. Whisk about 1 cup of the hot cream mixture into the yolk mixture to temper it, then pour the mixture back into the saucepan and whisk until thoroughly combined. The mixture should be thick enough to coat a wooden spoon. (Run your finger through the custard on the back of the spoon. The custard is thick enough when the line remains.) Pour the custard through a China cap or fine-mesh strainer into a large bowl. Place in an ice bath or refrigerate until chilled, stirring occasionally.

ICE-CREAM BASE

YIELD: 1 QUART

2 cups milk

2 cups heavy cream

1 vanilla bean, split lengthwise

11 to 12 large egg yolks
  (225 grams or about 1 cup)

1 cup sugar

MAKE THE VANILLA ICE CREAM. Stir the vanilla into the ice-cream base. Transfer to an ice-cream maker and freeze according to manufacturer's instructions.

VANILLA ICE CREAM

YIELD: 1 QUART

1 tablespoon vanilla extract

1 quart Ice-Cream Base

HOT FUDGE SAUCE

YIELD: ABOUT 2 CUPS

4 ounces unsweetened chocolate

8 ounces (2 sticks) unsalted butter

½ cup Dutch-processed cocoa

1½ cups sugar

1 cup light cream

MAKE THE HOT FUDGE SAUCE. Melt the chocolate and butter in a small saucepan over very low heat, stirring frequently. Mix the cocoa and sugar together. Add the cocoa mixture and light cream to the chocolate-butter mixture. Cook, stirring frequently, for about 15 minutes. The sauce can be used immediately or refrigerated in an airtight container for up to several weeks.

ASSEMBLY

10 Fudge Cake squares

Vanilla Ice Cream

3 ripe bananas, quartered lengthwise
    and sliced into chunks

2 cups Hot Fudge Sauce

ASSEMBLE THE BANANA CHOCOLATE FUDGE SPLIT. For each banana split, slice a fudge cake square on the diagonal to make 2 triangular wedges. Place the wedges opposite one another in a dessert bowl, as if the square were split open. Fill the center with vanilla ice cream, cover with banana chunks, and smother with hot fudge sauce.

◆ FOR AN OVER-THE-TOP BANANA-FLAVOR EXPERIENCE, I LIKE TO SERVE THE SPLIT WITH THE BANANA ICE CREAM (PAGE 28) FROM THE BANANA CAKE RECIPE.

BIRDSEED CAKE

This unusually named cake launched my pastry-making career. It started out as my take on the Gâteau Marjolaine (French for "sweet marjoram"), immortalized by legendary Chef Fernand Point of La Pyramide restaurant in Vienne, France. In the early 1950s, it was considered by many to be the finest restaurant, turning Vienne, a quiet little town midway between Paris and the Riviera, into a food mecca. Point's Marjolaine was a *jaconde* (nutted meringue), which, by the way, contained no marjoram or herb of any kind and was filled with variously flavored creams. I found a recipe for the Marjolaine in Mary and Vincent Price's *Treasury of Great Recipes* and put my own spin on it by changing the cake to a chocolate almond génoise and taking liberties with the fillings. This cake was served at a little tearoom in Bethesda, Maryland, and the late Ann Crutcher, food editor of the long-gone *Washington Star* newspaper, wrote about it. The orders started pouring in, and the next thing I knew, I was in business. When my sons, Jay and Danny, were small, they loved to eat the trimmings of this almond-flavored cake. They accompanied the snack with shouts of "birdseed, birdseed," from one of the TV shows popular at that time, and always invited their friends over to share the "birdseed." The mother of one of their playmates actually called and asked if she could order the birdseed cake. And that's how the cake got its name.

SPECIAL EQUIPMENT: CANDY THERMOMETER

MAKE THE GÉNOISE. Sift the flour and cocoa into a bowl; set aside. Place the eggs and sugar in the bowl of an electric mixer. Place the bowl in a larger bowl with enough very hot water to come at least 2 inches up the side of the bowl and place over low heat. Whisk the mixture until the sugar has dissolved and the eggs are warm and dark yellow, about 3 minutes.

Place the bowl in an electric mixer fitted with the whisk attachment and whip the eggs on high speed until tripled in volume and cool to the touch. Reduce the mixer to low speed and add the almond paste by tablespoonfuls. This should be done rather quickly, to deflate the batter as little as possible. Beat on low speed for 1 minute. Some small lumps of almond paste will remain, but the batter

CHOCOLATE ALMOND GÉNOISE

YIELD: ONE 13 x 9–INCH CAKE

1½ cups (180 grams) cake flour

2 tablespoons Dutch-processed cocoa

7 large eggs (350 grams or 1½ cups)

1¼ cups sugar

½ cup (4 ounces) almond paste, grated on the largest holes of a box grater

2 tablespoons unsalted butter, melted and cooled to lukewarm

See Preparation at the top of the next page.

PREPARATION. Preheat the oven to 350°F. Butter a 13 X 9–inch baking pan. Line the bottom with parchment paper and butter the paper.

◆ I USE THE UNDERSIDE OF A HALF-SHEET OR JELLY-ROLL PAN COVERED WITH PARCHMENT PAPER TO TURN THE CAKE. THEN I IMMEDIATELY INVERT THE CAKE ONTO ANOTHER PAN OR CUTTING BOARD COVERED WITH PARCHMENT PAPER. THIS WAY THE MOIST, STICKY UNDERSIDE IS ON TOP, MAKING IT EASIER TO SLICE AND LIFT EACH PIECE WHEN IT COMES TIME TO SERVE THE CAKE.

will look smooth, shiny, and tan-colored. Working quickly, alternately add the flour mixture and butter in three additions, beginning and ending with the flour mixture and beating on low speed until just combined; then finish mixing by hand.

Pour the batter into the prepared pan and bake for 18 to 20 minutes, rotate the pan from front to back, and bake for another 5 minutes or until the top is lightly browned and the cake pulls away slightly from the sides of the pan. Let the cake cool in the pan on a cooking rack for about 10 minutes, then invert onto a rack to cool completely. Wrap in plastic wrap and refrigerate for at least 1 hour before using. It can be refrigerated for several hours, up to 1 day.

CRÈME GANACHE

YIELD: 3 CUPS

2 cups 40%–milkfat heavy cream

1 pound bittersweet chocolate, preferably Callebaut 60/40, Valrhona Caraibe, or Scharffen Berger 70%, finely chopped

MAKE THE GANACHE. Bring the cream to a boil in a 4-quart saucepan. When the cream boils up the side of the pan, immediately remove from the heat and add the chocolate all at once. Stir with a wire whisk until the chocolate has melted, continuing to whisk until the mixture is smooth, without any lumps of chocolate. Pour the ganache into a bowl and let cool to room temperature, uncovered, so no condensation forms. The ganache will firm up as it cools. When at room temperature, cover the ganache with plastic wrap and refrigerate until firm, 2 to 3 hours. You can hasten cooling by pouring the ganache into a half-sheet or jelly-roll pan and chilling for 1 hour.

To use the ganache, scoop out the needed amount with a metal spoon that has been dipped in hot water and place in a microwave-safe bowl. This recipe can be doubled or tripled successfully.

MAKE THE BUTTERCREAM. Combine the sugar and water in a small saucepan and stir to mix well. Place the saucepan over high heat and bring to a boil, stirring to dissolve the sugar. Wash any undissolved sugar from the side of the pan with the pastry brush dipped in water. Do not stir the syrup after it boils.

Meanwhile, beat the egg yolks on medium speed in the bowl of an electric mixer fitted with the whisk attachment until light and pale yellow, about 3 minutes, and then reduce the speed to low. When the sugar syrup reaches firm-ball stage (242°F on a candy thermometer—the bubbling syrup will become shiny and almost plastic looking), remove from the heat. Immediately pour the syrup into the egg yolks in a thin, steady stream down the inside of the bowl to prevent spattering. Increase the mixer speed to medium high and continue to beat until the yolks are at room temperature, which will take about 15 minutes. The bowl will be cool to the touch. Reduce the mixer speed to low and add the butter several tablespoons at a time, beating until all the butter has been incorporated, scraping down the side of the bowl if necessary.

EGG-YOLK BUTTERCREAM
YIELD: 4 CUPS

½ cup sugar

¼ cup water

12 large egg yolks (240 grams or 1 cup)

1 pound (4 sticks) unsalted butter, at room temperature

PREPARATION. Have ready a pastry brush and cup of cold water.

◆ HERE I USE THE EGG-YOLK BUTTERCREAM, WHICH FREEZES BEAUTIFULLY AND CAN BE THAWED OVERNIGHT IN THE REFRIGERATOR. I HAVE EVEN ZAPPED FROZEN BUTTERCREAM IN THE MICROWAVE, WITH PERFECT RESULTS.

MAKE THE NOUGATINE. Place the sugar, water, and corn syrup in a heavy-bottomed medium saucepan and stir until well combined. Place over medium heat and continue to stir until the sugar comes to a boil. As the mixture cooks, wash down the side of the pan with a pastry brush dipped in water to dissolve any sugar. Continue to boil without stirring, gently shaking the pot to evenly distribute the sugar while it cooks. (Do not stir.) Watch carefully and remove the pan from the heat when you begin to see small puffs of smoke coming from the sugar. At this point the sugar should be medium brown in color, not burned. Quickly stir in the almonds, then pour the mixture onto the prepared pan. Cool completely.

CONTINUED

NOUGATINE
YIELD: 5 CUPS

2½ cups sugar

½ cup water

2 tablespoons light corn syrup or glucose

3 cups sliced blanched almonds

PREPARATION. Coat an 18 X 13–inch jelly-roll or half-sheet pan with vegetable oil. Have ready a pastry brush and cup of cold water.

Break the cooled pieces of nougatine into 6 large pieces and loosely wrap in plastic wrap. Then place in a plastic bag and smash the nougatine with a heavy mallet or hammer to break it into small ¼-inch pieces. Store in an airtight container wrapped in the plastic wrap. The nougatine will keep for several weeks at room temperature.

RUM SYRUP

YIELD: ¾ CUP

4 tablespoons sugar

4 tepid tablespoons water

3 tablespoons dark rum, such as Myers's

MAKE THE RUM SYRUP. Dissolve the sugar in the water in a small bowl. Add the rum and set aside.

KIRSCH SYRUP

YIELD: ⅓ CUP

1 tablespoon sugar

2 tablespoons water

3 tablespoons kirsch

MAKE THE KIRSCH SYRUP. Dissolve the sugar in the water in a small bowl. Add the kirsch and set aside.

ASSEMBLY

Chocolate Almond Génoise

2 cups Crème Ganache

¾ cup Rum Syrup

1 tablespoon dark rum,
    such as Myers's

4 cups Egg-Yolk Buttercream

⅓ cup Kirsch Syrup

1 tablespoon kirsch

1 cup crushed Nougatine

½ cup confectioners' sugar

ASSEMBLE THE CAKE. Use a long serrated knife to split the génoise horizontally in half. (I use a cake turntable to shift or turn the cake as I'm slicing it. This makes it easier to get an even cut.) Trim the edges and cut each layer in half lengthwise. (You now have 4 cake rectangles in all.)

Heat 1 cup of the ganache in a microwave on medium power in 5-second intervals until melted; set aside.

Place 1 cake rectangle on a rectangular wooden board or cardboard cut to size (about 13 inches in length) and brush with 2 tablespoons of the rum syrup on top. Stir 1 tablespoon of the rum into 1 cup of the buttercream, then stir in ⅓ cup of the melted ganache; mix well. Spread evenly over the cake layer. Place the second cake layer on top of the buttercream. Drizzle the remaining rum syrup on top. Use a handheld electric mixer or wire whisk to whip the remaining 1 cup of unmelted ganache until it lightens and holds its shape. Spread the ganache over the cake layer and place the third layer on top. Brush with 2 tablespoons of the kirsch syrup. Mix the remaining 1 tablespoon of kirsch with another 1 cup of buttercream and the crushed nougatine and spread it on top of the layer. Top with the remaining cake layer.

Mix the remaining ⅔ cup of melted ganache with the remaining buttercream and spread it over the sides of the cake. Dust the top with the confectioners' sugar. Refrigerate for several hours or up to 24 hours. To serve, slice into ½-inch portions.

VARIATION. *I like to use two kinds of buttercream for a layer cake: one made with egg whites and one with egg yolks. I prefer to use the egg-yolk buttercream as a filling because it's silkier and richer. I use the meringue buttercream to cover the cake when I need an ivory shade on the outside.*

MAKE THE MERINGUE BUTTERCREAM. Combine the sugar and water in a small saucepan and stir to mix well. Place the saucepan over high heat and bring to a boil, stirring to dissolve the sugar. Wash any undissolved sugar from the side of the pan with a pastry brush dipped in water. Do not stir the syrup after it boils.

Meanwhile, beat the egg whites on low speed in the bowl of an electric mixer fitted with the whisk attachment until opaque and foamy. When the sugar syrup reaches firm-ball stage (242°F on a candy thermometer—the bubbling syrup will become shiny and almost plastic looking), remove from the heat. Immediately pour the syrup into the egg whites in a thin, steady stream down the inside of the bowl to prevent spattering. Increase the mixer speed to medium high and continue to beat the mixture until at

MERINGUE BUTTERCREAM

YIELD: 4 CUPS

2 cups sugar

4 tablespoons water

12 egg whites (360 grams or 1½ cups)

1½ to 2 pounds (6 sticks) butter

PREPARATION. Have ready a pastry brush and cup of cold water.

◆ You must be careful to guard against crystallization (the formation of coarse sugar crystals) in your sugar syrup. It is important to eliminate any grains of sugar on the inside of the pan before the syrup boils, and then not stir the syrup after it boils because stirring can also cause crystallization.

room temperature, which will take about 15 minutes. The bowl will be cool to the touch. Reduce the mixer speed to low and add the butter several tablespoons at a time, beating until all the butter has been incorporated and scraping down the side of the bowl if necessary.

If you see the buttercream come together smoothly after only 1½ pounds of butter have been added, you don't need to add the rest.

CARAMEL NUT CAKE

SERVES 10 TO 12

Jean-Louis Palladin, the youngest two-star Michelin chef ever to come to this country, was an innovator, a real character, and a friend. His restaurant Jean-Louis, at The Watergate in Washington, D.C., garnered immense respect in the food world and made the city a destination point for outstanding trendsetting food. During my tenure as pastry chef at the restaurant, I created this cake by using a caramel sauce mixed with butter, a technique taught to me by my good friend Patrick Musel, one of the first top-rated pastry chefs to come to Washington in the late 1970s. I love the raisins soaked in rum and the addition of walnuts, which make for a seriously rich cake. The chocolate glaze reminds me of a picture of a cake in a *Gourmet* magazine from the mid-1970s. Jean-Louis loved this seriously rich, somewhat sweet cake. I was always careful to save him a slice. Jean-Louis Palladin passed away in 2001. His legacy to the world of cooking cannot be overstated, and he is truly missed.

MAKE THE FRUIT AND NUT MIX. Combine the raisins, walnuts, and rum in a small bowl and set aside to soak for 2 hours (no longer); strain.

FRUIT AND NUT MIX
YIELD: 2 CUPS

1 cup raisins

1 cup walnuts, lightly toasted
  and chopped

¼ cup dark rum, such as Myers's

MAKE THE GÉNOISE. Sift the flour onto parchment or waxed paper; set aside.

Place the eggs, vanilla, and sugar in the bowl of an electric mixer. Place the bowl over a hot water bath and whisk by hand until the sugar has dissolved and the eggs are warm and dark yellow, about 3 minutes. When the mixture is homogenized and is lightly translucent, it is ready to beat in the mixer.

Place the bowl in the mixer fitted with the whisk attachment and beat on high speed until the mixture triples in volume, about 5 minutes. Reduce the mixer to very low speed and whisk for 1 more minute. Be careful not to overbeat the eggs at this point. CONTINUED

YELLOW GÉNOISE
YIELD: TWO 9-INCH ROUND CAKE
LAYERS

2 cups plus 3 tablespoons cake flour
  (243 grams)

8 large eggs (396 grams or 1¾ cups)

2 teaspoons vanilla extract

1 cup plus 3 tablespoons sugar
  (242 grams)

See Preparation at the top of the next page.

PREPARATION. Position a rack in the middle of the oven and preheat the oven to 350°F. Lightly butter two 9 X 3–inch round cake pans. Line the bottoms with parchment, and butter the paper.

◆ IF YOUR PANS HAVE BEEN PROPERLY SEASONED, IT IS NOT NECESSARY TO LINE THEM WITH PARCHMENT FOR THE GÉNOISE; JUST BUTTER THEM. THE TRICK TO SEASONING A PAN IS TO USE ONLY HOT WATER TO CLEAN IT AND NEVER TO USE SOAP.

With the mixer still on lowest speed, add the flour to the egg mixture in a quick and steady stream, using the parchment paper to funnel it in. Be careful not to overmix the batter. Stop the mixer while the flour is still visible in the batter. Remove the bowl from the mixer and use a rubber spatula to finish folding in the flour, being sure to scrape the batter from the bottom of the bowl and fold over the top.

Divide the batter evenly between the prepared pans. Bake for 25 minutes, or until the cakes are springy to the touch and golden, and a cake tester inserted in the center comes out clean. Do not open the oven door until the cakes have domed.

Let the cakes cool in their pans on cooling racks for about 5 minutes, then invert onto racks. Lift off the pans and remove the parchment, then invert the cakes onto racks so they are right side up. Cool completely. The cooled cakes can be filled, or wrap the layers tightly in plastic wrap and refrigerate for up to 2 days or freeze for up to 1 month.

CARAMEL SAUCE

YIELD: 5 CUPS

5 cups sugar

1 cup water

1 quart heavy cream

PREPARATION. Have ready a pastry brush, cup of cold water, a long-handled wire whisk, heavy-duty oven mitts, and a towel to cover your entire arm.

MAKE THE CARAMEL SAUCE. Combine the sugar and water in a heavy-bottomed large saucepan. Place over medium heat and mix well with a long-handled spoon until the sugar has completely dissolved. Meanwhile, dip a pastry brush in water and run it around the inside of the pot just above the level of the sugar to wash away any undissolved sugar. This will prevent the sugar from crystallizing.

Pour the cream into a large measuring cup or pitcher; set aside. As the sugar boils, gently move the pot back and forth over the burner to evenly distribute the ever-darkening syrup. Once the sugar begins to boil, no longer stir it. When it smells like caramel, is dark amber in color, and gives off little wisps of smoke, immediately remove the

pan from the heat. The caramel will burn very quickly at this point.

Standing back a bit with your arm covered, add the heavy cream quickly, whisking rapidly as you pour. The sugar will bubble up and may spatter, but continue to whisk until all the cream has been absorbed and the caramel is smooth. Let the caramel cool, then transfer to an airtight container and refrigerate for up to several weeks.

CRÈME GANACHE

YIELD: 2 TO 2½ CUPS

2 cups 40%–milkfat heavy cream

1 pound bittersweet chocolate, preferably Callebaut 60/40, Valrhona Caraibe, or Scharffen Berger 70%, finely chopped

MAKE THE GANACHE. Bring the cream to a boil in a large saucepan. When the cream boils up the side of the pan, immediately remove from the heat and add the chocolate all at once. Stir with a wire whisk until the chocolate has melted and the mixture is smooth and without tiny lumps of chocolate. Pour into a bowl and let cool to room temperature, uncovered, so no condensation forms. (The ganache will firm up as it chills.) When it reaches room temperature, cover the ganache with plastic wrap and refrigerate until firm, about 1 hour.

When you are ready to use the ganache, scoop out the needed amount with a metal spoon that has been dipped in hot water and place in a microwave-safe bowl. This recipe can be doubled or tripled successfully.

CARAMEL BUTTERCREAM

YIELD: 4½ TO 5 CUPS

3 cups Caramel Sauce, at room temperature

9 ounces (2 sticks plus 2 tablespoons) unsalted butter, at room temperature

MAKE THE BUTTERCREAM. Put the caramel sauce in the bowl of an electric mixer fitted with the whisk attachment and beat on medium speed until lightened in color and thickened, about 2 minutes. Beat in the butter 2 to 3 tablespoons at a time. If the buttercream looks somewhat separated, don't worry, as it just needs to be lightly warmed for 20 seconds over a hot water bath, while stirring it, to smooth it out. If it continues to look separated, add several more tablespoons of room-temperature butter and whip until smooth. Set aside.

MAKE THE RUM SYRUP. Dissolve the sugar in the water in a small bowl. Add the rum and set aside.

RUM SYRUP

YIELD: ABOUT 1¼ CUPS

2 tablespoons sugar

⅔ cup water

3 tablespoons dark rum, such as
    Myers's

ASSEMBLE THE CAKE. Use a long serrated knife to split each génoise layer in half horizontally. Place 1 cake layer on a cake plate or 9-inch cardboard cake round and brush with some of the rum syrup. Spread ½ cup of the caramel buttercream on top and sprinkle one-third of the fruit and nut mix evenly over the top, pressing it into the butter-cream. Drizzle about ¼ cup of the caramel sauce over the top and cover with ½ cup of the caramel buttercream.

Repeat with the remaining 3 layers without using the fruit and nut mix on the top layer. Brush the remaining rum syrup over the top layer. Use a narrow metal spatula to thinly cover the side and top of the cake with the remaining caramel buttercream. Refrigerate for several hours, or overnight, before putting on the final crème ganache glaze.

About 4 hours before serving, melt the crème ganache by placing it over a hot water bath and stir until smooth. If necessary, thin the ganache with a few tablespoons of heavy cream to make it pourable. Pour the ganache over the top of the cake, letting it drizzle down the side. Any ganache that falls onto the plate can be scooped up and refrigerated or frozen and reused at another time. Refrigerate for at least 1 hour or up to four hours before serving.

ASSEMBLY

2 Yellow Génoise layers

1¼ cups Rum Syrup

4½ to 5 cups Caramel Buttercream

2 cups Fruit and Nut Mix

¾ cup Caramel Sauce

2 to 2½ cups Crème Ganache

CASSATA

One of the tremendous influences on my baking was a book series published in the 1970s called the *Time-Life Series Foods of the World*. Not just a great read, the recipes could be counted as very reliable and authentic. I remember always being fascinated with the Sicilian Cassata in the *Cooking of Italy* book. It was a velvety pound cake filled with sweetened ricotta cheese, very similar to that found in cannoli. It took a while for me to perfect this recipe because I had a certain flavor and texture in mind—not something I had already tasted but something I wanted to taste. I simply couldn't get the combination right until a little cream cheese was added to the mix. I finally worked out a recipe that made me say, "That's the one!" I wanted a filling very close to the taste of cannoli but one that was still very much a cassata. This works because it is softer, more sensual, and definitely more flavorful. Use a good-quality ricotta cheese; it makes all the difference.

VANILLA CAKE

YIELD: TWO 8½ X 4½-INCH LOAVES

3 cups (420 grams) all-purpose flour

½ teaspoon baking soda

8 ounces (2 sticks) unsalted butter,
   at room temperature

2 tablespoons vegetable oil

2¾ cups sugar

6 large eggs (300 grams or 1⅓ cups)

1½ teaspoons vanilla extract

1 cup sour cream, at room temperature

3 tablespoons tepid milk

PREPARATION. Position a rack in the middle of the oven and preheat the oven to 350°F. Butter two 8½ X 4½-inch loaf pans.

MAKE THE CAKE. Sift the flour and baking soda onto a sheet of parchment or waxed paper; set aside.

Cream the butter, vegetable oil, and sugar on medium speed in the bowl of an electric mixer fitted with the whisk attachment until light and fluffy. Add the eggs two at a time and beat for 1 minute after each addition. Add the vanilla. Alternately, add the flour mixture, sour cream, and milk, ending with the flour mixture. Beat until thoroughly mixed, scraping down the inside of the bowl if necessary. Remove the bowl from the mixer and use a rubber spatula to scrape the bottom of the bowl to ensure that the ingredients are thoroughly blended.

Divide the batter evenly between the prepared pans. Bake for 15 minutes, rotate the pans from front to back, and bake for 15 minutes more, or until the cakes are lightly golden, pull away slightly from the sides of the pans, and a cake tester inserted in the center comes out clean. Let the cakes cool in their pans on cooling racks for about 20 minutes, then invert onto racks to cool completely.

◆ I ALWAYS LIKE TO HAVE THIS VANILLA CAKE ON HAND. AS A MOIST AND LIGHT YELLOW CAKE, ITS VERSATILITY IS LIMITLESS. TRY IT AS AN OLD-FASHIONED BIRTHDAY CAKE WITH A CHOCOLATE FUDGE FROSTING, THE FOUNDATION FOR A WHIPPED-CREAM-AND-FRUIT CAKE, OR AS SCRUMPTIOUS CUPCAKES, AND YOU'LL SEE WHY I CAN'T DO WITHOUT THIS CAKE.

MAKE THE FILLING. Put the ricotta and cream cheese in a bowl and mix well with a spatula. Sift in the confectioners' sugar and mix well. Combine the cream, Marsala, vanilla, and salt in a small bowl, then stir into the ricotta mixture. Add the cinnamon. Set aside.

CHEESE FILLING

YIELD: 3 CUPS

16 ounces ricotta cheese

1 (3-ounce) package cream cheese, at room temperature

½ cup confectioners' sugar

½ cup heavy cream

2 tablespoons Marsala wine

1 teaspoon vanilla extract

Pinch of salt

½ teaspoon ground cinnamon

MAKE THE FROSTING. Combine the cream and sugar in a small saucepan and bring to a boil. Reduce the heat and simmer for 6 minutes. Remove from the heat and add the chocolate, butter, and vanilla. Use a whisk to combine the mixture over very low heat, making sure that the butter and chocolate have thoroughly melted and the mixture is smooth. Mix in the confectioners' sugar. Transfer to a container and refrigerate, uncovered, for 1 hour or until room temperature, before using. The frosting should be room temperature when you begin to beat it.

Place the frosting in the bowl of an electric mixer fitted with the whisk attachment and whip until light. Set aside.

CHOCOLATE FUDGE FROSTING

YIELD: 2½ CUPS

1 cup heavy cream

¾ cup sugar

5 ounces finely chopped unsweetened chocolate

4 ounces (1 stick) unsalted butter

2 teaspoons vanilla extract

½ cup confectioners' sugar

ASSEMBLY

½ cup currant jelly

½ cup Marsala wine

2 loaves Vanilla Cake

3 cups Cheese Filling

2½ cups Chocolate Fudge Frosting

ASSEMBLE THE CASSATA. Use the back of a spoon or a rubber spatula to press the jelly through a strainer into a microwave-safe bowl. Add the Marsala and stir to combine, then heat it just enough to melt the jelly so it liquefies in the microwave or on the stove.

Even out the cakes by slicing off the domed tops, then slice each cake horizontally in thirds to make 3 even layers. (You now have 6 layers of cake in all.)

Set aside a top cake layer. Place 1 cake layer, cut side up, on a cake plate or rectangular cake board. Brush with the jelly mixture and top with a thin layer, about one-fifth, of the cheese filling, spreading it with an offset metal spatula to smooth it out. Repeat the layering four more times, brushing the layers with jelly and covering them with filling. Turn the reserved evened-off top layer bottom side up and firmly place on top. Brush with the remaining jelly mixture. (You should have 6 cake layers with 5 layers of filling.) Refrigerate the cassata for 2 hours. Cover the entire cake with chocolate fudge frosting. Refrigerated, the cake will remain fresh for up to 3 days. To serve, bring the cake to room temperature and cut into ½- to ¾-inch slices.

For the neatest slices, use a serrated knife and cut with a sawing motion, allowing the knife to do the work without putting too much pressure on the cake.

CHOCOLATE BABKA

MAKES 2 LOAVES, 6 SLICES EACH. SERVES 12

This recipe was inspired by the chocolate babka in Joan Nathan's *The Jewish Holiday Baker*. It contains apricot and chocolate and is absolutely wonderful for brunch or dessert. A good babka should have a soft, yeasty, tender dough redolent of the filling inside. The filling and streusel should be made first, as you don't want the yeast dough ready before the filling is prepared. I actually like to prepare the filling and streusel the day before and refrigerate them overnight. Then, while I am making the dough, the filling and streusel are brought to room temperature. The dough is twisted and placed in a loaf pan, then dusted with streusel and baked. It rises high in the pan and is simply wonderful to eat warm from the oven. It freezes so well that it is a perfect dessert to have on hand. Just thaw it wrapped in aluminum foil, then, when it comes to room temperature, heat it, still foil-wrapped, at 325°F for 15 minutes.

MAKE THE FILLING. Puree the preserves in a food processor until smooth. Combine the cake crumbs, pureed preserves, and butter in a small bowl and mix until smooth; set aside.

BABKA FILLING

YIELD: 2½ CUPS

¾ cup apricot preserves

1 cup dry pound cake crumbs (the Cassata, on page 44, or The Cleveland Park Cream Cakes, on page 66, make suitable crumbs)

3 ounces (6 tablespoons) unsalted butter, melted

MAKE THE TOPPING. Place the flour and sugar in a small bowl and mix well. Add the butter using your fingers to mix it together until crumbly; set aside.

STREUSEL TOPPING

YIELD: ABOUT 1 TO 1½ CUPS

6 tablespoons (57 grams) all-purpose flour, sifted

3 tablespoons sugar

3 tablespoons unsalted butter, diced and chilled

BABKA DOUGH

YIELD: ENOUGH FOR 2 LOAVES

1¾ cups plus 2 tablespoons (265 grams)
  all-purpose flour, sifted

¾ cup (90 grams) cake flour, sifted

⅛ teaspoon salt

⅓ cup sugar

¼ ounce or 2½ teaspoons active
  dry yeast, or 1 cake (0.6 ounce)
  fresh yeast

1 tablespoon warm water (90°F to
  110°F)

½ cup milk, heated and cooled to
  room temperature

2 to 3 large eggs (125 grams
  or slightly over ½ cup)

¾ teaspoon vanilla extract

4 ounces (1 stick) unsalted butter,
  at room temperature

MAKE THE DOUGH. Combine the all-purpose and cake flours, salt, and all but 1 tablespoon of the sugar in the bowl of an electric mixer fitted with the paddle attachment and mix on medium speed. In a small bowl, stir the yeast with the warm water and reserved tablespoon of sugar just until the sugar and yeast have dissolved. Reduce the mixer to low speed, add the yeast mixture, milk, eggs, and vanilla, and beat until the dough is smooth, shiny, and elastic, about 20 minutes.

Add the butter by spoonfuls until thoroughly incorporated, then beat on low speed for about 5 minutes. When finished, the dough should be silken and rich like very thick ice cream. Transfer to a large bowl, cover with plastic wrap, and set aside. When the dough has doubled in bulk, after 2 hours, punch it down, cover, and refrigerate for 1 hour.

ASSEMBLY

4 ounces bittersweet chocolate

Babka Dough

2½ cups Babka Filling

1 tablespoon unsalted butter, melted

1 to 1½ cups Streusel Topping

PREPARATION. Preheat the oven to 350°F. Line two 8½ X 4½–inch loaf pans with overlapping, perpendicular pieces of parchment paper, with one piece lining the bottom and two short sides and the second piece lining the bottom and two long sides. Don't let the paper come more than 1 inch above the top of the pan.

ASSEMBLE THE BABKA. Grate the chocolate by hand on the large holes of a box grater or in a food processor. If using a food processor, be careful not to overprocess or you might run the risk of the chocolate's melting. Set the grated chocolate aside. Remove the dough from the refrigerator and divide it in half. On a lightly floured surface, roll one piece of the dough into a 12 X 8–inch rectangle. Use an off-set metal spatula to spread half the filling over the dough within ½ inch of the edges. Sprinkle with half the grated chocolate. Beginning with a long side, roll it up tightly. Holding one end of the babka in each hand, twist it lengthwise to create a spiral. Place the babka in a prepared pan. It is important to press the babka down firmly in the pan at this point. Brush the top with some of the melted butter and sprinkle with half the streusel topping. Make the second babka with the remaining dough, filling, chocolate, butter, and streusel. Cover loosely with plastic wrap.

Let the loaves rise at room temperature until doubled in volume, about 1 hour. Bake for about 45 minutes, or until a cake tester inserted in the center comes out clean. Allow the babka to cool for 30 minutes before cutting. Slice the babka and serve warm.

◆ I BAKE THE BABKA IN A HIGH-BLOWER CONVECTION OVEN FOR 20 MINUTES, ROTATE THE PANS, THEN BAKE FOR ABOUT 25 MINUTES OR MORE, TURNING THE BLOWER TO LOW IN THE LAST 15 MINUTES OR SO. IF YOU ARE LUCKY ENOUGH TO OWN A CONVECTION OVEN OR AN OVEN WITH CONVECTION CAPABILITIES, DEFINITELY USE IT HERE.

◆ I OFTEN LIKE TO CUT THE BABKA INTO HEARTY SLICES AND SERVE WITH SCOOPS OF HOMEMADE CHOCOLATE-CHIP ICE CREAM. I ADD 2 CUPS OF CHOPPED CHOCOLATE TO 1 PINT OF FRESHLY TURNED, STILL SOFT VANILLA ICE CREAM (PAGE 259). I SOMETIMES ALSO THROW IN CHOPPED WHITE AND MILK CHOCOLATES, TO MAKE IT TRIPLE CHOCOLATE-CHIP ICE CREAM.

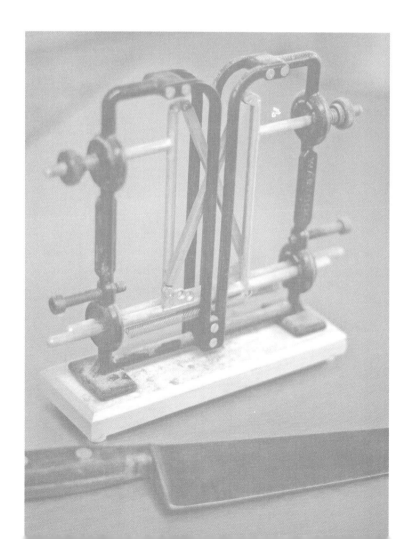

CHOCOLATE MARBLE CAKE WITH MILK CHOCOLATE— CHIP ICE CREAM

SERVES 10 TO 12

For this recipe, I wanted a classic light, fluffy marble cake like the ones we all remember having as children. I researched old cookbooks for recipes but with limited success, as I was just not happy with the depth of flavor or the texture of the cakes. After much experimentation and adding and subtracting of ingredients, I came up with this recipe. Here the marbleized chocolate is deep, yet light and chocolatey at the same time: the result of finding a really good, light and fluffy chocolate-cake batter and swirling it with a light-colored vanilla-cake batter. This was the result I was after. As far as I'm concerned, this is one of the best marble cakes ever.

SPECIAL EQUIPMENT: ICE-CREAM MAKER

MARBLE CAKE

YIELD: 13 X 9–INCH CAKE

1¾ cups (210 grams) cake flour

2 teaspoons baking soda

2 ounces unsweetened chocolate, chopped

1¼ cups plus 2 tablespoons sugar

5 tablespoons hot water

6 tablespoons unsalted butter, at room temperature

¼ cup neutral vegetable oil

1 large egg (50 grams or ¼ cup)

¾ cup milk

1 teaspoon vanilla extract

3 large egg whites (90 grams or generous ⅓ cup)

PREPARATION. Preheat the oven to 350°F. Butter a 13 X 9–inch baking pan.

MAKE THE CAKE. Sift the flour and baking soda into a bowl; set aside.

Put the chocolate in a microwave-safe dish and heat at medium power at 10-second intervals, stirring between each interval until the chocolate melts, being careful not to let it burn. When the chocolate still has some bits visible, reduce the cooking intervals to 5 seconds, stirring well between each. Stir 2 tablespoons of the sugar and all the hot water into the melted chocolate until blended. Set aside to cool.

Cream the butter, oil, and ¾ cup sugar on medium speed in the bowl of an electric mixer fitted with the paddle attachment until light and fluffy. Add the egg and mix to combine. Add the flour mixture alternately with the milk in three additions, starting and ending with the flour and beating well after each addition until smooth. Add the vanilla.

Place the egg whites in the bowl of an electric mixer fitted with the whisk attachment and whip on high speed until foamy and beginning to hold a shape. Gradually add the remaining ½ cup sugar and beat until the whites form stiff, glossy peaks. Fold the beaten whites into the cake batter all at once. Stir ⅓ of the cake batter into the cooled chocolate mixture.

Spoon the cake batter into the prepared pan, alternating the light and dark batters. Use a knife to cut a wide zigzag shape through the batters once to create a marbled effect. Bake for 15 minutes, rotate the pan from front to back, and bake for 10 minutes more, or until the cake pulls away slightly from the sides of the pan and a cake tester inserted in the center comes out clean. Let the cake cool in the pan on a cooling rack for 15 minutes, then unmold onto a rack and cool completely. Slice the cake crosswise in half to make two 9 X 6½–inch rectangles. Cover loosely with plastic wrap until ready to frost.

MAKE THE FROSTING. Place the chocolate into a microwave-safe bowl and heat at medium power at 10-second intervals until melted. Stir in the confectioners' sugar and water until blended. Add the yolks one at a time, beating well with a whisk after each addition. Add the butter 1 tablespoon at a time, stirring until incorporated. Add the vanilla, then whip the frosting to lighten it.

◆ I HAVE FOUND THAT WHILE REFRIGERATING THIS TYPE OF CAKE HELPS TO KEEP ITS FLAVOR, THE TEXTURE IS NEVER THE SAME. IT'S BEST TO MAKE AND SERVE THE CAKE THE SAME DAY, OR FREEZE IT AND THAW TO SERVE. FREEZING DOES SEEM TO PRESERVE THE LIGHT TEXTURE BETTER THAN THE REFRIGERATOR.

FROSTING

YIELD: 2½ CUPS

3 ounces unsweetened chocolate, chopped
1½ cups confectioners' sugar
2½ tablespoons hot water
3 large egg yolks (60 grams or ¼ cup)
4 tablespoons unsalted butter, at room temperature
2 teaspoons vanilla extract

VARIATION. *You can also use the Chocolate Fudge Frosting from the Cassata recipe (page 45).*

MILK CHOCOLATE-CHIP ICE CREAM

YIELD: ABOUT 1 QUART

2 cups milk

2 cups heavy cream

1 vanilla bean, split lengthwise

11 to 12 large egg yolks (225 grams
   or 1 cup)

1 cup sugar

1 pound good-quality milk chocolate,
   finely chopped

◆ I LOVE TO SERVE THIS CAKE
SLICED INTO LONG, NARROW
FINGERS AND ACCOMPANIED WITH
A SCOOP OF CHOCOLATE-CHIP ICE
CREAM PLACED AT ONE OF THE
SHORT SIDES OF THE CAKE, LIKE
DOTTING AN I.

◆ THIS MARBLE CAKE AND SOME
RICH VANILLA ICE CREAM CAN ALSO
BE USED FOR DELECTABLE ICE-
CREAM SANDWICHES. TO MAKE
SANDWICHES, SLICE THE CAKE INTO
WIDER SQUARE CUTS AND ADD HOT
FUDGE SAUCE FROM THE BANANA
CHOCOLATE FUDGE SPLIT (PAGE
32). THE FUDGE SAUCE COVERS THE
ICE CREAM, AND THE SECOND PIECE
OF CAKE GOES OVER THAT.

MAKE THE ICE CREAM. Place the milk and cream in a heavy medium saucepan. Use the back of a knife to scrape out the seeds from the vanilla bean and add the seeds and pod to the saucepan. Bring to a rolling boil over medium-high heat. Let the mixture rise up the side of the pan, then immediately remove it from the heat.

Meanwhile, beat the egg yolks and sugar on high speed in the bowl of an electric mixer fitted with the whisk attachment until very thick and pale, about 5 minutes. The mixture will triple in volume, hold its shape when dropped from the whisk, and be very stiff.

Bring the bowl over to the saucepan. Whisk about 1 cup of the hot cream mixture into the yolk mixture to temper it, then pour the mixture back into the saucepan and whisk until thoroughly combined. The mixture should be thick enough to coat a wooden spoon. (Run your finger through the custard on the back of the spoon. The custard is thick enough if the line remains.)

Pour the custard through a fine-mesh stainless-steel strainer or China cap into a large bowl. Place in an ice bath or refrigerate until chilled, stirring occasionally. When chilled, transfer the mixture to an ice-cream maker and freeze according to manufacturer's instructions. As soon as the ice cream has finished churning, stir in the milk chocolate. Transfer the ice cream to an airtight container and freeze.

ASSEMBLY

2 Marble Cake layers

2½ cups Frosting

Milk Chocolate–Chip Ice Cream

ASSEMBLE THE CAKE. Place a cake layer on a cake plate or cardboard cake round. Spread ⅓ of the frosting over the cake layer and place the second layer on top. Spread the remaining frosting over the top and sides of the cake. Serve at room temperature with ice cream on the side.

CHOCOLATE RASPBERRY TORTE

I love this truly light chocolate fudge cake for its moist crumb, raspberry-jam buttercream, and chocolate-truffle cream topping. Chocolate and raspberry is a flavor combination made in heaven. The tart raspberry flavor accentuates the richness of the chocolate without overwhelming it. I started making this cake in the early 1980s but was never fully satisfied with the depth of chocolate flavor that I got from using a chocolate génoise. This chocolate cake is perfect, as it is delicate, light, and chocolatey. It also makes a great birthday cake. To complement the raspberry flavor, I serve it with fresh raspberry sorbet.

SPECIAL EQUIPMENT: CANDY THERMOMETER • ICE-CREAM MAKER

MAKE THE CAKE. Stir 2 tablespoons of the sugar and hot water into the melted chocolate and blend well; set aside. Sift the flour and baking soda into a bowl; set aside.

Cream the butter, ¾ cup of the sugar, and the oil on high speed in the bowl of an electric mixer fitted with the paddle attachment until light, about 2 minutes. Add the egg and vanilla and continue beating until fluffy. Turn off the mixer, add the chocolate mixture, and fold in by hand, scraping the bottom of the bowl to ensure that it is thoroughly combined. Add the flour mixture alternately with the milk in three additions, mixing by hand and beginning and ending with the flour mixture.

Place the egg whites in the bowl of an electric mixer fitted with the whisk attachment and whip on high speed until foamy and beginning to hold a shape. Gradually add the remaining ½ cup sugar and beat until the whites form stiff, glossy peaks.

Fold the beaten whites into the batter all at once until incorporated. Divide the batter evenly among the prepared pans. Bake for 18 to 20 minutes or until a cake tester inserted in the center comes out clean. (This is a light moist cake with a fluffy crumb.) Cool the layers in their pans on cooling racks for 10 minutes, then turn out

CHOCOLATE CAKE

YIELD: THREE 8-INCH ROUND CAKE LAYERS

2 tablespoons sugar

6 tablespoons hot water

3 ounces unsweetened chocolate, melted

2 cups (240 grams) cake flour

2 teaspoons baking soda

6 tablespoons unsalted butter, at room temperature

1¼ cups sugar

¼ cup neutral vegetable oil

1 large egg (50 grams or about ¼ cup)

2 teaspoons vanilla extract

1 cup milk

3 large egg whites (90 grams or a generous ⅓ cup)

PREPARATION. Position racks in the middle and lower third of the oven and preheat the oven to 350°F. Butter three 8 X 2–inch round cake pans.

onto racks and cool completely. At this point, the layers can be filled or wrapped individually in plastic wrap and frozen for up to 3 months.

EGG-YOLK BUTTERCREAM

YIELD: 4 CUPS

½ cup sugar

¼ cup water

12 large egg yolks (240 grams or 1 cup)

1 pound (4 sticks) unsalted butter,
   at room temperature

PREPARATION. Have ready a pastry brush
   and cup of cold water.

◆ I USUALLY HAVE MY YOLKS
BEATING AT LOW SPEED DURING
THE EARLY STAGES OF THE SYRUP
COOKING. DEPENDING ON THE
STOVETOP'S HEAT STRENGTH, THIS
CAN TAKE ANYWHERE FROM 2 TO 5
MINUTES. THE LESS WATER ADDED
TO THE SUGAR, THE SHORTER THE
SYRUP'S COOKING TIME. ONCE THE
SYRUP COMES TO A BOIL, I TURN THE
MIXER UP TO MEDIUM-HIGH SPEED.

MAKE THE BUTTERCREAM. Place the sugar and water in a small saucepan and stir to mix well. Place the saucepan over high heat and bring to a boil, stirring to dissolve the sugar. Wash any sugar from the insides of the pan with a pastry brush dipped in water. Do not stir the syrup after it boils.

Meanwhile, beat the egg yolks on low speed in an electric mixer fitted with the whisk attachment until light and pale, about 5 minutes. (The yolks should reach this point at the same time that the sugar syrup reaches the firm-ball stage or 242°F on a candy thermometer.) Immediately pour the syrup into the egg yolks. Increase the speed to medium high and continue to beat until the yolks reach room temperature, about 15 minutes. If the bowl has cooled to room temperature, the yolks are done. Reduce the speed to low and add the butter several tablespoons at a time, beating until all the butter has been incorporated and scraping down the inside of the bowl if necessary. Set aside.

CRÈME GANACHE

YIELD: ABOUT 8 CUPS

6 cups heavy cream

3 pounds bittersweet chocolate,
   preferably Callebaut 60/40,
   Valrhona Caraibe, or Scharffen
   Berger 70%, finely chopped

MAKE THE GANACHE. Bring the cream to a boil in a large saucepan. When the cream boils up the side of the pan, immediately remove from the heat and add the chocolate all at once, stirring with a wire whisk until the chocolate melts and the mixture is smooth with no small bits of chocolate remaining.

Pour the ganache into a bowl and cool to room temperature (uncovered, so no condensation forms). Cover with plastic wrap and refrigerate until firm, about 3 hours. To hasten cooling, I sometimes pour the chocolate on a half-sheet or jelly-roll pan and refrigerate it, which makes it cool in about 1 hour. Scoop out the needed amount with a metal spoon that has been dipped in hot water. This recipe can be doubled or tripled successfully.

MAKE THE SORBET. Mix all ingredients in a large bowl, stirring well. Make the sorbet sweeter than you would like, as some of the sweetness is lost in the freezing. Transfer the mixture to an ice-cream maker and freeze according to manufacturer's instructions.

ASSEMBLE THE TORTE. Mix 1 cup of the raspberry jam, the water, and 2 tablespoons of the framboise in a small bowl.

Soften the ganache in the microwave until it is about 76°F. It should not be melted, just soft enough to beat with a whisk. Beat either by hand, or in the bowl of an electric mixer fitted with the whisk attachment at medium speed, until fluffy and lighter in color.

Place 1 cake layer on a plate or cake board. Use an off-set metal spatula to spread half of the jam mixture over the layer. Combine the remaining 1 cup raspberry jam with 1½ cups buttercream. Gently fold in the raspberries and the remaining 2 tablespoons framboise. Spread the buttercream over the raspberry jam. Place a second cake layer on top of the buttercream. Spread the remaining jam mixture over the layer, then spread 1 cup of the whipped crème ganache over the jam. Place the final layer on top. Combine the remaining 1½ cups buttercream, the remaining 2 cups whipped ganache, and the rum. Spread smoothly over the top of the cake. Refrigerate for 2 hours.

Transfer the cake to a cooling rack set over an 18 X 13–inch half-sheet or jelly-roll pan. Place the remaining

RASPBERRY SORBET

YIELD: ABOUT 1 QUART

4 cups raspberry puree, such as frozen Boiron Raspberry Puree (2 pints)

2¼ cups sugar, or more to taste

2 tablespoons framboise (clear raspberry brandy)

3 cups water

1 tablespoon lemon juice

ASSEMBLY

2 cups seedless raspberry jam

¼ cup water

4 tablespoons framboise

7 cups Crème Ganache

3 Chocolate Cake layers

3 cups Egg-Yolk Buttercream

½ pint fresh raspberries

1 tablespoon dark rum, such as Myers's

¾ cup heavy cream

Raspberry Sorbet

VARIATION. *The cake can also be covered with a thin coat of chocolate buttercream and decorated with chocolate cutouts or curls if you like.*

VARIATION. *A dramatic way to embellish this cake is to cover the side with large chocolate fans immediately after glazing it. Any kind of thin chocolate shape could be used around the side of the glazed cake to decorate it. For example, you can spread the melted chocolate onto parchment paper and either spread it out into fan-like shapes or cool it slightly and cut with a pastry cutter into heart shapes or other forms. Refrigerate the shapes until ready to use.*

4 cups ganache in a microwave-safe bowl and heat at medium power until just warm, stirring occasionally. Watch the ganache carefully so it does not overheat in the microwave. Stir in the heavy cream until well blended. Pour the warm glaze over the top of the cake. Using a few quick strokes with a clean offset metal spatula, spread the glaze evenly over the cake, so it flows down the side. Refrigerate until the glaze sets.

This cake is best served at room temperature. To serve, cut the cake into wedges and accompany each slice with a scoop of raspberry sorbet. Refrigerated, the cake will remain fresh for up to 2 days. This cake also freezes well, for up to one month.

CHOCOLATE TOFFEE TORTE

Almost a fallen soufflé, this dense, deep, dark chocolate torte is without a doubt one of my signature cakes. Filled with mocha buttercream chock-full of morsels of homemade English toffee, and topped with a thin layer of ganache, it's pretty hard to resist. The toffee recipe makes more than is called for in the torte, but it keeps well and is great to have on hand for a last-minute dessert.

SPECIAL EQUIPMENT: CANDY THERMOMETER

MAKE THE TORTE. Melt the chocolate in a large bowl set over a saucepan of simmering water, stirring frequently. When the chocolate has melted, remove from the heat and leave the chocolate over the hot water. (You can put the chocolate into a microwave-safe bowl and heat on medium power in 10-second intervals, stirring frequently, until melted.)

Meanwhile, beat the butter with ¼ cup of the sugar on medium speed in the bowl of an electric mixer fitted with the paddle attachment until light and fluffy. Add the egg yolks and beat for 1 minute. Add the almonds and rum and beat for about 3 minutes longer.

Beat the egg whites on medium speed in a clean bowl of the electric mixer fitted with the whisk attachment until foamy and white. Gradually add the remaining ¼ cup sugar, beating until the whites form stiff and glossy peaks.

Add the melted chocolate to the butter mixture and mix with a rubber spatula until well combined. Fold one-quarter of the chocolate mixture into the egg whites, and then fold the egg whites into the chocolate mixture all at once, folding gently to avoid deflating the meringue.

Pour the batter into the prepared cake pan and bake for 18 to 22 minutes, or until a cake tester inserted in the center comes out with some moist crumbs clinging. The cake should be a bit underdone. The surface of the cake will be

TORTE

YIELD: 8-INCH ROUND CAKE

10 ounces bittersweet chocolate, chopped

4 ounces (1 stick) unsalted butter, at room temperature

½ cup sugar

5 large egg yolks (100 grams or scant ½ cup)

⅓ cup blanched almonds, finely ground

2 tablespoons dark rum, such as Myers's

5 large egg whites (150 grams or ⅔ cup)

PREPARATION. Preheat the oven to 300°F. Butter an 8 X 3–inch round cake pan. Line the bottom with parchment paper and butter the paper.

cracked, and when shaken it should be a little wobbly. Cool the cake in its pan on a cooling rack for 1 hour, then carefully turn the cake out onto a cake plate or 8-inch cardboard cake round. Wrap in plastic wrap and refrigerate while preparing the toffee and buttercream. The wrapped cake can be refrigerated for up to 1 week or frozen for up to 1 month.

ENGLISH TOFFEE

YIELD: 2 CUPS

1 cup granulated sugar

¼ cup water

1 tablespoon light corn syrup

1 teaspoon vanilla extract

6 ounces (1½ sticks) unsalted butter

2 cups walnut halves

PREPARATION. Grease an 18 X 13–inch half-sheet or jelly-roll pan with vegetable oil and set aside. Have ready a pastry brush and cup of cold water.

MAKE THE TOFFEE. Place the sugar, water, corn syrup, and vanilla in a heavy-bottomed large saucepan and stir well to dissolve the sugar. Cook the mixture over high heat, stirring often, until it comes to a boil, washing down the inside of the pot with a pastry brush dipped in cold water. Let the mixture boil for 1 minute. Add the butter, stirring to combine. Wash down the side of the pan one last time and continue to boil, stirring often. Make sure to scrape the bottom of the pan to keep the mixture from burning. When the mixture reaches 290°F on a candy thermometer and is the color of a brown paper bag, remove from the heat and stir in the walnuts.

Immediately turn the mixture onto the prepared pan and let cool completely. Break the toffee into pieces and wrap in plastic wrap. It will keep for several weeks at room temperature if wrapped in plastic wrap and stored in an airtight container. Do not refrigerate.

CRÈME GANACHE

YIELD: 5 TO 6 CUPS

4 cups heavy cream

2 pounds Callebaut 60/40 bittersweet chocolate, finely chopped

MAKE THE GANACHE. Bring the cream to a boil in a large saucepan. When the cream boils up the side of the pan, immediately remove from the heat and add the chocolate, stirring with a wire whisk until the chocolate has melted and the mixture is smooth with no small bits of chocolate remaining. Pour the ganache into a bowl and let cool to room temperature (uncovered, so no condensation forms). Cover the bowl with plastic wrap and refrigerate the ganache until firm, about 3 hours. You can hasten cooling by pouring the ganache into a half-sheet or jelly-roll pan and chilling for 1 hour. When you are ready to use the ganache, scoop out the needed amount with a metal spoon that has been dipped in hot water and place it in a microwave-safe bowl. This recipe can be doubled or tripled successfully.

MAKE THE BUTTERCREAM. Place the sugar and water in a small saucepan and stir to mix well. Place the saucepan over high heat and bring to a boil, stirring to dissolve the sugar. Wash any sugar from the side of the pan with a pastry brush dipped in water. Do not stir the syrup after it boils.

Meanwhile, place the egg yolks in the bowl of an electric mixer fitted with the whisk attachment and mix on low speed until light and pale yellow, about 5 minutes. The yolks should reach this point at the same time that the sugar syrup reaches the firm-ball stage (242°F on a candy thermometer). Immediately pour the syrup in a thin, steady stream down the inside of the bowl into the egg yolks. Increase the speed to medium high and continue to beat until the mixture is at room temperature, about 15 minutes. If the bowl has cooled to room temperature, the egg yolks are ready. Reduce to medium speed and add the butter several tablespoons at a time, beating until all the butter has been incorporated and scraping down the inside of the bowl if necessary. Set aside.

EGG-YOLK BUTTERCREAM

YIELD: 4 CUPS

½ cup sugar

¼ cup water

12 large egg yolks (240 grams or 1 cup)

1 pound (4 sticks) unsalted butter, at room temperature

PREPARATION. Have ready a pastry brush and cup of cold water.

Torte

4 cups Egg-Yolk Buttercream

5 cups Crème Ganache

2 cups crushed English Toffee

½ cup heavy cream

Chocolate shavings (optional)

◆ IT'S ALWAYS A GOOD IDEA TO HAVE A SUPPLY OF BUTTERCREAM ON HAND. REFRIGERATED AND WRAPPED IN PLASTIC WRAP, IT WILL REMAIN FRESH FOR UP TO 1 WEEK, FROZEN FOR UP TO 1 MONTH. TO BRING IT BACK TO A SPREADABLE CONSISTENCY, THAW AT ROOM TEMPERATURE, WARM BRIEFLY IN THE MICROWAVE, THEN WHIP IT WITH A WHISK.

ASSEMBLE THE TORTE. Place the torte on a cake plate or cardboard cake round. Melt ½ cup of the ganache in a microwave-safe bowl and heat at 10-second intervals to approximately 94°F. Place the buttercream in a large bowl and fold in the melted ganache. Fold in the crushed toffee. Use a metal offset spatula to spread the buttercream mixture over the top of the chilled cake, smoothing it with a metal spatula. Refrigerate, uncovered, for at least 2 hours, or up to 24 hours.

Using room-temperature ganache (74°F), whip with either a whisk or a handheld mixer 2 cups of the crème ganache until light and fluffy and smooth it over the top and side of the cake. Refrigerate the cake again for about 2 hours or up to overnight. Leave the cake uncovered until it is firm, then cover loosely with plastic wrap.

Place the remaining 2½ cups of ganache in a microwave-safe bowl and heat at 10-second intervals to approximately 94°F. Stir the cream into the 2½ cups of melted ganache. Place the cake on a cooling rack set over a tray and pour the ganache glaze over the top of the chilled cake. Use a long metal icing spatula to smooth the top of the cake to remove any excess glaze. Add chocolate shavings to embellish the sides of the cake, if desired.

◆ IT IS IMPORTANT TO CHILL THE CAKE, UNCOVERED, UNTIL THE GLAZE SETS, WHICH TAKES AT LEAST 3 HOURS. REFRIGERATED AND COVERED, THE CAKE WILL REMAIN FRESH FOR UP TO 1 WEEK, BUT THE GLAZE WILL CRACK AFTER A FEW DAYS. BE SURE TO BRING THE CAKE TO ROOM TEMPERATURE BEFORE SERVING, FOR THE BEST FLAVOR. UNGLAZED, THE CAKE FREEZES BEAUTIFULLY IF WRAPPED WELL, FOR UP TO 1 MONTH.

CHOCOLATE VIENNESE CAKE

This is my version of the famous Sacher Torte. I had the joy of actually eating a piece at the Hotel Sacher in Vienna in 1991. I expected to be disappointed because I had heard and read about this very cake for years. How could it possibly be as good as the reverent descriptions? Yet, it was wonderful! It was a very light, moist, and deeply chocolatey cake sandwiched with a layer of apricot preserves and glazed with a smooth chocolate coating. My cake has the same lightness and moistness but a slightly different texture, as I use cornstarch instead of flour, which gives it lightness as well as a soft and tender crumb. And the combination of the bittersweet chocolate glaze and the apricot filling is lovely. My rendition is sophisticated-looking but simple to make. The technique I use to make this cake is unusual. Typically, you would start by whipping room-temperature butter and sugar together and then adding melted chocolate. Here, I melt the chocolate then add butter to it, creating an almost mayonnaise-like emulsion, which I think gives the cake its marvelously airy, almost mousse-like texture. I enjoy eating this cake as much as I savored the cake that glorious day in Vienna!

SPECIAL EQUIPMENT: PASTRY BAG FITTED WITH A STAR TIP, SUCH AS WILTON #22 OR ATECO #22

MAKE THE CAKE. Combine the chocolate, light cream, and rum in a medium bowl and set over a bowl of hot water, stirring frequently, until the chocolate has completely melted. Remove from the heat and add the chilled butter one piece at a time, beating with a whisk or handheld electric mixer after each addition until it is thoroughly incorporated.

Whisk the egg yolks and 1 tablespoon of the sugar in a large bowl until light and lemon-colored. Fold the egg-yolk mixture into the chocolate mixture and whisk until smooth and fluffy. Immediately fold all the cornstarch into the chocolate mixture until blended well. If you feel the chocolate begin to stiffen, warm it by setting it over a bowl of hot water until it is fluid enough to accept the egg whites without breaking them down. If the chocolate goes below about 96°F, it may be too cool, and therefore too stiff, to mix the whites into. (The fluidity of the chocolate

CHOCOLATE VIENNESE CAKE

YIELD: TWO 8-INCH ROUND CAKE LAYERS

11 ounces bittersweet chocolate, preferably Valrhona Caraibe, Scharffen Berger 70%, or Lindt Excellence, chopped

½ cup light cream or half-and-half

1 tablespoon dark rum, such as Myers's

4 ounces (1 stick) unsalted butter, diced and chilled

5 large eggs, separated (100 grams or scant ½ cup yolks; 150 grams or ⅔ cup whites)

⅓ cup sugar

½ cup cornstarch, sifted

See Preparation at the top of page 63.

is very important here, as well as in any recipe that has beaten egg whites added to a chocolate mixture.)

Whip the egg whites on high speed in the bowl of an electric mixer fitted with the whisk attachment until foamy and beginning to hold a shape, then gradually add the remaining sugar until the whites form stiff and glossy peaks. Fold ¼ of the meringue into the chocolate mixture with a rubber spatula to lighten it. Gently fold in the remaining whites until no longer visible, being careful not to overmix.

Divide the batter evenly between the prepared pans. Bake for about 18 minutes, or until a cake tester inserted in the center comes out with a few moist crumbs clinging, being careful not to overbake the layers. Cool the cakes in their pans on cooling racks for about 10 minutes, then invert onto racks and remove the parchment. Let the cakes cool completely. The cakes will fall as they cool, which is normal.

MAKE THE GLAZE. Combine the cream, sugar, and corn syrup in a small saucepan and cook over very low heat, stirring frequently with a wooden spoon until the sugar has dissolved, about 3 minutes. Remove from the heat and add the chocolate and vanilla. Let the mixture sit for about 1 minute to allow the chocolate to melt. Stir until smooth and then let the mixture cool until pourable.

ASSEMBLE THE CAKE. Place 1 cake layer on an 8-inch cardboard cake round or cake plate. Use an offset metal spatula to spread the apricot preserves over the top of the cake. Place the second layer, bottom side up, on top.

Set the cake on a cooling rack set over a half-sheet or jelly-roll pan to catch the excess glaze. Pour the chocolate

PREPARATION. Preheat the oven to 350°F. Butter two 8 X 2–inch round cake pans and line with parchment paper.

BITTERSWEET CHOCOLATE GLAZE

YIELD: 2 CUPS

1 cup heavy cream

¼ cup sugar

1 teaspoon light corn syrup

8 ounces bittersweet chocolate, preferably Valrhona Caraibe, Valrhona Manjari, or Scharffen Berger 70%, finely chopped

1 teaspoon vanilla extract

ASSEMBLY

2 Chocolate Viennese Cake layers

½ cup apricot preserves

2 cups Bittersweet Chocolate Glaze

◆ IF THE PRESERVES ARE
ESPECIALLY CHUNKY, I PUREE THEM
FIRST IN A MINI FOOD PROCESSOR.

◆ ALTHOUGH IT WILL STAY FRESH
IF REFRIGERATED AND WRAPPED
TIGHTLY IN PLASTIC WRAP FOR UP
TO SEVERAL DAYS, I DO THINK THIS
CAKE IS BEST SERVED THE DAY IT
IS MADE.

glaze over the top of the cake, letting it run down the side of the cake, smoothing out the top with a spatula as needed. Refrigerate the cake until the glaze sets, about 3 hours, or refrigerate for up to several hours. Remove from the refrigerator 1 to 2 hours before serving.

For a more finished look, pour about a third of the chocolate glaze over the top of the cake and smooth it out with a metal spatula, spreading it just to the edge. Refrigerate the cake until the glaze just sets, about 15 minutes. Meanwhile, transfer the remaining chocolate glaze to a bowl of an electric mixer. Thicken the glaze by chilling it in the refrigerator for about 10 minutes, or by resting it in a bowl of ice water for several minutes. Place the bowl with the thickened mixture in the mixer fitted with the whisk attachment and beat the glaze on high speed until it is thick and fluffy, about 2 minutes. Remove the cake from the refrigerator and spread most of the whipped glaze around the side of the cake. Fill a pastry bag fitted with a star tip, such as a Wilton #22, with the remaining glaze and pipe a decorative rim around the top edge of the cake. Refrigerate the cake until the glaze sets, about 1 hour, or refrigerate for up to several hours; remove from the refrigerator about 1 to 2 hours before serving.

I often plate this elegant dessert with a side of sweetened whipped cream and a dollop of apricot cream. Traditionally, however, it is served only with *Schlagober* (sweetened whipped cream).

SWEETENED WHIPPED CREAM

YIELD: 2 CUPS

2 cups heavy cream

1 tablespoon confectioners' sugar

MAKE THE WHIPPED CREAM. Place the cream and sugar in a large bowl and whisk to stiff peaks.

◆ ADDING CONFECTIONERS' SUGAR TO WHIPPED CREAM HELPS TO STABILIZE IT. GRANULATED SUGAR TENDS TO BREAK DOWN WHIPPED CREAM, CAUSING MOISTURE TO SEPARATE OUT, WHEREAS CONFECTIONERS' SUGAR ABSORBS THE MOISTURE BECAUSE IT CONTAINS CORNSTARCH.

MAKE THE APRICOT CREAM. Puree the preserves in a food processor until smooth. Combine the cornstarch and sherry in a small saucepan; stir until smooth. Add the apricot puree, orange zest and juice, and lemon juice. Cook over medium heat, stirring constantly, until thick, about 4 minutes. Pour into a bowl and cover with plastic wrap to keep a skin from forming. Cool to room temperature, and then refrigerate for several hours before using. Refrigerated, it will stay fresh for 1 week.

APRICOT CREAM

YIELD: 1 CUP

¾ cup apricot preserves

2 tablespoons cornstarch

⅓ cup Harvey's Bristol Cream sherry

Finely grated zest and freshly squeezed juice of 1 orange

2 tablespoons freshly squeezed lemon juice

THE CLEVELAND PARK CREAM CAKES

I suppose these little cakes are most like Boston cream pie, which really isn't a pie at all but a custard-filled yellow cake covered with chocolate glaze. Here it is made of a simple, rather light pound cake that is baked in jumbo muffin cups, then filled with custard and glistened with a little warm chocolate that is poured over the tops and allowed to run down the sides. It's a wonderful old-fashioned dessert. This recipe was submitted on behalf of Chef Frank Ruta and me to *Cooking from the Heart,* a cookbook by Share our Strength, an organization dedicated to eradicating childhood hunger in the United States.

SPECIAL EQUIPMENT: TWO JUMBO (3-INCH) MUFFIN PANS, PREFERABLY STRAIGHT-SIDED

PASTRY CREAM

YIELD: 2 CUPS

½ cup sugar

¼ cup (30 grams) cake flour, sifted

2 cups milk

8 large egg yolks (160 grams
  or ¾ cup)

1 teaspoon vanilla extract

MAKE THE PASTRY CREAM. Combine the sugar and flour in a bowl and stir with a whisk to remove any lumps. Bring the milk to a boil in a large saucepan.

Meanwhile, place the egg yolks in the bowl of an electric mixer fitted with the whisk attachment and mix on high speed for about 2 minutes. Add the flour mixture and continue to beat on high until the mixture is thick, heavy, and pale. Remove the bowl from the mixer and bring it over to the stove. When the milk has come to a rolling boil, rising up the side of the pan, reduce the heat to low.

Whisk about ½ cup of the hot milk into the egg mixture to temper it, then pour the mixture back into the saucepan and continue to cook for about 2 minutes on medium-low heat, stirring constantly, until the custard begins to bubble or "burp." Cooking the mixture for this additional time removes any floury aftertaste.

Remove the pan from the heat and whisk in the vanilla. Pour the custard into a bowl and press a piece of plastic wrap directly onto the surface, leaving a very small area uncovered to allow the heat to escape to prevent a skin from forming on the surface. Let cool completely, then cover with plastic wrap and refrigerate until cold.

MAKE THE CRÈME ANGLAISE. Pour the milk into a heavy nonreactive medium saucepan and bring to a rolling boil over medium-high heat. Let the mixture rise up the side of the pan, then immediately remove from the heat.

Meanwhile, beat the egg yolks with the sugar on high speed in the bowl of an electric mixer fitted with the whisk attachment until very thick and pale, 3 to 4 minutes. The mixture will triple in volume and form a ribbon when dropped from the whisk.

Bring the bowl over to the stove. Whisk about ½ cup of the hot milk into the yolk mixture to temper it, then pour the mixture back into the saucepan. Stir until thick enough to coat a wooden spoon. (Run your finger through the custard on the back of the spoon. The custard is thick enough when the line remains.) Immediately pour the custard through a fine-mesh strainer or China cap into a large bowl and whisk to cool. Add the vanilla and refrigerate, stirring occasionally, until cold, then cover. Refrigerated, the anglaise will remain fresh for up to 3 days.

CRÈME ANGLAISE

YIELD: ABOUT 3 CUPS

2 cups milk

5 large egg yolks (100 grams or scant ½ cup)

½ cup sugar

1 teaspoon vanilla extract

MAKE THE HOT FUDGE SAUCE. Melt the chocolate and butter in a small saucepan over very low heat, stirring frequently. Mix the sugar and cocoa together. Add the cocoa mixture and light cream to the chocolate mixture and cook, stirring frequently, for about 15 minutes. Add the confectioners' sugar, stirring well to combine. The sauce will remain fresh in an airtight container refrigerated for up to several weeks.

HOT FUDGE SAUCE

YIELD: ABOUT 2 CUPS

4 ounces unsweetened chocolate, chopped

8 ounces (2 sticks) unsalted butter

1½ cups sugar

½ cup Dutch-processed cocoa

1 cup light cream

½ cup confectioners' sugar

PRESERVED ORANGE SLICES

YIELD: ABOUT 3½ CUPS

4 navel oranges

1¼ cups cold water

1 cup sugar

3 tablespoons freshly squeezed
  lemon juice

2 tablespoons Grand Marnier

MAKE THE ORANGE SLICES. Cut each orange crosswise into 6 thick rounds. Place the slices in a nonreactive medium saucepan with enough cold water to cover. Bring to a boil over medium-high heat, reduce the heat to medium, and cook for 1 hour. Drain. Set the orange slices aside.

Combine the water, sugar, and lemon juice in the same saucepan. Cook over medium heat, stirring until the sugar dissolves. Add the orange slices and cook until the slices are very tender but not falling apart, about 1 hour. Remove from the heat and allow the slices to cool in the syrup. Add the Grand Marnier. Transfer to a covered glass container and refrigerate until ready to use.

VANILLA CAKES

YIELD: FIFTEEN 3-INCH CAKES

2 cups (240 grams) cake flour

2½ teaspoons baking powder

5 large eggs (250 grams), separated

1 cup sugar

4 ounces (1 stick) unsalted butter,
  melted and slightly cooled

¼ cup neutral vegetable oil

1 teaspoon vanilla extract

¾ cup buttermilk

PREPARATION. Position a rack in the middle of the oven and preheat the oven to 350°F. Line fifteen 3-inch muffin cups with jumbo paper liners.

◆ I LIKE TO USE HEAVY-DUTY, STRAIGHT-SIDED 3-INCH MUFFIN CUPS FOR THIS RECIPE RATHER THAN THE USUAL SLOPE-SIDED MUFFIN CUPS, SO THAT THEY REALLY LOOK LIKE LITTLE CAKES RATHER THAN MUFFINS.

MAKE THE CAKES. Sift the flour and baking powder into a bowl; set aside. Beat the egg yolks and ¼ cup of the sugar in the bowl of an electric mixer fitted with the whisk attachment at medium-high speed until thick enough to form a ribbon when it falls from the whisk, at least 2 minutes. Add the melted butter, oil, and vanilla, mixing until combined. Add a third of the flour mixture until combined, then add half the buttermilk and mix well; add the second third of the flour mixture, mix well again, add the remaining buttermilk, mix well, and end with the last third of the flour mixture, beating until smooth.

Place the egg whites in a clean bowl of the electric mixer fitted with the whisk attachment and whip on high until foamy and white. Gradually add the remaining ¾ cup sugar and beat until the whites form stiff, glossy peaks. Gently fold the egg whites into the cake batter all at once. Divide the batter among the prepared muffin cups, filling them two-thirds full.

Bake for 15 minutes, rotate the pans from front to back, then bake for another 5 minutes, or until the cakes are golden and a cake tester inserted in the center comes out clean. Let the cakes cool in their pans on cooling racks for 5 minutes. Remove the cakes from their pans and cool completely on racks. Cover loosely with plastic wrap and set aside.

◆ To ensure that each cake is exactly the same size, I spoon the batter into a pastry bag fitted with a ½-inch plain tip (ateco #26) and pipe it into the muffin cups.

ASSEMBLE THE CAKES. Remove the cakes from their paper liners and slice them horizontally in thirds. Place the largest layers (the tops of the cakes), cut side up, on plates and top each with 2 heaping tablespoons of pastry cream. Place the middle layers on the cream and top each with 2 heaping tablespoons of preserved orange. Place the final cake layer, cut side down, over the oranges. Pour 3 tablespoons of crème anglaise around the base of the cakes. Spoon 2 tablespoons of hot fudge sauce over the tops of the cakes, allowing it to run down the sides and into the crème anglaise. These cakes are best served the day they are made.

ASSEMBLY

15 Vanilla Cakes

2 cups Pastry Cream

About 3½ cups chopped Preserved
    Orange Slices

2 cups Crème Anglaise

2 cups Hot Fudge Sauce

DEMAYO CHOCOLATE CAKE

T his cake is named in honor of my friend Melissa DeMayo, a former New York City pastry
chef of great talent I met years ago at a meeting of the Bakers Dozen East. Melissa,
along with Penelope Pate Green, was instrumental in forming the organization—Nick
Malgieri's brainchild—an informal group where women in the pastry business could get
together and brainstorm about recipes, techniques, and the industry. During a visit with
Melissa in Pennsylvania, she asked if I would like the recipe for the greatest chocolate cake.
"Absolutely," I said. This marvelous, foolproof cake is tender and moist and has an intense
chocolate flavor. Here I've paired it with Melissa's coconut custard–cream filling for
an updated version of German chocolate cake. Chocolate lovers may want to pair it
with a luxurious chocolate mousse filling or an old-fashioned chocolate frosting.

DEMAYO CAKE

YIELD: THREE 8-INCH ROUND CAKE
LAYERS

2 cups sugar

1⅔ cups (200 grams) cake flour

1 cup Scharffen Berger natural cocoa

2 teaspoons baking soda

1 teaspoon baking powder

¼ teaspoon salt

1 cup buttermilk

1 cup water, at room temperature

3 large eggs (150 grams or ⅔ cup)

2 teaspoons vanilla extract

4 ounces (1 stick) unsalted butter,
melted and cooled to tepid

PREPARATION. Preheat the oven to
350°F. Butter three 8 X 2–inch round
cake pans. Line the bottoms with
parchment paper and butter the paper.

MAKE THE CAKE. Sift the sugar, flour, cocoa, baking soda, baking powder, and salt into a 10-quart bowl (or the largest you have). Mix together well.

Whisk the buttermilk, water, eggs, and vanilla in a medium bowl until just combined. Immediately whisk the egg mixture into the flour mixture until smooth, scraping down the inside of the bowl with a rubber spatula. Add the butter and stir with the whisk until well combined. The batter will be somewhat thin.

Divide the batter evenly among the prepared pans, gently shaking them to level the batter if necessary. Bake for 15 to 18 minutes, or until the cakes are springy to the touch, start to pull away from the sides of the pans, and a cake tester inserted in the center comes out clean.

Let the cakes cool in their pans on cooling racks for 10 minutes. Invert them onto racks, remove the parchment, and invert them again so they are right side up. The cakes can be filled or wrapped tightly in plastic wrap and refrigerated for 1 day or frozen for up to 1 month.

MAKE THE FILLING. Whisk the egg yolks in a large bowl until well combined. Set aside. Combine the butter, half-and-half, sugar, and vanilla in a medium saucepan and bring to a full boil over medium-high heat. Reduce the heat to a simmer and cook for about 1 minute.

Bring the bowl with the egg yolks over to the stove. Whisk about 1 cup of the hot cream mixture into the egg yolks to temper them, then pour the mixture back into the saucepan. Cook over medium heat, stirring often with a whisk, until slightly thickened, about 1 minute. Remove from the heat and whisk in the coconut, stirring until the filling is thoroughly mixed. As you stir, the coconut will absorb the custard and the filling will thicken. To chill the filling quickly and uniformly, pour it onto an 18 X 13–inch half-sheet or jelly-roll pan and spread evenly with a rubber spatula. Cover with plastic wrap and refrigerate for at least 1 hour, or until cool.

ASSEMBLE THE CAKE. Place 1 cake layer on an 8-inch cardboard cake round or cake plate. Use a stiff offset metal spatula to spread one-third of the chilled custard filling evenly over the cake. If the filling seems so stiff that it might damage the cake, gradually add the heavy cream to loosen it a bit. Place the second cake layer on top and spread another third of the custard over the cake. Place the final cake layer on top and spread the remaining custard over the top of the cake, leaving the side bare.

Sprinkle the shaved coconut over the top of the cake. Cover loosely with plastic wrap and refrigerate until ready to serve. Slice into hearty wedges and serve at a little cooler than room temperature. Refrigerated, the cake will stay fresh for 2 to 3 days.

CUSTARD FILLING

YIELD: 4 CUPS

6 large egg yolks (120 grams or ½ cup)

6 ounces (1½ sticks) unsalted butter

2 cups half-and-half

1 cup sugar

1 teaspoon vanilla extract

2½ cups shredded unsweetened coconut (preferably unsulphured)

VARIATION. *For a little extra crunch, add 1 cup chopped pecans to the custard.*

ASSEMBLY

3 DeMayo Cake layers

4 cups Custard Filling

2 to 3 tablespoons heavy cream (optional)

1 cup large shavings desiccated unsweetened coconut (preferably unsulphured)

◆ I LIKE TO ACCOMPANY EACH SLICE OF CAKE WITH A
SCOOP OF COCONUT SORBET (PAGE 292) AND A CREAM
CHEESE BROWNIE (PAGE 292) STALK. TO MAKE A STALK,
CUT A BROWNIE INTO ½-INCH SLICES. PLACE THE CAKE
AT THE TOP OF THE PLATE, THE TWELVE-O'CLOCK
POSITION. SPRINKLE ABOUT 2 TABLESPOONS OF
SHREDDED COCONUT ON THE CENTER OF THE PLATE
TO HELP KEEP THE SORBET IN PLACE. PLACE AN OVAL
SCOOP OF SORBET ON TOP OF THE COCONUT AND
STAND THE BROWNIE STALK AGAINST THE SORBET.

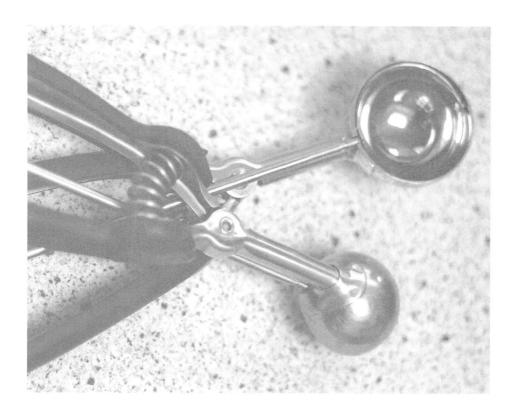

HONEY CAKE WITH GINGER PEACH ICE CREAM

MAKES 2 LOAVES, 6 SLICES EACH. SERVES 10 TO 12

A good honey cake is worth its weight in gold. This is an adaptation of Grandma Faye's recipe. Grandma Faye was the grandmother of Linda Krinn, the wife of Mal Krinn, who baked for the fun of it at both the Wheaton and Cleveland Park Bakery. She was, by all accounts, a stellar and rather elegant baker. I've tweaked the ingredients of the original cake a little, making this new version one of the loveliest honey cakes I've ever eaten. Here, it's matched with a fruity spiced ice cream, but it's also delicious plain or served with a scoop of light citrus sorbet.

SPECIAL EQUIPMENT: ICE-CREAM MAKER

MAKE THE ICE CREAM. Combine the milk, cream, and ¼ cup of the sugar in a heavy medium saucepan and bring to a boil over medium-high heat. When the mixture boils up the side of the pan, immediately turn off the heat.

Meanwhile, beat the egg yolks and the remaining ¾ cup sugar on high speed in the bowl of an electric mixer fitted with the whisk attachment until very thick and pale, 3 to 4 minutes. The mixture will triple in volume and form a thick ribbon when dropped from the whisk.

Bring the bowl over to the stove. Whisk about 1 cup of the hot cream mixture into the yolk mixture to temper it, then pour the mixture back into the saucepan and whisk to cook the yolks thoroughly. The mixture should be thick enough to coat a wooden spoon. (Run your finger through the custard on the back of the spoon. The custard is thick enough when the line remains.) Pour the custard through a fine-mesh strainer or China cap into a large bowl. Place in an ice bath and refrigerate until chilled, but preferably for 8 hours, stirring occasionally.

GINGER PEACH ICE CREAM

YIELD: ABOUT 1 QUART

2 cups milk

2 cups heavy cream

1 cup sugar

11 to 12 large egg yolks (225 grams or 1 cup)

6 very ripe, medium peaches, peeled and diced into ½-inch pieces

¼ cup candied ginger, very finely chopped

CONTINUED

Transfer the mixture to an ice-cream maker and freeze according to the manufacturer's instructions. Gently stir the peaches and ginger into the soft ice cream as soon as it is removed from the machine. Transfer the ice cream to an airtight container and freeze for at least 1 hour or up to 24 hours.

HONEY CAKE

YIELD: TWO 9 X 5–INCH LOAVES

2 cups (240 grams) cake flour

½ teaspoon baking soda

½ teaspoon ground cinnamon

½ teaspoon ground ginger

½ teaspoon ground allspice

4 large eggs (200 grams or ⅞ cup)

1 cup sugar

1 cup honey

1 cup neutral vegetable oil

PREPARATION. Preheat the oven to 350°F. Butter two 9 X 5–inch loaf pans, line the pans with 2 pieces of parchment paper, and butter the paper.

◆ I SOMETIMES SERVE THIS CAKE SLICED INTO STRIPS (FINGERS), USING THE STRIPS TO FORM A RECTANGLE ON A PLATE. EACH SIDE OF THE RECTANGLE SHOULD BE TWO STRIPS HIGH TO FORM A WALL. THEN I FILL THE CENTER WITH SCOOPS OF LIME SORBET OR CITRUS SORBET (PAGE 26).

ASSEMBLY

2 Honey Cake loaves

Ginger Peach Ice Cream

MAKE THE HONEY CAKE. Sift the flour, baking soda, cinnamon, ginger, and allspice into a bowl; set aside. Place the eggs and sugar in the bowl of an electric mixer fitted with the whisk attachment. Beat on high speed until the mixture is light and fluffy. Reduce the speed to low and add the honey, then the oil. Mix on low speed for 2½ minutes, then on medium speed for an additional 2½ minutes. Fold in the flour mixture by hand in several additions, mixing well with a spatula. Spoon the batter into the prepared pans, dividing it evenly.

After much experimentation, I have found that filling the pans no more than half full ensures that the cakes will not collapse during baking due to lack of rising space or that they will be done before their crust becomes overly dark.

Bake for 30 to 40 minutes, or until domed, set, and a cake tester inserted in the center comes out clean. (The loaves will crack during baking.) Do not open the oven doors until the cakes have domed as this could cause them to collapse. Cool the loaves in their pans on cooling racks for 1 hour. Unmold the cakes onto racks and wrap tightly in plastic wrap while they are still slightly warm, to preserve moistness, until ready to serve. At room temperature, the cakes will remain fresh for up to 3 days, or you can freeze them for up to 1 month.

ASSEMBLE THE DESSERT. Cut the loaves into slices and serve at room temperature along with scoops of ice cream.

LEMON BUTTERCREAM TORTE

This cake is pure lemon, with its cake layers doused in lemon syrup made with freshly squeezed lemon juice and just enough sugar to take away the very tart edge. The layers are topped with marmalade and lemon curd and then coated with lemon buttercream. The bright flavor of fresh lemon juice permeates the layers, a flavor that is incomparable and takes the dessert to another level. For special occasions, I like to slather the cake with the lemon buttercream, then decorate it with a starburst of candied grapefruit peel on the top and coat the sides with sugared toasted almonds.

SPECIAL EQUIPMENT: CANDY THERMOMETER • PASTRY BAG FITTED WITH A STAR TIP (ATECO #24)

MAKE THE GÉNOISE. Sift the flour into a bowl. Set aside.

Place the eggs, sugar, and lemon zest in the bowl of an electric mixer. Place the bowl over a hot water bath and whisk the mixture by hand until the sugar has dissolved and the eggs are warm and dark yellow, about 2 minutes. When the mixture is homogenized and lightly translucent, it is ready to beat in the mixer.

Beat the egg mixture on high speed in an electric mixer fitted with the whisk attachment until the mixture triples in volume, about 5 minutes. Reduce the mixer to low and continue beating for 1 minute. Be careful not to overbeat the eggs at this point. Delicately but quickly add the flour, turning off the mixer before the flour is fully incorporated. Use a rubber spatula or bowl scraper to gently finish mixing the batter, being careful not to deflate all the wonderful airiness that has been developed. (Using a scraper helps to get to the very bottom of the bowl so there are no stray particles of flour remaining.)

Gently divide the batter between the prepared pans. Bake for 20 minutes, or until the cakes are springy to the touch, golden, pull away slightly from the sides of the pans, and a cake tester inserted in the center of the cakes comes out clean. Do not open the oven door until the cakes have domed.

YELLOW GÉNOISE

YIELD: TWO 9-INCH ROUND CAKES

2 cups plus 3 tablespoons cake flour (243 grams)

8 large eggs (396 grams or 1¾ cups)

1 cup plus 3 tablespoons sugar (242 grams)

2 teaspoons finely grated lemon zest

PREPARATION. Position a rack in the middle of the oven and preheat the oven to 350°F. Lightly butter two 9 X 3–inch cake pans.

CONTINUED

Let the cakes cool in their pans on cooling racks for just 5 minutes, then unmold them and invert them onto racks so they are right side up. Cool completely. The cakes can be filled, or wrapped tightly in plastic wrap and refrigerated for up to 2 days, or freeze them for up to 1 month.

LEMON CURD JEAN-LOUIS

YIELD: ABOUT 2 CUPS

1 cup lemon juice (from about 5 large lemons) and zest from 2 lemons

4 ounces (1 stick) unsalted butter

3 large eggs (150 grams or ⅔ cup)

3 large egg yolks (60 grams or ¼ cup)

2 to 2¼ cups sugar

◆ WHEN COOKING CITRUS JUICE, I USE ONLY NONREACTIVE PANS AND STAINLESS-STEEL STRAINERS, SUCH AS STAINLESS-STEEL OR CERAMIC-COATED STEEL; ALUMINUM REACTS WITH ACID, LEAVING A METALLIC AFTERTASTE.

MAKE THE LEMON CURD. Finely grate the zest of 2 lemons, then squeeze enough juice from the lemons to equal 1 cup of strained juice. Place the lemon juice, zest, and the butter in a heavy nonreactive medium saucepan and heat on low until the butter has completely melted. Have ready a fine-mesh stainless-steel strainer or China cap set over a bowl.

Meanwhile, mix the eggs, yolks, and 1 cup sugar on low speed in an electric mixer fitted with the whisk attachment until just combined. If whisked past this point, the curd will end up cloudy, instead of transparent and almost jelly-like.

Bring the bowl over to the stove. Whisk about 1 cup of the hot lemon mixture into the egg mixture to temper it, then pour the mixture back into the saucepan. Increase the heat to medium high and whisk well to combine. At this point, add the remaining 1¼ cups sugar a little at a time, tasting as you go. Adjust the quantity according to taste, as lemons can be more or less sour at different times of the year. The curd should taste sweet at first and tart at the end. Make it a little bit sweeter than you think it should be, as some of the sweetness will be lost in the chilling.

Continue cooking the curd over medium heat, whisking constantly until thickened, 3 to 5 minutes. Stir vigorously, touching all points of the bottom of the pan to make sure the mixture doesn't burn. As the curd begins to thicken and you see steam rise from the saucepan, immediately remove from the heat. (Do not let the curd come to a boil.)

Quickly pour the curd through the stainless-steel strainer, using a rubber spatula to help press the mixture through. Press a piece of plastic wrap directly onto the surface of the curd, leaving a small vent. Set aside at room temperature until cool, then cover completely and refrigerate until cold and firm. Refrigerated, the curd will remain fresh for up to 2 weeks. It cannot be frozen.

MAKE THE MARMALADE. Use a vegetable peeler to remove the colorful outer skin of the orange, leaving the bitter white pith. Then use a small paring knife to cut away the pith and discard. Chop the orange flesh and thinly slice the peel. Combine the sugar, lemon juice, orange flesh, and peel in a nonreactive large saucepan and bring to a boil, stirring constantly. Reduce the heat to very low and simmer, stirring frequently and skimming off the scum as it accumulates, until the juices have thickened and the marmalade is clear, at least 1 hour. Spoon the marmalade into a bowl and refrigerate until cold.

ORANGE MARMALADE

YIELD: ABOUT 1 CUP

2 pounds navel oranges, or 4 to
    5 oranges

1¼ cups sugar

1 lemon, juiced

MAKE THE BUTTERCREAM. Combine the sugar and water in a small saucepan and stir to mix well. Place the saucepan over high heat and bring to a boil, stirring to dissolve the sugar. Wash any undissolved sugar from the inside of the pan with a pastry brush dipped in water. Do not stir the syrup after it boils.

Meanwhile, place the egg yolks in the bowl of an electric mixer fitted with the whisk attachment and beat on low speed. (They will thicken.) When the sugar syrup reaches a firm-ball stage (242°F on a candy thermometer—the bubbling syrup will take on a shiny and almost

EGG-YOLK BUTTERCREAM

YIELD: 4 CUPS

½ cup sugar

¼ cup water

12 large egg yolks (240 grams or 1 cup)

1 pound (4 sticks) unsalted butter,
    at room temperature

PREPARATION. Have ready a pastry brush
and cup of cold water.

plastic-looking quality), immediately pour the syrup into the egg yolks in a thin, steady stream down the inside of the bowl to prevent spattering, beating constantly. Increase the mixer speed to medium high and continue to beat the mixture until cooled to room temperature, about 15 minutes. If the bowl is cool to the touch, the yolk mixture is ready. Reduce the mixer speed to low and add the butter, several tablespoons at a time, beating until all the butter has been incorporated, scraping down the inside of the bowl if necessary.

ASSEMBLY

1 cup freshly squeezed lemon juice (from about 5 large lemons)

1½ cups water

½ cup sugar

4 cups Egg-Yolk Buttercream

About 2 cups Lemon Curd Jean-Louis

Confectioners' sugar (optional)

2 Yellow Génoise cakes

1 cup Orange Marmalade

VARIATION. *Divide the batter between two 18 × 13–inch half-sheet or jelly-roll pans. Bake at 350°F for about 5 minutes, then rotate the pan from front to back and bake for another 5 minutes. When it cools, I brush one layer with lemon syrup, spread with a layer of buttercream and a layer of lemon curd, then top it off with the second layer of cake. A final smooth coat of lemon buttercream goes over the top, and the cake is then chilled. Cut it into rectangles about 3½ × 2 inches and top each rectangle with Candied Grapefruit Peel (page 112).*

ASSEMBLE THE TORTE. Combine ⅔ cup of the lemon juice with the water and sugar in a bowl to make a light syrup. Set aside. Combine the buttercream with ⅔ cup of the lemon curd and the remaining ⅓ cup lemon juice; mix well. If the buttercream separates, set the bowl over hot water for a minute and whisk well. You may want to adjust the sweetness or tartness of the lemon buttercream to your own taste with a bit of confectioners' sugar.

Use a serrated knife to slice each cake horizontally in half to create four layers. Place 1 layer on a cake plate or cardboard cake round and brush with some lemon syrup. Use a stiff metal icing spatula to spread about 1 cup lemon buttercream on top, then spread ½ cup lemon curd over the buttercream. Place a second cake layer on the curd and brush with the lemon syrup. Spread with the orange marmalade. Place the third cake layer on top of the marmalade. Brush with lemon syrup, spread with 1 cup lemon buttercream, and then ½ cup lemon curd. Top with the final cake layer and brush with lemon syrup. Refrigerate for 30 minutes. Spread a thin coat of the remaining lemon buttercream over the top and side of the cake and refrigerate for 20 minutes more. Finish the cake by spreading ⅔ cup of the lemon buttercream over the cake smoothly and decorate with swirls using the remaining ⅓ cup of the lemon buttercream and an Ateco star tip #24.

APRICOT ORANGE TORTE (PAGE 22)

CRANBERRY BARS WITH CRANBERRY SORBET (PAGE 130)

CHOCOLATE ORANGE FONDANT OVALS (PAGE 164)

GOAT CHEESE CHEESECAKE SANDWICHES WITH
PUMPKINSEED BRITTLE (PAGE 320)

MONT BLANC (PAGE 116)

COFFEE ÉCLAIRS AFTER ROBERT (PAGE 166)

CHOCOLATE RASPBERRY TORTE
(PAGE 53)

CREAM CHEESE PUFF (PAGE 310)

BLACK-AND-WHITE COCONUT SURPRISES (PAGE 290)

THAT COOKIE PLATE CLOCKWISE FROM TOP: BRUSSELS, CHOCOLATE SPRITS, VANILLA NUTS, GINGERSNAPS, AND WELLINGTONS (PAGE 138)

CHOCOLATE BABKA (PAGE 47)

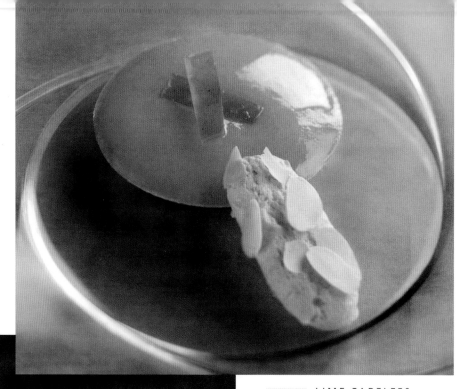

LIME TARTLETS
(PAGE 109)

TRIPLE CHOCOLATE TERRINE (PAGE 210)

MARYLAND STRUDEL WITH MANCHEGO CHEESE AND
SEASONAL GRAPES (PAGE 114)

SCHNECKEN WITH VANILLA ICE CREAM AND GINGER CARAMEL SAUCE (PAGE 257)

RED-AND-WHITE RICE PARFAITS WITH CRANBERRY LEATHER
(PAGE 200)

BIRDSEED CAKE (PAGE 33)

MACAROON MERINGUE TORTE

When I was sixteen, my mother took me to New York City as a graduation present. We went to the theater and afterwards, as a special treat, to Sardi's. I was thrilled beyond words. One of the specialties was a dessert called *Boccone Dolce*, a meringue, strawberry, and whipped cream affair enhanced with a crackle of chocolate. I never forgot it. I thought about making my own version of the cake with Amaretti di Saronno cookies added to the meringue. This clever idea was given to me by Barbara Witt, the owner of The Big Cheese, a restaurant in Washington, D.C. The cookies impart a wonderful almond taste while leaving the meringue light and dry. I've also substituted well-dried homemade macaroons, but the oil in the macaroons breaks down the meringue too much. The reason this doesn't happen with the amaretti cookies is because they don't contain any nut oil. They are made from apricot kernels, which impart a delicious bitter-almond flavor. I crush the cookies in a blender and add them to the beaten meringue. The baked and cooled meringue rounds are coated with a thin layer of chocolate and allowed to set before being layered with whipped cream and strawberries. The chocolate imparts a wonderful flavor to the cake while helping keep the meringue crisp. I think it's a fine tribute to Sardi's.

SPECIAL EQUIPMENT: PASTRY BAG FITTED WITH A ½-INCH PLAIN TIP (ATECO #26)

MAKE THE MERINGUE. Place the egg whites in the bowl of an electric mixer fitted with the whisk attachment. Whip on high speed until foamy and beginning to hold a shape. Set aside 1 tablespoon of the sugar. Add the vanilla and continue beating, gradually adding the remaining 7 tablespoons sugar until the whites form stiff, glossy peaks.

Mix the crushed cookies with the reserved 1 tablespoon sugar and the cornstarch in a separate bowl. Use a large rubber spatula to gently fold the cookie mixture into the meringue a little at a time, being careful not to deflate the meringue.

CONTINUED

✦ MAKE SURE THE BOWL USED FOR BEATING THE EGG WHITES IS CLEAN AND FREE FROM ANY FAT, AS FAT BREAKS DOWN EGG WHITES, PREVENTING THEM FROM WHIPPING UP PROPERLY.

MERINGUE

YIELD: THREE 8-INCH MERINGUE ROUNDS

6 large egg whites (180 grams or ¾ cup), at room temperature

½ cup sugar

¼ teaspoon vanilla extract

¼ cup finely crushed Amaretti di Saronno cookies (about 10)

1 tablespoon cornstarch

PREPARATION. Preheat the oven to 175°F. Line two 18 X 13–inch half-sheet or jelly-roll pans with parchment paper.

Gently scoop the meringue into a pastry bag fitted with a ½-inch plain tip, Ateco #26, filling the bag two-thirds full.

Pipe small dabs of meringue in the corners of the pans, then press the parchment paper firmly in place.

Starting in the center and working your way around in a spiral, pipe a meringue circle on a prepared pan, holding the tip of the bag about 1 inch or so off the paper, letting the meringue drop down from the tip. This will give the meringue more height. (Piping meringue takes a little practice, so don't get discouraged if your first attempts aren't picture-perfect.) Pipe 2 more meringue circles.

Bake the meringue rounds for about 1½ hours, or until they are firm and dry and release easily from the parchment, rotating the pans from front to back every 30 minutes. Allow the meringue rounds to cool, and further dry them overnight in the oven turned off. The meringue rounds are now ready to be filled. Or they can be placed in an airtight container and refrigerated or frozen for up to 1 week.

◆ BAKING MERINGUE ROUNDS PROPERLY CAN BE TRICKY
SINCE THEY MUST BE BAKED LONG ENOUGH SO THAT
THEY ARE COMPLETELY DONE ON THE INSIDE. THIS
TAKES A LONG, SLOW BAKING TIME. ONE WAY TO ENSURE
COMPLETE COOKING IS TO TURN THE OVEN OFF AFTER
1½ HOURS AND LEAVE THE MERINGUE ROUNDS IN THE
OVEN OVERNIGHT. IF I FIND THEY NEED MORE BAKING
WHEN I CHECK THEM IN THE MORNING, I TURN THE
OVEN ON AND BAKE THEM FOR ANOTHER 30 MINUTES
AT 175°F.

ASSEMBLE THE TORTE. Place the chocolate in a small microwave-safe bowl and heat at medium power at 20-second intervals, stirring frequently, until melted and smooth. Place a meringue round on a cake plate. Use an offset metal spatula to spread one-third of the melted chocolate over the meringue. Set aside. Repeat with the remaining 2 meringue rounds and chocolate. Set aside.

Beat the cream, confectioners' sugar, and liqueur at medium-high speed in the bowl of an electric mixer fitted with the whisk attachment until stiff peaks form.

When the chocolate has set on the first meringue round, cover it with a ¼- to ½-inch layer of the whipped cream and half of the sliced strawberries. Place the second meringue round on top and cover with another layer of whipped cream and the remaining sliced strawberries.

Set the last meringue round on top and cover the top and side with the remaining whipped cream. Gently press the almonds on the side of the torte and arrange the whole strawberries on top.

◆ FOR AN EXTRA FLOURISH, THE WHOLE STRAWBERRIES CAN BE DIPPED IN CHOCOLATE, THEN PLACED ON THEIR SIDES AROUND THE TOP OF THE TORTE.

ASSEMBLY

8 ounces bittersweet Valrhona, Lindt, or Scharffen Berger chocolate, finely chopped

3 Meringue rounds

3 cups heavy cream

2 tablespoons confectioners' sugar, sifted

2 tablespoons Amaretto Di Saronno liqueur

2 pints strawberries, hulled and sliced, setting aside whole the 8 biggest strawberries

1 cup sliced blanched almonds, toasted

◆ ADDING CONFECTIONERS' SUGAR TO WHIPPED CREAM HELPS TO STABILIZE IT. GRANULATED SUGAR TENDS TO BREAK DOWN WHIPPED CREAM, CAUSING MOISTURE TO SEPARATE OUT, WHEREAS CONFECTIONERS' SUGAR ABSORBS THE MOISTURE BECAUSE IT CONTAINS CORNSTARCH.

ORANGE CAKE
WITH ORANGE SORBET

SERVES 15

This recipe uses a very unusual technique to make an orange sponge cake. Here, a sugar syrup leavens the eggs and gives the cake height, while orange zest lends it a hint of citrus and ground almonds contribute richness. Paired with a light sorbet, this cake is perfect during the winter months, when fresh citrus fruits are plentiful. I prefer using straight-sided muffin cups because I think they make the cakes look like miniature tortes and less like cupcakes. Straight-sided muffin pans are available from J.B. Prince Company in New York City and through their web site.

SPECIAL EQUIPMENT: TWO JUMBO (3-INCH) STRAIGHT-SIDED MUFFIN PANS •
CANDY THERMOMETER • ICE-CREAM MAKER

ORANGE CAKES

YIELD: FIFTEEN 3-INCH CAKES

8 large egg yolks (160 grams or ⅔ cup),
    at room temperature

1 cup plus 1 tablespoon sugar

¼ cup water

1 cup (120 grams) cake flour, sifted

Pinch of salt, sifted with the cake flour

1 cup ground blanched almonds,
    approximately 1½ cups of whole
    almonds

1 tablespoon finely grated orange zest

8 large egg whites (240 grams or 1 cup),
    at room temperature

PREPARATION. Preheat the oven to 350°F. Generously butter fifteen 3-inch muffin cups. Have ready a pastry brush and cup of cold water.

MAKE THE CAKES. Place the egg yolks in the bowl of an electric mixer fitted with the whisk attachment and beat on high speed until the yolks are very thick and pale, 4 to 5 minutes. The yolks will double in volume and form a ribbon when dropped from the whisk.

Meanwhile, combine 1 cup of the sugar and the water in a small saucepan and stir well. Bring to a boil over medium-high heat, stirring to dissolve the sugar. Cook until it reaches the soft-ball stage (238°F on a candy thermometer), washing away any undissolved sugar from the inside of the pan with a pastry brush dipped in water. Do not stir the syrup after it boils.

When the syrup has reached the soft-ball stage, remove from the heat and add to the beating egg yolks in a slow, continuous stream down the inside of the bowl to prevent spattering, beating until the mixture is cool and doubled in volume, about 10 minutes. Use a spatula to fold in the flour and salt, delicately but quickly, until thoroughly blended. Gently fold in the ground almonds and orange zest, combining the mixture well. Set aside.

Place the egg whites in a clean bowl of the electric mixer fitted with a whisk attachment and whip on high speed until foamy and beginning to hold a shape. Gradually add the remaining 1 tablespoon sugar and whip until the whites form stiff peaks. Gently fold the beaten egg whites all at once into the batter until combined.

Fill each prepared muffin cup about half full with batter. Bake for about 15 minutes, rotate the pans from front to back, and bake for another 5 minutes, or until domed, golden, and a cake tester inserted in the center comes out clean. Let the cakes cool in their pans on cooling racks for 5 minutes, then unmold onto racks and cool completely. Cover loosely with plastic wrap until ready to use. Refrigerated, the cakes will remain fresh for up to 2 days, or freeze for up to 1 month.

VARIATION. *If you are a true citrus lover, make an orange glaze of 2 cups confectioners' sugar and ⅓ cup orange juice and drizzle over the cakes. Add a teaspoon of grated orange zest for heightened flavor.*

◆ ONE WAY THAT I USE TO DETERMINE WHEN A SUGAR MIXTURE HAS REACHED THE SOFT-BALL STAGE, OR 238°F, IS TO DROP A SMALL SPOONFUL OF THE SYRUP INTO A CUP OF COLD WATER. I REACH IN AND TRY TO PINCH THE SUGAR TOGETHER, ROLLING IT AROUND BETWEEN MY THUMB AND FOREFINGER. IF IT FORMS A SOFT BALL, IT'S READY. IF IT STAYS SHAPELESS, IT NEEDS A LITTLE MORE TIME TO COOK.

MAKE THE COMPOTE. Peel and segment the oranges. Combine them with the lime zest, cinnamon, cardamom, and cumin in a bowl. Taste the mixture to see if you find it too tart. If needed, add a little sugar. Store at room temperature for up to 2 hours, or until ready to serve.

ORANGE COMPOTE

YIELD: 2½ CUPS

5 large navel oranges

Finely grated zest of 1 lime

1 teaspoon ground cinnamon

½ teaspoon ground cardamom

¼ teaspoon ground cumin

Sugar to taste

MAKE THE SORBET. Place all the ingredients in a large bowl and stir to combine. Make the sorbet sweeter than you would like, as some of the sweetness is lost in the freezing. Transfer the mixture to an ice-cream maker and freeze according to manufacturer's instructions.

ORANGE SORBET

YIELD: 1 QUART

4 cups freshly squeezed orange or blood-orange juice

½ to 1 cup sugar, or more to taste

2 tablespoons Grand Marnier

ASSEMBLY

15 Orange Cakes

2½ cups Orange Compote

Orange Sorbet

ASSEMBLE THE DESSERT. Use a serrated knife to split the cooled cakes horizontally in half. Place a mound of orange compote on the bottom half of a cake layer and cover with the top of the cake layer, pressing down on the top. Repeat with remaining cakes. Serve with the orange sorbet.

PAIN DE GENES WITH GINGERED WATERMELON RIND

This is one of those simple French country cakes that I love. It is a delicate almond pound cake made with a generous amount of freshly ground almonds, which I prefer over store-bought almond flour. *Pain de Genes* is French for "Genoa bread." It's a very rich, not too sweet confection that is perfect with a cup of tea. The watermelon rind tastes very unusual, and I love the gingery crunch it lends. Make the rind during the summer, when watermelon is plentiful. Stored in the refrigerator, it keeps for several months. Keep in mind that the rind has to sit overnight in the refrigerator before it is cooked, so plan your time accordingly.

MAKE THE CAKE. Beat the butter on medium speed in the bowl of an electric mixer fitted with the paddle attachment, then add 1½ cups of the confectioners' sugar and beat until creamy. Add the eggs one at a time, beating for 30 seconds after each addition. Add the sherry, and then the ground almonds, mixing well. Remove the bowl from the mixer and fold in the flour by hand.

Spread the sliced almonds in the prepared pan, then scrape the cake batter on top, spreading it evenly. Bake the cake for about 25 minutes, or until puffed, light golden brown, and a cake tester inserted in the center comes out clean. Let the cake cool in its pan on a cooling rack for about 15 minutes, then invert onto a rack to cool completely. Sift the remaining ½ cup confectioners' sugar over the top of the cake.

◆ SOMETIMES I TOAST THE SLICED ALMONDS IN THE OVEN AT 350°F FOR 5 MINUTES OR SO, JUST UNTIL LIGHT GOLDEN, THEN COOL THEM BEFORE PLACING THEM IN THE PAN.

PAIN DE GENES

YIELD: 8-INCH ROUND CAKE

4 ounces (1 stick) unsalted butter, at room temperature

2 cups confectioners' sugar

5 large eggs (250 grams or 1⅛ cups)

2 tablespoons cream sherry

2 cups ground blanched almonds, about 1⅔ cups whole almonds

⅔ cup (80 grams) cake flour, sifted

1 cup sliced blanched almonds

PREPARATION. Preheat the oven to 350°F. Butter an 8 X 2–inch round cake pan, line with parchment paper, and butter the paper.

GINGERED
WATERMELON RIND

YIELD: 3 TO 4 CUPS, DEPENDING ON
SIZE OF WATERMELON

1 medium watermelon, approximately
    7 pounds

4 quarts boiling water

5 cups sugar

1 quart cold water

2 limes, sliced

1 tablespoon chopped peeled fresh
    ginger

½ teaspoon salt

PREPARATION. Have ready a pastry brush
    and cup of cold water.

MAKE THE WATERMELON RIND. Cut away and discard the green skin from the watermelon, leaving the white portion intact. Remove the pink flesh and reserve for another use. Cut the white rind into 2 X ¼–inch strips. You should have about 29 ounces of rind. Refrigerate the rind in cold water overnight to crisp it.

On the following day, cook the rind in the 4 quarts of boiling water in a large pot for 10 minutes, or until just tender. Drain the rind and rinse with cold water. Set aside. Place the sugar in the pot with 1 quart of cold water. Bring to a boil over high heat, stirring until the sugar dissolves.

Add the watermelon, lime slices, ginger, and salt and simmer, stirring, for 30 minutes until the melon rind is tender. Remove from heat. Cool completely. The rind can be refrigerated in jars or an airtight container for up to 3 months.

ASSEMBLY

Pain de Genes
2 cups Gingered Watermelon Rind
Fresh fruit

ASSEMBLE THE DESSERT. Serve the cake with the gingered watermelon rind and fresh fruit on the side. The cake will remain fresh for up to 3 days in the refrigerator if well wrapped in plastic wrap, but bring it to room temperature before serving, for the best flavor. It is also delicious warmed slightly in a 325°F oven, wrapped in foil, for 5 minutes.

PISTACHIO CAKES

The artist Claude Monet was something of a gourmand. The book *Monet's Table*, a magnificent riot of color photography, includes a green-colored cake called Vert-Vert, made by the cook at his home in Giverny. The cake was flavored with pistachios, colored with spinach juice, and was supposedly a favorite of the artist's, who had his cook prepare it for special occasions. This cake is my version; just a bit lighter and without the green marzipan coating. I added the pistachio ice cream because it seemed to work so well with the cake.

SPECIAL EQUIPMENT: TWO JUMBO (3-INCH) STRAIGHT-SIDED MUFFIN PANS

MAKE THE CAKES. Sift the flour and baking soda into a bowl; set aside.

Place the eggs and sugar in the bowl of an electric mixer. Place the bowl over a hot water bath and whisk by hand until the sugar has dissolved and the eggs are warm and dark yellow, about 3 minutes. When the mixture is homogenized and is lightly translucent, it is ready to beat in the mixer.

Place the bowl in the mixer fitted with the whisk attachment and beat on high speed until the mixture triples in volume, about 5 minutes. Reduce the mixer speed to medium and beat for 1 minute more.

Reduce the mixer speed to low and gradually but quickly add the flour mixture, turning off the mixer before the flour is fully incorporated. Gently fold in the pistachios and the orange-flower water just until the batter is fully blended, being sure to scrape the batter from the bottom of the bowl and fold it over the top.

Divide the batter evenly among the prepared muffin cups, filling them no more than half full. Bake for about 15 minutes, rotate the pans from front to back, then bake for another 5 minutes, or until the cakes feel springy to the touch, are golden, and a cake tester inserted in the center comes out clean. (Do not open the oven door until the cakes have domed.)

CONTINUED

PISTACHIO CAKES

YIELD: EIGHTEEN 3-INCH CAKES

1 cup (120 grams) cake flour

1 teaspoon baking soda

8 large eggs (400 grams or 1¾ cups)

1 cup sugar

1½ cups unsalted raw pistachios, finely ground

1 teaspoon orange-flower water

PREPARATION. Position a rack in the middle of the oven and preheat the oven to 350°F. Butter eighteen 3-inch muffin cups.

Let the cakes cool in their pans for just 5 minutes. Unmold the cakes onto cooling racks and place right side up to cool completely. If not ready to use, wrap the cakes tightly in plastic wrap and refrigerate. Refrigerated, the cakes will stay fresh for up to 2 days.

I like to serve these as individual cakes filled with pistachio ice cream. I call it my Pistachio Ice Cream Sandwich, and I surround it with Crème Anglaise (page 67) flavored with orange-flower water, and garnish the plates with pistachio-stuffed dates from Mahallabyya (page 203).

SPECIAL EQUIPMENT: ICE-CREAM MAKER

PISTACHIO ICE CREAM

YIELD: 1 QUART

2 cups milk

2 cups heavy cream

11 to 12 large egg yolks (225 grams or 1 liquid cup)

1 cup sugar

2 teaspoons almond extract

2 cups unsalted pistachios, toasted and chopped

MAKE THE ICE CREAM. Place the milk and cream in a heavy nonreactive medium saucepan. Bring to a rolling boil over medium-high heat. Let the mixture rise up the side of the pan, then immediately remove from the heat.

Meanwhile, beat the egg yolks and sugar on high speed in the bowl of an electric mixer fitted with the whisk attachment until very thick and pale, about 5 minutes. The mixture will triple in volume and hold its shape when dropped from the whisk. It should be very stiff.

Bring the bowl over to the saucepan and gradually whisk about 1 cup of the hot cream mixture into the yolk mixture to temper it, then pour the mixture back into the saucepan and whisk until combined. The mixture should be thick enough to coat a wooden spoon. (Run your finger through the custard on the back of the spoon. The custard is thick enough when the line remains.)

Pour the custard through a fine-mesh strainer or China cap into a large bowl. Place in an ice bath or refrigerate, uncovered, until chilled, then add the almond extract. Transfer the mixture to an ice-cream maker and freeze according to the manufacturer's instructions. When the ice cream has finished churning and is still soft, fold in the pistachios.

PUMPKIN CHEESECAKE WITH PECAN SQUARES

Here, strips of rich and gooey pecan squares are placed atop creamy pumpkin-flavored cheesecake squares. Crystallized ginger, chopped up and added to the cake batter, elevates the pumpkin cheesecake to another level by bringing out the pumpkin flavor and melding perfectly with the creaminess of the cheesecake. The dark rum, on the other hand, lends the pecan squares an extra kick. Serve this dessert at Thanksgiving for a twist on the traditional pumpkin and pecan pies.

SPECIAL EQUIPMENT: 10-INCH SQUARE CAKE PAN

MAKE THE CRUST FOR THE PECAN SQUARES. Place the butter and confectioners' sugar in the bowl of an electric mixer fitted with the paddle attachment and mix on low speed until light and creamy. Add the flour and salt and mix just until combined, then finish combining the mixture by hand.

Use your hands to press the dough evenly into the prepared pan. Place a piece of parchment over the dough, then roll a small rolling pin or thick dowel about 10 inches long (the rolling pin or dowel should be narrower than the width of the pan for easy rolling) over the dough to even it out. The bottom dough should be about ¼-inch thick. Press the excess dough up against the sides of the pan.

Refrigerate the dough for at least 30 minutes, or until firm.

Meanwhile, preheat the oven to 275°F. Bake the crust for 15 minutes, rotate the pan front to back, and bake for another 15 minutes, or until golden and firm to the touch. Set aside on a cooling rack.

CRUST

YIELD: 18 X 13–INCH RECTANGLE

1 pound (4 sticks) unsalted butter, at room temperature

1 cup confectioners' sugar, sifted

4 cups (560 grams) all-purpose flour, sifted

¼ teaspoon salt

PREPARATION. Generously butter an 18 X 13–inch half-sheet or jelly-roll pan. Line the bottom with two layers of parchment paper and butter the paper.

PECAN SHEET

6 ounces (3 sticks) unsalted butter

1½ cups light brown sugar

1 cup dark corn syrup

2½ tablespoons dark rum, such as
  Myers's

4 large eggs (200 grams or ¾ cup
  plus 2 tablespoons)

2 teaspoons vanilla extract

¼ teaspoon salt

6 cups pecan halves

Crust

PREPARATION. Preheat the oven to
325°F.

MAKE THE PECAN SHEET. Place the butter, sugar, corn syrup, and rum in a medium saucepan and bring to a boil over medium-high heat. Just after it boils, remove from the heat and cool to room temperature. When the mixture has cooled, beat the eggs on high speed in the bowl of an electric mixer fitted with the whisk attachment until light and frothy, about 4 minutes. Reduce the speed to low and mix in the sugar mixture, vanilla, and salt.

Spread the pecan halves evenly over the baked crust, then pour the filling over the pecans. Bake for about 20 minutes, or until bubbling. The filling should be slightly loose for the best flavor and texture. Set aside on a rack to cool.

After the pecan sheet has cooled at room temperature, go around the sides of the pan with a knife to loosen it.

PUMPKIN CHEESECAKE

YIELD: 10-INCH SQUARE

2½ pounds cream cheese, at room
  temperature

1½ cups sugar, or more to taste

4 large eggs (200 grams or ⅞ cup),
  at room temperature

3 large egg yolks (60 grams or ¼ cup),
  at room temperature

2 cups solid-pack pumpkin

1 cup sour cream, at room temperature

1 tablespoon dark rum, such as Myers's

1 teaspoon vanilla extract

2 tablespoons finely chopped
  crystallized ginger

1 teaspoon ground ginger

1 tablespoon ground cinnamon

¼ teaspoon ground mace

See Preparation at the top of the next page.

MAKE THE PUMPKIN CHEESECAKE. Place the cream cheese and sugar in the bowl of an electric mixer fitted with the paddle attachment and beat at medium speed until very smooth. Add the eggs, egg yolks, pumpkin, sour cream, rum, and vanilla and mix well. Add both gingers, the cinnamon, and mace, beating until well combined.

Pour the cheesecake into the prepared pan. Place a shallow pan of water on the lower oven rack in the oven and place the cheesecake on the middle rack. Bake for 20 minutes, then reduce the temperature to 250°F. Rotate the pan from front to back and bake for 1 hour and 20 minutes more. Leave at room temperature for 1 hour, then refrigerate, uncovered.

◆ I ALWAYS BAKE MY CHEESECAKES WITH A SHALLOW PAN OF WATER EITHER UNDERNEATH THEM OR WITH THE CAKE PAN IMMERSED IN A LARGER PAN OF WATER AND PLACED ON A LOWER SHELF, TO ENSURE THAT THEY BAKE EVENLY. IT HELPS TO PREVENT CRACKING, TOO. BAKED THIS WAY, THE CHEESECAKE IS PALE AND SMOOTH ON TOP AND CREAMY WITHIN.

PREPARATION. Position racks in the middle and lower third of the oven and preheat the oven to 350°F. Line a 10-inch square pan with a double thickness of plastic wrap, extending it so it just comes up to the top edges of the pan. Snip off any excess so it doesn't hang over the sides of the pan.

ASSEMBLE THE DESSERT. Loosen the plastic wrap from around the edges of the pan by pulling it away from the sides, then invert the cheesecake onto a parchment-lined cutting board. Remove the plastic wrap, being careful around the edges not to catch the corners of the cheese-cake in the plastic. Cut into 2-inch squares. You will have sixteen 2-inch cheesecake squares and eight edge pieces, each approximately 1 inch. I put two edge pieces togeth-er, giving me a total of 20 cheesecake squares.

Cut the pecan sheet into 2-inch squares—you will have a total of 40 squares. Place a pecan square on a serving plate, place a cheesecake square on top of the pecan square, and place a second pecan square on top of the cheesecake. Repeat with the remaining cheesecake squares and pecan squares.

◆ WHEN CUTTING THE PECAN SHEET INTO SQUARES, I LIKE TO USE A 2-INCH-WIDE SPATULA AS A GUIDE AND CUT THE PECAN SHEET USING THE EDGE OF A THIN-BLADED PASTRY SCRAPER. I PREFER THIS METHOD TO CUTTING WITH A KNIFE, AS IT'S EASIER TO SIMPLY PRESS DOWN ON THE SCRAPER TO CUT THROUGH THE SQUARE. THE CUT IS ALSO A BIT MORE PRECISE AND CLEAN. THE PECAN SQUARES CAN BE TRIMMED VERY PRECISELY WHEN COLD. THEY FREEZE BEAUTIFULLY.

ASSEMBLY

Pumpkin Cheesecake

Pecan Sheet

PIES AND TARTS

his is a short chapter, but certainly not because I don't love pies and tarts. It might be because most of the tartlets and pastry-based desserts in this book appear within the Warm Desserts and Dessert Sandwiches chapters (pages 216 and 278, respectively). In some ways, these are the desserts that I would most likely order if I were out to dinner. I think I am enthralled by pies and tarts because my mother never made them. I thought a lot about them as a child because my storybooks described apple pies and cherry pies, so they were something of a mystery to me, and I *really* wanted my mother to make them.

When I was around eight years old, I happened upon a little carnival, where I saw a wheel of fortune. I bought a ticket and won! The prize was a big bag of groceries, and one of the items was something called a "pie stick." On the box was a picture of a delicious-looking cherry pie, so I couldn't wait to get home. The pie stick was actually a mixture of flour, salt, and shortening in the form of a bar, and all you had to do was break it up in a bowl and add a specified amount of water and, presto! You had pie dough, ready to roll out and bake. To me, this was magic! I wish I could tell you what I made, but I honestly don't remember.

I do recall that my mother was less enthusiastic about the pie stick, as well as most of the other stuff in the bag. Her lack of zeal, however, did nothing to diminish my love of pies. In fact, I recall that the very first sweets I ever baked on my own after I graduated from college were miniature fruit tartlets. I loved custard-filled crusts and glazed fruit toppings. Then I made a cheesecake pie that called for decorations of candied violets. I was so enthralled with how the violets looked on the pie, and I seem to recall that the instructions suggested using candied angelica split lengthwise and cut into diamonds to form leaves.

Oddly enough, when I was first married and had just set up housekeeping, I was very unsure about making a two-crust fruit pie, and only made one years later—an apple pie whose fragrance filled the kitchen.

What I like to do now is to make one-crust pies, tarts, and tartlets. I fully bake the crusts and make the fillings separately. Filled at the last moment, the crusts always remain flaky and crisp, not soggy or raw, which unfortunately can happen when juicy fruit filling is spooned into an uncooked pie shell and baked. The exception was when Rose Levy Berenbaum wrote up our bakery as one of ten places in the United States to get a good pumpkin pie. That was the year of the PP (Pumpkin Pie) Olympics. I made one hundred pies from scratch that morning. But that is a story for another time!

CANDY TARTLETS

This is a super-rich confection borne of my childhood memories of the candy bars Chunky and Baby Ruth. Their ingredients—raisins, nuts, and milk chocolate—were something I probably thought about way too much, as I recall. Here I turn milk chocolate into a mousse that is lightened with whipped cream and filled with fruits and nuts. I sometimes use walnuts instead of English toffee, which cuts some of the sweetness. The pastry crust is made all the more flaky due to a high percentage of vegetable shortening. As a result, this little tartlet goes a long way!

SPECIAL EQUIPMENT: 4-INCH ROUND PASTRY CUTTER • TWELVE 4-INCH FLUTED TARTLET PANS

MAKE THE PÂTE BRISÉE. Place the flour, sugar, and salt in the bowl of an electric mixer fitted with the paddle attachment and mix on low speed. Add the shortening and butter to the dry ingredients. On low speed, cut the butter and shortening into the mixture until the dough looks coarse and crumbly. If you like, remove the bowl from the mixer and break up the fat particles with your fingers to distribute the fat more evenly. Stir in just enough ice water to form the mixture into a ball. The dough will be crumbly and will barely hold together.

Remove the dough from the bowl and place it on a clean, dry work surface. Then, with the heel of your hand, smear a small amount on the work surface by pushing it away from you until the dough appears homogenized—that is, smooth and not crumbly. Continue smearing small portions of the dough until all of it has been smoothed. This should take about 3 minutes. Gather the dough into a ball, flatten slightly, and wrap in plastic wrap. Use the dough right away, or refrigerate or freeze. If chilled, allow the dough to sit until at room temperature, to soften a bit.

Kneading dough by smearing it with the heel of your hand is a French technique called *fraisage*. It not only

PÂTE BRISÉE

YIELD: ENOUGH FOR 12 TARTLET
SHELLS (THIS GIVES YOU A FEW EXTRA
IN CASE OF BREAKAGE)

1½ cups (210 grams) all-purpose
   flour, sifted

⅛ cup sugar

¼ teaspoon salt

⅓ cup plus 1 tablespoon (2½ ounces)
   shortening, chilled

2 ounces (½ stick) unsalted butter,
   diced and chilled

⅛ cup (2 tablespoons or 1 ounce)
   ice water

◆ UNBELIEVABLY, THE DOUGH IS
READY TO ROLL OUT IMMEDIATELY.
I DON'T CHILL THIS ONE—IT'S MUCH
EASIER TO ROLL WHEN FIRST MADE.
IT IS SUCH A SHORT DOUGH THAT
THE GLUTEN ADDS VERY LITTLE
ELASTICITY, SO CHILLING IT TO
RELAX THE GLUTEN IS UNNECESSARY.

forms the dough into a smooth, cohesive mass, but it develops just enough structure in the dough so it is less likely to tear or crack while being rolled and lifted.

TARTLET SHELLS

YIELD: TWELVE 4-INCH TARTLET SHELLS

Pâte Brisée

PREPARATION. Position a rack in the middle of the oven and preheat the oven to 275°F.

MAKE THE TARTLET SHELLS. Roll out the dough on a lightly floured work surface to ⅛-inch thickness. Use a 4-inch round cutter to cut out 12 rounds. Use a metal spatula to lift the rounds and transfer them to the pans, being sure not to stretch the dough. Use your fingertips to press the dough firmly onto the bottom and against the sides of the pans. Then use the back of a knife to trim off any excess dough from around the edge. Prick the dough all over with a fork, cover with plastic wrap, and refrigerate for at least 1 hour, or until very firm. Or place in the freezer for up to 1 day and bake frozen.

When ready to bake, line the tartlet shells with aluminum foil and fill with uncooked rice or dried beans. Place the shells on an 18 X 13–inch half-sheet or jelly-roll pan for easier handling. Bake for 20 minutes, rotate the pans from front to back, and and bake for another 20 minutes. Remove the foil with its contents and bake for about another 2 minutes, or until the shells are light brown and firm to the touch.

Let the shells cool in their pans on a cooling rack for 10 minutes, then unmold the shells and cool completely on a rack. If a shell seems to stick a little to the pan, turn it over into your hand and gently tap the bottom with your other hand to help release it.

◆ I SERVE THESE TARTLETS WITH A DOLLOP OF LIGHTLY SWEETENED, LIGHTLY WHIPPED CREAM AND DRIZZLED WITH HOT FUDGE SAUCE. YOU CAN ALSO SPOON THE FILLING INTO ANY KIND OF EDIBLE CONTAINERS SUCH AS TULIP CUPS (PAGE 147), CHOCOLATE CUPS (PAGE 195), OR ALMOND LACE COOKIE CYLINDERS (PAGE 126).

MAKE THE FILLING. Plump the raisins in the hot water in a small bowl for 30 minutes. Place the chocolate in a bowl set over a bowl of hot, not boiling, water and stir frequently until melted and smooth. (Or place the chocolate in a microwave-safe bowl and heat at medium power at 10-second intervals, stirring frequently until melted. Use caution, as milk chocolate burns more quickly than bittersweet or semisweet chocolate.) Set aside.

Whip the cream in the bowl of an electric mixer fitted with the whisk attachment until soft peaks form. Remove the bowl from the mixer and fold the cream into the warm chocolate with a rubber spatula until no streaks of cream show. Drain the raisins and gently fold them, with the chopped toffee, into the mixture.

MAKE THE HOT FUDGE SAUCE. Melt the chocolate and butter together in a medium saucepan over low heat, stirring occasionally. Mix the sugar and cocoa together and add to the saucepan along with the light cream. Cook, stirring frequently, for 15 minutes. Reduce the heat to very low and keep the sauce warm until ready to use. If not using right away, refrigerate in an airtight container for up to several weeks.

ASSEMBLE THE DESSERT. Spoon the filling into the shells, filling them to the top and mounding it a bit. Refrigerate for 2 hours or up to 8 hours.

Remove the filled tartlets from the refrigerator 30 minutes before serving. When ready to serve, drizzle about 2 tablespoons of fudge sauce over each tartlet and set each on a plate. Pass the remaining fudge sauce alongside.

FILLING

YIELD: APPROXIMATELY 3 CUPS

1 cup raisins

½ cup hot water

1 pound milk chocolate, chopped into 1-inch pieces

2 cups heavy cream

1 cup coarsely chopped English Toffee (page 58) or 1 cup plain English toffee plus 1 cup chopped plain pecans or walnuts, toasted

HOT FUDGE SAUCE

YIELD: 2½ CUPS

4 ounces unsweetened chocolate, chopped into medium chunks (1-inch pieces)

8 ounces (2 sticks) unsalted butter, melted

1½ cups sugar

½ cup Dutch-processed cocoa

1 cup light cream

ASSEMBLY

3 cups Filling

8 Tartlet Shells

2½ cups Hot Fudge Sauce

CHEESE DANISH SUCRÉE

I love the filling in a cheese Danish so much that I would much rather eat the filling than the dough. This Danish does the trick with Grand Marnier and orange zest as delicious additions to an already mouth-watering cheese filling. I find these cheese Danish tartlets easier to plate than traditional cheesecake, and the name *sucrée* lends the dessert a little sophistication.

SPECIAL EQUIPMENT: 4-INCH ROUND PASTRY CUTTER • TWELVE 4-INCH TARTLET PANS

SWEET PASTRY DOUGH

YIELD: ENOUGH FOR 12 TARTLET SHELLS (THIS GIVES YOU A FEW EXTRA IN CASE OF BREAKAGE)

10 ounces (2½ sticks) unsalted butter, at room temperature

1 cup confectioners' sugar, sifted

1 large egg (50 grams or ¼ cup)

1 large egg yolk (20 grams or 2 tablespoons)

1½ teaspoons vanilla extract

4 cups (480 grams) cake flour, sifted

PREPARATION. Position a rack in the middle of the oven and preheat the oven to 275°F.

MAKE THE DOUGH. Place the butter and confectioners' sugar in the bowl of an electric mixer fitted with the paddle attachment and beat on very low speed until well combined. Beat in the egg, egg yolk, and vanilla until just combined. Gradually add the flour in three additions, mixing until the flour is barely incorporated into the mixture. Remove the bowl from the mixer and finish mixing the dough with a rubber spatula until well blended. Shape the dough into a disk, wrap in plastic wrap, and refrigerate for at least 1 hour or up to 2 days. The dough can be frozen for up to 1 month.

TARTLET SHELLS

YIELD: TWELVE 4-INCH TARTLET SHELLS

Sweet Pastry Dough

MAKE THE TARTLET SHELLS. Remove the dough from the refrigerator and divide it into 3 equal pieces. Work with 1 piece of dough at a time, keeping the other pieces refrigerated. Cut the dough into small pieces and work them with the heel of your hand against the work surface to make them more malleable and easier to work with. Shape the dough into a disk and repeat with the remaining pieces. Each piece yields about 4 tartlet shells. You will get a yield of between 12 to 16 tartlet shells.

Roll each disk of dough out on a slightly flowered surface to ⅛-inch thickness. Cut out a total of 12 rounds with a 4-inch round pastry cutter. Use a metal spatula to lift the rounds and transfer them to twelve 4-inch tartlet pans. Use your fingertips to firmly press the dough onto the bottom and sides of the pans, pushing the excess up over the edges of the pans. Use the back of a knife to trim off any excess dough from around the edges. Prick the dough all over with a fork, cover with plastic wrap, and refrigerate for at least 1 hour, until well chilled and firm, or up to 24 hours.

Place the tartlet shells on an 18 X 13–inch half-sheet or jelly-roll pan. Bake for 8 minutes, rotate the pan from front to back, and bake for 7 minutes more, or until the shells are light golden and set. Let the shells cool in their pans on a cooling rack for no more than 15 minutes. Remove the shells from their pans, wrap in plastic wrap, and refrigerate, unless you plan to use them immediately.

◆ I HAVE FOUND THAT A LOWER BAKING TEMPERATURE NOT ONLY KEEPS THE TARTLET SHELLS FROM BURNING BUT GIVES THEM A MUCH MORE EVEN COLOR, TOO.

IF THIS KIND OF PASTRY IS LEFT IN THE TARTLET PANS FOR TOO LONG AFTER BAKING, IT TENDS TO SPLIT AND CRACK. REMOVE THE SHELLS FROM THE PANS, WRAP IN PLASTIC WRAP, AND PUT THEM IN THE REFRIGERATOR RIGHT AWAY TO ALLEVIATE THIS PROBLEM.

◆ AFTER I HAVE CUT OUT MY DOUGH ROUNDS, I TAKE THE EXCESS DOUGH AND COMBINE IT WITH A PIECE THAT I HAVE CHILLED. THIS WAY I DON'T HAVE A PIECE OF DOUGH THAT IS REWORKED WITH TOO MUCH FLOUR, AND THE DOUGH ALSO STAYS COOLER.

CHEESE FILLING

YIELD: ABOUT 3 CUPS

1 cup golden raisins

¼ cup Grand Marnier

2 (8-ounce) packages cream cheese,
    at room temperature

¼ cup dry-curd cottage cheese,
    at room temperature

2 tablespoons sour cream, at room
    temperature

1 tablespoon unsalted butter,
    at room temperature

½ cup sugar

1 large egg yolk (20 grams or
    2 tablespoons)

2 tablespoons (19 grams) all-purpose
    flour, sifted

1 teaspoon vanilla extract

Finely grated zest of 1 orange

PREPARATION. Preheat the oven
    to 325°F.

ASSEMBLY

3 cups Cheese Filling

8 Tartlet Shells

MAKE THE FILLING. Soak the raisins in the Grand Marnier for 30 minutes.

Meanwhile, place the cream cheese, cottage cheese, sour cream, and butter in the bowl of an electric mixer fitted with the paddle attachment and beat on medium speed for 1 minute. Add the sugar and the egg yolk and beat for 1 minute. Add the flour and vanilla and mix well with a rubber spatula, scraping the bottom and side of the bowl. Add the orange zest and the soaked raisins, along with any Grand Marnier remaining in the bowl, and combine well.

ASSEMBLE THE TARTLETS. Spoon enough cheese filling into the tartlet shells to fill them two-thirds full. Place the filled tartlets on an 18 X 13–inch half-sheet or jelly-roll pan. Bake for about 7 minutes, rotate the pan from front to back, and bake for about 7 minutes more, or until the filling rises and is firm and light brown. Place the tartlets in their pans on a rack and cool them to room temperature. Chill for several hours before serving. Refrigerated, they will remain fresh for 2 days.

These tartlets are delicious on their own and are super for a brunch dessert.

CHESS CAKES

The term *cakes* is a misnomer here. These charming little English tea cakes are really tartlets filled with a raisin-and-nut-speckled custard. If made even smaller, they are perfect for a petit four plate. They are lovely when served alone or when surrounded by crème anglaise.

SPECIAL EQUIPMENT: 4-INCH ROUND PASTRY CUTTER • TWELVE 4-INCH TARTLET PANS

MAKE THE PÂTE BRISÉE. Place the flour, sugar, and salt in the bowl of an electric mixer fitted with the paddle attachment and combine on low speed. Add the shortening and butter to the dry ingredients. On low speed, cut the butter and shortening into the mixture until it looks coarse and crumbly. If you like, remove the bowl from the mixer and break up the fat particles with your fingers to distribute the fat more evenly. Add just enough ice water to combine and form the mixture into a ball.

Remove the dough from the bowl and place it on a clean, dry work surface. Then, with the heel of your hand, smear a small amount on the work surface by pushing it away from you until the dough appears homogenized— that is, smooth and not crumbly. Continue smearing small portions of it until all of the dough has been smoothed. This should take about 3 minutes. Shape the dough into a disk.

◆ UNBELIEVABLY, THE DOUGH IS READY TO ROLL OUT IMMEDIATELY. I DON'T CHILL THIS ONE. I FIND IT MUCH EASIER TO ROLL WHEN IT'S FIRST MADE. IT IS SUCH A SHORT DOUGH THAT THERE IS VERY LITTLE ELASTICITY FROM THE GLUTEN, SO CHILLING IT TO RELAX THE GLUTEN SEEMS UNNECESSARY.

PÂTE BRISÉE

YIELD: ENOUGH FOR 12 TARTLET SHELLS (THIS GIVES YOU A FEW EXTRA IN CASE OF BREAKAGE)

1½ cups (210 grams) all-purpose flour, sifted

⅛ cup sugar

¼ teaspoon salt

⅓ cup plus 1 tablespoon (2½ ounces) shortening, chilled

2 ounces (½ stick) unsalted butter, diced and chilled

⅛ cup (2 tablespoons or 1 ounce) ice water

PREPARATION. Position a rack in the middle of the oven and preheat the oven to 275°F.

MAKE THE TARTLET SHELLS. Roll out the dough on a lightly floured work surface to ⅛-inch thickness. Use a 4-inch round pastry cutter to cut out 12 rounds. Without stretching the dough, use a metal spatula to lift the rounds and fit them inside twelve 4-inch tartlet pans. Use your fingertips to press the dough firmly onto the bottoms and against the sides of the pans to thin the dough and so there will be excess going up the sides. Use the back of a knife to trim off any excess dough around the edges. Refrigerate for at least 1 hour, covered with plastic wrap, or until well chilled and firm. Or place in the freezer for 1 day and bake frozen.

Line the shells with aluminum foil and fill them with uncooked rice or dried beans. Place the tartlet shells on an 18 X 13–inch half-sheet or jelly-roll pan. Bake for 20 minutes, rotate the pan from front to back, and bake for another 20 minutes, or until the shells are lightly brown in color and firm to the touch when you lift the foil. Remove from the oven and immediately lift the foil with its contents from each shell.

Let the shells cool in their pans on a cooling rack for just 10 minutes, then remove from the pans and cool completely on the rack. If a shell seems to stick to its pan, turn the shell over into your hand and gently tap the bottom with your other hand to help release it. These shells are fragile, so pack carefully, stacking no more than two together if not using right away. These can be frozen or refrigerated in an airtight container for later use. Just pop them into a 275°F oven for about 1½ minutes, or microwave for 10 to 15 seconds.

TARTLET SHELLS

YIELD: TWELVE 4-INCH TARTLET SHELLS

Pâte Brisée

⬧ I MAKE TARTLET SHELLS SO OFTEN THAT I KEEP A CONTAINER READY WITH THE PIECES OF FOIL AND THE RICE OR BEANS, SO I CAN REUSE THEM.

FILLING

YIELD: 2 TO 2½ CUPS

1 cup dark raisins

1 cup boiling water

4 ounces (1 stick) unsalted butter,
   at room temperature

½ cup sugar

1 cup walnuts, chopped

3 large eggs (150 grams or ⅔ cup)

¼ cup heavy cream

1½ teaspoons vanilla extract

¼ teaspoon ground ginger

¼ teaspoon ground allspice

ASSEMBLY

8 Tartlet Shells

2 to 2½ cups Filling

PREPARATION. Preheat the oven
   to 325°F.

MAKE THE FILLING. Plump the raisins in the hot water for 5 minutes. Meanwhile, cream the butter and sugar at low speed in the bowl of an electric mixer fitted with the paddle attachment until light and fluffy. Drain the raisins and add to the butter mixture along with all the remaining ingredients, beating until well mixed.

MAKE THE CHESS CAKES. Place the tartlet shells on an 18 X 13–inch half-sheet or jelly-roll pan and fill each two-thirds full with filling. Bake for about 20 minutes, or until set. Transfer the tartlets to a cooling rack, and serve warm or at room temperature.

GALETTE BRETONNE

A galette is a flat disk-shaped cake similar to a rich shortbread cookie. Simple to make and delicious to serve, this galette is filled with rum-soaked raisins and glacéed grapefruit peel and baked in a fluted tart pan. There will be leftover rum; use it in the Palets aux Raisins cookies (page 154) or reserve for another use. I love to serve this cake warm at brunch with lightly sweetened whipped cream.

SPECIAL EQUIPMENT: 10-INCH FLUTED TART PAN WITH A REMOVABLE BOTTOM

MAKE THE GALETTE. Soak the raisins and grapefruit peel in the rum for 30 minutes.

Meanwhile, place the flour, sugar, salt, and butter in the bowl of an electric mixer fitted with the paddle attachment and beat on low speed until coarse and mealy. Mix in the egg yolks. Squeeze the raisins and grapefruit to remove all the excess rum; discard the rum or reserve for another use in the refrigerator. Add the fruit to the dough. Mix well.

Press the dough into the prepared pan. Brush the dough with the beaten egg, then use the tines of a fork to create a crosshatch pattern on its top. Bake for 25 to 30 minutes, or until well browned. Let the galette cool in the pan on a cooling rack for 10 minutes, then unmold. Cut into wedges and serve warm.

◆ THIS CAKE HAS SUCH A MARVELOUS FLAVOR THAT IT'S HARD TO SUGGEST SERVING IT WITH ANYTHING EXCEPT MAYBE APPLE MARMALADE (PAGE 150) OR LIGHTLY SUGARED CRUSHED STRAWBERRIES. AT ROOM TEMPERATURE, THE GALETTE WILL REMAIN FRESH FOR 1 DAY, OR REFRIGERATE FOR UP TO 3 DAYS. IF REFRIGERATING, BRING IT TO ROOM TEMPERATURE BEFORE SERVING. I WOULD EVEN HEAT IT BRIEFLY, COVERED IN FOIL, FOR ABOUT 2 MINUTES AT 325°F.

GALETTE

YIELD: 10-INCH ROUND CAKE

½ cup dark raisins

½ cup Candied Grapefruit Peel (page 112), finely chopped

¼ cup dark rum, such as Myers's

2 cups (280 grams) all purpose-flour, sifted

⅔ cup sugar

¼ teaspoon salt

8 ounces (2 sticks) unsalted butter, diced and chilled

5 large egg yolks (100 grams or ½ cup)

1 large egg (50 grams or ¼ cup), lightly beaten

PREPARATION. Position a rack in the middle of the oven and preheat the oven to 350°F. Generously butter a 10-inch fluted tart pan with a removable bottom.

LEMON CARAMEL TARTLETS

This dessert is unusual in that the filling is baked separately and added to the fully baked tartlet shells at the last minute. This method creates an incredibly crisp tartlet shell, something that is very difficult to achieve when baking a filling in an uncooked shell. The sweet dough recipe yields more dough than is needed for the tartlets, but I really like having extra dough since it freezes so well.

SPECIAL EQUIPMENT: 4-INCH ROUND PASTRY CUTTER • TWELVE 4-INCH TARTLET PANS • TWELVE 3-OUNCE SOUFFLÉ DISHES OR RAMEKINS

SWEET PASTRY DOUGH

YIELD: ENOUGH FOR TWELVE TARTLET SHELLS

10 ounces (2½ sticks) unsalted butter, at room temperature

1 cup confectioners' sugar, sifted

1 large egg (50 grams or ¼ cup)

1 large egg yolk (20 grams or 1 tablespoon)

1½ teaspoons vanilla extract

4 cups (480 grams) cake flour, sifted

MAKE THE DOUGH. Place the butter and confectioners' sugar in the bowl of an electric mixer fitted with the paddle attachment and beat on low speed until well combined. Beat in the egg, egg yolk, and vanilla until just combined. Add the flour in three additions, mixing until it is barely incorporated into the mixture. Remove the bowl from the mixer and finish mixing by hand with a rubber spatula until well blended, scraping the bottom and side of the bowl. Wrap the dough in plastic wrap and refrigerate for at least 3 hours or up to 24 hours.

TARTLET SHELLS

YIELD: TWELVE 4-INCH TARTLET SHELLS

Sweet Pastry Dough

PREPARATION. Position a rack in the middle of the oven and preheat the oven to 275°F.

MAKE THE SHELLS. Remove the dough from the refrigerator and divide the chilled dough into 3 equal pieces. Work with 1 piece of dough at a time, keeping the other pieces refrigerated. Cut the dough into small pieces and work them with the heel of your hand against the work surface to make them more malleable and easier to work with. Shape the dough into a disk and repeat with the remaining pieces. Each piece yields about 4 tartlet shells.

Roll each disk of dough out on a lightly floured surface to ⅛-inch thickness. Cut out a total of 12 rounds with a 4-inch round pastry cutter. Use a metal spatula to lift the rounds and transfer them to twelve 4-inch tartlet pans. Use your fingertips to firmly press the dough onto the bottoms and sides of the pans, pushing the excess up over the edges of the pans. Use the back of a knife to trim off any excess dough from around the edges. Prick the dough all over with a fork, cover with plastic wrap, and refrigerate for at least 1 hour, until chilled and firm, or up to 24 hours.

Place the tartlet shells on an 18 X 13–inch half-sheet or jelly-roll pan. Bake for 7 minutes, rotate the pan from front to back, and bake for 7 more minutes, or until the shells are light golden and set. Let the shells cool in their pans on a cooling rack for just 10 minutes, then remove the shells from the pans, and wrap immediately while still warm and set aside if using right away, or cover and refrigerate.

MAKE THE CARAMEL SAUCE. Place the sugar and water in a medium heavy-bottomed saucepan over medium heat and bring to a boil. While the sugar is heating, dip a pastry brush in water and run it around the inside of the saucepan just above the level of the sugar to wash away any undissolved sugar. This will prevent the sugar from crystallizing.

As the sugar begins to boil, gently move the pot back and forth over the burner to evenly distribute the ever-darkening syrup. Once the sugar boils, do not stir. When it smells like caramel, is dark amber in color, and gives off little wisps of smoke, immediately remove from the heat. The caramel could burn very quickly at this stage.

Put on the oven mitts and cover your whisking arm with a towel. Standing back a bit; quickly add the heavy cream, whisking rapidly as you pour. The sugar will bubble up and may spatter, but continue to whisk until all the

◆ I USE THE BACK OF A SMALL PARING KNIFE TO TRIM OFF THE EXCESS DOUGH AROUND THE EDGES OF THE TARTLET PANS. IT GIVES THE TARTLETS A CLEAN AND FINISHED LOOK.

CARAMEL SAUCE

YIELD: ABOUT 1¼ CUPS

1 cup sugar

½ cup water

1 cup heavy cream

1 teaspoon vanilla extract

PREPARATION. Have ready a pastry brush, a cup of cold water, a long-handled wire whisk, heavy-duty oven mitts, and a towel to cover your entire arm.

VARIATION. *Add 2 to 3 tablespoons of raspberry puree or the juice of a lemon or lime to the caramel sauce after it has cooled to give it another layer of taste.*

cream has been incorporated and the caramel is smooth. Add the vanilla. Let the sauce cool, then pour into an airtight container and refrigerate for up to a month.

LEMON CUSTARD

YIELD: ABOUT 1¾ CUPS

5 large egg yolks (100 grams or scant ½ cup)

1 large egg (50 grams or ¼ cup)

¾ cup sugar, or more to taste

¾ cup freshly squeezed and strained lemon juice (from about 8 lemons)

¾ cup heavy cream

PREPARATION. Position a rack in the middle of the oven and preheat the oven to 250°F.

◆ FOR QUICKER COOLING, NESTLE THE CUPS INTO A PAN FILLED WITH ICE.

MAKE THE LEMON CUSTARD. Whisk the egg yolks, egg, and sugar in a medium bowl. Add the lemon juice and whisk to combine. Add the cream and mix well. At this point, it may be necessary to add a bit more sugar, depending on the tartness of the lemons. Pour the mixture into a 4-cup glass measuring cup or pitcher.

Place twelve 3-ounce soufflé dishes or ramekins in a large, shallow baking pan. Pull out the middle oven rack, and place the pan on the rack. Carefully pour equal amounts of the lemon cream into the cups, filling them about two-thirds full. Fill the pan with 1 to 2 inches of water, cover with foil, and close the oven door.

Bake for about 25 minutes, then carefully rotate the pan from front to back and bake for 20 minutes more, or until the filling sets and just jiggles slightly in the center when shaken. Transfer the cups to a cooling rack and cool completely. Refrigerate for several hours or up to overnight.

ASSEMBLY

1¾ cups Lemon Custard

12 Tartlet shells

1¼ cups Caramel Sauce

◆ I SOMETIMES LIKE TO CENTER THE TARTLETS ON DESSERT PLATES AND USE A SQUEEZE BOTTLE TO DRIZZLE LINES OF SLIGHTLY WARM CARAMEL SAUCE DECORATIVELY OVER THE TOPS.

ASSEMBLE THE TARTLETS. When ready to serve, run a thin-bladed knife around the edges of the cups to loosen the lemon custard and dip the bottoms very briefly in hot water. Shake the lemon custard back and forth until you feel each one loosen, then quickly invert each custard into a shell.

Since getting the lemon custard into a tartlet shell without breaking the shell is a little tricky, sometimes I gently invert the custard into my hand and then carefully place it, centered, in the shell. Drizzle the caramel sauce over the top of the tartlets and serve.

LIME TARTLETS

When you bite into these tartlets, the first taste is of a crisp butter crust that crumbles and gives way to a cool, velvety lime cream that has a curiously sweet yet tart exotic flavor. These tartlets are ideal to make in winter, when flavorful fresh fruits are often hard to come by but citrus fruits are plentiful and at their best. Look for thin-skinned, plump limes, as they yield the most juice. Keep in mind that the sweetness of limes varies, so be sure to taste the lime curd as you cook it, so you can adjust the amount of sugar needed. I developed this recipe based on one given to me by Jean-Louis Palladin when I worked for him at Jean-Louis, at The Watergate. In my early years of baking, recipes such as this one often contained cornstarch or other thickeners, but I didn't like the aftertaste they left behind. Here, eggs combined with butter become the thickener, and while this curd is a little looser than others, it is a wonderful one to have on hand. The candied grapefruit peel was inspired by the wonderful version served at the Inn at Little Washington, Patrick O'Connell and Reinhardt Lynch's legendary ode to fine dining.

SPECIAL EQUIPMENT: 4-INCH ROUND PASTRY CUTTER • TWELVE 4-INCH TARTLET PANS

MAKE THE DOUGH. Place the butter and confectioners' sugar in the bowl of an electric mixer fitted with the paddle attachment and beat on low speed until well combined. Beat in the egg, egg yolk, and vanilla until just combined. Add the flour in three additions, mixing until it is barely incorporated into the mixture. Remove the bowl from the mixer and finish mixing the dough with a rubber spatula until well blended, scraping the bottom and side of the bowl. Wrap the dough in plastic wrap and refrigerate for at least 3 hours or up to 24 hours.

MAKE THE SHELLS. Remove the dough from the refrigerator and divide into 3 equal pieces. Work with 1 piece of dough at a time, keeping the other pieces refrigerated. Cut the dough into small pieces and work them with the heel of your hand against the work surface to make them more

SWEET PASTRY DOUGH

YIELD: ENOUGH FOR TWELVE TARTLET SHELLS

10 ounces (2½ sticks) unsalted butter, at room temperature

1 cup confectioners' sugar, sifted

1 large egg (50 grams or ¼ cup)

1 large egg yolk (20 grams or 1 tablespoon)

1½ teaspoons vanilla extract

4 cups (480 grams) cake flour, sifted

TARTLET SHELLS

YIELD: TWELVE 4-INCH TARTLET SHELLS

PREPARATION. Position a rack in the middle of the oven and preheat the oven to 275°F.

malleable and easier to work with. Shape the dough into a disk and repeat with the remaining pieces. Each piece yields about 4 tartlet shells.

Roll each disk of dough out on a lightly floured surface to ⅛-inch thickness. Cut out a total of 12 rounds with a 4-inch round pastry cutter. Use a metal spatula to lift the rounds and transfer them to twelve 4-inch tartlet pans. Use your fingertips to firmly press the dough onto the bottom and against the sides of the pans, pushing the excess up over the edges of the pans. Use the back of a knife to trim off any excess dough from around the edges. Prick the dough all over with a fork, cover with plastic wrap, and refrigerate for at least 1 hour, until well chilled and firm, or up to 24 hours.

Place the tartlet shells on an 18 X 13–inch half-sheet or jelly-roll pan. Bake for 7 minutes, rotate the pan from front to back, and bake for 7 more minutes, or until the shells are light golden brown and set. Let the shells cool in their pans on a cooling rack for just 10 minutes. Set aside if using right away, cover and refrigerate, or cover and freeze for up to 1 month.

LIME CURD

YIELD: 4 CUPS

Freshly grated lime zest from 4 limes (zest first before juicing)

2 cups freshly squeezed and strained lime juice (from about 10 limes)

8 ounces (2 sticks) unsalted butter

6 large eggs (300 grams or 1⅓ cups)

6 large egg yolks (120 grams or ½ cup)

4½ cups sugar, or to taste

MAKE THE CURD. Place the lime zest and juice and the butter in a heavy nonreactive medium saucepan over low heat, stirring occasionally, until the butter has completely melted. Have ready a fine-mesh stainless-steel strainer or China cap set over a bowl. CONTINUED

◆ I LIKE TO MAKE LIME CURD IN A HEAVY STAINLESS-STEEL SAUCEPAN OVER DIRECT HEAT. TYPICALLY IT IS COOKED IN A DOUBLE BOILER FOR AT LEAST 45 MINUTES. MY METHOD IS A LOT QUICKER, AND I HAVE NEVER HAD A PROBLEM COOKING IT THIS WAY. I JUST ADJUST THE FLAME, KEEPING IT HIGH ENOUGH TO COOK THE MIXTURE BUT NOT SO INTENSE THAT FLAMES SHOOT OUT AROUND THE SIDE OF THE POT. IF YOU HAVE AN ELECTRIC STOVE, I RECOMMEND USING MEDIUM HEAT.

◆ WHEN COOKING ANY TYPE OF CITRUS JUICE, BE SURE TO USE ONLY STAINLESS-STEEL OR ENAMEL PANS AND STRAINERS, AS ALUMINUM REACTS WITH THE ACID AND LEAVES AN UNPLEASANT METALLIC AFTER-TASTE.

◆ THIS VERSATILE LIME CURD CAN BE SPREAD BETWEEN GÉNOISE LAYERS, ADDED TO A SIMPLE BUTTERCREAM, OR USED TO FILL MERINGUE SHELLS.

Meanwhile, mix the eggs, yolks, and 3½ cups of the sugar on low speed in an electric mixer fitted with the whisk attachment until just combined. The finished curd will be transparent, almost jelly-like; overbeating the mixture will make the curd cloudy.

Bring the bowl over to the saucepan. Whisk several spoonfuls of the hot lime-juice mixture into the egg mixture to temper it, then pour the mixture back into the saucepan and whisk until well combined over medium heat.

Gradually add the remaining sugar, tasting as you go. An exact quantity is difficult to give, as the limes can be more or less sour at different times of the year. Usually another cup is about right. The curd should taste sweet but tart at the end of the taste. You always want to make it a little sweeter than you think, as some of the sweetness will be lost in the chilling.

Continue cooking the curd over medium heat, whisking continually until thickened. This may take up to 5 minutes. Be sure to whisk vigorously, touching all points of the bottom of the pan to make sure the mixture doesn't burn. When the curd begins to thicken and you see steam rise from the saucepan, immediately remove from the heat. (Do not let the curd come to a boil.) Quickly pour the curd into the stainless-steel strainer set over the bowl, using a rubber spatula to press the curd through. Press a piece of plastic wrap directly onto the surface of the curd to keep a skin from forming. Refrigerate the curd for 3 to 4 hours, until cold and firm. Refrigerated, the lime curd will stay fresh for up to 2 weeks. It should not be frozen.

CANDIED GRAPEFRUIT PEEL

YIELD: ABOUT 4 CUPS

2 large grapefruit, such as Indian River

3 cups cold water

6 cups sugar

MAKE THE CANDIED GRAPEFRUIT PEEL. Cut the grapefruit in half. Scoop out all the flesh, leaving the colorful rind.

Slice the peel into ¼-inch slices. Place the rind in a large saucepan, add enough cold water to cover, and bring to a boil. Continue to boil the peel for 20 minutes. Drain, rinse with cold water, and repeat the process twice more. After the third cooking, rinse the peel with cold water and set aside.

Pour 3 cups of cold water into the same saucepan and add the sugar. Cook over high heat, stirring until the sugar has dissolved. As soon as the mixture is clear and before it begins to boil, return the grapefruit peel to the pan and bring to a boil. Reduce the heat to medium and continue to cook, checking often, until the syrup has thickened. Reduce the heat to low and cook until the peel is translucent and the syrup is very thick and has almost evaporated. The total cooking time could be 1 hour or more. Do not stir after the syrup has boiled, as the peel should not be disturbed.

When the peel is translucent and the syrup has thickened, use a slotted spoon to transfer the peel to a cooling rack. Separate the peel and spread it out, so it can dry evenly. When the peel is completely dry, after a few hours or even up to overnight, layer it in an airtight container, separating the layers with parchment or waxed paper. Refrigerate.

◆ THICK-SKINNED GRAPEFRUIT ARE MUCH EASIER TO PEEL, AND IT IS ALSO EASIER TO PULL OUT THE FLESH WITH YOUR HANDS, YIELDING A COMPLETELY CLEAN INNER SHELL.

◆ BE CAREFUL, THE PEEL CAN BURN VERY QUICKLY ONCE THE SYRUP HAS THICKENED. IT IS HELPFUL TO SET A TIMER FOR 15-MINUTE INTERVALS, SO YOU CAN CHECK ON THE SUGAR SYRUP TO MAKE SURE IT DOES NOT BURN.

ASSEMBLE THE TARTLETS. A few hours prior to serving, spoon about ⅓ cup lime curd into each tartlet shell, using a small metal spatula to smooth the surface. Decorate each tartlet with some candied grapefruit peel.

ASSEMBLY
4 cups Lime Curd

12 Tartlet Shells

4 cups Candied Grapefruit Peel

◆ I SOMETIMES LIKE TO GO ALL OUT WHEN SERVING THESE TARTLETS. I FILL EACH SHELL WITH ABOUT ⅓ CUP LIME CURD, THEN USE A SMALL METAL OFFSET SPATULA TO SMOOTH THE LIME CURD OVER THE SHELL, DOMING IT IN THE CENTER TO GIVE IT A CLEAN FINISHED LOOK. I PLATE EACH TARTLET WITH A WELLINGTON (PAGE 141), PLACED ALMOST LIKE A HANDLE AT ONE EDGE OF THE TARTLET, AND THEN I CRISSCROSS CANDIED GRAPEFRUIT PEEL IN THE CENTER. JUST BEAUTIFUL AND SIMPLE.

MARYLAND STRUDEL WITH MANCHEGO CHEESE AND CHAMPAGNE GRAPES

MAKES 2 STRUDELS, 12 SLICES EACH. SERVES 10 TO 12

The inspiration for this strudel comes from a recipe called Mock Strudel in *The Elegant but Easy Cookbook*, by Marian Burros and Lois Levine. It is reminiscent of the strudel many of our grandmothers made. Dark and golden raisins, dried cranberries, walnuts, and apricot jam encased in a flaky, golden crust that has been baked slowly make this pastry hard to resist. The flaky dough and mincemeat-like filling suggest a kind of portable spiral tart. I like to serve the strudel with a soft, ripe manchego cheese and bundles of champagne grapes (when in season), an idea that came from an early 1970s *Gourmet* magazine article by Shirley Sarvis. The recipe calls for champagne grapes, but you can use any seasonal grapes available.

STRUDEL DOUGH

YIELD: TWO 12-INCH-LONG STRUDELS

4 ounces (1 stick) unsalted butter, melted

½ cup sour cream

1⅛ cups (158 grams) all-purpose flour, sifted

1½ teaspoons sugar

PREPARATION. Line one 18 X 13–inch half-sheet or jelly-roll pan with parchment paper.

MAKE THE DOUGH. Place the butter in a large microwave-safe bowl. Add the sour cream and heat at medium power in 10-second intervals, stirring between intervals, until warm. Whisk until thoroughly combined. Having the melted butter and sour cream warmer than room temperature keeps the mixture fluid and also prevents tiny lumps of butter from appearing in the finished dough.

Add the flour and sugar to the butter mixture, using a rubber spatula to incorporate them thoroughly. The dough will be light and look curdled. Gather the dough into a disk, wrap in plastic wrap, and refrigerate for at least 3 hours. Refrigerated, the strudel dough will remain fresh for up to 1 week or frozen for up to 1 month.

STRUDEL

YIELD: ENOUGH TO FILL TWO 12-INCH-LONG STRUDELS

½ (7.5-ounce) box golden raisins (1¼ cups)

See continuation of Ingredients and Preparation at the top of the next page.

MAKE THE STRUDEL. Combine the golden and dark raisins, currants, and dried cranberries in a large bowl. Set aside.

Divide the dough into 2 equal pieces and lightly flour the work surface. Work with 1 piece of dough at a time, keeping the other piece refrigerated. Cut 1 piece of dough into small chunks and work each chunk with your hands until smooth. Gather the dough into 1 piece and roll into a rectangle about 12 inches long, 8 inches wide, and a bit less than ⅛ inch thick (the thinner the better). This dough will retract a bit. Keep flouring your surface as you roll.

Use a stiff metal spatula to spread half of the apricot preserves over the dough, leaving a ½-inch border all around. Sprinkle half of the dried fruit mixture and half of the walnuts over the preserves and sprinkle with 1 teaspoon of the cinnamon. Fold the short sides of the dough just over the edges of the filling, then tightly roll the strudel lengthwise, jelly-roll fashion, using a pastry brush to remove any excess flour as you go. Place the roll, seam side down, on a prepared pan. Cover loosely with plastic wrap and refrigerate. Repeat with the remaining dough and filling, placing the roll on the pan. Refrigerate the strudels for about 10 minutes before baking.

Bake the strudels for 20 minutes, rotate the pan from front to back, and bake for another 20 minutes, or until light golden brown. Transfer the strudels to cooling racks. While still warm, use a serrated knife and with a sawing motion cut the rolls into 1-inch slices, cutting only three-quarters of the way through each slice. Finish slicing through each cut by pressing down hard with a sharp straight-edged knife.

Cool the strudel slices and layer between pieces of waxed paper in an airtight container. Refrigerated, the strudel will stay fresh for 1 week; frozen, it will remain fresh for up to 1 month.

½ (7.5-ounce) box dark raisins (1¼ cups)
½ (7.5-ounce) box dried currants (1¼ cups)
½ cup dried cranberries
Strudel dough
1 (12-ounce) jar apricot preserves
1 cup walnuts, finely chopped
1 teaspoon ground cinnamon

PREPARATION. Meanwhile, position racks in the middle and lower third of the oven and preheat the oven to 325°F.

◆ THIS IS ONE OF THOSE PASTRIES THAT I LOVE TO HAVE ON HAND. IT FREEZES SO BEAUTIFULLY; IT'S AS IF THE FLAVOR OF THE FRUIT FILLING INTENSIFIES OVER TIME, NOT UNLIKE MINCEMEAT OR A HEAVILY LADEN FRUITCAKE.

◆ IT IS IMPORTANT TO SLICE THE STRUDEL WHILE STILL WARM. AS THE STRUDEL COOLS, THE FILLING THICKENS AND IT BECOMES HARDER TO SLICE WITHOUT THE FLAKY DOUGH CRACKING AND CRUMBLING.

ASSEMBLE THE DESSERT. Serve the strudel slices with manchego cheese and bundles of grapes.

ASSEMBLY
24 Strudel slices
Manchego cheese
Champagne grapes

MONT BLANC

This is a time-honored French dessert that I've turned into individual servings. The classic version consists of chestnut cream piped out in a multitude of thin coils, spiraling upward in a cup or small bowl and topped with *crème chantilly* (lightly sweetened whipped cream). Here, chestnut cream is mounded to a peak, placed in a paper-thin sweet dough shell, and served with a little whipped cream on the top to symbolize snow. And that's how it got its name, as *mont blanc* means "white mountain" in French. The use of fresh chestnuts makes a difference, but they require more work. They need to be cooked long enough to peel easily, and sometimes the inner skin needs to be cut off. I have also made these in 4-inch barquette (boat-shaped) tartlet pans.

SPECIAL EQUIPMENT: 4-INCH ROUND PASTRY CUTTER • TWELVE 4-INCH PLAIN ROUND TARTLET PANS OR BARQUETTE PANS • CANDY THERMOMETER • PASTRY BAG FITTED WITH A ¼-INCH PLAIN TIP (ATECO #22) • PASTRY BAG FITTED WITH A ⁷⁄₁₆-INCH STAR TIP (ATECTO #25)

SWEET PASTRY DOUGH

YIELD: ENOUGH FOR 12 TARTLET SHELLS

10 ounces (2½ sticks) unsalted butter, at room temperature

1 cup confectioners' sugar, sifted

1 large egg (50 grams or ¼ cup)

1 large egg yolk (20 grams or 1 tablespoon)

1½ teaspoons vanilla extract

4 cups (480 grams) cake flour, sifted

MAKE THE DOUGH. Place the butter and confectioners' sugar in the bowl of an electric mixer fitted with the paddle attachment and beat on low speed until well combined. Beat in the egg, egg yolk, and vanilla until just combined. Gradually add the flour in three additions, mixing just until it is barely incorporated into the mixture. Remove the bowl from the mixer and finish mixing with a rubber spatula until well blended, scraping from the bottom of the bowl. Shape the dough into a ball, wrap in plastic wrap, and refrigerate for at least 2 hours, until chilled and firm, or up to 12 hours.

TARTLET SHELLS

YIELD: TWELVE 4-INCH TARTLET SHELLS

Sweet Pastry Dough

PREPARATION. Position a rack in the middle of the oven and preheat the oven to 275°F.

MAKE THE SHELLS. Remove the dough from the refrigerator and divide into 3 equal pieces. Work with 1 piece of dough at a time, keeping the other pieces refrigerated. Cut the dough into small pieces and work them with the heel of your hand against a work surface to make them more malleable and easier to work with. Shape the dough into a disk and repeat with the remaining pieces. Each piece yields about 4 tartlet shells.

Roll each disk of dough out on a lightly floured surface to ⅛-inch thickness. Cut out a total of 12 rounds with a 4-inch round pastry cutter. Use a metal spatula to lift the rounds and transfer them to twelve 4-inch tartlet pans. Use your fingertips to firmly press the dough onto the bottom and sides of the pans, pushing the excess up over the edges of the pans. Use the back of a knife to trim off any excess dough from around the edges. Prick the dough all over with a fork, cover with plastic wrap, and refrigerate for at least 1 hour, until well chilled and firm, or up to 24 hours.

Place the tartlet shells on an 18 X 13–inch half-sheet or jelly-roll pan. Bake for 7 minutes, rotate the pan from front to back, and bake for 7 more minutes, or until the shells are light golden brown and set. Let the shells cool in their pans on a cooling rack for 10 to 15 minutes. (If left in the pans any longer, the shells will split and crack.) Remove the shells from the pans and set aside if using right away, otherwise cover and refrigerate or freeze.

MAKE THE CHESTNUT CREAM. To shell chestnuts, preheat the oven to 350°F. Cut a cross on the round side of each chestnut and spread out on a half-sheet or jelly-roll pan. (It's imperative to cut the cross in chestnuts, otherwise they will explode in the oven.) Pour ⅓ cup water over and bake for at least 30 to 35 minutes, or until the shells open. Remove the chestnuts from the oven, and shell and peel them after they cool down.

Place the chestnuts, 1 cup of water, the milk, and vanilla scrapings in a large saucepan and cook until the chestnuts become tender, about 15 minutes. (The time will depend upon how long the chestnuts bake in the oven. Sometimes they are soft enough to cook in only 5 minutes or so.)

Meanwhile, combine the remaining ⅓ cup water and the sugar in a small heavy saucepan and heat to boiling over medium-high heat. Cook for about 5 minutes, or

CHESTNUT CREAM

YIELD: APPROXIMATELY 4 CUPS

1 pound chestnuts, shelled and peeled
    (buy 1½ pounds of chestnuts); or
    2 (8-ounce) cans of chestnut puree,
    such as Clément Faugier

1⅓ cups water (if using chestnut puree,
    leave out the water)

1⅓ cups milk

1 vanilla bean, split lengthwise and
    scraped

1 cup sugar

¼ cup dark rum, such as Myers's

4 ounces (1 stick) unsalted butter,
    at room temperature

¾ cup heavy cream

See Preparation at the top of the next page.

until the syrup reaches the soft-ball stage (238°F on a candy thermometer). Brush down the inside of the pan with a pastry brush dipped in water.

Mash the tender chestnuts in their cooking liquid and stir in the sugar syrup and rum. Transfer the chestnut mixture to the bowl of an electric mixer fitted with the paddle attachment and beat on medium speed until mixed well. Add the butter and cream and continue to beat the mixture until fluffy, about 3 minutes. Set aside.

ASSEMBLY

1 cup heavy cream

1 tablespoon confectioners' sugar

1 tablespoon dark rum, such as Myers's

2½ to 3 cups Chestnut Cream

Tartlet Shells

½ pint fresh raspberries

ASSEMBLE THE MONT BLANC. Place the cream, confectioners' sugar, and rum in the bowl of an electric mixer fitted with the whisk attachment and beat on high speed until stiff peaks form. Set the whipped cream aside.

Fill a pastry bag fitted with a ¼-inch plain tip, such as Ateco #22, with the chestnut cream. Pipe into the pastry shells, using a circular motion if using round tartlet shells or a back-and-forth motion if using barquette pans, mounding it about 3 inches high. Spoon the whipped cream into a pastry bag fitted with a 7/16-inch star tip (Ateco #25). Place 1 or 2 raspberries on top of the chestnut puree and cover with a swirl of whipped cream.

On occasion, I like to surround the Mont Blanc with fresh raspberries and some chunky raspberry coulis that contains the raspberry seeds.

RASPBERRY COULIS

YIELD: ABOUT ¾ TO 1 CUP

2 pints fresh raspberries

1 tablespoon framboise (clear raspberry brandy)

2 to 3 tablespoons sugar, or to taste

MAKE THE RASPBERRY COULIS. Place the raspberries in a bowl and mash with a fork. Add the framboise and sugar to taste. There is no need to cook, puree, or strain this coulis. The sugar will lightly cook the raspberries and bring out their sweetness.

ORANGE FRANGIPANE TART

SERVES 8

This tart evolved from my experimentations with something called a Mazarin Tart, a dense ground almond–filled confection baked in a springform pan and topped with an apricot glaze. I decided to give it a distinct bitter-almond filling, use a tart pan or pie plate instead of a cake pan, and cover the top with fresh fruit and a glaze. Here almond paste and just a hint of orange-flower water is used in the filling, sweet segmented navel oranges blanket the top, and a touch of Grand Marnier added to the apricot glaze contributes shine and fragrance.

SPECIAL EQUIPMENT: 10-INCH TART PAN WITH A REMOVABLE BOTTOM

MAKE THE DOUGH. Place the butter and confectioners' sugar in the bowl of an electric mixer fitted with the paddle attachment and beat on low speed until well combined. Beat in the egg, egg yolk, and vanilla until just combined. Gradually add the flour in three additions, mixing just until it is barely incorporated into the mixture. Remove the bowl from the mixer and finish mixing the dough with a rubber spatula until well blended. Gather the dough into a ball, flatten slightly, and wrap in plastic wrap. Refrigerate for at least 1 hour or up to 12 hours.

SWEET PASTRY DOUGH

YIELD: ENOUGH FOR 1 TART SHELL

10 ounces (2½ sticks) unsalted butter, at room temperature

1 cup confectioners' sugar, sifted

1 large egg (50 grams or ¼ cup)

1 large egg yolk (20 grams or 1 tablespoon)

1½ teaspoons vanilla extract

4 cups (480 grams) cake flour, sifted

MAKE THE TART SHELL. Remove the dough from the refrigerator and cut it into small pieces and work them with the heel of your hand against a work surface, making them more malleable and therefore easier to work with. Combine the pieces to form a disk.

Roll out the disk of dough on a lightly floured surface into a 12-inch round, about ⅛-inch thick. Dust the dough with flour, then transfer the dough to the tart pan by carefully positioning the top end of the dough round over the rolling pin and loosely rolling the entire round onto the rolling pin. Gently unroll the dough over a 10-inch tart

TART SHELL

YIELD: 10-INCH SHELL

Sweet Pastry Dough

PREPARATION. Position a rack in the middle of the oven and preheat the oven to 275°F.

◆ You can also run a rolling pin back and forth over the top of the tart pan to cut off any overhanging dough. It is a quick and easy way to achieve a nice clean edge.

◆ The longer the dough is chilled, the better it will hold its shape while baking. The egg and yolk seem to give the dough stability, which helps it to hold its form, so I have found it unnecessary to fill the shell with weights.

◆ I used to bake these tart shells only partially before filling them, but I began baking them fully because even though they bake further once they're filled, they never burn or overbake, and the shell always remains crisp.

pan with a removable bottom. Dip your hands in flour and press the dough very gently down onto the bottom and against the side of the pan, making sure to press the dough into the bottom edge at the base of the pan. Use the back of a knife to trim off any excess dough from the edge of the pan.

Prick the dough all over with a fork, cover with plastic wrap, and chill for at least 1 hour or until firm, or up to 24 hours.

Bake for 15 minutes, rotate the pan from front to back, and bake for about 10 minutes longer, or until golden and firm to the touch. Place the tart shell in the pan on a cooling rack and cool completely. Set aside.

◆ Do not confuse almond paste, which is used in this recipe, with marzipan. Almond paste is made of ground almonds and sugar, while marzipan has a higher ratio of sugar and some glucose and is used for decoration, either by being formed into shapes or rolled out and draped over a cake. Homemade almond paste is delicious but more delicate, so it doesn't provide the intense flavor I want here.

ORANGE FRANGIPANE TART

YIELD: 10-INCH TART

2 (8-ounce) cans almond paste

3 large eggs (150 grams or ⅔ cup)

½ cup confectioners' sugar

4 ounces (1 stick) unsalted butter,
   at room temperature

1 large navel orange

1 teaspoon orange-flower water

Tart Shell

PREPARATION. Position a rack in the middle of the oven and preheat the oven to 325°F.

MAKE THE TART. Coarsely grate the almond paste on a box grater and place in the bowl of an electric mixer fitted with the paddle attachment. Add the eggs, confectioners' sugar, and butter and beat on low speed until well combined. There should be no small bits of almond paste visible.

Finely grate enough zest from the orange to equal ½ teaspoon and mix into the almond mixture. Reserve the orange for the tart assembly. Stir the orange-flower water into the almond paste mixture and pour into the cooled tart shell. Bake for about 20 minutes, or until the tart shell is brown and the filling is golden and firm. Cool the tart in the pan on a cooling rack. Then, holding the center of the tart pan, push up to release the tart from the pan side.

MAKE THE GLAZE. Use the back of a large spoon or rubber spatula to press the preserves through a strainer set over a small saucepan. Add the Grand Marnier and cook over medium heat, stirring often, until thickened. Reduce the heat to low, stirring occasionally, until ready to use. The glaze can be made ahead. Refrigerated, it will remain fresh for up to 3 weeks. When ready to use, reheat to boiling.

ASSEMBLE THE TART. Segment the oranges by first cutting away the peel. Then with a sharp knife, slice along the side of each membrane to release the segments into a bowl. Arrange the segments on the tart in overlapping concentric rounds, covering the entire tart. Brush the oranges with the hot apricot glaze. This tart is best served at room temperature and will remain fresh, if refrigerated, for up to 2 days.

◆ I LIKE TO SERVE THIS TART WITH A CITRUS COMPOTE OF ORANGES, TANGERINES, AND GRAPEFRUIT WITH JUST A HINT OF ORANGE-FLOWER WATER AND A QUENELLE (SCOOP) OF ORANGE SORBET (PAGE 83).

APRICOT GLAZE

YIELD: 1½ CUPS

1 (12-ounce) jar apricot preserves
¼ cup Grand Marnier

ASSEMBLY

Reserved navel orange plus 4 large
   navel oranges
Orange Frangipane Tart
1½ cups Apricot Glaze, heated to
   boiling

PRUNE TURNOVERS WITH FROZEN ARMAGNAC SABAYON

This turnover doubles as a delicious prune hamantashen during the Jewish holiday of Purim. The filling has multiple uses, but in this recipe it's stuffed into a thin round of cream-cheese dough to form turnovers and baked until it is light golden. The frozen sabayon is very intense but an interesting foil for the simple turnover, adding a creamy, winey Armagnac essence, a layering that enhances the prune flavor.

SPECIAL EQUIPMENT: 3-INCH ROUND PASTRY CUTTER

ARMAGNAC SABAYON

YIELD: ABOUT 3 CUPS

8 large egg yolks (160 grams or ⅔ cup)

½ cup sugar

1 cup dry white wine, such as
Pouilly-Fuissé

¾ cup stiffly whipped cream

2 tablespoons Armagnac, the best
you can afford

PREPARATION. Have ready a large bowl embedded in an even larger bowl of ice. Line an 8-inch square baking pan with a double layer of plastic wrap, letting the excess hang over the edges of the pan.

MAKE THE SABAYON. Whisk the egg yolks with the sugar in a heavy-bottomed nonreactive medium saucepan until well blended. Add the wine and cook over low heat, whisking constantly, until the mixture is thick and has at least doubled in volume. There should not be any residual liquid in the bottom of the pan.

Pour the sabayon into the large bowl that is sitting in the ice. Whisk constantly until cool. Gently fold in the whipped cream and Armagnac. Spread the mixture in the prepared pan. Smooth the top, cover with plastic wrap, and place in the freezer until frozen, about 8 hours.

VARIATION. *I have sometimes nestled Armagnac-soaked pitted prunes in the sabayon for an even more intense Armagnac flavor.*

VARIATION. *You can substitute dried figs for the prune filling with great results.*

TURNOVER FILLING

YIELD: APPROXIMATELY 2 CUPS

1 (12-ounce) package pitted prunes,
chopped

*See continuation of Ingredients at the top
of the next page*

MAKE THE FILLING. Place all the ingredients in a medium saucepan and cook over low heat, stirring constantly, until the mixture forms a thick puree, about 5 minutes.

Cool the filling to room temperature, then refrigerate until ready to use.

◆ I FIND THAT SOMETIMES THE PRUNES DON'T BECOME COMPLETELY PUREED. IF THAT HAPPENS, A QUICK TURN IN THE FOOD PROCESSOR IS ALL THEY NEED.

½ cup orange marmalade

½ cup blanched sliced almonds, finely chopped

3 tablespoons freshly squeezed lemon juice

1 teaspoon finely grated orange zest

½ teaspoon ground cinnamon

MAKE THE DOUGH. Place the butter and cream cheese in the bowl of an electric mixer fitted with the paddle attachment and cream on low speed until light and fluffy. Add the flour and mix until combined. Wrap the dough in plastic wrap and refrigerate for about 2 hours, or until cold and firm.

DOUGH

YIELD: ENOUGH FOR 24 TURNOVERS

8 ounces (2 sticks) unsalted butter, at room temperature

1 (8-ounce) package cream cheese, at room temperature

2 cups (280 grams) all-purpose flour, sifted

MAKE THE TURNOVERS. Roll out the chilled dough on a lightly floured surface to ⅛-inch thickness. Use a 3-inch round pastry cutter to cut the dough into 24 rounds.

Place a generous teaspoon of the cooled filling in the center of each dough round. Brush the edges of each round with water. Form the dough rounds into tri-cornered hats by folding in 3 edges of the pastry, or form the dough into turnovers by folding one-half of the round over the filling and then pressing the edges together tightly to seal them. Place the turnovers on the prepared pans. Bake for about 20 minutes, or until very lightly browned. Transfer the turnovers to cooling racks and dust lightly with confectioners' sugar.

PRUNE TURNOVERS

Dough

2 cups Turnover Filling

Confectioners' sugar

PREPARATION. Preheat the oven to 325°F. Line two 18 X 13–inch half-sheet or jelly-roll pans with parchment paper.

ASSEMBLE THE DESSERT. Carefully lift the frozen sabayon out of the pan by the plastic wrap and quickly cut into 2-inch squares. Place a square on each plate and place 2 turnovers on either side.

I like to plate the dessert simply with the turnover set against the square of sabayon like a T.

ASSEMBLY

Armagnac Sabayon

24 Prune Turnovers

COOKIES AND CANDIES

What could be more fun or more satisfying than a wonderful cookie? A plate of cookies with a glass of milk or a steaming cup of tea is just as comforting as it gets. And gifts of cookies are among the most cherished of treats. All the cookies in this chapter really fit the bill, as they are some of my favorites. Some of the cookies are very simple, and some are a bit more complicated, but all are worth the effort. The two fruit bar cookies in the chapter, for example, are wonderful served as dessert. And the graham crackers will truly make you a believer. Many of the recipes in this book have cookies as one of their components. But because I didn't want to cross-reference recipes and have you go back and forth through the book, lots of cookies are included in other chapters as subrecipes. These cookies are for the most part tiny, something of an anachronism in today's world of giant cookies.

ALMOND LACE COOKIES

These cookies make the perfect addition to a cookie plate, and they are also tempting when filled with flavored whipped cream. As the cookie bakes, delicate holes form, giving them a lacy look, hence their name. The cookie has a Scandinavian heritage, something I discovered while going through a Swedish baking book from 1950.

⅔ cup slivered blanched almonds, finely chopped

½ cup sugar

4 ounces (1 stick) unsalted butter

2 tablespoons light cream

1 tablespoon (10 grams) all-purpose flour

1 teaspoon vanilla extract

PREPARATION. Position a rack in the middle of the oven and preheat the oven to 275°F. Line three 18 X 13–inch half-sheet or jelly-roll pans or large cookie sheets with parchment paper.

MAKE THE COOKIES. Combine all the ingredients in a heavy small saucepan and place over low heat, stirring until the butter melts. Continue cooking until the mixture is bubbly and pulls away from the side of the pan. Remove from the heat.

Drop teaspoonfuls of the dough 1 inch apart on the prepared pans. Bake 1 pan at a time for 6 to 8 minutes, or until the cookies are light brown. Working quickly, use a wide spatula to remove the warm cookies, 1 at a time, from the pan, and curve each around a clean broom handle or thick dowel rod to form cylinders. If the cookies become too hard to shape, return them to the oven for 30 seconds or so. Let the formed cookies cool for about 1 minute, then slide them off the dowel. Handle them carefully, since they can break quite easily. The cookies can be stored airtight for several days in a cool, dry place.

CASSIS BARS
WITH CASSIS SORBET

I got the inspiration for this dessert after tasting a lemon bar made by Pastry Chef Terri Horn at 1789, a Georgetown restaurant. I thought it was wonderful and asked her how she'd made them. She told me she had taken the recipe for lemon curd from my book *Special Desserts* and baked it in a pastry crust! I decided to try the technique using other tart fruits for the curd. Here I use cassis fruit puree, which then gets baked in a rich, buttery crust. The flavor is both intensely strong and delicate. For a dinner hosted by Share Our Strength (the phenomenal organization dedicated to eradicating childhood hunger in the United States), this dessert was served to two hundred people who simply loved it. It was a very formal black-tie dinner given for the most generous supporters of the organization, many of them sophisticated restaurant-goers. It plated beautifully and was a breeze to serve. Any strong-flavored fruit, such as passion fruit or red currant, would work as well in this recipe.

SPECIAL EQUIPMENT: ICE-CREAM MAKER

MAKE THE CRUST. Place the butter and sugar in the bowl of an electric mixer fitted with the paddle attachment and mix on low speed until light and creamy. Add the flour and salt and mix until just combined. Finish mixing by hand, making sure all the flour is incorporated.

Remove the dough from the bowl and use your hands to press it into the prepared pan. Place a piece of parchment over the dough and roll a small rolling pin or thick dowel rod (no more than 10 inches long) across the top of the dough to even it out to ¼-inch thickness. A length of 10 inches or less ensures you can roll the dough without having the edges of the tray in the way. Push the excess dough up high around the edges. This method ensures a crust that is of uniform thickness and therefore bakes evenly.

Refrigerate the dough for at least 30 minutes, or until firm and well chilled. Bake for 15 minutes, rotate the pan

CRUST

YIELD: ONE 18 X 13–INCH RECTANGLE

1 pound (4 sticks) unsalted butter, at room temperature

1 cup confectioners' sugar, sifted

4 cups (560 grams) all-purpose flour, sifted

¼ teaspoon salt

PREPARATION. Preheat the oven to 275°F. Generously butter an 18 X 13–inch half-sheet or jelly-roll pan, line the bottom with parchment paper, and butter the paper.

from front to back, and bake for another 15 minutes, or until golden and firm to the touch. Set the baked crust aside on a cooling rack.

CASSIS FILLING

YIELD: ABOUT 6 CUPS

4 cups frozen cassis puree, such as
 Boiron frozen puree, thawed

4 ounces (1 stick) unsalted butter

1 tablespoon freshly squeezed
 lime juice

7 large eggs (350 grams or 1⅓ cups)

2¾ cups sugar

MAKE THE FILLING. Place the cassis puree, butter, and lime juice in a heavy nonreactive medium saucepan and heat on low heat until the butter has completely melted.

Meanwhile, mix 6 of the eggs and the sugar in the bowl of an electric mixer fitted with the whisk attachment on low speed until just combined. Do not overwhip, or the mixture will form an emulsion.

Bring the egg mixture over to the saucepan. Whisk about 1 cup of the hot cassis mixture into the egg mixture to temper it, then pour the mixture back into the saucepan. Set the pan over medium heat and whisk until thoroughly combined. Continue cooking the filling over medium heat, whisking continuously, until thickened. This may take up to 5 minutes. Be sure to stir vigorously, touching all points of the bottom of the pan to make sure the mixture doesn't burn. The custard will begin to thicken and you will feel it thickening under the whisk. When the custard thickens and steam rises from the saucepan, immediately remove from the heat. Do not let the custard come to a boil. Quickly pour the filling into a bowl and cool at room temperature. You can hasten the cooling by refrigerating the bowl or placing it in an ice-water bath. When the mixture has cooled, lightly beat the remaining egg and stir it into the cassis mixture.

CASSIS BARS

YIELD: 30 BARS

Crust

6 cups Cassis Filling

PREPARATION. Preheat the oven
 to 325°F.

MAKE THE BARS. Pour the filling over the baked crust. Bake for 20 minutes, rotate the pan from front to back, and bake for 10 minutes more, or until the filling has set. Let the bars cool completely on a cooling rack, then cut into thirty 3-inch squares. The bars can be stored in the refrigerator for about 1 week.

MAKE THE SORBET. Place all the ingredients in a large bowl and stir to combine. Transfer the mixture to an ice-cream maker and freeze according to manufacturer's instructions.

ASSEMBLE THE DESSERT. Serve the bars at room temperature. Cut a bar in half on the diagonal and place it in the center of a plate, opened at a 20° angle like a fan, and place a quenelle (or scoop) of sorbet between the 2 triangles.

CASSIS SORBET

YIELD: ABOUT 1 QUART

2 cups frozen cassis puree, thawed

1¾ cups sugar

1 cup freshly squeezed orange juice

1 cup water

¼ cup sherry, preferably Harvey's
   Bristol Cream or Hidalgo

ASSEMBLY

30 Cassis Bars

Cassis Sorbet

CRANBERRY BARS
WITH CRANBERRY SORBET

MAKES 30 BARS. SERVES 15

Cranberry is one of my favorite flavors when it comes to baking because it has such a deep, unique essence and gorgeous color. This recipe pairs a satiny cranberry filling with an incredibly buttery crust to make a delectable fruit bar, a "cousin" to the Cassis Bars (page 127). A great plated dessert, it's also wonderful cut in small squares and served with That Cookie Plate (page 138) or as a colorful addition to a Thanksgiving dessert offering.

SPECIAL EQUIPMENT: ICE-CREAM MAKER

CRUST

YIELD: 18 X 13–INCH RECTANGLE

1 pound (4 sticks) unsalted butter,
     at room temperature

1 cup confectioners' sugar, sifted

4 cups (560 grams) all-purpose flour,
     sifted

¼ teaspoon salt

PREPARATION. Preheat the oven
     to 275°F. Generously butter an
     18 X 13–inch half-sheet or jelly-roll
     pan. Line the bottom with parchment
     paper and butter the paper.

MAKE THE CRUST. Place the butter and confectioners' sugar in the bowl of an electric mixer fitted with the paddle attachment and mix on low speed until light and creamy. Add the flour and salt and mix until just combined. Remove the bowl from the mixer and finish incorporating the dry ingredients by hand.

Remove the dough from the bowl and use your hands to press the dough evenly into the prepared pan. Place a piece of parchment over the dough and roll a small rolling pin or thick dowel rod of no more than 10 inches long across the dough to even it out to no thicker than ¼ inch on the bottom. (A length of 10 inches or less ensures you can roll the dough without having the edges of the tray in the way.) Push excess dough up high around the edges. This method ensures a uniform, less thick, evenly baked crust.

Refrigerate the dough for at least 30 minutes, or until well chilled and firm. Bake for about 15 minutes, rotate the pan from front to back, and bake for another 15 minutes, or until golden and firm to the touch. Set the baked crust aside on a cooling rack.

MAKE THE PUREE. Combine the cranberries, water, and sugar in a large saucepan and cook over medium-high heat, stirring occasionally, until the cranberries start to pop. Puree the cranberry mixture in a food processor until smooth and strain through a fine-mesh sieve into a bowl. Measure out 3 cups of the puree for the bars, and set aside. Measure out ¼ cup of the puree for the coulis, and set aside.

MAKE THE COULIS. Add the orange juice to the cranberry filling, then refrigerate. (The liquid needs to be added right away to the puree or it thickens.)

MAKE THE BARS. Whisk the eggs with the sugar in a large bowl until mixed well. Stir the 3 cups cranberry puree into the egg mixture until well combined and pour over the crust. Bake for 25 minutes, rotate the pan from front to back, and bake for 15 minutes longer, or until set and firm. Set aside on a cooling rack until completely cool. When cooled, refrigerate for 2 hours, or until chilled. Cut the sheet, using a sharp, thin-bladed knife, into 30 approximately 2½ X 2¼–inch pieces.

◆ CHILLING THE FILLING THOROUGHLY ENSURES THAT YOU WILL GET NICE CLEAN EDGES WHEN YOU CUT IT INTO BARS.

CRANBERRY PUREE
YIELD: 3¼ CUPS

2 (12-ounce) bags fresh or frozen cranberries

1 cup water

1 cup sugar

CRANBERRY COULIS
YIELD: ¾ CUP

½ cup fresh orange juice

¼ cup Cranberry Puree

CRANBERRY BARS
YIELD: 30 BARS

8 large eggs (400 grams or 1¾ cups)

1½ cups sugar

3 cups Cranberry Puree

Crust

PREPARATION. Preheat the oven to 325°F.

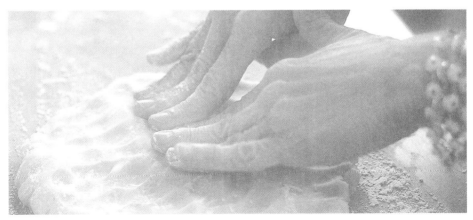

CRANBERRY SORBET

YIELD: ABOUT 1 QUART

2 (12-ounce) bags fresh or frozen
   cranberries

3 cups cold water

2¾ cups sugar, or more to taste

½ cup sherry, such as Harvey's Bristol
   Cream, Lustau, or Hidalgo

1 teaspoon freshly squeezed lemon
   juice

◆ THESE BARS ALSO MAKE A GREAT
BASE FOR A CREAMY SQUARE OF
CHEESECAKE. IF YOU FEEL LIKE
GOING ALL OUT FOR A SPECIAL
OCCASION, TOP EACH BAR WITH
A BEAUTIFUL LITTLE ICED ROSE-
SHAPED BUTTER COOKIE, PLACE ON
TOP OF A SQUARE OF CHEESECAKE,
AND CALL IT VERY BERRY
CHEESECAKE.

ASSEMBLY

30 Cranberry Bars

Cranberry Sorbet

¾ cup Cranberry Coulis

MAKE THE SORBET. Combine the cranberries, 2 cups of the water, and 2 cups of the sugar in a large saucepan. Cook over medium-high heat, stirring occasionally, until the cranberries start to pop. Puree the cranberry mixture in a food processor until smooth and strain through a fine-mesh sieve set over a bowl.

Add the remaining ¾ cup sugar, the remaining 1 cup water, the sherry, and lemon juice to the cranberry puree, stirring to combine. Taste and adjust the sweetness, adding more sugar if necessary. Set the mixture aside until cool, then transfer to an ice-cream maker and freeze according to manufacturer's instructions.

◆ IN THE FALL, WHEN FRESH CRANBERRIES ARE
PLENTIFUL, I FREEZE LARGE QUANTITIES OF THEM
SO I HAVE ENOUGH TO USE THROUGHOUT THE YEAR
WITH NO LOSS IN QUALITY.

ASSEMBLE THE DESSERT. Plate two cranberry bars overlapping on a plate with a scoop of the cranberry sorbet and a few drops of the cranberry coulis.

◆ TO ADD SOME HEIGHT TO THE PLATE, I SET A TWIST
OF FRUIT LEATHER ATOP THE BAR. FANCIFUL!

HOMEMADE HONEY GRAHAMS

Who doesn't love to bite into a crisp honey-graham cookie? Reminiscent of our child-hoods, it is a cookie we never seem to outgrow. After much experimentation, I finally achieved what I think is the perfect combination of honey-graham flavor and crisp yet soft texture. Whether you enjoy these cookies with a cold glass of milk or pulverized and lining dessert cups, you'll find these grahams are always great to have on hand.

SPECIAL EQUIPMENT: PIZZA WHEEL CUTTER

MAKE THE HONEY GRAHAMS. Sift the all-purpose and graham flours, baking soda, baking powder, and salt into a bowl. Set aside.

Mix butter, shortening, and sugar on low speed in the bowl of an electric mixer fitted with the paddle attachment until smooth and homogenized. Add the honey and malt syrup and mix well. Add the flour mixture, then the water and vanilla, beating until just mixed well.

On a lightly floured work surface, roll out the dough to ¼-inch thickness.

Use a pizza wheel cutter to cut the dough into 2-inch squares. Place the squares on the prepared pan and bake for 12 to 15 minutes, or until an even medium brown and firm to the touch. Transfer the cookies to a rack and cool completely.

◆ IF YOU'RE USING THE RECIPE TO MAKE CRUMBS FOR THE GRAHAM-CRACKER CUPS FOR THE SOUR CREAM BLUEBERRY CUPS (PAGE 208), YOU DON'T NEED TO BE CONCERNED ABOUT THE EXACT SIZE OF THE CUT COOKIE—IT DOESN'T HAVE TO BE PERFECTLY SQUARE.

◆ I LIKE TO STORE THESE COOKIES WELL WRAPPED IN AN AIRTIGHT CONTAINER IN THE REFRIGERATOR. THEY KEEP FOR UP TO 2 WEEKS.

3 cups (420 grams) all-purpose flour

¼ cup plus 1 tablespoon graham flour (34 grams)

2 teaspoons baking soda

1 teaspoon baking powder

¼ teaspoon salt

4½ ounces (1 stick plus 1 tablespoon) unsalted butter, melted

3 tablespoons vegetable shortening, melted

½ cup plus 1 tablespoon sugar

Scant ¼ cup honey

1 tablespoon barley malt syrup or brown rice syrup*

Generous ⅓ cup (6 to 7 tablespoons) water

2 teaspoons vanilla extract

PREPARATION. Preheat the oven to 275°F. Line two 18 X 13–inch half-sheet or jelly-roll pans or large cookie sheets with parchment paper.

Available at health food or organic food stores.

PEANUT BUTTER CREAM TRUFFLES WITH SHORTBREAD AND RASPBERRY GELÉE

SERVES 12

What is it about peanut butter that makes people love it so? Perhaps it is because it is one of the comfort foods of our childhoods. The peanut-butter truffle in this recipe was the brainchild of pastry chef Melissa DeMayo, who was trying to duplicate the inside of a Reese's Peanut Butter Cup. I loved it and asked her if I could use it in a recipe for *Chocolatier* magazine's tenth-anniversary celebration issue. Here, I've covered the truffles in chopped peanuts and used peanut butter made with freshly ground peanuts, instead of processed peanut butter. The raspberry gelée is simply a fruit paste, which is easy to make, and oh so good with the peanut flavor.

For guaranteed success with this recipe, source the glucose from a baking supply store. Ordinary corn syrup is too thin, and the result would be a looser gelée that would not set properly. When making the raspberry gelée, be sure to use a scale to weigh the ingredients to ensure the amounts are accurate.

SPECIAL EQUIPMENT: PIZZA WHEEL CUTTER • CANDY THERMOMETER

MAKE THE SHORTBREAD. Place the butter and sugar in the bowl of an electric mixer fitted with the paddle attachment and mix on low speed for about 2 minutes, or until combined. Add the flour, peanut butter, and vanilla and mix until almost blended, about 1 minute. Remove the bowl from the mixer and finish mixing the dough by hand to be sure it's well combined.

Roll the dough out on a lightly floured surface to ¼-inch thickness. Cut the dough into 2½-inch squares using a pizza wheel cutter. Place the squares on the prepared pans, leaving a little space in between. Cover with plastic wrap and place in the freezer for 30 minutes. Remove the plastic wrap. Bake for 10 minutes, rotate the pan from

PEANUT BUTTER SHORTBREAD

YIELD: 24 COOKIES

8 ounces (2 sticks) unsalted butter, diced and chilled

⅔ cup sugar

2 cups (280 grams) all-purpose flour, sifted

⅔ cup natural unsalted smooth peanut butter

1 teaspoon vanilla extract

See Preparation at the top of the next page.

PREPARATION. Preheat the oven to 275°F. Line two 18 X 13–inch half-sheet or jelly-roll pans or large cookie sheets with parchment paper.

front to back, and continue baking for 10 minutes, or until firm to the touch. Transfer the squares to racks and cool completely. Store in an airtight container until ready to use. Refrigerated, they will remain fresh for up to 1 week, frozen for up to 1 month.

RASPBERRY GELÉE

YIELD: ABOUT 24 SQUARES

4¼ cups (scant 2 pounds) plus ⅓ cup (generous 2½ ounces) sugar

1 tablespoon plus 2 teaspoons (generous ¾ ounce) pectin powder

3⅓ cups (26½ ounces) raspberry puree

1 cup plus 1 tablespoon (8⅞ ounces) glucose

1 tablespoon unsalted butter

15 grams of tartaric acid (Weinstein), or 1 tablespoon freshly squeezed lemon juice

PREPARATION. Line a 13 X 9–inch shallow baking pan with parchment paper.

MAKE THE GELÉE. Place the ⅓ cup sugar and the pectin in a small bowl and whisk well to prevent lumps of pectin in the finished gelée.

Cook the raspberry puree in a medium saucepan over medium-high heat until it reaches 104°F on a candy thermometer. Add the pectin mixture to the saucepan, stirring vigorously with a whisk to prevent any lumps of pectin. Stir continuously for 1 minute. Bring the mixture to a boil and boil for 1 minute without stirring. Add the 4¼ cups sugar, the glucose, and the butter. Stir to combine, and continue cooking, without stirring, until it reaches 223°F.

Remove from the heat and add the tartaric acid, whisking until combined. Quickly pour the gelée into the prepared pan and set aside on a rack until completely cool. The gelée should not be cut until cool and firm.

◆ Weinstein Acid is named for my friend Susan Weinstein, who developed the acid. It is available at Albert Uster Imports (see Sources, page 333).

MAKE THE TRUFFLES. Coarsely chop 1 cup of the peanuts in a food processor. Transfer the chopped peanuts to a dish and set aside. Place the remaining 3 cups peanuts in the processor and puree until the mixture is as smooth as possible. The peanuts are smooth enough when their oil is released and the puree just begins to cling to the blade.

Mix 1½ cups of the peanut puree with the peanut butter on low speed in the bowl of an electric mixer fitted with the paddle attachment until blended. Add the brown and confectioners' sugars and the butter and mix until the mixture comes together and is well combined. Dust your hands with a little confectioners' sugar (to prevent them from sticking to the truffles) and form the mixture into 1½-inch balls, placing them on the prepared pan. To finish, roll the truffles in the reserved chopped peanuts. Refrigerated in an airtight container, they will remain fresh for up to 1 week or frozen up to 1 month.

◆ I LIKE TO MAKE PEANUT BUTTER BECAUSE I FIND PROCESSED VARIETIES TO BE TOO SOFT AND LOOSE, WITHOUT ENOUGH BODY TO GIVE THE TRUFFLES THEIR FIRMNESS. USING GROUND ROASTED PEANUTS ADDS THICKNESS TO THE JARRED PEANUT BUTTER. TOGETHER, THE FLAVORS MELD AND TAKE THE TASTE UP A LEVEL.

ASSEMBLE THE DESSERT. Use a thin-bladed knife to cut the gelée into twenty-four 2-inch squares. Sandwich 1 of the gelée squares between 2 of the peanut butter shortbread squares. Cut the remaining raspberry gelée squares in half on the diagonal and serve 2 triangles standing up on the side of the sandwich. Finish off by placing 3 peanut butter cream truffles off to one side.

PEANUT BUTTER CREAM TRUFFLES

YIELD: 36 TRUFFLES

4 cups unsalted freshly roasted peanuts
½ cup natural unsalted smooth
    peanut butter
¼ cup packed dark brown sugar
½ cup confectioners' sugar, sifted
2 ounces (½ stick) unsalted butter,
    at room temperature

PREPARATION. Line a half-sheet or jelly-roll pan with parchment paper.

VARIATION. *Try rolling the truffles in finely chopped bittersweet chocolate for a classic flavor combination.*

◆ TO ENSURE THAT MY TRUFFLES ARE OF UNIFORM SIZE, I USE A TABLESPOON-SIZE ICE-CREAM SCOOP TO FORM THEM, AND I GENTLY ROLL THEM BY HAND TO FINISH THEIR SHAPE.

ASSEMBLY

24 Raspberry Gelée squares
24 Peanut Butter Shortbread squares
36 Peanut Butter Cream Truffles

THAT COOKIE PLATE

At a time when it seems like the bigger the cookie, the better, my personal preference is for small and elegant cookies. I love offering a cookie plate with a tempting variety of my favorite cookies, along with a few caramel candies for interest. My favorite cookie plate contains Chocolate Sprits, Brussels, Wellingtons, Gingersnaps, Vanilla Nuts, and whatever other items I may have just made. I find that a special cookie plate is perfect for afternoon tea, as a light sweet snack, or as the finale to a special-occasion meal.

CHOCOLATE SPRITS

YIELD: 65 TINY COOKIES

¾ cup (105 grams) all-purpose flour

2 tablespoons Dutch-processed cocoa

½ teaspoon baking powder

1 ounce unsweetened chocolate, chopped

½ ounce bittersweet chocolate, chopped

¼ pound (1 stick) unsalted butter, at room temperature

⅓ cup sugar

⅛ cup (25 grams) from half of one whole egg

½ egg yolk (10 grams or ½ tablespoon)

1 teaspoon vanilla extract

PREPARATION. Preheat the oven to 275°F. Line two 18 X 13–inch half-sheet or jelly-roll pans or large cookie sheets with parchment paper.

SPECIAL EQUIPMENT: 16-INCH PASTRY BAG FITTED WITH A ½-INCH STAR TIP (ATECO #24)

MAKE THE CHOCOLATE SPRITS. Sift the flour, cocoa, and baking powder onto parchment paper and set aside. Place the unsweetened and bittersweet chocolates in a small bowl and set over a saucepan of almost simmering water, stirring frequently until melted and smooth. (Alternately, you can use the microwave.) Set aside until cooled slightly, but bear in mind that when the quantity is small, the chocolate cools quickly.

Cream the butter and sugar on low speed in the bowl of an electric mixer fitted with the paddle attachment until just incorporated. Add the egg, egg yolk, and vanilla and continue to mix for 1 to 2 minutes more, or until well combined. Remove the bowl from the mixer and stir in the melted chocolate with a rubber spatula. Add the flour mixture to the chocolate mixture one-quarter at a time, blending well after each addition. The batter will be thick and dark.

Fill a pastry bag fitted with a ½-inch star tip (Ateco #24) half full with batter. Since the dough is a rather stiff one, filling the bag only partway makes it easier to pipe. Pipe 1-inch strips of batter 1 inch apart on the prepared pans. Bake for 8 minutes, rotate the pans from front to

back, and bake for at least another 8 minutes, or until the cookies feel firm to the touch, rotating after the second 8 minutes if the cookies need more baking time.

Transfer the cookies to a rack to cool completely. The cookies will be fresh for 1 day at room temperature or can be tightly wrapped in plastic wrap, placed in an airtight container, and frozen for up to 1 month.

BRUSSELS

YIELD: 60 COOKIES

3¾ cups ground almonds (4½ cups whole almonds)

2⅔ cups sugar

5 large egg yolks (110 grams or ½ cup)

1 teaspoon finely grated lemon zest

1 to 2 teaspoons lightly beaten egg

1 (12-ounce) jar apricot preserves or raspberry jam

PREPARATION. Preheat the oven to 250°F. Line two 18 X 13–inch half-sheet or jelly-roll pans or large cookie sheets with parchment paper.

SPECIAL EQUIPMENT: PASTRY BAG FITTED WITH ¼-INCH PLAIN TIP (ATECO #24)

MAKE THE BRUSSELS. Place the ground almonds, sugar, egg yolks, and lemon zest in the bowl of an electric mixer fitted with the paddle attachment. Mix on low speed until combined. Add the beaten egg a drop at a time, adding just enough to bind the mixture. It should feel damp but not sticky.

Roll the dough into three 12-inch logs, about 1 inch in diameter. Wrap each log in plastic wrap and refrigerate at least 1 hour, or until firm.

Puree the apricot preserves in a food processor until smooth. Slice each log into ½-inch slices, place the slices on the prepared pans, and press a thumb into the center of each slice, making a well. Fill a pastry bag fitted with a ¼-inch plain tip (Ateco #24) with the apricot preserves. Pipe a small amount into the indentation in each cookie.

Bake for 5 minutes, rotate the pans from front to back, and bake for another 5 minutes, or just until the cookies feel firm to the touch. They should barely color. Transfer the cookies to racks to cool completely, then cover. Store in an airtight container in the freezer for up to 1 month.

MAKE THE WELLINGTONS. Place the almond paste, sugar, and lemon zest in the bowl of an electric mixer fitted with the paddle attachment. Beat on low speed until the almond paste is in tiny bits with no lumps. Slowly add the egg whites until the mixture is smooth, soft, and slightly loose. If necessary, add a drop more egg white. The mixture should pipe easily and hold its form.

Fill a pastry bag fitted with a ½-inch plain tip (Ateco #26) two-thirds full with batter. Pipe 2-inch-long and ¾-inch-wide cookies 1 inch apart on the prepared pans. Quickly sprinkle some sliced almonds over each cookie, pressing lightly to make sure the almonds adhere. Allow the unbaked cookies to dry overnight, uncovered, at room temperature.

The Following Day

BAKE THE WELLINGTONS. Bake the cookies for 7 minutes, rotate the pans from front to back, and bake for 5 or 6 minutes longer, or until barely colored and firm to the touch. Cool completely, then remove the cookies from the pans with a spatula. These cookies are fresh at room temperature for 1 day and can be stored in an airtight container in the freezer for up to 1 month.

WELLINGTONS

YIELD: 50 COOKIES

¾ cup (187 grams or 6½ ounces)
   almond paste, grated

¾ cup sugar

2 teaspoons finely grated lemon zest

2 to 3 large egg whites (75 grams
   or a scant ⅓ liquid cup*)

1 cup sliced blanched almonds

With this particular cookie type, the exact amount of egg white is critical to the success of the recipe.

PREPARATION. Line two 18 X 13–inch half-sheet or jelly-roll pans or large cookie sheets with parchment paper.

PREPARATION. Preheat the oven to 250°F.

◆ BOTH THE WELLINGTONS AND VANILLA NUTS ARE DUTCH MACAROONS, WHICH MEANS THAT THEY DRY OVERNIGHT BEFORE BAKING.

GINGERSNAPS

YIELD: 100 SMALL COOKIES

2 cups (280 grams) all-purpose flour

1 teaspoon baking soda

2 teaspoons ground ginger

1½ teaspoons ground cinnamon

½ teaspoon ground cloves

½ teaspoon dry mustard

6 ounces (1½ sticks) unsalted butter, at room temperature

1 cup packed dark brown sugar

¼ cup molasses, such as blackstrap

1 large egg (50 grams or ¼ liquid cup)

2 teaspoons finely chopped crystallized ginger

PREPARATION. Preheat the oven to 275°F. Line two 18 X 13–inch half-sheet or jelly-roll pans or large cookie sheets with parchment paper.

SPECIAL EQUIPMENT: PASTRY BAG FITTED WITH A ½-INCH PLAIN TIP (ATECO #26)

MAKE THE GINGERSNAPS. Sift the flour, baking soda, ginger, cinnamon, cloves, and dry mustard onto parchment paper. Set aside.

Cream the butter and brown sugar on low speed in the bowl of an electric mixer fitted with the paddle attachment. Add the molasses and egg and mix until just combined. Add the flour mixture to the butter mixture in two additions, mixing until combined. Remove the bowl from the mixer and use a rubber spatula to stir in the crystallized ginger, blending it in well.

Fill a pastry bag fitted with a ½-inch plain tip (Ateco #26) two-thirds full with the batter and pipe ½-inch mounds of the dough 2 inches apart on the prepared pans. Bake for about 10 minutes, or until the cookies feel dry and firm. Transfer the cookies to racks to cool completely. The cookies are fresh at room temperature for 1 day or can be stored in an airtight container in the freezer for up to 1 month.

MAKE THE VANILLA NUTS. Place the almond paste, granulated and confectioners' sugars, and orange zest in the bowl of an electric mixer fitted with the paddle attachment. Beat on low speed until the almond paste is in tiny particles with no lumps. Add the vanilla. Slowly add the egg whites until the mixture is smooth, soft, and slightly loose. It should pipe easily and hold its form.

Fill a pastry bag fitted with a ½-inch plain tip (Ateco #26) two-thirds full with batter and pipe cookies that are 1½ inches long and 1 inch wide on the prepared pans. (To achieve the 1-inch width with the ½-inch tip, use extra pressure while piping.) Allow the unbaked cookies to dry overnight, uncovered, at room temperature.

The Following Day

BAKE THE VANILLA NUTS. Use a small knife to make a clean, deep cut into the surface of each cookie. Bake for 7 minutes, rotate the pans from front to back, and bake for 7 more minutes, or until barely colored. Transfer the cookies to a cooling rack to cool completely. The cookies can be kept at room temperature for 1 day or stored in an airtight container in the freezer for up to 1 month. (The freezing lets them "hold" their flavor.)

◆ I HAVE FOUND IT HELPFUL TO USE A SPATULA TO LIFT THE COOKIES OFF THE PARCHMENT, SINCE THE SOFT UNDERSIDES ADHERE FIRMLY TO THE PARCHMENT PAPER.

VANILLA NUTS

YIELD: 50 COOKIES

¾ cup (187 grams or 6½ ounces) almond paste, grated

¾ cup granulated sugar

⅓ cup confectioners' sugar

1 teaspoon finely grated orange zest

½ teaspoon vanilla extract

2 to 3 large egg whites (75 grams or a scant ⅓ liquid cup*)

With this particular cookie type, the exact amount of egg white is critical to the success of the recipe.

PREPARATION. Line two 18 X 13–inch half-sheet or jelly roll pans or large cookie sheets with parchment paper.

PREPARATION. Preheat the oven to 225°F.

◆ ONE OF THE BAKERS AT PALENA, NOEL SANCHEZ, WHO IS A VANILLA-NUT EXPERT, MAKES A CRESCENT-SHAPED CUT IN THIS COOKIE, BUT HE IS CAREFUL NOT TO CUT ALL THE WAY TO THE ENDS. THE CUT ALLOWS THE INSIDE OF THE COOKIE, WHICH IS STILL SOFT, TO ERUPT OUTWARD WHILE THE COOKIE IS BAKING. IF THE CUT IS DONE RIGHT, AND NOEL'S ALWAYS ARE, THE INSIDE OF THE COOKIE ALWAYS PUFFS UP OUT OF THE CENTER AND NOT OFF TO THE SIDE.

COLD DESSERTS

his chapter contains recipes that go as far back as the 1970s, during the first of my forays into sweet baking when I worked at The Big Cheese restaurant, in Washington, D.C. As I look at these dessert recipes, I'm amazed at the varied styles included here: mousses, Bavarian creams, custards, and fruit desserts, as well as creamy frozen soufflés. But what all these desserts have in common is an unbeatable lightness of texture. It has been a challenge to create recipes that contain some delectable element of creaminess; some even have the flavors one might find in a classic Jell-O recipe! I remember eating chocolate pudding out of a small footed glass bowl when I was little, as well as custard pies (coconut and banana cream) and the loveliest chocolate icebox pudding at the Quixie restaurant, located at the Hutzler Brothers department store in Baltimore. (It's a pudding I cannot seem to replicate, though I will always try!) These desserts have evolved along the way—the amounts of sugar have been tweaked, new flavors incorporated, and the desserts' presentation updated for home entertaining—but they still remain very much the kind of honest handmade desserts I feel the most drawn to.

AMARETTO NOUGAT CUPS

Years ago I made this dessert as a tart for the dessert cart at the restaurant Jean-Louis at The Watergate, in Washington, D.C. But I really enjoy creating individual desserts *à la minute,* and that is how this sweet is served. The dessert is a tempting blend of textures. The tulip cups are thin and crisp, the génoise layer in the bottom of each cup is tender and delicate, and the whipped cream is an enticing mix of crunchy nougatine, whipped cream, finely chopped bittersweet chocolate, and just a hint of Amaretto. And though this dessert needs to be served immediately, all of the components can be prepared ahead of time.

SPECIAL EQUIPMENT: 2-INCH ROUND PASTRY CUTTER

NOUGATINE

YIELD: 2 CUPS

1¼ cups sugar

¼ cup water

1 teaspoon vanilla

1 tablespoon light corn syrup

1½ cups sliced blanched almonds

PREPARATION. Coat an 18 X 13–inch half-sheet or jelly-roll pan with vegetable oil and set aside. Have ready a pastry brush and a cup of cold water.

MAKE THE NOUGATINE. Place the sugar, water, vanilla, and corn syrup in a heavy medium saucepan and stir until well combined. Place over medium heat and cook, stirring constantly, until the sugar comes to a boil. As the mixture cooks, wash down the side of the pan with a pastry brush dipped in water to rinse away any undissolved sugar. Continue to boil, without stirring, gently agitating the pan to distribute the heat. Watch carefully and remove the pan from the heat when small puffs of smoke begin coming from the sugar, which should be a rich dark brown but not burned. Quickly stir in the almonds and immediately pour the nougatine onto the prepared pan. Cool completely.

When it is cool, break the nougatine into 4-inch pieces. Loosely wrap several pieces together in plastic wrap and place in a sturdy plastic bag. Store in an airtight container. When ready to use, leave the nougatine in the plastic wrap and break it into little morsels with a strong mallet or hammer, being careful not to turn them into powder.

At room temperature the nougatine will stay fresh for several weeks, but it tastes best when just made. Do not refrigerate, as the humidity will make it moist and gummy, causing it to stick together. If frozen in an airtight container, the nougatine will remain fresh for up to 1 month.

♦ YOU WILL HAVE MORE NOUGATINE THAN THIS RECIPE CALLS FOR, BUT IT'S SO GOOD TO HAVE ON HAND, IT'S A SHAME TO MAKE JUST A LITTLE. I LIKE TO MIX IT INTO BUTTERCREAM, FOLD SOME INTO MOUSSE, OR SPRINKLE IT ON A TART FOR A FINISHING TOUCH.

MAKE THE TULIP CUPS. Place the confectioners' sugar, butter, lemon zest, and vanilla in a large bowl and combine well with a wooden spoon. (Or use an electric mixer fitted with the paddle attachment on low speed, being careful not to overbeat the mixture.) Mix in the egg whites, then the flour, and then the egg yolk. The idea is to thoroughly incorporate all the ingredients without overworking the dough, so it is tender.

For each tulip, spread 1 heaping tablespoon of batter on the prepared pan, spreading it out with a small offset spatula to form a 6-inch round. Leave at least 2 inches between each round. Bake for about 6 minutes, or until the cookies are dry and the edges are brown.

Immediately after removing from the oven, form the cookies into tulip cups. At this point you need to work quickly because all the tulip cups must be formed while the cookies are still warm. Keeping the pan on the open oven door while you work will help to keep them warm and pliable. These cookies need to be baked in several batches in order to use this method, so wait until one batch of cookies is formed before baking the next batch.

Use a wide metal spatula to remove 1 cookie from the pan and immediately drape it over an inverted 6-inch-tall flat-bottomed glass to form a cup shape. Gently press the cookie against the side of the glass, folding it a bit where necessary to keep a neat, fluted shape. Remove the cookie from the glass, set on a rack to cool, and repeat with the

TULIP CUPS

YIELD: 16 CUPS (MORE THAN NEEDED IN CASE OF BREAKAGE)

¾ cup plus 2 tablespoons confectioners' sugar

7 tablespoons unsalted butter, at room temperature

½ teaspoon finely grated lemon zest

¼ teaspoon vanilla extract

3 large egg whites (90 grams or ⅓ cup)

½ cup plus 1 tablespoon (80 grams) all-purpose flour, sifted

1 large egg yolk (20 grams or 1 tablespoon)

PREPARATION. Preheat the oven to 275°F. Line an 18 X 13–inch half-sheet or jelly-roll pan or large cookie sheet with parchment paper. Have ready a 6-inch tall glass with a flat bottom.

next cookie. If the cookies cool too quickly to form into cups, reheat them for a few seconds in the oven with the oven door closed before proceeding.

Cool, then store in an airtight container in a cool, dry place. Do not refrigerate. The cookies are best made on a dry day, as they will collapse if exposed to humidity.

YELLOW GÉNOISE

YIELD: 18 X 13 X 1-INCH CAKE LAYER

8 large eggs (396 grams or 1¾ cups)

1 cup plus 2 tablespoons (242 grams) sugar

2 teaspoons vanilla extract

2 cups plus 3 tablespoons (243 grams) cake flour, sifted

PREPARATION. Position a rack in the middle of the oven and preheat the oven to 350°F. Lightly butter one 18 X 13–inch half-sheet or jelly-roll pan. Line the bottom of the pan with parchment paper and butter the paper.

◆ I USUALLY USE A PIECE OF CARD-BOARD SLIGHTLY LARGER THAN 18 X 13 INCHES, COVERED IN FOIL, TO PLACE THE CAKE ON FOR EASE OF HANDLING AND STORAGE. MAKE SURE THAT YOU HAVE A PIECE OF PARCHMENT PAPER UNDER THE CAKE WHEN YOU INVERT IT ONTO THE COOLING RACK AND UNDER IT AGAIN WHEN YOU TURN IT RIGHT SIDE UP.

MAKE THE GÉNOISE. Place the eggs, sugar, and vanilla in the bowl of an electric mixer. Set the bowl over a hot water bath and whisk by hand until the sugar has dissolved and the eggs are warm and dark yellow, about 3 minutes.

Place the bowl in the mixer fitted with the whisk attachment and beat on high speed until the mixture triples in volume, about 5 minutes. Reduce the speed to low and whisk for 1 more minute. Be careful not to over-beat the eggs at this point.

With the mixer still on low speed, delicately but quickly add the flour, turning off the mixer before it is fully incorporated. Use a rubber spatula to gently fold the batter to ensure that it is mixed throughout.

Scrape the batter into the prepared pan, wiping off any drips of batter around the rim or outside of the pan, as this will burn. Bake for 5 minutes, rotate the pan from front to back, and bake for 5 more minutes, or until the top of the cake has domed. The cake is done when springy to the touch, golden, and a cake tester inserted in the center comes out clean.

Let the cake cool in its pan on a cooling rack for about 10 minutes. Invert the cake onto a rectangular cake board or cardboard. Cool to room temperature. If not ready to use, wrap the cake tightly in plastic wrap and refrigerate. Refrigerated, it will stay fresh for up to 2 days, frozen for up to 1 month.

ASSEMBLE THE AMARETTO NOUGAT CUPS. Use a 2-inch round pastry cutter to cut out 10 rounds of génoise. (Carefully wrap and freeze the remaining cake for other use.) Place a round of génoise in the bottom of each tulip cup and, using 2 tablespoons of the Amaretto, brush each génoise round with a few drops.

Whip the cream at medium speed in the bowl of an electric mixer fitted with the whisk attachment until stiff. Gently but thoroughly fold in the nougatine, chocolate, remaining 2 tablespoons Amaretto, and the vanilla with a rubber spatula. Carefully spoon the mixture into the tulip shells. Serve immediately.

◆ THIS IS A GOOD TIME TO CUT OUT ROUNDS OR OVALS OF THE EXTRA GÉNOISE FOR OTHER DESSERTS, SUCH AS CHOCOLATE ORANGE FONDANT OVALS (PAGE 164) OR APPLE LIME MOUSSE (PAGE 150).

ASSEMBLY

Yellow Génoise layer

10 perfect Tulip Cups

4 tablespoons Amaretto di Saronno liqueur

3 cups heavy cream

1 cup Nougatine, crushed into ¼-inch pieces

1 cup finely chopped bittersweet chocolate, preferably Valrhona Caraibe or Scharffen Berger 70%

1 teaspoon vanilla extract

APPLE LIME MOUSSE

Over forty years ago, when I first started baking at home, I came across a really odd recipe for Key lime pie. It was a low-calorie version that used dietetic applesauce, diet lime Jell-O, and Dream Whip (a precursor to Cool Whip), a powdered flavoring that you added to milk and beat. The flavors were delightful, and I'm sorry to say that the pie wasn't bad either. But when I decided to recreate the dessert, I just couldn't help but make it with homemade applesauce, fresh lime juice, and heavy cream, at least 40 percent–milkfat! I also really liked the idea of turning it from a pie into a more formal mousse. I have always loved this dessert, either made in one large soufflé dish, molded in little metal ovals, spooned into 4-ounce soufflé dishes, or even in a pie crust! The flavors seem to burst in your mouth. To me, the dessert is tart, sweet, and creamy, with the texture of the applesauce adding another dimension.

SPECIAL EQUIPMENT: TEN 4-OUNCE DESSERT OR SOUFFLÉ DISHES OR ONE 8-CUP SOUFFLÉ DISH

APPLE MARMALADE

YIELD: ABOUT 4½ CUPS

12 medium-size McIntosh apples

¾ cup apricot preserves

Finely grated zest of 2 limes

MAKE THE MARMALADE. Peel and core the apples and cut into medium chunks. Place the chunks in a heavy large saucepan and cook, covered, over low heat for about 5 minutes, stirring often. When the apples have softened and can be broken up with a spoon, add the apricot preserves and lime zest. Cook, uncovered, over medium-high heat for 3 to 4 minutes, stirring frequently to cook down the juices. When cooked enough, the apples will form a firm mound on a spoon without any liquid visible.

Remove from the heat and cool slightly. Puree the apple marmalade in a food processor until smooth. Set aside.

MOUSSE

YIELD: 4½ CUPS

1 envelope unflavored gelatin

¼ cup cold water

See continuation of Ingredients at the top of the next page.

MAKE THE MOUSSE. Sprinkle the gelatin over the water in a small bowl and soften for 5 minutes. Place the bowl of gelatin in a larger bowl of hot water and stir with a rubber spatula until the gelatin has completely dissolved. (This will take a few minutes.) Combine the apple marmalade, the gelatin, sugar, light cream, lime juice, and vanilla in a medium bowl. Adjust the sugar as needed depending on the tartness of the limes. Make the mixture a little sweeter than you think is needed, as some of the sweetness will be lost when the mousse is chilled. Refrigerate for 30 minutes, or until the mixture is cool, stirring occasionally. To hasten the chilling, you can place the bowl in a large ice bath, stirring occasionally until cool.

When the apple mixture is cool, whip the heavy cream in the bowl of an electric mixer fitted with the whisk attachment until soft peaks form. Fold the whipped cream into the apple marmalade until well blended. Spoon into ten 4-ounce dessert dishes or one 8-cup soufflé dish. (The mousse will not come to the top of the mold.) Refrigerate until set, for at least 6 hours or overnight.

4 cups Apple Marmalade

2 cups sugar, or to taste

1 cup light cream

¾ cup freshly squeezed lime juice
(from about 5 large limes), strained
through a stainless-steel strainer

1 teaspoon vanilla extract

2 cups heavy cream

◆ TO DRESS UP THIS DESSERT, I SOMETIMES USE LITTLE OVAL OR ROUND METAL RINGS AND LINE THE SIDES WITH PIECES OF ACETATE*. I PLACE A PIECE OF GÉNOISE, CUT THE SAME SIZE AS THE RING, IN THE BOTTOMS OF THE RINGS, AND THEN FILL THEM WITH MOUSSE AND REFRIGERATE. WHEN UNMOLDED, THEY LOOK LIKE MINIATURE CAKES, WHICH MAKES THE PRESENTATION A BIT MORE SOPHISTICATED, PERFECT FOR A SPECIAL OCCASION.

*Available at J. B. Prince Co.

MAKE THE COULIS. Combine the apple marmalade, wine, and sugar. Add more sugar, if needed, to make a thin film of sauce.

APPLE COULIS
YIELD: ABOUT 1½ CUPS

Remaining Apple Marmalade
(about ½ cup)

1 cup sweet white wine, preferably
Beaume-de-Venise

½ cup sugar, or to taste

ASSEMBLE THE DESSERT. Unmold the dessert dishes onto individual plates (or spoon out if using a large soufflé dish) and surround with apple coulis.

ASSEMBLY
Mousse

1½ cups Apple Coulis

BANANA MOUSSE SURROUNDED
BY PALETS AUX RAISINS

SERVES 8

On the dessert cart at the restaurant Jean-Louis at The Watergate, in Washington, D.C., this mousse was made in a round mold and sliced like a cake. Because *palets aux raisin* cookies were one of Chef Jean-Louis Palladin's favorites, I came up with the idea of making what is essentially a sabayon (lightened egg yolks flavored with wine) enhanced with pureed bananas and surrounded with little individual "bracelets" of *palets aux raisin* cookies.

SPECIAL EQUIPMENT: 10 X 3–INCH ROUND CAKE PAN • 10 X 3–INCH SPRINGFORM PAN •
PASTRY BAG FITTED WITH A ¾-INCH PLAIN TIP (ATECO #29)

YELLOW GÉNOISE

YIELD: 10-INCH ROUND CAKE

8 large eggs (400 grams or 1¾ cups)

1 cup plus 2 tablespoons (242 grams)
    sugar

2 teaspoons vanilla extract

2 cups plus 3 tablespoons (243 grams)
    cake flour, sifted

¼ cup water

1 tablespoon dark rum, such as Myers's

PREPARATION. Position a rack in the
middle of the oven and preheat the
oven to 350°F. Lightly coat a 10-inch
round cake pan with butter. Line the
bottom of the pan with parchment
paper and butter the paper.

MAKE THE GÉNOISE. Place the eggs, sugar, and vanilla in the bowl of an electric mixer. Place the bowl over a hot water bath and whisk by hand until the sugar has dissolved and the eggs are warm and dark yellow, about 3 minutes. When the mixture is homogenized and lightly translucent, it is ready to beat in the mixer.

Place the bowl in the mixer fitted with the whisk attachment and beat on high speed until the mixture triples in volume, about 5 minutes. Reduce the mixer speed to low and continue whisking for 1 more minute. Be careful not to overbeat the eggs at this point.

With the mixer still on low, delicately but quickly add the sifted flour, turning off the mixer before the flour is fully incorporated. Use a rubber spatula to gently and thoroughly blend the batter, scraping the bottom and side of the bowl to ensure that it is mixed well.

Scrape the batter into the prepared pan. Bake for 20 to 25 minutes, or until the cake feels springy to the touch, is golden, and a cake tester inserted in the center comes out clean. Do not open the door until the cake has domed.

Let the cake cool in its pan on a rack for 10 minutes. Invert the cake onto a rack, remove the parchment, and invert it again so the cake is right side up. Cool completely. If not ready to use, wrap tightly in plastic wrap and refrigerate for up to 2 days, or freeze for up to 1 month.

Combine the water and rum in a cup. Slice the génoise horizontally in half (you will have two 1-inch-high layers). Brush the cut side of 1 layer with the rum mixture. Place the layer, cut side up, in a 10-inch springform pan. Wrap the remaining cake layer tightly in plastic wrap and freeze for another use.

MAKE THE MOUSSE CAKE. Combine the egg yolks, wine, and sugar in a heavy nonreactive medium saucepan. Whisk, or beat with a handheld mixer, over medium-high heat until thick and foamy, about 5 minutes. Remove from the heat.

Combine the rum and water in a small bowl and sprinkle with the gelatin. Let the gelatin soften for 5 minutes, then place in a hot water bath and stir until dissolved, which will take several minutes. Combine the gelatin mixture and egg mixture in a large bowl. Refrigerate until cool to the touch, about 30 minutes, stirring occasionally.

To hasten the chilling of the gelatin mixture, place ice cubes in a large bowl with plenty of cold water and set the smaller bowl into the larger bowl of ice water, stirring constantly until cool.

Whip the heavy cream at medium speed in the bowl of an electric mixer fitted with the whisk attachment until stiff peaks form. Puree the bananas in a food processor with the lemon juice until smooth. Fold the whipped cream and bananas into the cooled gelatin mixture. Pour into the springform pan over the génoise layer, spread evenly, and refrigerate overnight.

MAKE THE GLAZE. Press the preserves through a strainer set over a small saucepan. Stir in the water and bring to a boil over medium-high heat, stirring occasionally. Reduce the heat to very low to keep the glaze fluid until ready to use.

MOUSSE CAKE
YIELD: ABOUT 4½ CUPS

5 large egg yolks (100 grams or ½ cup)

1 cup plus 1 tablespoon dry white wine

½ cup sugar

2 tablespoons dark rum, such as Myers's

2 tablespoons cold water

1 envelope plus 1 teaspoon (10 grams or 1½ tablespoons) unflavored gelatin

2 cups heavy cream

2 very ripe bananas

1 tablespoon freshly squeezed lemon juice

Yellow Génoise layer

APRICOT GLAZE
YIELD: 2½ CUPS

2 (12-ounce) jars apricot preserves

½ cup water

RUM SUGAR

YIELD: 2 CUPS

2 cups confectioners' sugar

⅓ cup dark rum, such as Myers's

PALETS AUX RAISINS

YIELD: 60 COOKIES

4 ounces (1 stick) unsalted butter,
   at room temperature

1⅓ cups confectioners' sugar

2 large eggs (100 grams or ½ cup)

1 teaspoon vanilla extract

1⅓ cups plus 1 tablespoon (168 grams)
   cake flour, sifted

1 cup dried currants

1½ cups Apricot Glaze

2 cups Rum Sugar

PREPARATION. Position racks in the middle and lower third of the oven and preheat the oven to 325°F. Line two 18 X 13–inch half-sheet or jelly-roll pans or large cookie sheets with parchment paper.

ASSEMBLY

3 large perfectly firm-ripe bananas

Juice of 1 lemon

Mousse Cake

1 cup Apricot Glaze

Palets aux Raisins

MAKE THE RUM SUGAR. Stir the confectioners' sugar and rum in a small bowl until smooth. Cover with plastic wrap to keep it from drying out and set aside.

MAKE THE PALETS AUX RAISINS. Cream the butter on low speed in the bowl of an electric mixer fitted with the paddle attachment for 1 minute. Add the confectioners' sugar and mix well. Add the eggs and vanilla and mix for 1 more minute. With a rubber spatula fold in the flour in three additions. Stir in the currants until evenly mixed throughout the dough.

Fill a pastry bag fitted with a ¾-inch plain tip (Ateco #29) two-thirds full with the dough and pipe 1½-inch-diameter mounds about 2 inches apart on the prepared pans. Bake for 10 to 12 minutes, or until the edges are golden brown and the center is set.

GLAZE THE PALET AUX RAISINS. As soon as the cookies are removed from the oven and while still very hot, quickly brush with warmed apricot glaze and then immediately brush rapidly with the rum sugar. The melting sugar will form a lustrous coating. Transfer the cookies to racks to cool completely. Repeat the glazing with the rest of the cookies. These are best the day they're baked.

ASSEMBLE THE DESSERT. Just before serving, thinly slice the bananas and sprinkle them with lemon juice to prevent browning. Run a thin-bladed knife around the side of the springform pan, then remove the side of the pan. Transfer the mousse cake to a serving plate. Arrange overlapping slices of the bananas on top of the mousse cake in concentric circles around the top. Brush with the apricot glaze and arrange the palets aux raisins in a ring around the base of the mousse, forming a bracelet. Serve a plate of the palets aux raisins alongside the mousse cake.

CARAMEL TRIFLE

Here, a pouring custard soaks the cake layers, making this dessert rich, soft, and ever so sensual. It is also a very versatile dessert, as you can use whatever you like in the way of fruits. I can imagine diced ripe pears along with bananas and green grapes in the fall, and peaches, plums, and berries in the summer.

This dessert originated a long time ago. As the story goes, a celebrated hostess in England was in need of a dessert at the last moment and soaked some stale cake in liquor and then in custard and fruit. When complimented and asked what it was, she responded, "Oh, it's just a trifle."

SPECIAL EQUIPMENT: 10 X 3–INCH ROUND CAKE PAN • 10-INCH-WIDE AND 6-INCH-DEEP TRIFLE BOWL (24-CUP OR 6-QUART SIZE) • PASTRY BAG FITTED WITH A ½-INCH STAR TIP (ATECO #26)

MAKE THE GÉNOISE. Place the eggs, sugar, and vanilla in the bowl of an electric mixer. Set the bowl over a hot water bath and whisk the mixture by hand until the sugar has dissolved and the eggs are warm and dark yellow, about 3 minutes. When the mixture is homogenized and lightly translucent, it is ready to beat in the mixer.

Place the bowl in a mixer fitted with the whisk attachment and beat on high speed until the mixture triples in volume, about 5 minutes. Reduce the mixer to low speed and continue to whisk for 1 more minute. Be careful not to overbeat the eggs at this point.

With the mixer still on low speed, delicately but quickly add the flour, turning off the mixer before it is fully incorporated. Use a rubber spatula to gently fold the batter to ensure that it is thoroughly mixed. Make sure to get to the very bottom of the bowl so that there are no stray particles of flour.

Scrape the batter into the prepared pan. Bake for about 25 minutes, or until the cake is springy to the touch, golden, and a cake tester inserted in the center comes out clean. Do not open the oven door until the cake has domed.

YELLOW GÉNOISE

YIELD: 10-INCH ROUND CAKE

8 large eggs (396 grams or 1¾ cups)

1 cup plus 2 tablespoons (242 grams) sugar

2 teaspoons vanilla

2 cups plus 3 tablespoons (243 grams) cake flour, sifted

PREPARATION. Position a rack in the middle of the oven and preheat the oven to 350°F. Lightly brush a 10 X 3–inch round cake pan with melted butter. Line the bottom with parchment paper and butter the paper.

CONTINUED

Let the cake cool in its pan on a rack for 10 minutes. Invert the cake onto a rack, remove the parchment, and invert it again so that the cake is right side up. Cool to room temperature. If not ready to use, wrap the cake completely in plastic wrap and refrigerate for up to 2 days, or freeze for up to 1 month.

RICH POURING CUSTARD

YIELD: 1 QUART

2 cups milk

2 cups heavy cream

1 vanilla bean, split lengthwise

11 to 12 large egg yolks (225 grams or 1 cup)

¾ cup plus 3 tablespoons sugar

MAKE THE CUSTARD. Place the milk and cream in a heavy nonreactive large saucepan. With the back of a knife scrape out the seeds from the vanilla bean and place the seeds and pod into the saucepan. Bring to a rolling boil over medium-high heat. Let the mixture rise up the side of the pan, then immediately remove from the heat.

Meanwhile, in the bowl of an electric mixer fitted with the whisk attachment, beat the egg yolks with the sugar on high speed until very thick and pale, about 5 minutes. The mixture will triple in volume and hold its shape when dropped from the whisk. It should be very stiff.

Bring the bowl over to the saucepan. Whisk about 1 cup of the hot cream mixture into the yolk mixture to temper it, then pour the mixture back into the saucepan and whisk until combined. The mixture should be thick enough to coat a wooden spoon. (Run your finger through the custard on the back of the spoon. The custard is thick enough if the line remains.) Pour the custard through a fine-mesh strainer or China cap into a large bowl. Refrigerate until cool, stirring occasionally. Refrigerated, the custard will remain fresh for up to 3 days.

CARAMEL SAUCE

YIELD: 1½ CUPS

1 cup sugar

½ cup water

1 cup heavy cream

See Preparation at the top of the next page.

MAKE THE CARAMEL SAUCE. Combine the sugar and water in a small heavy-bottomed saucepan. Mix well with a long-handled spoon over medium heat until the sugar has completely dissolved. As the sugar is heating, dip a pastry brush in cold water and run it around the inside of the pot just above the level of the sugar. This will prevent the sugar from crystallizing. If not washed away, the sugar crystals can multiply and prevent the sugar from melting smoothly.

As the sugar begins to boil, increase the heat to high and continuously shake and rotate the pot around the burner to evenly distribute the ever-darkening syrup. Once the sugar begins to boil, no longer stir it. When the mixture smells like caramel, is dark amber in color, and gives off little wisps of smoke, immediately remove from the heat. The caramel could burn very quickly at this point. Make sure that your stirring arm is covered completely and that you are holding the whisk with heavy-duty oven mitts. Standing back a bit, quickly add the heavy cream, whisking rapidly as you pour. The sugar will bubble up and may spatter, but continue to whisk until all the cream has been absorbed and the caramel is smooth. Let the caramel cool. If not ready to use, refrigerate the sauce in an airtight container for up to 2 weeks.

ASSEMBLE THE TRIFLE. Place 2 cups of the cream in the bowl of an electric mixer fitted with the whisk attachment and beat on high until lightly whipped to soft peaks. Set aside.

Use a serrated knife to horizontally slice the génoise into 3 layers. Place 1 layer in the bottom of a trifle bowl about 10 inches in diameter and 6 inches deep. Mix the water and rum and sprinkle one-third over the cake layer. Place one-third of the sliced bananas on top in a single layer. Sprinkle about one-third of the strawberries and raspberries around the bananas, then sprinkle with ½ cup of the nuts. Drizzle one-third of the caramel sauce over the fruit. Fold the 2 cups of whipped cream into the custard and pour one-third of the custard mixture over the fruit.

CONTINUED

PREPARATION. Have ready a pastry brush, cup of cold water, a long-handled wire whisk, heavy-duty oven mitts, and a towel to wrap around any part of your arm that is exposed.

ASSEMBLY

4 cups heavy cream

Yellow Génoise

1 cup cold water

⅓ cup dark rum, such as Myers's

3 medium bananas, thinly sliced

1 pint strawberries, hulled

1 pint raspberries

1½ cups walnuts, chopped

1½ cups Caramel Sauce

1 quart Rich Pouring Custard

2 tablespoons confectioners' sugar

Chopped nuts and berries, for garnish
  (optional)

◆ THE TRIFLE CAN ALSO BE MADE WITH APRICOT PRESERVES, SHERRY-SOAKED SPONGE CAKE, AND PASTRY CREAM INSTEAD OF POURING CUSTARD, WHICH MAKES FOR A FIRMER TRIFLE. FOR THIS VERSION, USE BANANAS AND WALNUTS (NO OTHER FRUIT), AND IT IS WONDERFUL. THE TRIFLE WOULD ALSO BE DELICIOUS SERVED IN TULIP CUPS (PAGE 147).

Break the second layer of the génoise into 7 or 8 rough pieces. Place the pieces in the bowl and repeat the layers, using one-third of the remaining rum syrup, fruit, nuts, caramel sauce, and custard mixture. Break up the third layer of génoise and repeat with the remaining rum syrup, fruit, nuts, caramel sauce, and custard mixture.

Whip the remaining 2 cups heavy cream with the confectioners' sugar until stiff peaks form. Set aside ½ cup of the whipped cream. Smoothly spread the remaining whipped cream over the top of the trifle. Put the reserved ½ cup whipped cream into a pastry bag fitted with a ½-inch fluted star tip (Ateco #26) and decorate the top of the trifle with rosettes. The top can also be sprinkled with some additional chopped walnuts and berries, if you like. Refrigerate until ready to serve, or up to 1 day.

CHOCOLATE NAPOLEON

SERVES 8

This fabulous dessert is very rich, so a small slice goes a long way. The puff pastry is brushed with apricot glaze and filled with a lightened ganache, turning this into a chocolate mousse Napoleon. The success of this Napoleon depends on the incomparable quality of made-from-scratch puff pastry. Store-bought puff pastry is often made with shortening. Only an all-butter product is worth using here. The frozen Dufour all-butter puff pastry is a reliable substitute found in specialty food stores.

SPECIAL EQUIPMENT: CHEESE SLICER, TRUFFLE SLICER, MANDOLINE, OR ADJUSTABLE VEGETABLE SLICER

MAKE THE PUFF PASTRY. Place the all-purpose and cake flours, salt, and the diced butter in the bowl of an electric mixer fitted with the paddle attachment. Mix on low speed until the butter and flour mixture are well combined, about 3 minutes. The mixture should look coarse and crumbly. Add the water in a slow, continuous stream and mix until the dough is slightly damp, pliable, and gathers into a ball around the paddle attachment. If it looks too dry, use a spoon and slowly add more water, drop by drop. Touch the dough with your fingertips; it should be damp but not sticky.

Use the palm of your hand and your fingertips to pat and stretch the dough into a uniform square (the exact size is not important). Wrap the dough in plastic wrap and refrigerate for 30 minutes. (In cool weather, such as when the room temperature is below 65°F, I leave the dough out of the refrigerator.)

PREPARE THE BUTTER. Dust each stick of butter with a little all-purpose flour. Use a cheese slicer, truffle slicer, mandoline, or adjustable vegetable slicer to slice each cold stick of butter into 7 lengthwise slices. In all you will end up with 28 thin 5 X 1–inch slices of butter. Divide them into 3 groups (1 group will have 1 additional piece). Place

PUFF PASTRY

YIELD: 2 POUNDS PUFF PASTRY

3 cups (420 grams) all-purpose flour, sifted

1 cup (120 grams) cake flour, sifted

¼ teaspoon salt

4 tablespoons unsalted butter, diced and chilled

¾ cup chilled water

1 pound (4 sticks) cold unsalted butter

PREPARATION. Line two or three 18 X 13–inch half-sheet or jelly-roll pans or large cookie sheets lined with parchment paper.

each group on lightly floured parchment paper, long sides slightly overlapping, pressing the slices together to form three 7¾ X 5–inch "sheets" of butter. Refrigerate for just 20 minutes. (Again, when room temperature is below 65°F, leave them out.)

For the dough to perform at optimum level, the dough and butter should have the same amount of firmness and, most important, the same temperature. The puff pastry should need to be chilled for only about 15 minutes to roll out, unless the room is very cool; then keep for 15 minutes at room temperature. It has to be cool to the touch, not cold throughout. I have made this pastry when the butter was at the proper temperature but the dough was much colder, and it caused the butter to become too cold and break up in the dough. Once this happens, the dough will never be homogenized; that is, some of the butter will always remain visible in the dough, and this is what causes an uneven rise.

ADD THE BUTTER. Roll out the cool dough on a lightly floured surface to a rectangle about 20 inches long and 8 inches wide. See the diagram at left. Use a ruler as a guide and with your fingertip mark the dough crosswise into fourths (at 5, 10, 15, and 20 inches), without cutting all the way through (1). Place one 7¾ X 5–sheet of butter on the section of dough immediately left of center. Place the butter so it covers that entire section of dough (2). Fold over the section of dough to its left, bringing it toward the center, enclosing the butter in the dough. The dough should now be in 3 sections (3). Place a second sheet of butter in the middle section (4) and fold the right section of dough over the butter. You now have 2 sections of dough visible (5). Place the remaining sheet of butter on top of the left section (6) and fold the other half of the dough over to enclose it (7). The dough should measure roughly 9 X 6 inches.

Then, rolling forward with the rolling pin, roll the

DIAGRAM FOR ROLL/FOLD PASTRY

dough out to a rectangle approximately 18 inches long and 7 inches wide. Fold the rectangle into thirds to create a rectangle roughly 7 X 6 inches and rotate it 90°. Use a pastry brush and brush off any excess flour. Place the dough on a half-sheet or jelly-roll pan, cover with plastic wrap, and refrigerate for 15 minutes. The first turn (which is actually made up of four turns) has now been completed. Repeat the rolling, folding, turning, and chilling of the dough 2 more times. The exact dimensions of the dough are not as important as the smoothness and homogenization of the butter in the dough. The dough should be uniform in color, with no patches of butter showing through.

Place it on a prepared half-sheet or jelly-roll pan and wrap tightly in plastic wrap. Refrigerate for at least 5 hours or overnight.

PREPARE THE DOUGH. Remove the dough from the refrigerator and cut in half. Cut the chilled dough into 4 equal pieces. Return 3 pieces to the refrigerator while working with 1 piece. Roll out the dough into a strip about 14 inches long. The width and thickness are not important at this point. Brush off excess flour and fold into thirds. Roll this piece out again into a 14-inch-long strip, brush off any excess flour, and fold again in thirds. Refrigerate this piece while you roll and fold each of the other 3 pieces, keeping only one piece out of the refrigerator at a time. This is giving the dough 2 more turns and is the secret to getting a great, even rise.

Roll each piece of puff, with the folded side down, into a strip 15 inches long by 4 inches wide. Place each strip on the prepared pan and chill for 1 hour.

Meanwhile, preheat the oven to 400°F. When ready to bake, remove the pastry sheets from the refrigerator and or prick all over with a fork.

Bake the puff pastry strips for 15 minutes, rotate the pans from front to back, and bake for 8 more minutes. Reduce the oven temperature to 275°F and bake for

◆ WHEN I MAKE PUFF PASTRY, I PREFER TO CUT AND BAKE ALL THE PUFF WHEN IT'S FRESH AND THEN FREEZE THE EXTRA BAKED PIECES. THAT WAY I ALWAYS HAVE A PREPARED DESSERT COMPONENT READY TO USE AT A MOMENT'S NOTICE. YOU CAN ALSO USE HALF THE PUFF TO CUT NAPOLEON SQUARES.

PREPARATION. If you are baking all the puff, you will need four 18 X 13–inch pans lined with parchment paper.

If you are baking half the puff, line two 18 X 13–inch half-sheet or jelly-roll pans with parchment. Wrap one portion of the puff in plastic wrap and refrigerate for up to 2 days or freeze for up to 1 month.

another 30 minutes, or until dry looking and dark golden. Cool in the pans on racks for about 5 minutes.

If not using immediately, cool the strips completely, place in an airtight container, and refrigerate for up to 3 days, or freeze for up to 1 month.

◆ AFTER I CUT THE STRIPS AND TRIM THE EDGES EVENLY, I GATHER THE SCRAPS TOGETHER, WRAP THEM IN PLASTIC WRAP, AND FREEZE THEM. I USE THEM TO MAKE MINIATURE PALMIERS, OR SOMETIMES I SIMPLY SPRINKLE SUGAR ON THE TRIMMINGS AND BAKE AT 350°F UNTIL PUFFED AND GOLDEN. THEY ARE IRRESISTIBLE HOT FROM THE OVEN.

APRICOT GLAZE

YIELD: ABOUT 1 CUP

1 (12-ounce) jar apricot preserves
¼ cup Grand Marnier

◆ A GOOD APRICOT GLAZE IS JUST LIKE A FAVORITE KITCHEN TOOL THAT YOU WANT TO HAVE AT YOUR SIDE AT ALL TIMES. IT'S A GREAT BASIC COMPONENT FOR A MULTI-TUDE OF DIFFERENT DESSERTS. IT'S WONDERFUL FOR GLAZING FRUIT TARTS, SPREADING OVER OR BETWEEN CAKE LAYERS, OR AS A FRUITFUL ADDITION TO A SWEET, ESPECIALLY CHOCOLATE. IT'S A STAPLE IN MY KITCHEN.

MAKE THE GLAZE. Use the back of a large spoon to press the preserves through a fine-mesh strainer that has been set over a small saucepan. Add the Grand Marnier and cook over medium heat, stirring often, until thickened, about 8 minutes. Set aside. When ready to use, reheat to boiling. Refrigerated in an airtight container, any leftover glaze will keep fresh for up to 3 weeks.

MAKE THE GANACHE. Bring the cream to a boil in a large saucepan. Add the chopped chocolate and stir with a large stainless-steel spoon. When most of the chocolate has melted, continue stirring with a whisk until the mixture is completely smooth, making sure there are no small bits of chocolate remaining. Pour the chocolate cream into a large bowl and refrigerate until about 68°F, or just cool to the touch.

If the chocolate cream becomes too cold, it will harden and become too stiff to work. Soften it by setting it out at room temperature, by placing it in a bowl of very warm water and stirring, or by microwaving it on medium power for 10-second intervals, stirring between each interval. Do not heat to a temperature higher than 78°F.

MAKE THE WHIPPED CREAM. Place the cream, confectioners' sugar, and vanilla in the bowl of an electric mixer fitted with the whisk attachment. Use the back of a knife to scrape out the seeds from one of the bean halves and add to the cream mixture. Whip the cream until it forms stiff peaks. Use immediately.

ASSEMBLE THE NAPOLEON. To ensure crispness, assemble the Napoleon no more than 4 hours prior to serving.

Whip the crème ganache on high speed in the bowl of an electric mixer fitted with the whisk attachment until it is light and fluffy and has tripled in volume. Brush the tops of 3 of the 4 pastry strips with apricot glaze. Place 1 glazed puff strip on a platter and use a metal spatula to spread one-third of the whipped ganache evenly over the puff. Spread one-third of the whipped cream evenly over the ganache. Place the second layer of glazed puff on top of the whipped cream. Repeat with the crème ganache and whipped cream 2 more times, then place the unglazed puff strip on top. Dust with confectioners' sugar. Slice the Napoleon with a serrated knife into eight 1¾-inch pieces, using a delicate sawing motion. Serve within 4 hours.

CRÈME GANACHE

YIELD: ABOUT 6 CUPS

4 cups heavy cream

2 pounds bittersweet chocolate, such as Callebaut 60/40, chopped

WHIPPED CREAM

YIELD: 7 CUPS

4 cups heavy cream

3 tablespoons confectioners' sugar

1 teaspoon vanilla extract

1 vanilla bean, split lengthwise

ASSEMBLY

6 cups Crème Ganache

4 Puff Pastry strips

1 cup Apricot Glaze

7 cups Whipped Cream

½ cup confectioners' sugar

◆ YOU CAN RECRISP THE PUFF IN A 300°F OVEN FOR 5 MINUTES OR SO (EVEN WITH THE APRICOT GLAZE) IF NECESSARY.

CHOCOLATE ORANGE FONDANT OVALS

I've always had a fascination with oval shapes. And since so many people love chocolate mousse, I decided to combine the two. I've given the chocolate mousse a double dose of chocolate flavor by using bittersweet chocolate and unsweetened cocoa, then flavored it further with orange juice and Grand Marnier and poured it into small oval molds. Orange segments poached in white wine are served as an accompaniment to the mousse, but they would make a lovely light dessert on their own.

SPECIAL EQUIPMENT: PASTRY BAG FITTED WITH A ⁷⁄₁₆-INCH PLAIN TIP (ATECO #25) • 15 OVAL METAL MOLDS OR FIFTEEN 4- OR 6-OUNCE RAMEKINS • ACETATE LINERS (OPTIONAL)

MOUSSE

YIELD: APPROXIMATELY 6 CUPS

8 ounces bittersweet chocolate, preferably Valrhona Caraibe or Scharffen Berger 70%, chopped

4 ounces (1 stick) unsalted butter

1 cup cocoa powder or Dutch-processed cocoa powder

5 large egg whites (150 grams or ⅔ cup), at room temperature

¾ cup sugar

4 large egg yolks (80 grams or ⅓ cup)

1 tablespoon finely grated orange zest

¾ cup freshly squeezed orange juice

¼ cup Grand Marnier

2 cups heavy cream, whipped

MAKE THE MOUSSE. Combine the chocolate, butter, and cocoa powder in a large bowl and place over a bowl of hot, not boiling, water. Stir occasionally until the chocolate and butter have melted and the mixture is smooth. Remove from the heat.

Meanwhile, place the egg whites in the bowl of an electric mixer fitted with the whisk attachment and whip on high speed just until they are foamy and beginning to hold a shape. Gradually add ½ cup of the sugar and beat until the whites form stiff and glossy peaks. Reduce the speed to very low to gently whip until ready to use.

Whisk the egg yolks by hand in a large bowl with the remaining ¼ cup sugar until well mixed. Whisk a small amount of the egg-yolk mixture into the melted chocolate, then whisk it back into the egg-yolk mixture until blended. Whisk in the orange zest and juice and Grand Marnier. Fold in the egg whites all at once until no streaks of white remain. Fold in the whipped cream gently but thoroughly.

MAKE THE OVALS. Fill a pastry bag fitted with a $\frac{7}{16}$-inch plain tip (Ateco #25) two-thirds full with mousse and pipe it into 15 oval metal molds (pipe in enough to nearly over-flow the rims of the molds). Use a small offset spatula to remove any excess and even off the tops. Refrigerate, uncovered, until firm, about 3 hours. When set, cover each mousse with plastic wrap and refrigerate until ready to serve or up to 24 hours.

If you have acetate liners*, use them to line each oval mold before filling with mousse. When set, lift off the molds, peel away the liners, and plate the mousse. If using ramekins, do not unmold them for serving.

*Available at J. B. Prince Co.

MAKE THE ORANGES IN SYRUP. Remove the peel from 2 of the oranges with a lemon stripper, being careful not to cut into the white pith. Place the peel in a medium saucepan with enough boiling water to cover and cook for 3 min-utes. Drain and place on a paper towel. Set aside.

Peel the remaining 4 oranges; discard the peel. Cut away the pith from all 6 oranges. Combine the wine, sugar, and vinegar in a nonreactive large saucepan and bring to a boil, stirring, until the sugar dissolves. Add all 6 oranges and the reserved peel strips to the saucepan and coat with the syrup. Simmer over low heat for about 15 minutes, turning the oranges frequently.

Transfer the oranges and peel to a plate. Add the Grand Marnier to the syrup, stir well, and return the oranges to the syrup; let cool. Cover with plastic wrap and refrigerate overnight. The oranges should be very cold when served. Before serving, cut each orange into 5 pieces and return to the syrup.

ORANGES IN SYRUP

YIELD: 30 PIECES

6 navel oranges

1 cup dry white wine

¾ cup sugar

2 tablespoons red wine vinegar

3 tablespoons Grand Marnier

ASSEMBLE THE DESSERT. Unmold the ovals onto plates. Top each with 2 orange pieces and drizzle with syrup. Top each with a dollop of sweetened whipped cream, if desired.

ASSEMBLY

15 Mousse ovals (or ramekins)

30 pieces Oranges in Syrup

2 cups Sweetened Whipped Cream (page 64; optional)

COFFEE ÉCLAIRS
AFTER ROBERT

Our resident bread baker during the bakery operation, Robert de Lapeyrouse (known as Bob to all of us), spoke of a fond memory: eating coffee éclairs while growing up in France. "Was it mocha?" I asked, and he responded, "No. Coffee." So I made him this coffee éclair, and he pronounced it just like the ones from the old days! To Bob, the difference between mocha and coffee was like night and day, and more than once I heard him reminisce about how he missed the deep coffee flavor he could never seem to find in the United States . . . until now!

When making pâte à choux, the éclair paste, it is fine to make more than needed. Excess can be frozen, and it freezes beautifully.

SPECIAL EQUIPMENT: PASTRY BAG FITTED WITH A ⅝-INCH PLAIN TIP (ATECO #28) •
CANDY THERMOMETER • LARGE MARBLE SLAB • PASTRY BAG FITTED WITH ½-INCH
PLAIN TIP (ATECO #26) • PASTRY SCRAPER

ÉCLAIR SHELLS

YIELD: 12 TO 14 ÉCLAIRS

4 to 5 large eggs (200 grams and
   50 grams, separated, or 1 cup)

¾ cup water

3 ounces (¾ stick) unsalted butter

1 tablespoon sugar

¼ teaspoon salt

¾ cup (105 grams) all-purpose flour,
   sifted

PREPARATION. Preheat the oven to 375°F. Line two 18 x 13–inch half-sheet or jelly-roll pans or large cookie sheets with parchment paper.

MAKE THE PÂTE À CHOUX. Lightly beat 1 of the eggs and set aside. Place the water, butter, sugar, and salt in a medium saucepan and bring to a boil over medium-high heat. As soon as the butter has melted and the mixture comes to a boil, add the flour all at once, stirring constantly with a wooden spoon until the paste pulls away from the side of the pan, about 1 minute.

Place the paste in the bowl of an electric mixer fitted with the paddle attachment and beat on medium speed; add the remaining 4 eggs one at a time, making sure each egg is fully incorporated into the paste before adding the next. Add just enough of the beaten egg, 1 teaspoon at a time, to make the paste shiny, very smooth, and just thick enough to fall from the spoon. Reserve the remaining beaten egg for egg wash. The paste may be kept at room temperature, covered with plastic wrap, for up to several hours until ready to use.

MAKE THE ÉCLAIR SHELLS. Fill a pastry bag fitted with a ⅝-inch plain tip, such as Ateco #28, with the éclair paste and pipe twelve to fourteen 5-inch-long strips, placing them about 2 inches apart on the prepared pans. Brush quickly with the egg wash. Immediately bake for 20 minutes (do not open the oven door), then reduce the temperature to 350°F and bake for about 15 more minutes, or until golden, puffed, and light in weight (airy).

◆ EVEN WHEN THE ÉCLAIR SHELLS SEEM PUFFED AND BROWN, I LIKE TO OVERBAKE THEM JUST A BIT TO ENSURE THAT THEY HOLD THEIR FORM AND DON'T COLLAPSE FROM BEING UNDERDONE.

IN ORDER TO KEEP THE SHELLS CRISP, SLICE THEM HORIZONTALLY IN HALF AND SCRAPE OUT ANY SOFT INNER DOUGH.

MAKE THE COFFEE EXTRACT. Stir the espresso powder into the rum until dissolved. This makes a larger quantity than needed but it is great to have on hand. Stored in an airtight container in the refrigerator, it lasts indefinitely.

◆ YOU CAN PLAY WITH THE QUANTITIES HERE TO ADJUST THE STRENGTH OF THE EXTRACT, BUT I REALLY LIKE A STRONG, PURE COFFEE FLAVOR, AND A 2:1 RATIO DOES THIS TO A T. IT TAKES SOME TIME FOR THE ESPRESSO TO DISSOLVE, SO IF I'M IN A HURRY, I USE 1 TABLESPOON OF BOILING WATER TO HELP DISSOLVE THE ESPRESSO FASTER, AND THEN ADD THE RUM AND STIR WELL.

COFFEE EXTRACT

YIELD: 6 TABLESPOONS

¾ cup instant espresso powder

6 tablespoons dark rum, such as Myers's

MAKE THE PASTRY CREAM. Combine the sugar and cake flour in a bowl, whisking to remove any lumps to ensure the pastry cream is smooth.

Bring the milk to a boil in a large saucepan. Meanwhile, place the egg yolks in the bowl of an electric mixer fitted with the whisk attachment and whip on high speed for about 2 minutes. Add the flour mixture and continue whisking until the egg mixture is thick, heavy, and pale. Remove the bowl from the mixer and bring it over to the stove.

When the milk comes to a rolling boil and rises up the side of the pan, reduce the heat to low. Whisk several

PASTRY CREAM

YIELD: 2½ CUPS

½ cup sugar

¼ cup (30 grams) cake flour, sifted

2 cups milk

10 large egg yolks (200 grams or ⅞ cup)

2 tablespoons unsalted butter, at room temperature

2 tablespoons Coffee Extract

spoonfuls of the hot milk into the egg mixture to temper it, then return the tempered mixture to the saucepan and cook for about 2 minutes, stirring constantly, until the pastry cream begins to bubble or "burp." Continue cooking for 2 minutes to ensure that there is no floury aftertaste.

Remove the pan from the heat and whisk in the butter and coffee extract. Pour the pastry cream into a bowl and tightly press a piece of plastic wrap directly onto the surface, leaving only a small area uncovered to allow the heat to escape. This will prevent a skin from forming on the pastry cream. Refrigerate until chilled, then cover completely with plastic wrap. If refrigerated, the pastry cream may be made up to 4 days in advance.

FONDANT*

YIELD: 2½ CUPS

1 cup water

3 cups sugar

3 tablespoons light corn syrup

½ teaspoon Coffee Extract,
   or to taste

PREPARATION. Have ready a pastry brush and a cup of cold water.

*I have included a fondant recipe for glazing the éclairs, but the easiest and most reliable fondant is found in cake decorating stores or through commercial bakery supply houses (see Sources, page 333).

MAKE THE FONDANT. Mix the water, sugar, and corn syrup in a small saucepan and bring to a boil. Stir the mixture until it begins to boil, washing down the side of the pot several times with a brush dipped in water. Stop stirring only when the mixture comes to a boil. Cook until it reaches the soft-ball stage (238°F on a candy thermometer). Test this by dropping a bit of the mixture into a glass of cold water and pressing it between your thumb and forefinger.

Pour the fondant mixture onto a marble surface and let it cool until tepid, about 10 minutes. Use a pastry scraper to begin scraping the mass together and turning it onto itself. This could take 10 minutes or more. It will become progressively firmer until it turns opaque and is very hard, forming the fondant. Knead the fondant until it becomes smooth and pliable.

Season the fondant by wrapping it in damp cheesecloth, placing it in an airtight container, and refrigerating for a few hours. When ready to use, remove the cheesecloth and gently heat in the microwave or on the stovetop and add the coffee extract.

◆ To gently warm fondant, I like to heat it in a microwave-safe bowl on medium power for about 10 seconds at a time, stirring after each interval. It should be barely warm. The trick is to get a beautiful shine without overheating the fondant. Thin it down using a flavoring, in this case coffee extract. A perfect fondant is shiny after it has dried.

ASSEMBLE THE ÉCLAIRS. Recrisp the éclair shells by putting them in a 300°F oven for about 3 minutes. Let cool and then fill with pastry cream, using a spoon or a pastry bag fitted with a ½-inch plain tip (Ateco #26). Place the tops back on the filled éclairs and spoon a line of barely warm fondant across the top of each éclair. Set the éclairs aside for about 30 minutes to allow the fondant time to dry, then serve.

◆ These are best served right away, even though they can be refrigerated for up to 1 day. After that they will become soggy. But these are so good that even if slightly soggy, no store-bought éclair could compete. To vary the flavor, fill the éclairs with chocolate pastry cream and top with chocolate glaze. Or make the classic version with vanilla pastry cream and top with a Bittersweet Chocolate Glaze (page 63).

ASSEMBLY

12 to 14 Éclairs
2½ cups Pastry Cream, chilled
2½ cups Fondant, warmed

CRANBERRY PANNA COTTA

SERVES 8

Very trendy in the 1990s, panna cotta is an Italian dessert often made with mascarpone cheese. When working for Ann Cashion, chef and owner of Cashion's Eat Place in Adams Morgan, located in Washington, D.C., I added cranberry to the panna cotta and also discovered that sour cream changed the flavor of the custard in a way that I really liked. So perhaps *panna cotta* is a misnomer here, but I love the taste, and the color is so gorgeous; it never fails to please the palate or the eye.

SPECIAL EQUIPMENT: EIGHT 6-OUNCE RAMEKINS OR CUSTARD CUPS

CRANBERRY PUREE

YIELD: 2 CUPS

1 (12-ounce) bag fresh or frozen
   cranberries

¾ cup sugar

½ cup dry sherry

½ cup water

MAKE THE PUREE. Combine the cranberries, sugar, sherry, and water in a small nonreactive saucepan and cook until the berries pop, about 4 minutes. Puree the cranberry mixture in a food processor until smooth, then press through a strainer set over a bowl. Measure out 1½ cups of the puree for the panna cotta. Set aside the remaining puree for the sauce.

PANNA COTTA

YIELD: EIGHT 6-OUNCE RAMEKINS

1½ cups reserved Cranberry Puree

¾ cup heavy cream

½ cup sour cream

¼ cup freshly squeezed orange juice

2 ounces (4 tablespoons) unsalted
   butter

1 tablespoon unflavored gelatin,
   or 6 grams leaf (sheet) gelatin

¼ cup dry sherry

½ cup sugar, or to taste

MAKE THE PANNA COTTA. Place the cranberry puree, heavy cream, sour cream, orange juice, and butter in a nonreactive medium saucepan. Heat just until the butter melts, stirring to combine the mixture.

Meanwhile, sprinkle the gelatin over the sherry in a small bowl and let soften for 5 minutes. Set the bowl into a larger bowl of hot water and stir until the gelatin has completely dissolved, which will take several minutes. Add the melted gelatin to the warm cranberry mixture, stirring well. Add the sugar, being sure to sweeten the mixture well, as some of the sweetness will be lost in the chilling. Divide the mixture evenly among eight 6-ounce ramekins and refrigerate until set, about 6 hours, but preferably overnight.

MAKE THE SAUCE. Combine the cranberry puree, orange juice, sherry, and sugar in a small bowl. Add more sugar if needed.

CRANBERRY SAUCE

YIELD: APPROXIMATELY 1 CUP

½ cup reserved Cranberry Puree

½ cup freshly squeezed orange juice

1 tablespoon dry sherry

¼ cup sugar, or to taste

SERVE THE PANNA COTTA. Unmold the panna cotta by running the tip of a knife around the edges of the ramekins and then dipping each cup into hot water for a couple of seconds to loosen the custard. Turn the panna cotta out onto plates and serve with the cranberry sauce at room temperature.

ASSEMBLY

Eight 6-ounce Panna Cotta ramekins

1 cup Cranberry Sauce

CUSTARD-FILLED BABAS
WITH PEAR WILLIAM

This is such a lush dessert. *Baba au rhum* is a classic French dessert made with a soft yeast dough that is baked until golden brown and then soaked in warm rum syrup. Here we use eau-de-vie Pear William, a wonderful aromatic clear pear brandy from France. William is a variety of pear known in France as *Williams Bon Chrétien* and here in the United States as Bartlett. I use the classic yeast dough, but soak it in Pear William syrup and fill it with pear-flavored custard. Specialty stores such as Williams-Sonoma sell popover tins that work nicely for making these babas.

SPECIAL EQUIPMENT: 18 BABA MOLDS, POPOVER TINS, OR 2½-INCH MUFFIN CUPS

BABAS

YIELD: ABOUT 18 BABAS

1 cup dried currants

½ cup hot or warm water

1 tablespoon Pear William

1 cake (0.6 ounce) fresh yeast or
    1 envelope active dry yeast

¼ cup lukewarm water (no more
    than 100°F)

3 tablespoons sugar

2¼ cups (315 grams) all-purpose flour

¼ teaspoon salt

½ cup tepid milk

4 large eggs (200 grams or ⅞ cup),
    lightly beaten, at room temperature

6 ounces (1½ sticks) unsalted butter,
    cut into small pieces, at room
    temperature

PREPARATION. Generously butter
18 baba molds.

MAKE THE BABAS. Soak the currants in the hot water and Pear William for 30 minutes. Squeeze out the excess liquid and reserve to use in the soaking syrup. Set the currants aside.

Crumble the fresh yeast into a small bowl and stir in the lukewarm water and 1 tablespoon of the sugar. (Or sprinkle the dry yeast over the water in a small bowl and stir in 1 tablespoon of the sugar.) Set aside until creamy, about 1 minute.

Sift the flour, reserving ¼ cup. Sift the remaining flour, the remaining 2 tablespoons sugar, and the salt into a large bowl and make a well in the center. Pour in the yeast mixture, milk, and eggs and mix well. Gradually mix in the flour from around the edge of the well until thoroughly combined.

Transfer the dough to the bowl of an electric mixer fitted with the paddle attachment and mix on low speed until the mixture is smooth, shiny, and slightly sticky, about 10 minutes. If the dough is very sticky, add the reserved ¼ cup flour, a small amount at a time. Beat in the butter a couple of pieces at a time, until thoroughly incorporated. Add the drained currants.

Transfer the dough to a clean large bowl, cover with plastic wrap, and let rise until doubled in volume, about 1 hour. Punch down the dough, break off small golf ball–size pieces, and place in the prepared baba molds, filling them no more than halfway. Cover the pans loosely with plastic wrap and let rise until the dough reaches the tops of the molds.

⬧ IF YOU USE MUFFIN TINS INSTEAD OF BABA MOLDS, THE BABAS WILL END UP WIDER AND SHORTER THAN CLASSIC BABAS.

PREPARATION. Place two racks in the oven and preheat the oven to 375°F.

MAKE THE SOAKING SOLUTION. Combine the water and sugar in a small saucepan and bring to a boil. Remove from the heat. Combine the sugar syrup, Pear William, and the reserved soaking liquid in a large bowl.

SOAKING SOLUTION
YIELD: 5½ CUPS

4 cups water

1 cup sugar

½ cup Pear William

Reserved currant soaking liquid

BAKE THE BABAS. Bake the babas for about 15 minutes, or until the tops are golden brown and a cake tester inserted in the center comes out clean. Unmold the babas onto racks to cool for 15 minutes, then dip into the warm soaking solution, 4 or 5 at a time. Let the babas rise to the top, then keep pushing them down until extremely full and clearly unable to absorb any more liquid. Soak only the babas you plan to serve. Remove each baba from the solution and allow to drain on a rack with a half-sheet pan under it to catch the syrup to reuse. The babas can be chilled for later use or left at room temperature if to be served soon.

⬧ I HAVE FOUND THAT THE SUCCESS OF A GOOD BABA DEPENDS UPON THE FULLNESS OF THE SOAK, WHICH HAPPENS WHEN BOTH THE CAKE AND THE SOLUTION ARE WARM. SURPRISINGLY, BABAS CAN SOAK FOR UP TO 5 MINUTES WITHOUT DISINTEGRATING.

MAKE THE PASTRY CREAM. Combine the sugar and flour in a bowl, whisking to remove any lumps to ensure the pastry cream is smooth.

Bring the milk to a boil in a large saucepan. Meanwhile, place the egg yolks in the bowl of an electric mixer fitted with the whisk attachment and mix on high speed for about 2 minutes. Add the flour mixture and beat until the egg mixture is thick, heavy, and pale. Remove the bowl from the mixer and bring it over to the stove.

When the milk comes to a rolling boil and rises up the

PASTRY CREAM
YIELD: 3 CUPS

½ cup sugar

¼ cup (30 grams) cake flour, sifted

2½ cups milk

10 large egg yolks (200 grams or ⅞ cup)

2 tablespoons unsalted butter, at room temperature

¼ cup heavy cream

2 tablespoons Pear William

side of the pan, reduce the heat to low. Whisk several spoonfuls of the hot milk into the egg mixture to temper it, then pour the mixture back into the saucepan and continue to cook on medium-low heat, stirring constantly, until the pastry cream begins to bubble or "burp." Continue cooking for 2 minutes to ensure there is no floury aftertaste.

Remove the pan from the heat and whisk in the butter, cream, and Pear William until thoroughly incorporated. Pour the pastry cream into a bowl and tightly press a piece of plastic directly onto the surface, leaving a small area uncovered to allow the heat to escape. This will prevent a skin from forming on the pastry cream. Refrigerate until chilled, then cover completely with plastic wrap. Refrigerated, the pastry cream will remain fresh for up to 4 days.

PEAR COMPOTE

YIELD: ABOUT 2 CUPS

8 firm-ripe Bartlett pears (3½ pounds)

½ cup sugar

4 tablespoons unsalted butter

1 cup golden raisins

1 teaspoon freshly squeezed lemon
   juice

MAKE THE PEAR COMPOTE. Peel, core, and chop the pears into medium chunks. Set aside.

Place the sugar and butter in a heavy large saucepan and cook over medium heat, stirring constantly, until butter has melted and the sugar begins to brown. Add the pears and raisins and cook over low heat, stirring often, for about 2 minutes. (If the pears are perfectly ripe, it will take even less time than this.) When the pears have softened but still retain their shape, remove from the heat and stir in the lemon juice. Set aside.

ASSEMBLY

18 Babas

3 cups Pastry Cream

2 cups Pear Compote

ASSEMBLE THE BABAS. Cut each baba horizontally in half, place a large spoonful of the pastry cream in the bottom half, and replace the top. Place the babas on plates on their sides and deposit a large spoonful of the warm pear compote alongside. Delectable!

Place the egg whites in the bowl of an electric mixer fitted with the whisk attachment and whip on high speed until they are foamy and beginning to hold a shape. Gradually add the remaining ¼ cup sugar and beat until the whites form stiff, glossy peaks. Fold the beaten egg whites all at once into yolk mixture. Fold in the whipped cream.

FILL THE CUPS. Spoon the soufflé into the graham cracker cups and freeze, uncovered, until firm, at least 3 hours.

MAKE THE RELISH. Combine the cranberries, orange, and sugar in a food processor and process until chopped. Set aside.

SERVE THE LIME CUPS. When ready to serve, remove the soufflé-filled cups from the freezer, put on plates, and top each with a dollop of cranberry orange relish.

VARIATION. *These graham cracker cups would work equally well filled with Apple Lime Mousse (page 150).*

SOUFFLÉ-FILLED CUPS

4 cups Soufflé

10 Graham Cracker Cups

CRANBERRY ORANGE RELISH

YIELD: ABOUT 1½ CUPS

1 (12-ounce) bag fresh or frozen cranberries

1 unpeeled orange, cut into chunks, seeds removed

1 cup sugar

ASSEMBLY

10 Soufflé-Filled Cups

1½ cups Cranberry Orange Relish

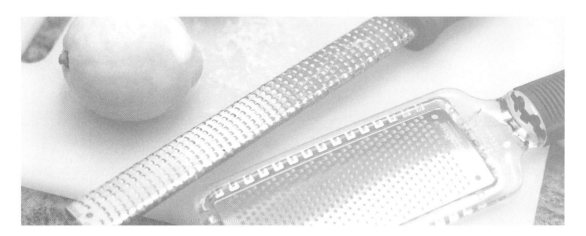

FROZEN GRAPEFRUIT SOUFFLÉ–FILLED TULIP CUPS

This recipe has been adapted from my cookbook *Soufflés*, published in 1989. It's a frozen soufflé served in tulip cups, but it could be served in graham cracker cups as well, if you like. The soufflé makes for a light and interesting winter dessert, and you could embellish it with Candied Grapefruit Peel (page 112) from the Lime Tartlet recipe. It can also be made in a loaf pan that is lined with plastic wrap or even in miniature soufflé dishes that have aluminum-foil collars taped to the outside top edges. If you use soufflé dishes, pile the soufflé high and then level it off straight across the foil collar. Remove the collar just before serving, to give the soufflé the dramatic height of baked soufflés.

SPECIAL EQUIPMENT: SILPAT BAKING MAT (SEE PAGE 201)

GRAPEFRUIT SOUFFLÉ

YIELD: ENOUGH TO FILL 8 TULIP CUPS
(ABOUT 3½ CUPS)

2 or 3 large grapefruit

6 large egg yolks (120 grams or ½ cup)

½ cup sugar

2 tablespoons Grand Marnier

1 cup heavy cream

3 egg whites (90 grams or generous ⅓ cup)

Few drops of freshly squeezed lemon juice

MAKE THE SOUFFLÉ. Finely grate enough zest from the grapefruit to equal 2 tablespoons, then squeeze enough juice to equal 1¼ cups. Place ½ cup of the grapefruit juice and the zest in a heavy nonreactive small saucepan and bring to a boil over medium-high heat. Boil until thick, syrupy, and reduced to about 2 tablespoons. Cool, then add the remaining ¾ cup grapefruit juice.

Whisk the egg yolks with ¼ cup of the sugar in a large bowl until very thick and pale. Stir the grapefruit syrup and the Grand Marnier into the egg yolks.

Whip the cream in a medium bowl to stiff peaks. Set aside in the refrigerator. Place the egg whites and lemon juice in the bowl of an electric mixer fitted with the whisk attachment and whip on high speed until foamy and beginning to hold a shape. Gradually add the remaining ¼ cup sugar and beat until the whites form stiff, glossy peaks. Fold in the whipped cream, then fold in the grapefruit-yolk mixture. Transfer the soufflé mixture to an airtight container and freeze for at least 4 hours.

TULIP CUPS

YIELD: 16 CUPS (MORE THAN NEEDED
IN CASE OF BREAKAGE)

¾ cup plus 2 tablespoons confectioners'
    sugar
7 tablespoons unsalted butter, at
    room temperature
½ teaspoon finely grated lemon zest
¼ teaspoon vanilla extract
3 large egg whites (90 grams or ⅓ cup)
½ cup plus 1 tablespoon (80 grams)
    all-purpose flour, sifted
1 large egg yolk (20 grams or
    1 tablespoon)

PREPARATION. Preheat the oven to 275°F.
Line an 18 X 13–inch half-sheet or jelly-
roll pan or large cookie sheet with
parchment paper. Have ready a 6-inch-
tall glass with a flat bottom.

MAKE THE TULIP CUPS. Place the confectioners' sugar, butter, lemon zest, and vanilla in a large bowl and mix well by hand. (Or use an electric mixer fitted with the paddle attachment and mix on very low speed until well combined, being careful not to overbeat.) Mix in the unbeaten egg whites, then add the flour. Finally, stir in the egg yolk. The idea is to thoroughly incorporate all the ingredients without overworking the dough, so it is tender.

For each tulip, spread 1 heaping tablespoon of batter onto the prepared pan, then spread it out with a small offset spatula to form a 6-inch round. Leave at least 2 inches between each round. Bake for about 6 minutes, or until the cookies are dry and the edges brown.

Immediately form the cookies into tulip cups when they are removed from the oven. At this point you need to work quickly because all the tulip cups must be formed while the cookies are still warm. Keeping the cookie sheet on the open oven door while you work will help to keep them warm and pliable. In order to use this method, these cookies need to be baked in several batches, so wait until the cookies from one batch are formed before baking the next batch.

Use a wide metal spatula to remove 1 cookie from the baking pan and immediately drape it over an inverted flat-bottomed glass to form a cup shape. Gently press the cookie against the side of the glass, folding it a bit where necessary to keep a neat, fluted shape. Remove the cookie from the glass and set it on a rack to cool. Repeat with the next cookie. If the cookies cool too quickly to form, reheat them for a few seconds in the oven before proceeding. Store the tulips in an airtight container in a cool dry place. Do not refrigerate. The cookies are best made on a dry day, as they will collapse if exposed to humidity.

ASSEMBLY

1½ cups Grapefruit Soufflé
8 perfect Tulip Cups
8 Candied Grapefruit Peels (page 112)

ASSEMBLE THE TULIP CUPS. When ready to serve, scoop the grapefruit soufflé by rounded spoonfuls into the tulip cups and garnish each with a piece of candied grapefruit peel. Serve immediately.

LIME BAVARIAN
WITH CRANBERRY SORBET

Back in the early 1960s, when I first started entertaining, one of my favorite desserts was lime sherbet with cranberry juice poured over it. As simple as it sounds, the combination was fantastic. This Bavarian is the very essence of lime, very deep and fragrant. It was one of the most popular desserts at both Jean-Louis at The Watergate and at Chanterelle Caterers. Serving it with cranberry sorbet seemed like the perfect way to combine the flavors, and it duplicates that early special memory perfectly.

SPECIAL EQUIPMENT: 10 X 3-INCH ROUND CAKE PAN • NONREACTIVE 10 X 3–INCH SPRINGFORM PAN • CANDY THERMOMETER • ICE-CREAM MAKER

MAKE THE GÉNOISE. Place the eggs, sugar, and vanilla in the bowl of an electric mixer. Place the bowl over a larger bowl of hot water and whisk by hand until the sugar has dissolved and the eggs are warm and dark yellow, about 3 minutes. When the mixture is homogenized and lightly translucent, it is ready to beat in the mixer.

Place the bowl in the mixer fitted with the whisk attachment and beat at high speed until the mixture triples in volume, about 5 minutes. Reduce the mixer to very low and continue to whisk for 1 more minute. Be careful not to overbeat the eggs at this point.

With the mixer still on very low speed, delicately but quickly add the sifted flour, turning off the mixer before the flour is fully incorporated. Use a rubber spatula to gently fold the batter to ensure that it is thoroughly mixed, making sure to scrape the very bottom of the bowl so that all of the flour is mixed into the batter.

Scrape the batter into the prepared pan. Bake for about 25 minutes, or until the cake feels springy to the touch, is golden, and a cake tester inserted in the center comes out clean. Do not open the oven door until the top of the cake has domed.

CONTINUED

YELLOW GÉNOISE

YIELD: 10 X 3-INCH ROUND CAKE

8 large eggs (396 grams or 1¾ cups)

1 cup plus 2 tablespoons (242 grams) sugar

2 teaspoons vanilla

2 cups plus 3 tablespoons (243 grams) cake flour, sifted

PREPARATION. Position a rack in the middle of the oven and preheat the oven to 350°F. Lightly brush a 10-inch round cake pan with melted butter. Line the bottom with parchment paper and butter the paper.

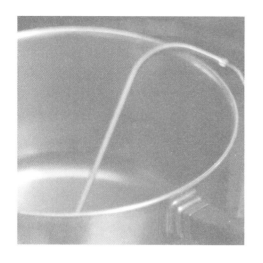

Let the cake cool in its pan on a cooling rack for 10 minutes. Invert the cake onto a rack, remove the parchment, and invert it again so the cake is right side up. Cool the cake completely. If not ready to use, wrap in plastic wrap. Refrigerated, the cake will stay fresh for up to 2 days, frozen for up to 1 month.

Use a serrated knife to cut the génoise horizontally in half to make two 1-inch-high layers. Place 1 layer in a 10-inch springform pan cut side up. Set aside. Wrap the remaining cake layer tightly in plastic wrap and freeze for another use.

CRÈME ANGLAISE

YIELD: 2 CUPS

1½ cups milk

1 cup sugar

5 large egg yolks (100 grams or ½ cup)

MAKE THE CRÈME ANGLAISE. Place the milk and ½ cup of the sugar in a heavy nonreactive medium saucepan. Bring to a rolling boil over medium-high heat. Let the mixture rise up the side of the pan, then immediately remove from the heat. Meanwhile, in the bowl of an electric mixer fitted with the whisk attachment, beat the egg yolks on medium-high speed with the remaining ½ cup sugar until very thick and pale, about 2 minutes.

Bring the bowl over to the saucepan. Whisk about ½ cup of the hot milk mixture into the yolk mixture to temper it, then return the mixture to the saucepan and whisk until combined. The mixture should be thick enough to coat a wooden spoon. (Run your finger through the custard on the back of the spoon. The mixture is thick enough when the line remains.) Pour the custard through a fine-mesh sieve or China cap and whisk into a large bowl. Place in an ice bath or refrigerate until chilled, stirring occasionally.

LIME BAVARIAN

YIELD: ABOUT 4½ CUPS

2 cups Crème Anglaise

See continuation of Ingredients at the top of the next page.

MAKE THE LIME BAVARIAN. Place the crème anglaise, milk, and lime zest in a nonreactive medium saucepan. Add 1⅔ cups of the lime juice to the saucepan and heat the mixture until it is warm (about 94°F on a candy thermometer).

Meanwhile, sprinkle the gelatin over the remaining ⅓ cup lime juice in a cup and let soften for 5 minutes. Place over a small bowl of hot water and stir until the gelatin dissolves, which will take several minutes. Add to the warmed milk mixture, then pour into a large bowl and refrigerate until well chilled, stirring frequently. (To hasten the chilling, set the bowl of Bavarian into a larger bowl filled with ice cubes and water. Chill until just cold, but not set, stirring occasionally.)

½ cup milk

Finely grated zest of 1 lime

2 cups freshly squeezed lime juice (from about 10 large limes), strained through a stainless-steel strainer

2 envelopes unflavored gelatin or 5 sheets dry (15 grams)

MAKE THE ITALIAN MERINGUE. Combine the sugar and water in a small saucepan and stir to mix well. Place the saucepan over high heat and bring to a boil, stirring to dissolve the sugar. Wash away any undissolved sugar from the inside of the pan with a pastry brush dipped in water. Do not stir the syrup after it boils.

Meanwhile, place the egg whites in the bowl of an electric mixer fitted with the whisk attachment and beat on high until stiff peaks form. When the sugar syrup reaches the soft-ball stage (238°F on a candy thermometer), pour the sugar syrup in a thin, steady stream down the inside of the bowl to prevent spattering, and beat the whites until the meringue becomes very dense, glossy, and smooth.

ITALIAN MERINGUE

YIELD: ABOUT ½ CUP

1½ cups sugar

¼ cup water

4 large egg whites (120 grams or ½ cup), at room temperature

PREPARATION. Have ready a pastry brush and cup of cold water.

ASSEMBLE THE BAVARIAN. Whip the cream in the bowl of an electric mixer fitted with the whisk attachment on medium-high speed until firm but not too stiff. Fold the whipped cream into the meringue, combining it well with a wire whisk. Using the largest bowl you have, fold the meringue mixture into the chilled Bavarian, and with a wire whisk combine it gently but thoroughly.

Mix the lime juice, water, and sugar together in a small bowl to make a soaking syrup. Brush the génoise layer in the springform pan with the soaking syrup.

BAVARIAN

1¾ cups heavy cream

½ cup Italian Meringue

4½ cups Lime Bavarian

2 tablespoons freshly squeezed and strained lime juice

2 tablespoons water

¼ cup sugar

Yellow Génoise layer

CONTINUED

Pour the Bavarian over the génoise, gently spreading it evenly. Refrigerate until set, for at least several hours or overnight.

CRANBERRY SORBET

YIELD: ABOUT 1 QUART

2 (12-ounce) bags fresh or frozen cranberries

2¾ cups sugar, or more to taste

5 cups water

¼ cup cream sherry

1 teaspoon freshly squeezed lemon juice

MAKE THE SORBET. Place the cranberries, sugar, and 4 cups of the water in a large saucepan and cook over medium heat, stirring occasionally, until the cranberries start to pop. Puree the mixture in a food processor, then press it through a fine-mesh strainer or China cap into a large bowl. Add the sherry and lemon juice and stir to combine. Add more sugar to taste, making the sorbet a little sweeter than you might think, as some of the sweetness will be lost in the chilling. Stir in the remaining 1 cup water and refrigerate until cool. Transfer the mixture to an ice-cream maker and freeze according to manufacturer's instructions.

ASSEMBLY

Bavarian

Cranberry Sorbet

SERVE THE DESSERT. Unmold the Bavarian by running a thin-bladed knife around the inside of the pan, then release the pan side. The Bavarian can be placed on a serving plate with the springform bottom or transferred to a platter by sliding 1 or 2 long metal spatulas under the cake and lifting it carefully.

Cut the Bavarian into wedges and serve with quenelles (scoops) of cranberry sorbet alongside.

MERINGUE BASKETS FILLED
WITH A LEMON CREAM TORTE

These meringue baskets are really an old-fashioned French dessert, very old school. I find myself going back more and more often to the older, more classic desserts. To me, the flavors are more authentic and purer. I suppose that I am old-fashioned that way, as I am happier with a flavor that is not corrupted with any new attention-getting ingredients added just for the sake of being different. This recipe is really for a vacherin (meringue shell), but instead of a meringue base and rings that are glued together with more meringue, here various-size meringue sheets are piped to resemble a basket-weave pattern. After the sheets are baked, they are trimmed and glued together with royal icing to form 4-walled rectangular baskets. You will want to start one week ahead. The technique may seem a little complicated, and I admit that it's more involved than most of my desserts, but the boxes are utterly charming and irresistible. And they would make wonderful containers for chocolate truffles as the finale to a sumptuous dinner with friends. The lid adds a whimsical touch. It is placed after the basket is filled: in this case with lemon cake and layers of fresh lemon cream. This is the perfect time to use that extra layer of génoise you have in the freezer! You will need to make this recipe several times, because the oven can hold only so many trays. For this reason, these baskets are made at least 24 hours ahead of time but can and should be made even days ahead, as long as the weather is dry. I have even kept them for a year, well covered.

SPECIAL EQUIPMENT: PASTRY BAG FITTED WITH A ⅝-INCH BASKET-WEAVE TIP (WILTON #2B) •
PASTRY BAG FITTED WITH A ⅛-INCH PLAIN TIP (WILTON #5) •
PASTRY BAG FITTED WITH A ⁷⁄₁₆-INCH BASKET-WEAVE TIP (WILTON #48)

MAKE THE MERINGUE BASKETS. Place the egg whites in an electric mixer fitted with the whisk attachment and whip on high speed until foamy and just beginning to hold a shape. Gradually add the granulated sugar and beat for at least 10 minutes, or until the meringue is glossy and very stiff. (Beating the meringue for this long ensures that it will be very strong and sturdy.) Remove the bowl from the mixer, sift the confectioner's sugar over the whites, and gently fold in all at once.

MERINGUE BASKETS

YIELD: 6 BASKETS

8 large egg whites (240 grams or 1 cup),
   at room temperature
1¾ cups granulated sugar
1 cup confectioners' sugar, sifted

See Preparation at the top of the next page.

CONTINUED

PREPARATION. Line two 18 X 13–inch half-sheet or jelly-roll pans or large cookie sheets with parchment paper.

Each basket consists of 6 pieces:

- a floor (base) about 3 inches long and 2½ inches wide
- two long walls (front and back) measuring 3½ inches long and 2 inches high
- two slightly shorter (side) walls measuring 2½ inches long and 2 inches high
- a lid that is 3½ inches long and 3 inches wide.

If you like, trace the pieces on the parchment with a dark pencil to use as a guide when piping, then turn the paper over on the pan. It's not necessary to trace every piece, just perhaps one of each size for guidance.

DIAGRAM FOR MERINGUE BASKET

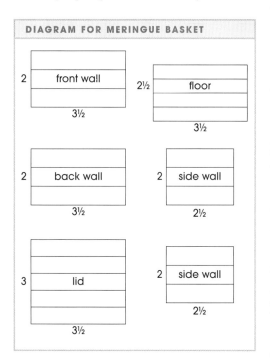

Fill a pastry bag fitted with the ⅝-inch basket-weave tip (Wilton #2B) two-thirds full with meringue.

MAKE THE FLOOR (BASE) OF THE BASKET: Create a rectangle 3½ X 2½ inches by piping four 3-inch-long strips next to one another, slightly overlapping them. (The width of the 4 strips together should equal 2½ inches.)

NEXT MAKE THE SIDE (SHORT) WALLS: Use the same tip to create a rectangle 2½ X 2 inches by piping three 2½-inch-long strips next to one another, slightly overlapping them. (The width of the 3 strips together should equal 2 inches, the height of the walls.) Repeat to create a second side wall.

MAKE THE FRONT (LONG) WALL: Create a rectangle 3½ X 2 inches by piping three 3½-inch-long strips next to each other, slightly overlapping them. (The width of the 3 strips together should equal 2 inches, the height of the wall.). Repeat to create the back (long) wall.

MAKE THE LID: Create a rectangle 3½ X 3 inches by piping five 3½-inch-long strips next to one another, slightly overlapping them. (The width of the 5 strips together should equal 3 inches.) The lid needs to be large enough to cover all 4 sides of the finished basket. (Making a lid for the basket is optional, but it definitely finishes off the dessert.) See diagram at left.

Fill a pastry bag fitted with a ⅛-inch plain tip (Wilton #5) half full with meringue. Create the first part of the basket-weave pattern by piping vertical strips about ½ inch apart over the 4 walls and lid. (The front and back walls will have 4 or 5 strips and the side walls about 3 strips.) Then, using a pastry bag fitted with a ⁷⁄₁₆-inch basket-weave tip (Wilton #48), pipe strips perpendicular to and between every other crosswise strip, alternating their placement to simulate a basket-weave pattern.

The procedure above will give you one basket. You will need to repeat it five more times: make 5 more floors, 20 more front or back walls, 20 more short walls, and 5 more lids, to make 6 baskets in all.

Meanwhile, preheat the oven to 150°F. If you have a gas oven, bake the meringues overnight. If using an electric oven, bake the meringues for 1 hour (or as low as the oven will go, but no lower than 150°F), then turn off the oven and let the meringues dry overnight in the oven. The next morning, turn the oven on to 150°F and bake the meringues for 1 hour, or until they lift off of the paper easily and feel very light. Rotate the pan from front to back after 30 minutes and watch carefully to make sure they do not color at all. Cool on racks for several hours and leave overnight. They should be dry so that when trimmed, they are as firm and dry as chalk.

◆ A 3-STRIP RECTANGLE WITH THE WILTON #2B TIP MAKES A 2-INCH WIDTH, A 4-STRIP RECTANGLE WITH THE WILTON #2B TIP MAKES A 2½-INCH WIDTH, AND A 5-STRIP RECTANGLE MAKES A 3-INCH WIDTH.

Day of Assembly

MAKE THE ROYAL ICING. Place the egg white in the bowl of an electric mixer. Add the confectioners' sugar 1 cup at a time, stirring with a wooden spoon until smooth. The mixture should be firm but still somewhat liquid, not too loose but not stiff. Use the whisk attachment and beat the icing on high until it stiffens.

The stiffer royal icing becomes, the harder it is to use as glue, because it becomes too dry. The consistency should be firm enough to hold its shape without dripping but not so stiff as to be hard to pipe and therefore too dry to adhere. If the icing is too thick, add a tiny bit of additional egg white to thin it out ever so slightly. (You need to add less egg white than you think.)

Royal icing dries out very quickly, so as soon as it is made, transfer to an airtight container and place a piece of plastic wrap pressed directly onto the surface. Refrigerated in an airtight container, it will remain fresh for up to 1 week.

ROYAL ICING
YIELD: ABOUT 1 CUP
1 large egg white (30 grams
    or ⅛ cup)
About 3 cups confectioners' sugar

ASSEMBLE THE MERINGUE BASKETS. When working with the various components of each meringue basket, set all the meringue rectangles on parchment paper. This will ensure easy removal of the boxes when dry, in case any royal icing has seeped out after gluing.

ASSEMBLED MERINGUE BASKETS
Meringue Basket rectangles
1 cup Royal Icing

Use a serrated knife to very gently trim the long and short walls straight. Very gently score through the tops of the meringues, then continue sawing using as little pressure as possible, until the trim is complete. (It is best to let the knife do the work, rather than put pressure on it.) Each piece should be straight edged so it can be glued to the others to form a basket. The 4 walls should also fit snugly against the base.

Fill a pastry bag fitted with a ⅛-inch plain tip (Wilton #5) half full with royal icing. Using the royal icing as the glue, glue 2 long walls and 2 short walls to the base and to each other to create a rectangular basket. Build the basket: Place a long wall upright and flush against a long edge of the base of the basket. Pipe a thin line of royal icing where the base and wall meet. Smooth the line of icing by pressing it into the crevice between the 2 pieces with your forefinger so it shows as little as possible. Then attach the second long wall in the same fashion. If necessary, use a paper cup or glass to support and hold the walls straight until the icing dries. Both walls should extend beyond the base a little on each side. Then, measure the 2 short walls, trimming them if needed, so they can be slid into each side, between the ends of the 2 long walls and against the base of the basket. Pipe icing between each wall and the base so the pieces of meringue are attached to each other. Fill in any gaps between the corners of the walls with more icing. Allow to dry undisturbed for 24 hours.

YELLOW GÉNOISE

YIELD: 18 X 13–INCH CAKE LAYER

8 large eggs (396 grams or 1¾ cups)

1 cup plus 2 tablespoons (242 grams) sugar

1 teaspoon vanilla extract

2 cups plus 3 tablespoons (243 grams) cake flour, sifted

See Preparation at the top of the next page.

MAKE THE GÉNOISE. Place the eggs, sugar, and vanilla in the bowl of an electric mixer. Place the bowl over a hot water bath and with a whisk beat the mixture by hand until the sugar has dissolved and the eggs are warm and dark yellow, about 3 minutes. When the mixture is homogenized and is lightly translucent, it is ready to whisk in the mixer.

Place the bowl in the mixer fitted with the whisk attachment and beat on high speed until the mixture triples in volume, about 5 minutes. Reduce the mixer to very low speed and whisk for 1 more minute. Be careful not to overbeat the eggs at this point.

With the mixer still on very low speed, delicately but quickly add the sifted cake flour, turning off the mixer before all the flour is incorporated. Use a rubber spatula to gently fold the batter by hand to ensure that it is thoroughly mixed, being sure to scrape any flour in the bottom of the bowl.

Scrape the batter into the prepared pan, spreading it evenly. Use the straight edge of a pastry scraper or a long, narrow metal spatula to evenly distribute and smooth out the cake batter. This ensures the cake will be level.

Bake for 5 minutes, rotate the pan from front to bake, and bake for another 5 minutes, or until the cake feels springy to the touch, is golden, and starts to pull away from the sides of the pan.

Let the cake cool in its pan on a rack for 10 minutes. Invert the cake onto a rack, remove the parchment, and invert it again so that the cake is right side up. Cool completely. If not ready to use, wrap in plastic wrap and refrigerate. Refrigerated it will stay fresh for up to 2 days, frozen for up to 1 month.

PREPARATION. Preheat the oven to 350°F. Butter an 18 X 13–inch half-sheet or jelly-roll pan, line the bottom with parchment paper, and butter the paper.

◆ I USUALLY USE A PIECE OF CARDBOARD SLIGHTLY LARGER THAN 18 X 13 INCHES, COVERED IN FOIL, TO PLACE THE CAKE ON FOR EASE OF HANDLING AND STORAGE. MAKE SURE THAT YOU HAVE A PIECE OF PARCHMENT PAPER UNDER THE CAKE WHEN YOU INVERT IT ONTO THE COOLING RACK AND UNDER IT AGAIN WHEN YOU TURN IT RIGHT SIDE UP.

MAKE THE LEMON CREAM. Place the lemon zest and juice and butter in a heavy nonreactive large saucepan and heat on low heat until the butter has completely melted. Have ready a deep bowl fitted with a fine-mesh stainless-steel strainer.

Meanwhile, mix the eggs, yolks, and sugar on low speed in an electric mixer fitted with the whisk attachment until just combined. Do not whisk the mixture on high speed or it will lose its translucency when cooked.

Bring the bowl over to the stove. Whisk several spoonfuls of the butter-lemon mixture into the egg mixture to temper it, then return the mixture to the saucepan, increase the heat to medium, and whisk well to combine.

LEMON CREAM

YIELD: 1½ CUPS

1 tablespoon finely grated lemon zest (from about 2 lemons)

1 cup freshly squeezed and strained lemon juice (from about 4 lemons)

4 ounces (1 stick) unsalted butter

3 large eggs (150 grams or ⅔ cup)

3 large egg yolks (60 grams or ¼ cup)

2 cups sugar, or more to taste

At this point taste the lemon cream to see if it needs more sugar. The curd should taste sweet and yet tart at the end of the taste. Make it a little sweeter than you think it should be, as some of the sweetness will be lost in the chilling.

Continue to cook the custard over medium heat, whisking continually, until thick and smooth. Be patient, as this may take up to 4 to 6 minutes. Be sure to stir vigorously, touching all points of the bottom of the pan to make sure the mixture doesn't burn. The cream will begin to thicken, which you will feel as you whisk. When it thickens and steam rises from the saucepan, immediately remove from the heat. (Do not let the cream come to a boil.) Quickly pour the cream into the stainless-steel strainer using a rubber spatula to press it through. Tightly press a piece of plastic wrap directly onto the surface. Chill in the refrigerator until it is cold and firm, about 4 to 5 hours. Refrigerated, the lemon cream will stay fresh for up to 1 week. It cannot be frozen.

ASSEMBLY

Yellow Génoise layer

½ cup freshly squeezed lemon juice

½ cup water

½ cup sugar

6 Assembled Meringue Baskets
(and lids, if you've made them)

1½ cups Lemon Cream

3 cups grapes and assorted berries

ASSEMBLE THE MERINGUE BASKETS. Cut the génoise into 6 pieces, each measuring 3½ by 2½ inches, to fit inside each basket. Mix the lemon juice, water, and sugar and, with a brush, lightly soak one side of the cake pieces. Place 1 piece of cake in each basket and add a ¼-cup layer of lemon cream, piping it in using a pastry bag if this is easier. Top the lemon cream with the grapes and berries. Angle a lid on top of each basket, if using. Serve at once.

PEAR MOUSSE HELEN IN CHOCOLATE CUPS

SERVES 8

The French have a classic dessert called Pear Belle Hélène, named after a beautiful woman named Hélène, it would seem. That dessert pairs (no pun intended) poached pears with chocolate sauce. Here, I've taken a frozen mousse flavored with pear puree and eau-de-vie de Pear William and poured it into chocolate cups and named it for my mother, Helen.

SPECIAL EQUIPMENT: EIGHT 6-OUNCE STYROFOAM CUPS • CANDY THERMOMETER

MAKE THE CHOCOLATE CUPS. Place the chocolate in a narrow, deep, microwave-safe bowl and microwave on medium power, stirring every 30 seconds, until the chocolate is thoroughly melted and lukewarm.

Dip the plastic-covered cups, one at a time, halfway into the lukewarm chocolate, then swirl the cup to coat the entire outside as evenly as possible. As you remove each cup from the chocolate, wipe the bottom across the rim of the bowl to remove any excess chocolate. The base should not have too thick a layer of chocolate or it will be hard to cut.

After each cup is dipped, set it on the prepared pan. When the chocolate is firm, place the pan in the refrigerator to chill the cups until set.

When chilled, carefully lift the plastic cup out of the chocolate, then gently twist the plastic wrap in order to remove it from the inside of each chocolate cup. Refrigerate the cups until ready to use. Refrigerated in an airtight container, they will remain fresh for up to 1 week.

MAKE THE PUREE. Combine the wine, water, lemon juice, and sugar in a large pot and bring to a boil over high heat. Boil for 5 minutes, then add the pears. Reduce the heat to

CHOCOLATE CUPS

YIELD: 8 CUPS

15 ounces bittersweet chocolate, preferably Callebaut 60/40, finely chopped

♦ THIS WILL BE MORE THAN YOU NEED BUT IT WILL MAKE IT EASY TO DIP THE 8 CUPS.

PREPARATION. Set eight 6-ounce Styrofoam cups on squares of plastic wrap and pull the wrap up tightly around the outside of the cups so that they are completely enclosed. Tuck the excess wrap inside the cups. The outside should be as smooth as possible. Line an 18 X 13–inch half-sheet or jelly-roll pan or large cookie sheet with parchment paper.

See Ingredients at the top of the next page.

CONTINUED

POACHED PEAR PUREE

YIELD: APPROXIMATELY 3 CUPS

2 cups dry white wine

2 cups water

1 tablespoon freshly squeezed
   lemon juice

½ cup sugar

6 to 8 ripe Bartlett or Anjou pears,
   peeled and cored (about 3 pounds)

PEAR MOUSSE

YIELD: ENOUGH TO FILL 8 CHOCOLATE
CUPS (ABOUT 3 CUPS)

½ cup heavy cream

⅓ cup sugar

2 tablespoons water

2 large eggs (100 grams or ½ cup)

1½ cups reserved Poached Pear Puree

2 tablespoons Pear William

1½ tablespoons freshly squeezed
   lemon juice

PREPARATION. Have ready a pastry brush
and cup of cold water.

ASSEMBLY

3 cups Pear Mousse

8 Chocolate Cups

1½ cups reserved Poached Pear Puree

a simmer and continue cooking for 15 minutes, or until the pears are tender. The amount of time it takes to poach the pears will depend upon how ripe they are. Transfer the pears and syrup to a bowl and refrigerate for several hours, or until chilled. This can be done the day before serving.

Remove the chilled pears from the syrup and puree them in a food processor until smooth. Reserve 1½ cups of the puree for the pear mousse. Save the extra puree, thinned with some of the poaching syrup, to serve with the pear cups.

MAKE THE MOUSSE. Whip the cream in a medium bowl to stiff peaks. Set aside in the refrigerator.

Combine the sugar and water in a small saucepan and stir to mix well. Place the saucepan over high heat and bring to a boil, stirring to dissolve the sugar. Wash away any undissolved sugar from the inside of the pan with a pastry brush dipped in water.

Meanwhile, beat the eggs in a large bowl using a hand-held mixer until they are thick and pale. When the sugar syrup reaches the firm-ball stage (242°F on a candy thermometer), remove from the heat and immediately pour into the eggs down the inside of the bowl in a thin, steady stream to prevent spattering, beating constantly. Continue beating until the mixture is cool.

Combine the pear puree, Pear William, and lemon juice in a small bowl. Fold the whipped cream into the pear mixture, then into the egg mixture just until they are combined.

ASSEMBLE THE DESSERT. Spoon the mousse into the chocolate cups, dividing it evenly. Smooth the tops. Place in 1 layer in an airtight container, and freeze for at least 4 hours or overnight before serving. Plate with the extra puree poured around the cup on each plate.

PEARS PRALINÉ

This dessert is really so simple. Everything except the whipped cream can be made a day ahead, and then, several hours before serving, everything gets put together. Crushed nougatine sprinkled over the poached pears glitters like amber jewels and adds unbeatable crunch and flavor.

SPECIAL EQUIPMENT: 3-INCH ROUND PASTRY CUTTER

POACH THE PEARS. Combine the wine, water, lemon juice, and sugar in a large pot, and bring to a boil over high heat. Boil for 5 minutes, then add the pears. Reduce the heat to a simmer and continue cooking for 15 minutes, or until the pears are tender. The amount of time it will take to poach the pears depends upon how ripe they are. Transfer the pears and syrup to a bowl and refrigerate for several hours, or until chilled. This can be done a day ahead.

POACHED PEARS

YIELD: 8 PEARS

2 cups dry white wine

2 cups water

1 tablespoon freshly squeezed
   lemon juice

½ cup sugar

8 ripe Bartlett or Anjou pears, peeled
   and cored (about 3½ pounds)

MAKE THE NOUGATINE. Place the sugar, water, and corn syrup in a heavy medium saucepan and stir until well combined. Place over medium heat and continue stirring until the sugar comes to a boil. As the mixture cooks, wash down the inside of the pan with a pastry brush dipped in water to wash away undissolved sugar.

Continue to boil without stirring, gently agitating the pan to distribute the heat. Watch carefully and remove the pan from the heat when you begin to see small puffs of smoke coming from the sugar, which should be rich dark brown in color but not burned. Quickly stir in the almonds and immediately pour the mixture onto the prepared pan. Let cool completely.

NOUGATINE

YIELD: 5 CUPS

2½ cups sugar

½ cup water

2 tablespoons light corn syrup

3 cups sliced blanched almonds

PREPARATION. Coat an 18 X 13–inch half-sheet or jelly-roll pan with vegetable oil. Set aside. Have ready a pastry brush and cup of cold water.

CONTINUED

When cool, break the nougatine into 4-inch pieces. Loosely wrap several pieces together in plastic wrap and place in a sturdy plastic bag. Store in an airtight plastic container. When ready to use the nougatine, leave the pieces in the plastic wrap and break them into little morsels with a strong mallet or hammer, being careful not to turn them into powder.

YELLOW GÉNOISE

YIELD: 18 X 13–INCH CAKE LAYER

8 large eggs (396 grams or 1¾ cups)

1 cup plus 2 tablespoons (242 grams) sugar

2 teaspoons vanilla extract

2 cups plus 3 tablespoons (243 grams) cake flour, sifted

PREPARATION. Position a rack in the middle of the oven and preheat the oven to 350°F. Lightly butter an 18 X 13–inch half-sheet or jelly-roll pan. Line the bottom of the pan with parchment paper and butter the paper.

MAKE THE GÉNOISE. Place the eggs, sugar, and vanilla in the bowl of an electric mixer. Place the bowl over a hot water bath and whisk by hand until the sugar has dissolved and the eggs are warm and dark yellow, about 3 minutes. When the mixture is homogenized and lightly translucent, it is ready to beat in the mixer.

Place the bowl in the mixer fitted with the whisk attachment and beat on high speed until the mixture triples in volume, about 5 minutes. Reduce the speed to very low and whisk for 1 more minute. Be careful not to overbeat the eggs at this point.

With the mixer still on very low, delicately but quickly add the sifted flour, turning off the mixer before the flour is fully incorporated. Use a rubber spatula to gently fold the batter to ensure that it is thoroughly mixed, scraping the batter from the bottom of the bowl and folding it over the top.

Scrape the batter into the prepared pan, spreading it evenly. Bake for 5 minutes, rotate the pan front to back, and bake for 5 more minutes, or until the cake feels springy to the touch, is golden, and begins to pull away from the sides of the pan.

Let the cake cool in the pan on a rack for 10 minutes. Invert the cake onto a rack, remove the parchment, and invert again so that the cake is right side up. Cool completely. If not ready to use, wrap tightly in plastic wrap and refrigerate. Refrigerated, it will stay fresh for up to 2 days, frozen for up to 1 month.

PREPARE THE GÉNOISE. Use a 3-inch round pastry cutter to cut out 8 rounds from the génoise. Freeze excess for other desserts, such as Caramel Trifle (page 155), Amaretto Nougat Cups (page 146), and Meringue Baskets Filled with a Lemon Cream Torte (page 189).

❖ I USUALLY USE A PIECE OF CARDBOARD SLIGHTLY LARGER THAN 18 X 13 INCHES, COVERED IN FOIL, TO PLACE THE CAKE ON FOR EASE OF HANDLING AND STORAGE. MAKE SURE THAT YOU HAVE A PIECE OF PARCHMENT PAPER UNDER THE CAKE WHEN YOU INVERT IT ONTO THE COOLING RACK AND UNDER IT AGAIN WHEN YOU TURN IT RIGHT SIDE UP.

ASSEMBLE THE DESSERT. Drain the pears, reserving the syrup. Cut a slice off the very bottom of each pear so they stand upright firmly. Stand the pears on a half-sheet or jelly-roll pan. Mix 1 tablespoon of the Pear William with the reserved pear syrup. Brush the génoise rounds with the syrup. Place a pear on each round. Refrigerate until ready to serve, up to 3 hours.

About 1 or 2 hours before serving, whip the cream at medium speed in a large bowl of an electric mixer until stiff peaks form. Beat in the confectioners' sugar and the remaining 2 tablespoons Pear William. Just before serving, use a small metal spatula to cover each pear completely with the whipped cream. Sprinkle each pear generously with the crushed nougatine. This should be done at the last minute to keep the nougat crunchy. Use a wide spatula to transfer each pear to a plate.

ASSEMBLY

8 Poached Pears

3 tablespoons Pear William

Yellow Génoise layer

2 cups heavy cream

2 tablespoons confectioners' sugar, sifted

2 cups crushed Nougatine

PREPARATION. Have ready a half-sheet or jelly-roll pan.

RED-AND-WHITE RICE PARFAITS
WITH CRANBERRY LEATHER

This is one of those desserts where one taste just isn't enough. Elegant yet simple to make, this creamy parfait is really an almond-enhanced rice pudding layered with a sweet-tart cranberry compote. A twist of cranberry leather makes it restaurant-worthy by giving it height and color.

SPECIAL EQUIPMENT: SILPAT BAKING MAT (SEE PAGE 201)

RICE PUDDING

YIELD: ABOUT 3 CUPS

1 cup sliced blanched almonds

1 quart milk

½ cup sugar

¾ cup jasmine rice

¼ cup cream sherry

1 cup heavy cream

PREPARATION. Position a rack in the middle of the oven and preheat the oven to 325°F. Have ready a half-sheet or jelly-roll pan.

MAKE THE RICE PUDDING. Spread the almonds on a half-sheet or jelly-roll pan and toast for about 10 minutes, or until golden brown. Watch carefully, as almonds tend to burn quickly. Set aside for assembly.

Place the milk and sugar in a medium saucepan and bring to a boil over medium heat. Add the rice, stirring several times, then reduce the heat and simmer, stirring occasionally, for about 30 minutes or until all the milk has been absorbed and there is no hard kernel in the center of the grains of rice. Immediately pour the rice into a bowl to cool it down quickly. Add the sherry and mix well. Cool the mixture to room temperature.

Whip the cream in a medium bowl until soft peaks form. Fold the cream into the rice mixture. Refrigerate the rice pudding while making the cranberry sauce.

CRANBERRY SAUCE

YIELD: ABOUT 1½ CUPS

1 (12-ounce) package fresh or frozen cranberries

1 cup dried apricots, cut into quarters

1 cup sugar

1 cup water

MAKE THE SAUCE. Combine the cranberries, apricots, sugar, and water in a medium saucepan and bring to a boil over medium heat. Boil until the cranberries pop and the mixture has thickened, about 5 minutes. Cool to room temperature.

MAKE THE CRANBERRY LEATHER. Combine the cranberries with the water and bring to a boil over medium heat. Cook until the cranberries pop and are very soft, about 10 minutes. Set the cranberries aside until cool, then puree in a food processor until smooth. Return the puree to the pan, add the sugar, and cook the mixture, stirring frequently, until very thick and no moisture remains. Spread the puree very thinly and evenly onto the Silpat using an offset metal spatula.

◆ A SILPAT IS A SILICONE BAKING MAT THAT COMES IN SEVERAL SIZES AND IS USED INSTEAD OF PARCHMENT PAPER. IT IS ESPECIALLY USEFUL FOR VERY DAMP MIXTURES THAT NEED TO DRY OUT RATHER THAN BAKE. AND SILPATS CAN BE REUSED HUNDREDS OF TIMES. HERE, YOU WILL NEED TWO BAKING MATS THAT FIT 18 X 13-INCH PANS. SILPATS ARE AVAILABLE AT BAKERY AND RESTAURANT SUPPLY STORES, AT COOKWARE STORES, AND ONLINE.

Bake for at least 1 hour, or until dry. Cool the leather, then carefully remove it from the sheet. Cut out various random squares and rectangles with scissors and layer between sheets of parchment paper in an airtight container. The leather will remain fresh for up to several weeks.

ASSEMBLE THE PARFAITS. Alternately layer the rice pudding, almonds, and cranberry sauce in 6 goblets or wineglasses, beginning and ending with the pudding, so that there are two or three layers of rice pudding and two layers of cranberry sauce, depending on the size of the glass. Refrigerate until ready to serve, or up to 3 hours. Garnish the parfaits with cranberry-leather cutouts.

CRANBERRY LEATHER

YIELD: 1 THIN RECTANGLE ABOUT 16 X 11 INCHES (THE LEATHER WON'T FILL THE ENTIRE 18 X 13-INCH PAN)

½ (12-ounce) package fresh or frozen cranberries

2 tablespoons water

½ cup sugar

PREPARATION. Line an 18 X 13–inch half-sheet or jelly-roll pan with a Silpat baking mat. Preheat the oven to 200°F.

◆ FOR ADDED INTEREST, USE A SQUEEZE BOTTLE TO DRAW RANDOM LINES OF A DIFFERENT-COLORED FRUIT PUREE ACROSS THE CRANBERRY PUREE. A LIGHT-COLORED FRUIT, SUCH AS APRICOT OR NECTARINE, LOOKS BEST SQUIGGLED WITH THE RED PUREE. I GARNISH THE PARFAITS WITH SPRIGS OF MINT AND PLAYFUL SHAPES OF MULTICOLORED CUTOUTS OF THE CRANBERRY LEATHER.

ASSEMBLY

3 cups Rice Pudding

1 cup toasted almonds

1½ cups Cranberry Sauce

Cranberry Leather cutouts

◆ I HAVE CUT TRIANGLES AND FORMED CONE SHAPES THAT CAN BE PLACED STANDING UP ON TOP OF THE PUDDING.

RICE FLOUR MAHALLABYYA WITH PISTACHIO-STUFFED DATES

SERVES 8 TO 10

Years ago I frequented a Middle Eastern restaurant in Washington, D.C. One of the desserts was a very light, somewhat gelatinous pudding delicately flavored with flower water and topped with a shower of chopped pistachios. I always ordered it, as I loved its fragrance and smooth texture and was never too full to have some. It took me a while to replicate the special quality of that dessert, but after researching recipes in several of my older cookbooks, I came up with this version. The use of pistachio-stuffed dates instead of chopped pistachios gives the dessert a little more formality. Be aware that there are many different rice flours available and that they produce different results when cooked. Use Thai rice flour, which is available in Asian markets.

SPECIAL EQUIPMENT: TEN 6-OUNCE RAMEKINS OR GOBLETS

RICE PUDDING

YIELD: TEN 6-OUNCE RAMEKINS

½ cup (60 grams) Thai rice flour

3½ cups milk

6 tablespoons sugar

2 teaspoons orange-flower water
  or rose water

Ground cinnamon

MAKE THE RICE PUDDING. Whisk the rice flour into 1 cup of the milk in a small bowl until dissolved. Place the remaining 2½ cups milk and the sugar in a medium saucepan and bring to a boil over medium heat, stirring occasionally to dissolve the sugar. Once the milk comes to a full boil, reduce the heat to low and add the rice-flour mixture. Simmer, stirring constantly, until the mixture is very thick, about 5 minutes. Stir in the flower water, then pour the pudding into ten 6-ounce ramekins. Sprinkle the tops with cinnamon and refrigerate for about 4 hours, or until set.

MAKE THE STUFFED DATES. Place the pistachios on a pan and toast for 3 minutes, or until lightly colored. Combine the pistachios and sugar in a food processor and process until very finely chopped. Add the flower water and process until a smooth paste forms.

Use a sharp knife to split each date down the center. Spread the date open, remove the pit, and stuff a spoonful of the filling into the center. Press the cut edges of the date together to enclose the filling. Repeat with remaining dates.

SERVE THE DESSERT. To serve, garnish each pudding with 2 stuffed dates beside it.

PISTACHIO-STUFFED DATES

YIELD: 20 STUFFED DATES

2 ounces unsalted shelled pistachios

1 tablespoon sugar

1 teaspoon orange-flower water or rose water

20 large fresh Medjool dates

PREPARATION. Preheat the oven to 300°F. Have ready an 18 X 13–inch half-sheet or jelly-roll pan.

RUM RAISIN
NESSELRODE TRIFLE

Nesselrode pudding is one of those desserts that most people have heard of but probably haven't tasted. Nesselrode was a Russian count who was something of a gourmet and had many dishes named after him. Nesselrode pudding is a chestnut-and-custard pudding, but here I've introduced fruit to add some tartness. The rum-soaked fruit goes well with chestnut custard, and the génoise is soft enough to soak up the liquid perfectly. This dessert is guaranteed to be rich and satisfying enough to sate any sweet tooth. Chestnut puree is available in some supermarkets and in specialty food stores. You can substitute an 8-ounce can for the homemade version, if you prefer.

CHESTNUT PUREE

YIELD: ABOUT 2 CUPS

½ pound chestnuts, peeled and skinned
  (¾ pound unpeeled)

⅓ cup water

1⅓ cups milk

1 vanilla bean, split lengthwise

PREPARATION. Preheat the oven
  to 350°F.

PEEL AND SKIN THE CHESTNUTS. Cut a cross on the round side of each chestnut and spread them out on a half-sheet or jelly-roll pan. Pour the water over the chestnuts and bake for 30 minutes, or until the shells open. When the chestnuts cool down, remove the outer shells and thin papery layers a few at a time.

MAKE THE CHESTNUT PUREE. Place the peeled chestnuts and 1 cup of the milk in a medium saucepan. Use the back of a knife to scrape the seeds from the vanilla bean. Add the seeds and pod to the pan and cook until the chestnuts are tender, about 15 minutes. Puree the chestnut mixture in a food processor, adding the remaining ⅓ cup milk, and set aside.

MAKE THE GÉNOISE. Place the eggs, sugar, and vanilla extract in the bowl of an electric mixer. Place the bowl over a hot water bath and whisk by hand until the sugar has dissolved and the eggs are warm and dark yellow, about 3 minutes. When the mixture is homogenized and is lightly translucent, it is ready to beat in the mixer.

Place the bowl in the mixer fitted with the whisk attachment and beat on high speed until the mixture triples in volume, about 5 minutes. Reduce the speed to very low and whisk for 1 more minute. Be careful not to overbeat the eggs at this point.

Delicately but quickly add the sifted flour, turning off the mixer before the flour is incorporated. Use a rubber spatula or scraper to gently fold the batter to ensure that it is thoroughly mixed, scraping the batter from the bottom of the bowl and folding it over the top.

Scrape the batter into the prepared pan. Bake for 5 minutes, rotate the pan front to back, and bake for 5 more minutes or until it feels springy to the touch, is golden, and the cake begins to pull away from the sides of the pan.

Let the cake cool in the pan on a rack for 10 minutes. Invert the cake onto a rack, and invert again so that the cake is right side up. Cool completely. If not ready to use, wrap tightly in plastic wrap and refrigerate. Refrigerated, it will stay fresh for up to 2 days; frozen, for up to 1 month.

CONTINUED

YELLOW GÉNOISE

YIELD: 18 X 13-INCH CAKE LAYER

8 large eggs (396 grams or 1¾ cups)

1 cup plus 2 tablespoons (242 grams) sugar

1 teaspoon vanilla extract

2 cups plus 3 tablespoons (243 grams) cake flour, sifted

PREPARATION. Position a rack in the middle of the oven and preheat the oven to 350°F. Lightly butter an 18 X 13–inch half-sheet or jelly-roll pan. Line the bottom with parchment paper and butter the paper.

MAKE THE CUSTARD. Place egg yolks in bowl of an electric mixer fitted with the whisk attachment and beat on medium speed until light and pale yellow. Set aside half of the sugar. Add the remaining sugar to the yolks and beat until the mixture is thick, pale, and forms a ribbon when dropped from the whisk.

Heat the cream and the milk with the reserved sugar in a medium saucepan over medium heat until small bubbles form around the edge of the pot. Remove from the heat. Bring the bowl over to the saucepan and whisk about 1 cup of the hot cream mixture into the yolk mixture to temper it, then pour the mixture back into the saucepan and whisk until thoroughly combined. Set aside.

MAKE THE FILLING. Soak the currants, raisins, and cranberries in the rum for 30 minutes, stirring frequently.

Combine the custard with the fruit-rum mixture, then add in the chestnut puree and vanilla extract. Transfer to a bowl and refrigerate for 1 hour, or until chilled.

ASSEMBLE THE TRIFLE. Cut the génoise into 1½-inch squares.

Whip the cream with the confectioners' sugar until stiff peaks form. Fold half of the whipped cream into the chestnut filling until mixed well. In 12 individual glass bowls or goblets, layer the pieces of génoise and the custard–whipped cream mixture, starting and ending with the mixture, and then top it off with the remaining whipped cream.

CUSTARD
YIELD: 2½ CUPS

4 large egg yolks (80 grams
   or ⅓ cup)
⅔ cup granulated sugar
1 cup heavy cream
1 cup milk

CHESTNUT FILLING
YIELD: 3½ CUPS

½ cup dried currants
½ cup golden raisins
½ cup dried cranberries
¼ cup dark rum, such as Myers's
2½ cups Custard
1 cup Chestnut Puree or 1 (8-ounce)
   can Clément Faugier Chestnut
   Puree
1 teaspoon vanilla extract

ASSEMBLY

Yellow Génoise layer
2 cups heavy cream
1 tablespoon confectioners' sugar
3½ cups Chestnut Filling

◆ I HAVE ALSO MADE THESE IN
PLASTIC-LINED 6-OUNCE SOUFFLÉ
DISHES OR RAMEKINS, THEN TURNED
THEM OUT ONTO PLATES AND SERVED
WITH WHIPPED CREAM FLAVORED
WITH A LITTLE MYERS'S DARK RUM.

SOUR CREAM BLUEBERRY CUPS

Years ago, when I worked at the restaurant The Big Cheese, I made this as a blueberry pie in a sweet pastry crust. Now I like to grind my own homemade graham crackers to form individual graham cracker crumb cups, fill them with blueberries drenched in red currant jelly, top them with sour cream, and bake briefly. The customers clamor for them.

SPECIAL EQUIPMENT: TEN 4-OUNCE TIN OR DISPOSABLE ALUMINUM RAMEKINS OR CERAMIC SOUFFLÉ CUPS • ICE-CREAM MAKER

GRAHAM CRACKER CUPS

YIELD: 10 CUPS

3 cups crushed Homemade Honey Grahams (page 133; 1 recipe will be enough)

¼ cup sugar

4 ounces (1 stick) unsalted butter, melted

MAKE THE GRAHAM CRACKER CUPS. Combine the crushed honey grahams, sugar, and butter in a medium bowl and mix well. Divide into 10 portions. Line ten 4-ounce well-buttered tin or aluminum cups with the mixture, pressing the crumbs well with your fingertips to form a thickness of ¼ inch. Use another cup (the same size) to press the graham crumbs to ensure an even thickness throughout. Place the cups on a half-sheet or jelly-roll pan and refrigerate for 1 hour.

Meanwhile, preheat the oven to 325°F. Bake the crusts for 5 minutes to set them, then transfer to a cooling rack. Keep the oven on.

FILLED GRAHAM CRACKER CUPS

YIELD: 10 CUPS

1 (12-ounce) jar best-quality red currant jelly

2 pints blueberries plus additional for serving

10 Graham Cracker Cups

2 cups sour cream

3 tablespoons brown sugar

½ teaspoon ground cinnamon

MAKE THE FILLING. Place the jelly in a small saucepan and bring to a boil over high heat. Reduce the heat to medium and cook until the jelly has completely melted and slightly thickened, about 3 minutes. Set aside.

Rinse and drain the berries in a colander. Pick them over to remove any stems or small leaves, then place in a bowl. Pour the jelly over the berries, mixing well.

FILL THE CUPS. Spoon the berry mixture into the baked graham cracker cups.

Combine the sour cream, brown sugar, and cinnamon in a separate bowl and spoon over the berry-jelly mixture. Place the filled cups on a half-sheet or jelly-roll pan. Bake for 5 minutes, rotate the pan from front to back, then bake for 5 minutes longer. Cool the blueberry cups on a rack for 20 minutes, or until barely warm. Run a small knife around the edges of the tins and unmold the cups by turning them upside down gently and lifting off the tins. Invert them carefully onto the palm of your hand. Set the cups on the pan, then refrigerate for at least 2 hours, or until very cold. Unmold the blueberry cups when they are still warm to the touch. If you let them cool too long in their tins, they will be difficult to remove.

MAKE THE BUTTERMILK ICE CREAM. Place the milk and cream in a heavy nonreactive medium saucepan. Use the back of a knife to scrape out the seeds from the vanilla bean and add the seeds and pod to the saucepan. Bring to a rolling boil over medium-high heat. Let the mixture rise up the side of the pan, then immediately remove from the heat.

Meanwhile, in the bowl of an electric mixer fitted with the whisk attachment, beat the egg yolks with the sugar on high speed until very thick and pale, about 5 minutes. The mixture will triple in volume and hold its shape when dropped from the whisk. It should be very stiff.

Bring the mixing bowl over to the saucepan and whisk about 1 cup of the hot cream mixture into the yolk mixture to temper it, then return the mixture to the saucepan and whisk until combined. Pour through a fine-mesh strainer or China cap into a large bowl. Place in an ice bath or refrigerate, uncovered, to cool it down, then add the buttermilk. Refrigerate for a few hours, or until completely cool, stirring occasionally. Transfer the mixture to an ice-cream maker and freeze according to manufacturer's instructions.

SERVE THE SOUR CREAM BLUEBERRY CUPS. Serve the chilled sour cream blueberry cups on plates, with fresh blueberries scattered around the plate and scoops of buttermilk ice cream off to the side.

BUTTERMILK ICE CREAM
YIELD: 1 QUART

1¼ cups milk

2 cups heavy cream

1 vanilla bean, split lengthwise

11 to 12 large egg yolks (225 grams or 1 cup)

Generous ¾ cup sugar

¾ cup buttermilk

ASSEMBLY
10 Filled Graham Cracker Cups

Fresh blueberries

Buttermilk Ice Cream

TRIPLE CHOCOLATE TERRINE

SERVES 8

I first made this dessert for my friend the chef Jean-Louis Palladin in 1982, when working at the restaurant Jean-Louis at The Watergate. I believe we were the first restaurant in Washington to make such a dessert, and I continued to see versions of it in restaurants for years to come. It is a lovely, creamy, mousse-like pâté made of white, milk, and bittersweet chocolates layered to look like an old-fashioned Neopolitan ice-cream loaf from the 1950s. The flavors are pure and stand out because of their simplicity. It is so easy to make and yet tastes so good. After all these years it still stands the test of time.

CHOCOLATE TERRINE

YIELD: 9 X 5–INCH LOAF

5 ounces white chocolate

5 ounces milk chocolate

5 ounces bittersweet chocolate

2¾ cups heavy cream

PREPARATION. Lay a length of double-thickness plastic wrap large enough to cover the bottom and sides of a 9 X 5–inch loaf pan on a work surface. Smooth out any air bubbles. Fit the plastic wrap into the loaf pan, lining the bottom and sides and allowing it to extend over the sides of the pan. Press the plastic wrap in well to get rid of any air bubbles. Set aside.

MAKE THE TERRINE. Chop the white, milk, and bittersweet chocolates separately and place each in a separate microwave-safe bowl. Whip ¾ cup of the heavy cream until soft peaks form. Set aside.

Microwave the white chocolate on medium power for 20 seconds, then 10 seconds, stirring between each interval. As soon as the chocolate begins to melt, decrease the interval time to 5 seconds each. The chocolate should be warm and completely melted without being burned. As soon as the white chocolate is melted, fold in the whipped cream quickly, so as not to solidify the chocolate with the coldness of the cream, until no streaks of chocolate show. Pour into the prepared loaf pan and smooth the top with a 2-inch-wide offset metal spatula. Refrigerate.

Whip another ¾ cup of the heavy cream until soft peaks form. Set aside. Repeat the melting process with the milk chocolate, then fold in the whipped cream. Pour it over the white chocolate layer and smooth with a spatula. Refrigerate.

Barely whip the remaining 1¼ cups cream to less-than-soft peaks, until the tracks of the whisk are just visible in the cream. Remove ½ cup of the cream and set aside. Melt the bittersweet chocolate using the same method as with the white and milk chocolates. The chocolate should be very warm to best mix with the whipped cream.

Working very quickly, pour the very warm chocolate into the remaining whipped cream and immediately begin whisking the mixture very quickly and thoroughly to combine the chocolate and cream, until no chocolate bits are visible. (This must be done quickly so the chocolate goes in smoothly.) Add the reserved ½ cup whipped cream, whisking it in thoroughly until blended.

Pour the bittersweet chocolate mixture over the milk-chocolate mixture in the pan and smooth the top. Cover and refrigerate for 8 hours or overnight. Turn the terrine out onto a serving platter, remove the plastic wrap, and cut into 1-inch slices.

◆ IT MAY BE HELPFUL TO ENLIST THE AID OF A SECOND PERSON TO POUR THE CHOCOLATE IN WHILE YOU BEAT THE CREAM. IF IT IS NOT DONE VERY QUICKLY, THE CHOCOLATE WILL HARDEN AND FORM LITTLE CHIPS IN THE CREAM.

SERVE THE TERRINE. Place a slice on each plate and surround with raspberry coulis.

ASSEMBLY

Chocolate Terrine

1 cup Raspberry Coulis (page 118)

TURKISH RICE AND ROSE-WATER PUDDING

This rice pudding has a smooth gelatin-like crown and is very refreshing after a heavy meal. The pudding is creamy and loose, and the rose water lends it a uniquely Middle Eastern fragrance. Serve it plain, the way I like it, or with a plate of Vanilla Nuts (page 143).

SPECIAL EQUIPMENT: TEN ¾-CUP OR 6-OUNCE GOBLETS

TURKISH RICE

YIELD: 4½ CUPS

2 quarts half-and-half or light cream

½ cup sugar

⅓ cup basmati rice

2 teaspoons rose water

MAKE THE RICE. Bring the cream and sugar to a boil in a heavy large saucepan over medium-high heat. Reduce the heat and cook, stirring occasionally, for 30 minutes. Add the rice and continue cooking until the rice is very soft and has almost disintegrated, about 30 minutes or longer. Continue stirring occasionally until cool and the pudding coats the spoon heavily. Stir in the rose water and mix well. Divide the mixture among ten ¾-cup or 6-ounce goblets. Refrigerate.

ROSE-WATER PUDDING

YIELD: ABOUT 1¾ CUPS

2 cups low-fat milk

⅓ cup sugar

2 tablespoons cornstarch

3 large egg yolks (60 grams or ¼ cup)

1 teaspoon rose water

MAKE THE PUDDING. Bring the milk to a boil in a small saucepan over medium-high heat. Whisk the sugar and cornstarch by hand in the bowl of an electric mixer. Add the egg yolks and fit the mixer with the whisk attachment. Beat on high speed until the mixture is thick, pale yellow, and forms a ribbon when dropped off the whisk.

Bring the bowl over to the saucepan and whisk about 1 cup of the hot milk into the yolk mixture to temper it, then return the tempered mixture to the saucepan and whisk until combined. Bring the mixture to a boil, stirring vigorously for 1 minute. Remove the pudding from the heat and continue to stir, adding the rose water.

ASSEMBLY

1¾ cups Rose-Water Pudding

10 Turkish Rice–filled goblets

ASSEMBLE THE DESSERT. Pour a layer of the pudding over the rice mixture in the goblets, filling them to the top. Refrigerate. Serve as is, or with Vanilla Nuts (page 143).

VACHERIN SNOW EGGS

This is a meringue lover's dream. Here, crisp chocolate meringue ovals are filled with milk-poached meringue ovals, which are then floated in a sea of crème anglaise. They are simple *oeufs à la neige* in their own little chocolate meringue boats!

SPECIAL EQUIPMENT: PASTRY BAG FITTED WITH A ½-INCH PLAIN TIP (ATECO #26)

MAKE THE MERINGUE OVALS. Place the egg whites and vanilla in the bowl of an electric mixer fitted with the whisk attachment and beat on medium-high speed until light and foamy. Gradually add the sugar and continue beating for 8 to 10 minutes. The egg whites will be very stiff and shiny.

Fold in the cocoa all at once with a rubber spatula until well mixed. Fill a pastry bag fitted with a ½-inch plain tip (Ateco #26) two-thirds full with meringue and pipe the meringue in a spiral to form ten 3-inch-long and 2-inch-wide oval shapes on the prepared pans 2 inches apart. Pipe out the meringue in a slow, continuous flow as if you were writing, holding the tip about 1 inch above the parchment. Then pipe 50 plain finger-shaped ovals about 2½ inches long and ½ inch wide.

Bake for 1 hour. Turn off the oven and leave the meringue ovals to dry overnight. When done, the ovals should be firm to the touch and release easily from the parchment. If they don't release easily, bake for 1 hour more. Let cool on the pans on cooling racks. (The ovals will expand a little bit while baking, ending up about 3 inches in diameter.)

CONTINUED

MERINGUE OVALS

YIELD: 10 LARGE AND 50 SMALLER MERINGUE OVALS

8 large egg whites (240 grams or 1 cup), at room temperature

1 teaspoon vanilla extract

1¾ cups sugar

½ cup natural or Dutch-processed cocoa

PREPARATION. Line four 18 X 13–inch half-sheet or jelly-roll pans or large cookie sheets with parchment paper. Preheat the oven to 150°F.

◆ THE MERINGUE OVALS CAN BE MADE SEVERAL DAYS AHEAD. LAYER THEM BETWEEN SHEETS OF PARCHMENT PAPER IN AN AIRTIGHT CONTAINER AND REFRIGERATE. STORING AT ROOM TEMPERATURE KEEPS THEM DRIER, BUT REFRIGERATING THEM RETAINS THEIR FLAVOR BETTER.

SNOW EGGS (POACHED MERINGUE OVALS)

YIELD: 10 SNOW EGGS

2 quarts milk

⅓ cup plus ¾ cup sugar

2 vanilla beans, split lengthwise

6 large egg whites (180 grams or ¾ cup), at room temperature

Pinch of salt

MAKE THE SNOW EGGS. Combine the milk and ⅓ cup of the sugar in a large shallow pot about 4 inches deep. Use the back of a knife to scrape out the vanilla bean seeds and add to the pot. Bring the milk to a boil, then reduce the heat to a simmer.

Meanwhile, place the egg whites and salt in the bowl of an electric mixer fitted with the whisk attachment and beat on medium-high speed until foamy and beginning to hold a shape. Gradually add the remaining ¾ cup sugar, 2 tablespoons at a time, and continue to beat until very stiff and glossy peaks form.

Form ovals by scooping the meringue with a soup spoon, then release into the simmering milk mixture with the help of another spoon. Poach the meringue ovals for 2 minutes, turn carefully, and then poach for another 2 minutes. Transfer with a slotted spoon to paper towels to drain. Reserve the milk mixture.

CRÈME ANGLAISE

YIELD: 4 CUPS

Milk

Reserved poaching liquid

10 large egg yolks (200 grams or ⅞ cup)

¾ cup sugar

1 tablespoon dark rum, such as Myers's

MAKE THE CRÈME ANGLAISE. Add enough milk to the poaching liquid to equal 4 cups, then pour into a heavy nonreactive medium saucepan. Bring to a boil over medium-high heat. Remove from the heat.

Meanwhile, in the bowl of an electric mixer fitted with the whisk attachment, beat the egg yolks with the sugar on high speed until very thick and pale. The mixture will triple in volume and form a ribbon when dropped from the whisk. This will take 3 to 4 minutes. Add the rum.

Bring the yolk mixture over to the stove. Whisk about 1 cup of the hot milk into the yolk mixture to temper it, then pour the tempered mixture back into the saucepan, whisking well to cook the eggs. The mixture should be thick enough to coat a wooden spoon. (Run your finger through the mixture on the back of the spoon. The mixture is thick enough when the line remains.) Pour through a fine-mesh strainer or China cap into a large bowl and whisk to cool. Refrigerate until chilled. Refrigerated, the crème anglaise will remain fresh for up to 3 days.

ASSEMBLE THE DESSERT. Set a meringue oval on each plate and top with a snow egg. Surround each snow egg with 5 meringue ovals for fingers, pressing them into place (like a fence) around the snow eggs. Pour crème anglaise over the eggs, and tilt the plate to allow the anglaise to coat the plate.

ASSEMBLY

60 Meringue Ovals

10 Snow Eggs

4 cups Crème Anglaise

WARM DESSERTS

The warm desserts in this chapter are both home-style and sophisticated. Many employ yeast as the leavener, others contain butter folded into dough to create layers that bake to flaky perfection, and some have egg whites added to give them lift. A good many of the offerings here are heavier, stick-to-the-ribs wintertime desserts (ice cream pairs with them especially well). I have also included soufflés, which although served hot, are lighter and more delicate by their very nature. In several of the recipes, soufflés are baked in individual tartlet shells for a unique and delicious way to enjoy them, as it is sort of like being able to eat the dish! And though the desserts here are all different, what they have in common is an intensity of flavor that I think is the most important quality of any sweet offering.

ALMOND PITHIVIER WITH PROSECCO–ALMOND GRAPPA SABAYON

SERVES 8

Antoon Van Tol, a wonderful old Dutch chef and pastry cook who owned a bakery specializing in Dutch desserts in Wheaton, Maryland, always made this classic almond log. He received much notoriety and acquired a devoted metropolitan Washington–area clientele because his offerings were of such high quality. His unique technique for making puff pastry was one I embraced early on and share with you here. I love this almond log. And with a little tweaking by changing the filling, the form, and the presentation, a classic old-world pastry has been turned into an elegantly sleek dessert.

SPECIAL EQUIPMENT: CHEESE SLICER, TRUFFLE SLICER, MANDOLINE, OR ADJUSTABLE VEGETABLE SLICER

PUFF PASTRY

YIELD: ENOUGH FOR 8 PITHIVIER

3 cups (420 grams) all-purpose flour, sifted

1 cup (140 grams) cake flour, sifted

1 teaspoon salt

4 tablespoons unsalted butter, diced and chilled

¾ cup chilled water

1 pound (4 sticks) cold unsalted butter

PREPARATION. Line an 18 X 13–inch half-sheet or jelly-roll pan with parchment paper.

MAKE THE PUFF PASTRY. Place the all-purpose and cake flours, salt, and the diced butter in the bowl of an electric mixer fitted with the paddle attachment. Mix on low speed until the butter and flour are well combined, about 3 minutes. The mixture should look coarse and crumbly. Add the water in a slow, continuous stream and mix until the dough is slightly damp, pliable, and gathers into a ball around the paddle attachment. If it looks too dry, use a spoon and slowly add more water, drop by drop. Touch the dough with your fingertips. It should be damp but not sticky.

Use the palm of your hand and your fingertips to pat and stretch the dough into a uniform square; the size is not important. Wrap the dough in plastic wrap and refrigerate for 15 minutes.

PREPARE THE BUTTER. Dust each stick of butter with a little all-purpose flour. Use a cheese slicer to thinly slice each stick of butter lengthwise into 7 slices. You should end up with 28 thin 5 X 1–inch slices of butter in total. Divide them into 3 groups (1 group will have 1 additional slice). Place each group on parchment paper, long sides slightly overlapping, and press them together to form three 7¾ X 5-inch "sheets" of butter. Refrigerate for just 20 minutes. (You want the butter to be the same amount of firmness and coolness as the dough.)

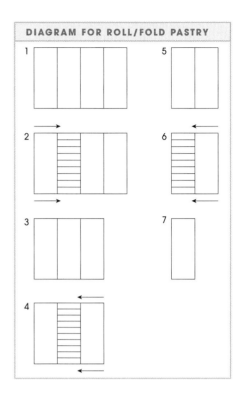

ADD THE BUTTER. Roll out the slightly chilled dough on a lightly floured surface to a rectangle about 20 inches long and 8 inches wide. See the diagram at right. Use a ruler as a guide to mark the dough crosswise into fourths without cutting all the way through (1). Place one 7¾ X 5-inch sheet of butter on the section of dough immediately to the left of center. Arrange the butter so it covers that entire section of dough (2). Fold over the flap of dough to its left, bringing it toward the center of the dough, enclosing the butter in the dough. The dough should now be divided in 3 sections (3). Place a second sheet of butter in the middle section (4) and fold the right section of dough over the butter. You now have 2 sections of dough visible (5). Place the remaining sheet of butter on top of the left section (6) and fold the other half of the dough over to enclose it (7). The dough should measure roughly 9 X 6 inches.

Rolling forward with a rolling pin, roll out the dough into a rectangle approximately 18 inches long and 7 inches wide. Fold the rectangle into thirds to create a rectangle roughly 7 X 6 inches and rotate it 90°. Use a pastry brush to brush off any excess flour. Place the dough on a half-sheet or jelly-roll pan, wrap in plastic wrap, and refrigerate for 15 minutes. The first turn (which is actually made up of 4 turns) has now been completed. Repeat the rolling, folding, turning, and chilling of the dough 2 more times. The dimensions here are not as important as the smoothness and homogenization of the butter into the dough. The dough should be uniform in color, with no patches of butter showing through.

Place it on a parchment-lined half-sheet or jelly-roll pan and wrap tightly in plastic wrap. Refrigerate for at least 5 hours or overnight.

APRICOT FILLING

YIELD: ABOUT 2 CUPS

12 ounces dried apricots, chopped

½ cup orange marmalade

⅓ cup sliced and blanched almonds,
    finely chopped

3 tablespoons freshly squeezed
    lemon juice

1 teaspoon finely grated orange zest

½ teaspoon ground cinnamon

MAKE THE APRICOT FILLING. Place all the ingredients in a medium saucepan. Cook the mixture over low heat, stirring occasionally, until it forms a thick paste, about 5 minutes. Spoon the mixture into a bowl and set aside until cool, then cover and refrigerate until ready to use.

ALMOND PASTE

YIELD: ABOUT 7 CUPS

4 ⅔ cups ground blanched almonds (at
    least 6 cups whole almonds)

1½ cups sugar

1 teaspoon finely grated lemon zest

2 large eggs (100 grams or ½ cup),
    lightly beaten

MAKE THE ALMOND PASTE. Place the almonds, sugar, and lemon zest in the bowl of an electric mixer fitted with the paddle attachment. Mix on low speed until the ingredients are mixed well. Add the beaten eggs drop by drop until the mixture comes together. Add the egg slowly to keep the almond paste from becoming too moist. All of the egg may not be needed. If the almond paste is too soft, it will expand while baking and break through, splitting the puff. To check the consistency of the almond paste, take some paste in your hand and squeeze it. It should be firm yet malleable and not at all sticky. Remove the almond paste from the bowl, wrap in plastic wrap, and chill for at least 1 hour.

LEMON CREAM

YIELD: ABOUT 2 CUPS

About 4 large lemons

4 ounces (1 stick) unsalted butter

3 large eggs (150 grams or ⅔ cup)

3 large egg yolks (60 grams or ¼ cup)

1⅔ cups sugar

PREPARATION. Have ready a bowl fitted with a fine-mesh stainless-steel strainer or China cap.

MAKE THE LEMON CREAM. Finely grate 1 tablespoon of zest from the lemons and squeeze and strain enough juice to equal 1 cup. Place the lemon zest and juice with the butter in a heavy nonreactive medium saucepan and heat over low heat until the butter has melted. Reduce the heat to low.

Mix the eggs, yolks, and 1 cup of the sugar in the bowl of an electric mixer fitted with the whisk attachment on the lowest speed until just combined. Do not whisk the mixture for more than 15 minutes. The final cream should be transparent, almost jelly-like; overbeating will cause the cream to become cloudy.

Bring the bowl over to the stove. Whisk several spoonfuls of the hot lemon mixture into the egg mixture to temper it, then return the tempered mixture to the saucepan. Increase the heat to medium and whisk well to combine. At this point gradually add the remaining ⅔ cup sugar, tasting as you go. Lemons can be more or less sour at different times of the year, but usually another ⅔ cup is right. The cream should taste sweet and yet tart at the end of the taste. Make it a little sweeter than you think it should be as some of the sweetness will be lost in the chilling.

Continue to cook the custard over medium heat, whisking constantly until thickened. Be patient, as this may take about 3 minutes or so. Be sure to stir vigorously, touching all points of the bottom of the pan to make sure the mixture doesn't burn. The lemon cream will begin to thicken, which you will feel as you whisk. When the cream thickens slightly and steam rises from the saucepan, immediately remove from the heat. Do not let the lemon cream come to a boil. Quickly pour the cream into the strainer, using a rubber spatula to press it through. Tightly press a piece of plastic wrap directly onto the surface. Refrigerate for several hours, or until it is cold and firm. Refrigerated, the lemon cream will stay fresh for up to 2 weeks; it cannot be frozen.

MAKE THE SABAYON. Put the yolks, sugar, and Prosecco into a nonreactive large saucepan and place over medium-low heat. Whisk constantly for 4 to 6 minutes, until the sauce is thick enough to leave a ribbon when dropped from the whisk and you don't see any liquid in the bottom of the pan when you pull the whisk through. Immediately set the pan into the bowl of ice water and whisk until cool. Fold in the whipped cream first and then the grappa. Set aside.

◆ WHEN COOKING WITH CITRUS JUICES, USE ONLY NONREACTIVE PANS SUCH AS STAINLESS STEEL OR ENAMEL-COATED METAL, AS ALUMINUM REACTS WITH ACID AND LEAVES A METALLIC AFTERTASTE.

PROSECCO-ALMOND GRAPPA SABAYON

YIELD: 2 CUPS

8 large egg yolks (240 grams or ¾ cup)

½ cup sugar

¾ cup Prosecco (Italian sparkling wine)

½ cup heavy cream, lightly whipped

2 tablespoons almond grappa

PREPARATION. Have ready a bowl of ice water.

PITHIVIER ASSEMBLY

7 cups Almond Paste

2 cups Apricot Filling

Puff Pastry

1 large egg, lightly beaten, for
   egg wash

2 cups Lemon Cream

PREPARATION. Line two 18 X 13–inch half-sheet or jelly-roll pans with parchment paper.

◆ EACH SHEET OF PUFF PASTRY WILL PRODUCE TWO 10½-INCH LOGS OF PITHIVIER. WITH 2 SHEETS YOU WILL HAVE A TOTAL OF 4 LOGS. WHEN EACH LOG IS CUT IN 4 PIECES, YOU GET 16 PIECES IN ALL.

◆ IF THE APRICOT PASTE IS AT ALL STICKY, SPRINKLE THE WORK SURFACE WITH CONFECTIONERS' SUGAR AND USE A PASTRY SCRAPER TO HELP YOU TO HANDLE THE PASTE WITH EASE.

ASSEMBLE THE PITHIVIER. Divide the almond paste into fourths and roll each portion into a 10-inch log about ¾ inch in diameter. A light dusting of confectioners' sugar on the work surface will keep the almond paste from becoming sticky. Set aside.

Roll the apricot filling into very thin strips, about 10 inches long and ¼ inch in diameter. Wrap each strip in plastic wrap and refrigerate until needed.

Take 1 almond paste log and press an apricot strip on top. Repeat with each almond paste log, pressing tightly to make sure the log and strip adhere. Wrap the rolls in plastic wrap and refrigerate for 1 hour.

On a lightly floured work surface, roll out the puff pastry into 2 rectangles that are each 12 inches long, 10 inches wide, and ⅛ inch thick. (See diagram on page 223.) Refrigerate both sheets for 30 minutes.

Place one sheet of puff pastry with a 12-inch side nearest you. (1) Beginning at the bottom (long) side of the rectangle, brush the first 5 inches of puff with the egg wash. Center an almond-apricot roll along the side nearest you, 1 inch from the bottom and sides, and spread a thin line of lemon cream over the log. Fold the 2 side edges of puff over the ends of the almond roll, then roll up half-sheet or jelly-roll fashion to completely enclose the roll (2). (This will use up 5 inches, or half, of the puff pastry.) Use a pizza wheel to separate the roll from the unfilled portion of the puff sheet. Fold the 2 open ends of the roll under and brush with egg wash to seal them. This will give you a 10-inch log. Place the log, seam side down, on the prepared pan. Place in the refrigerator while you assemble the remaining logs with the second sheet. Once all the logs are on the prepared pan, brush with the egg wash and refrigerate for 30 minutes.

Meanwhile, position a rack in the middle of the oven and preheat the oven to 350°F. Bake for about 20 minutes, then reduce the oven temperature to 275°F and bake for at least another 15 to 20 minutes, or until golden and firm to the touch. (The rolls should not sag in the middle and should hold their shape when lifted.) Place the logs in their pans on a cooling rack and cool them to room temperature.

SERVE THE DESSERT. Use a serrated knife to cut off both ends of a roll so each piece can stand upright without wobbling. Cut the roll crosswise in half. Then cut each half crosswise in half on a diagonal for a total of 4 pieces that are all able to stand on end (3). Repeat with the remaining logs. Stand 2 pithivier halves on each plate (diagonally, cut side facing up) and surround with a fluff of sabayon.

◆ I LIKE TO FLOUR A PIECE OF PARCHMENT PAPER AND PLACE THE CHILLED PUFF PASTRY ON THE PAPER TO FORM THE ROLL.

ASSEMBLY

Assembled Pithivier
2 cups Prosecco–Almond Grappa
    Sabayon

◆ FOR A QUICK AND EASY TREAT, SPRINKLE ANY LEFTOVER PUFF WITH A LITTLE CINNAMON SUGAR, CUT INTO STRIPS, AND BAKE IN A 350°F OVEN FOR ABOUT 12 MINUTES, OR UNTIL CRISP AND GOLDEN.

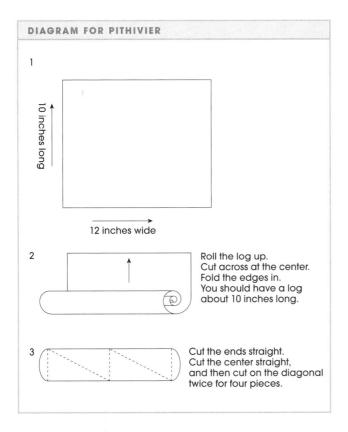

DIAGRAM FOR PITHIVIER

1

10 inches long

12 inches wide

2
Roll the log up.
Cut across at the center.
Fold the edges in.
You should have a log about 10 inches long.

3
Cut the ends straight.
Cut the center straight, and then cut on the diagonal twice for four pieces.

BRIOCHE DOME WITH FRUIT

Traditional brioche is a rich, fine-textured, buttery yeast dough, typically baked in a cylindrical mold lined with paper to extend its height or in a narrow rectangular loaf pan. I developed this recipe because I love to fill breads with all kinds of ingredients. Here, I transform brioche into airy boules, little domed breads with creamy, fruity centers. This brioche mousseline recipe comes from Sparky Boxhall, an American who lived in France with her husband. A well-studied cook, Sparky managed to make her way into many a fine French restaurant kitchen and came away with incredible knowledge and skill. She returned to the United States and, in the 1960s, started teaching cooking classes in the Washington, D.C. area. Anyone into cooking in the seventies will definitely remember her. Although I have made a few subtle changes, this is essentially the recipe she taught in her brioche mousseline class. The brioche is made with a levain (sponge), which gives it the wonderful aroma and earthy flavor that develops only over a long, leisurely rising period. When paired with rum-soaked dried fruit and a sweet pastry cream filling, this brioche makes for a wonderfully unique dessert.

PASTRY CREAM

YIELD: 3 CUPS

½ cup sugar

¼ cup (about 30 grams) cake flour, sifted

2 cups milk

10 large egg yolks (200 grams or ⅞ cup)

2 tablespoons unsalted butter

MAKE THE PASTRY CREAM. Combine the sugar and flour in a bowl, whisking to remove any lumps. This technique will ensure the pastry cream is smooth.

Bring the milk to a boil in a large saucepan. Meanwhile, place the egg yolks in the bowl of an electric mixer fitted with the whisk attachment and mix on high speed for about 2 minutes. Add the flour mixture and continue to beat on high until the egg mixture is thick, heavy, and pale. Remove the bowl from the mixer and bring it over to the stove.

When the milk comes to a rolling boil and rises up the side of the pan, reduce the heat to low. Whisk several spoonfuls of the hot milk into the egg mixture to temper it, then pour the tempered mixture back into the saucepan and continue to cook on medium-low heat, stirring constantly, until the pastry cream begins to bubble or "burp." Continue cooking for 2 minutes to remove any floury aftertaste.

Remove the pan from the heat and whisk in the butter. Pour the custard into a bowl and tightly press a piece of plastic wrap directly onto the surface, leaving a small area uncovered for the heat to escape. This will prevent a skin from forming. Refrigerate for several hours, or until chilled. Cover completely with plastic wrap. The pastry cream may be made up to 4 days in advance and kept refrigerated until ready to use.

MAKE THE DRIED FRUIT MIXTURE. Combine the dark and golden raisins and the cranberries in a small bowl. Add the hot water and rum. Let soak for 2 hours. The dried fruit will become plump and be imbued with just a hint of rum. The fruit mixture should be made the day before.

DRIED FRUIT MIXTURE
YIELD: ABOUT 2¾ CUPS

¾ cup dark raisins

¾ cup golden raisins

½ cup dried cranberries

¾ cup hot water

2 tablespoons dark rum, such as Myers's

MAKE THE DOUGH. Place the cake and all-purpose flours, the sugar, and salt in the bowl of an electric mixer fitted with the paddle attachment attachment. Add the milk, eggs, and egg yolks and beat on very low speed for 25 minutes. Make the levain while the dough is beating.

◆ I FIND THE SIMPLEST WAY TO HEAT MILK TO TEPID IS IN THE MICROWAVE. HEAT ON HIGH POWER AT 10-SECOND INTERVALS UNTIL IT IS LUKEWARM TO THE TOUCH.

BRIOCHE MOUSSELINE (BRIOCHE DOUGH)

2 cups (240 grams) cake flour, sifted

2 cups (280 grams) all-purpose flour, sifted

¼ cup sugar

1 teaspoon salt

¼ cup lukewarm milk (70°F to 80°F)

6 large eggs (300 grams or 1⅓ cups)

2 large egg yolks (40 grams or generous ⅛ cup)

MAKE THE LEVAIN. Crumble the yeast into a small bowl, sprinkle with the sugar, and beat with a wooden spoon. It will form a creamy paste, then become a thin syrup.

Place the flour on a lightly floured surface or in a medium bowl. Make a well in the center of the flour and pour the yeast mixture into the well, making sure to get every last drop of yeast out of the bowl. Use your fingers to incorporate the flour from around the edge of the well

LEVAIN

1 cake (0.6 ounce) fresh yeast or 1 envelope active dry yeast

1 teaspoon sugar

¾ cup (105 grams) all-purpose flour

⅓ cup lukewarm milk (70°F to 80°F)

14 ounces (3½ sticks) unsalted butter, at room temperature

◆ I LIKE TO USE FRESH WET COMPRESSED OR CAKE YEAST. IT CAN BE FOUND IN MOST SUPERMARKETS IN THE DAIRY SECTION, BUT IF YOU PREFER, YOU CAN SUBSTITUTE DRY YEAST. PLACE 1 PACKAGE OF ACTIVE DRY YEAST IN A BOWL. ADD 2 TABLESPOONS WARM WATER, STIR WELL TO DISSOLVE, THEN WAIT A FEW MINUTES UNTIL IT BECOMES SMOOTH AND CREAMY AND RISES A LITTLE IN THE BOWL.

into the yeast. At the same time, slowly pour in the milk with the other hand as you continue to bring in the flour. You may not need to use all the milk.

Knead the levain on a lightly floured surface with the heel of your hand until it is smooth and elastic and comes together into a ball, about 2 minutes. The dough should be moist enough to hold together but not sticky to the touch. If it becomes too sticky, sprinkle in more flour as needed, being careful not to make the dough too dry.

Place the levain in a large bowl filled two-thirds full with warm water (no hotter than about 100°F) and let rise for 10 to 15 minutes. At first, the levain will be a small wad of heavy dough that sinks to the bottom of the bowl. And then, almost magically, it will grow and rise to the surface, bubbling all over. But the rise to the surface isn't an indication that it is ready. When it is ready, it will become light. The dough will no longer be compacted but rather porous and spongy; it will have turned into a levain. This usually happens around the same time that the brioche dough is ready, in 20 to 25 minutes.

INCORPORATE THE LEVAIN INTO THE DOUGH. When the brioche dough has become soft, elastic, very shiny, and begins to pull away from the side of the bowl, it is ready to accept the levain. Lift the finished levain out of the water and carefully place it in a small bowl. Break off small pieces (tablespoon size) of the levain and drop them into the bowl of dough with the mixer still on, allowing each piece to be incorporated before adding another. Continue to beat on very low speed until the dough is very soft, supple, and sticky. When the dough rises up the paddle attachment, begins to come together into a ball, and makes a slapping sound against the side of the bowl, it is ready to accept the butter. This should take about 5 minutes.

INCORPORATE THE BUTTER INTO THE DOUGH. Use your fingertips to pull off small pieces of the butter and drop them into the dough one by one, beating constantly. Make sure that each piece of butter is incorporated before adding the next piece. If the butter begins to stick to the side of the bowl and the dough doesn't come together, use a rubber spatula to scrape down the bowl. At this point you may think you've done something wrong. The dough probably looks too loose and buttery, has all pulled apart, and looks like it will never come together. Be patient. In about 5 minutes, the straggly mass of dough will transform itself into a beautiful, smooth, glistening, creamy mass of dough. Touch the dough with your fingertips. It should feel soft and delicate and not stick to your fingers.

Transfer the dough to a clean large bowl and cover with plastic wrap. Let it rise for several hours, or until doubled in bulk. The edges of the dough, which rise first, should be gently tucked under every so often to ensure that the dough rises evenly. When the dough has doubled in bulk, deposit it onto a lightly floured surface and gently knead it a few times. Return it to the bowl, cover with plastic wrap, and refrigerate for several hours until doubled in bulk again.

ASSEMBLE THE BRIOCHE DOME WITH FRUIT. Remove the dough from the refrigerator. Deposit the dough on a lightly floured surface and lightly knead it. Cover with plastic wrap and let rest for 15 minutes. Squeeze out any excess liquid from the plumped raisins and cranberries. The fruit mixture should be dry, with no liquid visible. Remove the chilled pastry cream from the refrigerator and add the fruit mixture, mixing well.

Divide the dough into 16 equal pieces, each weighing approximately 90 grams. I usually weigh out the dough pieces for the sake of uniformity of size.

Form each piece of dough into a ball by rolling it in the palms of your hands. Flatten out a ball with the heel of

ASSEMBLY

2¾ cups Dried Fruit Mixture

3 cups Pastry Cream (all of the cream may not be used)

1 large egg, lightly beaten, for egg wash

PREPARATION. Preheat the oven to 350°F. Line two 18 X 13–inch half-sheet or jelly-roll pans or large cookie sheets with parchment paper.

your hand and stretch it out gently with your fingertips. Place a generous tablespoon of pastry cream in the center of the dough round. Lift up the sides of the round and gradually bring into the center, over the filling. Pinch the edges together, then give it a little twist to enclose the cream and fruit in the brioche. Turn the boule upside down and place on the prepared pans. Repeat with the remaining dough balls and pastry cream–fruit filling mixture. Cover the boules loosely with plastic wrap and let rise for 30 minutes. You will have extra filling left, which will be used to plate the boules.

Meanwhile, preheat the oven to 350°F. Lightly brush the boules with the egg wash. Bake for about 20 minutes, or until golden and light to the touch.

To reheat the boules, place on 2 parchment-lined half-sheet or jelly-roll pans, cover with foil, and rewarm in a 275°F oven for approximately 10 minutes.

SERVE THE BOULES. Serve the Brioche Dome with Fruit warm from the oven. Split open with a knife horizontally and insert some extra pastry cream–fruit filling before replacing the cut top.

CHAUSSON OF PEAR

The title Chausson of Pear is not exactly accurate, since in French a *chausson* is more of a turnover than a swirl of pastry. I have taken a little poetic license here, as this dessert is comprised of a mound of hot pear marmalade with a Danish pastry curl leaning up against it. This makes for a wonderfully satisfying fall dessert, when pears are at their freshest and most flavorful. Seek out pears at your local farmers' market for the best flavor.

SPECIAL EQUIPMENT: CHEESE SLICER, TRUFFLE SLICER, MANDOLINE, OR ADJUSTABLE VEGETABLE SLICER • 2-INCH ROUND OR SQUARE PASTRY CUTTER

PREPARE THE BUTTER. Dust each stick of butter with a little all-purpose flour. Use a cheese slicer, truffle slicer, mandoline, or adjustable vegetable slicer to slice each cold stick of butter into 7 lengthwise slices. You will end up with 14 thin 5 x 1–inch slices of butter in total. Divide them into 3 groups (2 groups will have 5 slices and 1 will have 4). Place each group on parchment paper, long sides slightly overlapping. Press the slices together to form three 5 x 4–inch "sheets" of butter. Refrigerate for 20 minutes.

MAKE THE DANISH DOUGH. Place the all-purpose and cake flours, the salt, and the 1 tablespoon diced butter in the bowl of an electric mixer fitted with the paddle attachment and mix on very low speed. Crumble the yeast into a small bowl, add 1 tablespoon of the sugar, and stir until it forms a thin syrup. Working quickly, add the yeast mixture, milk, water, the remaining ⅓ cup sugar, egg, and vanilla. Mix until the dough gathers around the paddle attachment, about 2 minutes. Add additional water if necessary. The dough should feel damp and slightly sticky to the touch.

DANISH DOUGH

YIELD: ENOUGH FOR 12 DANISH CURLS

½ pound (2 sticks) cold unsalted butter plus 1 tablespoon diced butter

2 cups (280 grams) all-purpose flour, sifted

½ cup (60 grams) cake flour, sifted

⅛ teaspoon salt

2 cakes (0.6 ounce each) fresh yeast

⅓ cup plus 1 tablespoon sugar

¼ cup cold milk

¼ cup chilled water plus 3 to 4 tablespoons more (enough to bring the dough together so that it's moist but not sticky)

1 large egg (50 grams or ¼ cup)

1 teaspoon vanilla extract

PREPARATION. Line an 18 X 13–inch half-sheet or jelly-roll pan or large cookie sheet with parchment paper.

CONTINUED

◆ IT MAY SEEM UNUSUAL TO ADD
CHILLED WATER TO A YEAST DOUGH,
BUT THE IDEA IS TO KEEP THE
DOUGH FROM RISING UNTIL YOU
BEGIN TO SHAPE AND LET IT RISE.
YOU WANT THE BIG RISE TO HAPPEN
WHEN THE DOUGH IS BAKING.

Remove the dough from the bowl and with your hand, pat and stretch it into a uniform square; the size is not important. Place the dough on an 18 X 13–inch half-sheet or jelly-roll pan, wrap in plastic wrap, and refrigerate for just 15 minutes. If the room is cold, I don't refrigerate the dough until it's completed.

◆ THIS IS USUALLY THE TIME WHEN I REMOVE THE PREPARED BUTTER FROM THE REFRIGERATOR AND LET IT SOFTEN JUST A BIT SO THE CONSISTENCY IS THE SAME AS THE DOUGH'S, BUT IT ALSO DEPENDS UPON THE TEMPERATURE OF THE ROOM. IF THE ROOM IS 80°F, THEN I KEEP THE BUTTER IN THE REFRIGERATOR. IF THE ROOM IS COOL, 63°F, FOR EXAMPLE, THEN I LEAVE THE BUTTER OUT FOR 2 HOURS.

DIAGRAM FOR ROLL/FOLD PASTRY

ADD THE BUTTER TO THE DANISH DOUGH. Roll out the chilled dough on a lightly floured surface to a rectangle about 16 inches long and 5 inches wide. See the diagram at left. Use a ruler as a guide to mark the dough crosswise into fourths without cutting all the way through the dough (1). Place one 5 X 4–sheet of room-temperature butter on the section of dough immediately left of center. Place the butter so it covers that entire section of dough (2). Fold over the section of dough to its left, bringing it toward the center, enclosing the butter in the dough. The dough should now have 3 sections (3). Place a second sheet of butter in the middle section (4) and fold the right section of dough over the butter. You now have 2 sections of dough visible (5). Place the remaining sheet of butter on top of the left section (6) and fold the other half of the dough over to enclose it (7). The dough should be roughly 7 X 5 inches.

Rolling forward with a rolling pin, roll the dough out to a rectangle approximately 14 inches long by 5 inches wide. Fold the rectangle into thirds to create a rectangle

MAKE THE SOUFFLÉ. Place the egg yolks and 2 tablespoons of the sugar in a large bowl and whisk until very thick and pale. Whisk in the cream cheese and vanilla and mix well. Set aside.

Place the egg whites with the lemon juice in the bowl of an electric mixer fitted with the whisk attachment and whip on high speed until foamy and beginning to hold a shape. Gradually add the remaining 2 tablespoons sugar and beat until the whites form firm, glossy peaks.

Fold the egg whites into the cream-cheese mixture all at once.

ASSEMBLE THE SOUFFLÉ. Fill a pastry bag fitted with a ½-inch plain tip (Ateco #26) with the soufflé mixture. Pipe into the baked shells to the top of the shell. Bake for 6 to 8 minutes, or until puffy and browned.

Serve the tartlets dusted with confectioners' sugar and accompanied by fresh cherries.

CHEESECAKE SOUFFLÉ

YIELD: ENOUGH FOR 8 TARTLETS
(ABOUT 4 CUPS)

4 large egg yolks (80 grams or ⅓ cup)

4 tablespoons sugar

2 (3-ounce) packages cream cheese,
    at room temperature

1 teaspoon vanilla extract

6 large egg whites (180 grams or ¾ cup)

1 teaspoon freshly squeezed
    lemon juice

ASSEMBLY

4 cups Cheesecake Soufflé

8 Tartlet Shells

Confectioners' sugar for dusting

Stoned (pitted) sweet red cherries,
    preferably Bing, for serving

PREPARATION. Position a rack in the middle of the oven and preheat the oven to 400°F. Have the baked tartlet shells ready on a half-sheet or jelly-roll pan.

FRUITED CROISSANT
BREAD PUDDING

Yes, this is another bread pudding recipe. But using croissants takes this pudding to another level, especially if you've made the croissants yourself. The Brittany cake (page 294) is a classic croissant recipe. The apple compote keeps the pudding moist, so this dessert keeps for a good week. You can even reheat it in the microwave with great results. Paired with vanilla caramel ice cream, this is a dessert guests will hope you serve time and time again.

SPECIAL EQUIPMENT: TWELVE 3-INCH RAMEKINS OR 6-OUNCE SOUFFLÉ DISHES •
ICE-CREAM MAKER

APPLE COMPOTE

YIELD: 1½ TO 2 CUPS

6 apples, preferably Fuji, McIntosh,
  or Gala

2 tablespoons unsalted butter

¼ cup sugar

1 cup dried cranberries

½ cup apricot preserves

1 tablespoon finely grated orange zest

MAKE THE COMPOTE. Peel, core, and cut the apples into ¼-inch slices. Set aside.

Place the butter and sugar in a heavy large saucepan and cook over medium heat until the butter has melted and the sugar begins to brown and become caramelized. Add the apples and cranberries and cook over low heat, stirring often, for about 2 minutes. Add the apricot preserves and orange zest. Continue cooking until the apples have lost much of their moisture, 1 or 2 more minutes. Remove from the heat.

◆ THIS APPLE COMPOTE, DRAINED OF ALL ITS EXCESS LIQUID, CAN BE USED FOR COUNTLESS DESSERTS. EXPERIMENT AT HOME WITH OTHER FRESH OR DRIED FRUITS. USE IT IN DESSERT SANDWICHES, AS A FILLING FOR COOKIES OR ROLLS, OR SERVE WARM OVER ICE CREAM. IT WILL BE A WONDERFUL ADDITION TO YOUR DESSERT REPERTOIRE.

CROISSANT BREAD PUDDING

YIELD: ENOUGH FOR 12 RAMEKINS
(ABOUT 9 CUPS)

6 large croissants, cut into 1-inch cubes

6 large eggs (300 grams or 1⅓ cups)

2 tablespoons cream sherry, preferably
  Harvey's Bristol Cream or Lustau
  Capataz Andrés

⅔ cup packed light brown sugar

2 cups milk

2 cups heavy cream

1½ to 2 cups Apple Compote

PREPARATION. Position a rack in the middle of the oven and preheat the oven to 325°F. Generously butter twelve 3-inch ramekins or 6-ounce soufflé dishes all the way up to the top and over the edges.

◆ TRY TO PLACE PIECES OF THE BREAD, RATHER THAN APPLE SLICES, ON THE VERY BOTTOMS OF THE CUPS. THE PUDDINGS WILL RELEASE EASIER.

MAKE THE BREAD PUDDING. Place the cut-up croissants in a very large bowl and set aside. Place the eggs and sherry in a large bowl and whisk well. Set aside.

Place the brown sugar, milk, and cream in a medium saucepan and bring to a boil over medium-high heat. Reduce the heat to low. Bring the bowl with the egg mixture over to the saucepan. Whisk about 1 cup of the hot milk mixture into the egg mixture to temper it, then return the tempered mixture to the pot and cook over low heat, whisking well to combine. Pour the custard mixture through a fine-mesh stainless-steel strainer or China cap into a bowl.

Pour the custard over the croissant pieces in the bowl, stirring to make sure they are all well coated. Add the apple compote, stirring until well combined. Let the mixture sit for 30 minutes to allow the croissants time to absorb the liquid. Fill the prepared ramekins to the tops, pressing the pudding mixture down tightly. (If you have extra pudding, put it into a 6- or 8-inch round cake pan and bake.)

Place the ramekins in a 2-inch-deep baking pan. Place the pan on the oven rack, then add enough hot water to come halfway up the sides of the ramekins. Bake the bread pudding for approximately 45 minutes to 1 hour, or until browned on top. Serve immediately or refrigerate, uncovered, until thoroughly cooled. When well chilled, cover with plastic wrap. Refrigerated, the puddings will remain fresh for up to 3 days.

MAKE THE ICE CREAM. Place the cream and milk in a medium saucepan. Use the back of a knife to scrape the seeds from the vanilla bean. Add the pod and the seeds to the pan. Heat the milk mixture over medium-high heat until it comes to a boil and rises up in the pot, then remove from the heat.

Meanwhile, place the sugar and egg yolks in the bowl of an electric mixer fitted with the whisk attachment and beat on high speed until thick and pale. The sugar should be thoroughly dissolved.

Bring the bowl over to the saucepan. Gradually whisk about 1 cup of the hot milk mixture into the egg mixture to temper it, then return the tempered mixture to the pot, whisking continuously (still off the heat) until the mixture coats the back of a spoon, 2 to 3 minutes. (Run your finger through the custard on the back of the spoon. The custard is thick enough when the line remains.) Pour the custard through a fine-mesh stainless-steel strainer or China cap into a large bowl. Chill in an ice bath or place in the refrigerator until cold. When well chilled, add the vanilla and caramel sauce. Place in an ice-cream maker and freeze according to manufacturer's instructions.

VANILLA CARAMEL ICE CREAM

YIELD: 1 QUART

2 cups heavy cream

2 cups milk

2 vanilla beans, split lengthwise

1 cup sugar

11 to 12 large egg yolks (225 grams or 1 cup)

1 teaspoon vanilla extract

1 cup Caramel Sauce (page 40), cold

SERVE THE BREAD PUDDING. Microwave the puddings, a few at a time, on high power—briefly (20 seconds) if the puddings are barely warm or for about 45 seconds if they are cooler—until heated through. Run a knife around the sides of the ramekins, then invert the puddings into small dessert bowls and lift off the ramekins. Top each pudding with a square of caramel ice cream.

✦ YOU CAN BUY AN EXCELLENT SQUARE ICE-CREAM SCOOP FROM J.B. PRINCE.

ASSEMBLY

12 Croissant Bread Pudding ramekins
Vanilla Caramel Ice Cream

VARIATION. *For a fancier presentation, pour a spoonful of Raspberry Coulis (page 118) over the vanilla caramel ice cream.*

FRIED MOCHA CUSTARD SQUARES

Have you ever had it in your head to try some obscure—even weird—idea for a dessert? I obsessed over making fried custard squares for quite some time, but each time I mentioned it to colleagues, the response was tepid, to say the least. When I finally made it, I was sure it would be pretty mediocre, but I loved it. It was soft, crunchy, and delicately coffee flavored . . . just really different. I kept eating it even though I couldn't explain why I liked it so much. It's a little unusual and, when served warm, very good! This dessert calls for a 12 X 8 X 1–inch pan, known as a quarter-sheet pan in bakeries and restaurants. It is found in most cookware shops.

MOCHA CUSTARD SQUARES

YIELD: 24 SQUARES

½ cup cornstarch

3 cups milk

½ cup sugar

2 tablespoons instant espresso powder

½ vanilla bean, split lengthwise and scraped

1 tablespoon dark rum, such as Myers's

1 teaspoon vanilla extract

4 large eggs (200 grams or ⅞ cup)

4 cups fine dry bread crumbs made from buttery brioche or day-old croissants

6 tablespoons unsalted butter, or more if needed

PREPARATION. Line a 12 X 8 X 1–inch pan with plastic wrap. Line one half-sheet or jelly-roll pan with parchment paper and another with a layer of paper towels.

MAKE THE CUSTARD SQUARES. Combine the cornstarch and 1 cup of the milk in a small saucepan and whisk until the cornstarch has dissolved. Stir in the remaining 2 cups milk, the sugar, instant espresso, and the vanilla bean scrapings.

Bring the mixture to a boil over high heat, stirring constantly. Cook until the custard bubbles and thickens heavily. Cook for 2 more minutes, then remove from the heat. Add the rum and vanilla and mix well. Pour into the plastic-lined pan. Refrigerate until very firm, at least 4 hours or overnight.

When the custard is firm, lift up the edges of the plastic wrap to gently release the custard. Place a piece of parchment paper on top of the pan, cover it with a cutting board and flip the custard over onto the board. Lift off the baking pan and remove the plastic wrap. Dip a large knife in hot water and, using a 2-inch-wide metal spatula as your guide, cut the custard into 2-inch squares, dipping and cleaning the knife in the water as you go. This will ensure nice clean cuts.

Lightly beat the eggs in a shallow bowl or pie plate. Dip the custard squares one at a time into the beaten eggs once, and then coat twice with the crumbs. Place the squares on the parchment-lined pan. Melt the butter in a heavy large skillet on medium-high heat. When the foam subsides, add 3 or 4 custard squares to the skillet and brown for 2 to 3 minutes on each side, carefully turning them over. Let drain on the paper towel–lined pan while continuing to sauté the remaining squares. Set aside.

MAKE THE CHOCOLATE SAUCE. Bring the cream to a boil in a medium saucepan over medium-high heat. Remove from the heat and add the chocolate and rum, stirring until the chocolate has melted and the mixture is smooth. Keep warm until ready to use.

CHOCOLATE SAUCE

YIELD: 3½ CUPS

3 cups heavy cream

8 ounces bittersweet chocolate, chopped

2 tablespoons dark rum, such as Myers's

ASSEMBLE THE DESSERT. If needed, recrisp the custard squares in a 325°F oven for 3 minutes. Place 2 custard squares on each plate and dust with a little confectioners' sugar. Top each square with a drizzle of chocolate sauce and a dollop of whipped cream.

ASSEMBLY

24 Mocha Custard Squares

Confectioners' sugar

3½ cups Chocolate Sauce

Lightly sweetened whipped cream

LEMON SOUFFLÉ TARTLETS

W hat I love about this tartlet is the triple filling: meringue, lemon cream, and a lemon meringue–cream mixture. Served warm from the oven with lemon sorbet, it's a light and delicate yet deeply flavored and satisfying dessert.

SPECIAL EQUIPMENT: 4-INCH ROUND PASTRY CUTTER • TEN 4-INCH FLUTED TARTLET PANS

TARTLET SHELLS

YIELD: 10 TARTLET SHELLS (YOU WILL GET A FEW EXTRA IN CASE OF BREAKAGE)

1½ cups (210 grams) all-purpose flour, sifted

⅛ cup sugar

¼ teaspoon salt

⅓ cup plus 1 tablespoon (2½ ounces) vegetable shortening, chilled

2 ounces (½ stick) unsalted butter, diced and chilled

⅛ cup (2 tablespoons or 1 ounce) ice water

◆ I PREFER TO ROLL OUT THIS DOUGH RIGHT AWAY. IF NOT ROLLING RIGHT AWAY, GATHER IT INTO A BALL, FLATTEN SLIGHTLY, AND WRAP IN PLASTIC WRAP. IF CHILLED, IT SHOULD BE BROUGHT TO ROOM TEMPERATURE BEFORE ROLLING.

PREPARATION. Position a rack in the middle of the oven and preheat the oven to 275°F.

MAKE THE PÂTE BRISÉE. Place the flour, sugar, and salt in the bowl of an electric mixer fitted with the paddle attachment and mix on low speed. Add the shortening and butter to the flour. On low speed cut the butter and shortening into the flour until it looks coarse and crumbly. If you like, remove the bowl from the mixer and break up the fat particles with your fingers to distribute the fat more evenly. Stir in just enough ice water to form the mixture into a ball. The dough will be crumbly and will barely hold together.

Remove the dough from the bowl and place on a clean, dry work surface. Then, with the heel of your hand, smear a small amount of the dough on the work surface by pushing it away from you until it looks homogenized—that is, smooth and not crumbly. Continue smearing small portions of the dough until all of it has been smoothed. This should take about 3 minutes. (This technique of kneading dough, or *fraisage*, not only forms the dough into a smooth, cohesive unit, but also develops just enough structure so that the dough is less likely to tear or crack while being rolled and lifted.)

MAKE THE TARTLET SHELLS. Roll out the dough on a lightly floured work surface to ⅛-inch thickness. Use a 4-inch round pastry cutter to cut out 10 rounds, rerolling the dough scraps as necessary. Use a metal spatula to lift and transfer the rounds to ten 4-inch fluted tartlet pans, being sure not to stretch the dough. Use your fingertips to firmly press the dough down onto the bottoms and against the sides of the tartlet pans. Use a knife to trim off any excess around the edges. Prick the dough all over with a fork and refrigerate until firm, for at least 1 hour, or up to 1 day.

When ready to bake, line the tartlet shells with aluminum foil and fill with uncooked rice or dried beans. Place the tartlet shells on an 18 X 13–inch half-sheet or jelly-roll pan and bake for 20 minutes, rotate the pan from front to back, and bake for another 20 minutes. Lift the foil with the rice from one of the shells to test for doneness. If necessary, continue to bake until the shells are lightly brown in color and firm to the touch. Let the shells cool in their pans for just 10 minutes, then unmold and cool completely on a rack. (These tartlet shells are fragile, so they need to be removed from their pans while still warm.) Set aside.

MAKE THE SOUFFLÉ. Finely grate enough zest from the lemons to equal 1 tablespoon, then squeeze and strain through a stainless-steel strainer enough juice to equal ¾ cup. Whisk the eggs, ½ cup of the sugar, the lemon zest, and all but a few drops of the lemon juice in a large bowl until smooth.

Fill with about 1 inch of water a skillet or roasting pan large enough to hold the bowl with the egg mixture. Bring the water to a simmer over medium-low heat. Place the bowl in the skillet and whisk until the lemon cream becomes very thick, about 10 minutes. Don't let it come to a boil or it will curdle. Remove from the heat, strain through a fine-mesh stainless-steel strainer or China cap set over a bowl, and cool to room temperature.

CONTINUED

◆ YOU CAN HASTEN THE COOLING BY PUTTING THE BOWL INTO A LARGER BOWL OF ICE AND WATER.

LEMON SOUFFLÉ (LEMON CREAM, LEMON MERINGUE-CREAM, AND MERINGUE)

YIELD: ENOUGH TO FILL 8 TARTLET SHELLS

About 4 or 5 large lemons

4 large eggs (200 grams or ⅞ cup)

½ cup plus 2 tablespoons sugar

2 large egg whites (60 grams or ¼ cup)

PREPARATION. Position a rack in the middle of the oven and preheat the oven to 375°F. Have the baked tartlet shells ready on a half-sheet or jelly-roll pan.

◆ A MICROPLANE GRATER IS AN EFFICIENT, EASY-TO-USE TOOL TO ZEST FRUIT.

WARM DESSERTS | 243

VARIATION. *To dress these up even more, serve the tartlets warm out of the oven with quenelles (or scoops) of Citrus Sorbet (page 26) off to the side.*

When the lemon cream has cooled, whip the egg whites with the few drops of reserved lemon juice on high speed in the bowl of an electric mixer fitted with the whisk attachment until foamy and beginning to hold a shape. Gradually add the remaining 2 tablespoons sugar and beat until the whites are firm and very glossy. Transfer half of the meringue to a bowl and set aside.

Fold half of the lemon cream into half of the meringue.

ASSEMBLY

8 Tartlet Shells

Lemon Cream

Lemon Meringue–Cream

Meringue

MAKE THE LEMON SOUFFLÉ TARTLETS. Fill the tartlet shells one-third full with a layer of lemon cream, top with an equal layer of lemon meringue–cream, and finish with an equal layer of meringue. Bake for 3 to 5 minutes, or until the meringue has browned. These lemon soufflé tartlets are best eaten the day they're made, otherwise the tartlet shells lose their crispness and become soggy.

ORANGE ESSENCE SOUFFLÉ

My friend and co-author of *Soufflés*, Richard Chirol, developed the wonderful, versatile orange essence that flavors this soufflé and gives it its memorable taste. Simple to prepare and quick to bake, this impressive-looking soufflé makes a great last-minute dessert. And the orange sablé cookies that I have included as a serving possibility are a citrusy, buttery addition.

SPECIAL EQUIPMENT: EIGHT 6-OUNCE SOUFFLÉ DISHES

MAKE THE ORANGE ESSENCE. Finely zest the oranges, making sure to remove only the orange part, leaving the white pith. Set aside.

Juice the oranges. Set aside about one-quarter of the juice and place the remaining juice in a small saucepan with the zest. Bring to a boil over medium-high heat, watching carefully until reduced to about ¼ cup. It should be very thick and syrupy. Remove from the heat, let cool, then add enough of the reserved juice to equal ⅓ cup. Set aside any remaining juice for another use.

ORANGE ESSENCE

YIELD: ⅓ CUP

3 large bright-skinned
   navel oranges

MAKE THE SOUFFLÉ. With a handheld whisk, beat the egg yolks with 2 teaspoons of the sugar and the lemon juice in a large bowl until very thick and light in color. Whip the whites on high speed in the bowl of an electric mixer fitted with the whisk attachment until foamy and beginning to hold a shape. Gradually add the remaining ¼ cup plus 2 teaspoons sugar, beating until the whites form stiff, glossy peaks. Stir the orange essence into the yolks, mixing well, then fold in the whites all at once. Spoon or pipe the mixture into the prepared dishes and bake for 8 to 10 minutes, or until puffy and browned. Serve at once.

SOUFFLÉ

YIELD: EIGHT 6-OUNCE SOUFFLÉS

4 large egg yolks (80 grams or ⅓ cup)
¼ cup plus 4 teaspoons sugar
1 tablespoon freshly squeezed
   lemon juice
8 large egg whites (240 grams or 1 cup)
⅓ cup Orange Essence

PREPARATION. Preheat the oven to
   400°F. Butter and sugar eight 6-ounce
   soufflé dishes. Refrigerate until ready
   to use.

nother nice way to serve the soufflés is plated with these cookies off to the side. Or serve with the Orange Compote (page 83) or Orange Sorbet (page 83) instead of the cookies for a different presentation at another time.

ORANGE SABLÉ COOKIES

YIELD: 40 TO 50 COOKIES

8 ounces (2 sticks) unsalted butter,
　　at room temperature

¾ cup confectioners' sugar

2 large egg yolks (40 grams or ⅛ cup)

2 tablespoons finely grated orange zest
　　(from about 2 large oranges)

Pinch of salt

2 cups (280 grams) all-purpose flour,
　　sifted

PREPARATION. Preheat the oven to 275°F. Line two 18 X 13–inch half-sheet or jelly-roll pans with parchment paper.

MAKE THE ORANGE SABLÉ COOKIES. Cream the butter and sugar on low speed in the bowl of an electric mixer fitted with the paddle attachment until light and fluffy. Add the egg yolks one at a time, beating until well blended. Add the orange zest and salt and mix until well blended. Add the flour and mix until combined.

Divide the dough and roll each piece into a log approximately 1½ inches in diameter. Wrap each log tightly in plastic wrap and refrigerate until firm, at least 1 hour or up to overnight.

Cut the logs into ¼-inch rounds and place 1½ inches apart on the prepared pans. Bake for 10 minutes, rotate the pans from front to back, and bake for another 10 minutes, or until firm and light golden. Transfer the cookies to a rack to cool completely. Storing cookies at room temperature results in loss of flavor; extra cookies can be placed in an airtight container and frozen for up to 1 month.

PEACH SOUFFLÉ TARTLETS WITH GINGER PEACH ICE CREAM

The addition of Grand Marnier–soaked cake cubes enhances the soufflé's fragrant peach perfume. All the flavor of the liqueur remains in the soaked cubes so it's not weakened by the other soufflé ingredients. The only other way to achieve this level of Grand Marnier essence would be to use a larger quantity of the liqueur. But that would cause the soufflé to break down, become loose, and therefore unable to rise sufficiently. The ginger peach ice cream is an added bonus, but the tartlets are lovely served on their own.

SPECIAL EQUIPMENT: 4-INCH ROUND PASTRY CUTTER • TWELVE 4-INCH FLUTED TARTLET PANS • ICE-CREAM MAKER

MAKE THE PÂTE BRISÉE. Place the flour, sugar, and salt in the bowl of an electric mixer fitted with the paddle attachment. Mix on low speed. Add the shortening and butter to the flour. On low speed cut the butter and shortening into the mixture until the dough looks coarse and crumbly. If you like, break up the fat particles with your fingers to distribute the fat more evenly. Stir in just enough ice water to form the mixture into a ball. The dough will be crumbly and will barely hold together.

Remove the dough from the bowl and place it on a clean, dry work surface. Then, with the heel of your hand, smear a small amount of it on the work surface by pushing it away from you until it looks homogenized—that is, smooth and not crumbly. Continue smearing small portions of the dough until all of it has been smoothed. This should take about 3 minutes. (This technique of kneading dough, called *fraisage* in French, not only forms the dough into a smooth, cohesive unit but also helps it develop just enough structure so that it is less likely to tear or crack while being rolled and lifted.)

TARTLET SHELLS

YIELD: 12 TARTLET SHELLS (THIS GIVES YOU 4 EXTRA IN CASE OF BREAKAGE)

1½ cups (210 grams) all-purpose flour, sifted

⅛ cup sugar

¼ teaspoon salt

⅓ cup plus 1 tablespoon (2½ ounces) vegetable shortening, chilled

2 ounces (½ stick) unsalted butter, chilled, diced

⅛ cup (2 tablespoons or 1 ounce) ice water

CONTINUED

When you've worked all the dough, gather it into a ball, flatten slightly, and wrap in plastic wrap. This dough can be rolled out immediately. In fact, I prefer to roll it right away. If chilled, it should be brought to room temperature before rolling.

PREPARATION. Position a rack in the middle of the oven and preheat the oven to 275°F.

MAKE THE TARTLET SHELLS. Roll out the dough on a lightly floured work surface to ⅛-inch thickness. Use a 4-inch round pastry cutter to cut out 12 rounds. Without stretching the dough, use a metal spatula to lift and transfer the rounds to twelve 4-inch fluted tarlet pans. With your fingertips, firmly press the dough down onto the bottoms and against the sides of the tartlet pans. Use a knife to trim off any excess around the edges. Prick the dough all over with a fork and refrigerate until firm, for at least 1 hour or up to 1 day.

Line the tartlet shells with aluminum foil and fill with uncooked rice or dried beans. Place the tartlet shells on an 18 X 13–inch half-sheet or jelly-roll pan. Bake for 15 minutes, rotate the pan from front to back, and bake for another 15 minutes. Lift the foil with the rice from one of the shells to test for doneness. If necessary, bake further, until the shells are lightly brown and firm to the touch. Let the shells cool in their tartlet pans on a rack for just 10 minutes, then unmold and cool completely on a rack. (These tartlet shells are fragile, so they need to be removed from their pans while still warm.)

SOUFFLÉ

YIELD: ENOUGH TO FILL 8 TARTLET
SHELLS

6 very ripe fragrant peaches
(preferably Freestone)

½ cup (½-inch) cubes of homemade
sponge cake or Yellow Génoise
(page 39)

2 tablespoons Grand Marnier

1 large egg yolk (20 grams or 1
tablespoon)

2 tablespoons sugar

2 large egg whites (60 grams or ¼ cup)

1 tablespoon freshly squeezed
lemon juice

FILLED TARTLET SHELLS

YIELD: 8 TARTLETS

8 Tartlet Shells

Soufflé

PREPARATION. Preheat the oven to
400°F. Have the tartlet shells ready
on a half-sheet or jelly-roll pan.

MAKE THE SOUFFLÉ. Peel the peaches. To remove the skins easily, drop the peaches into boiling water for 1 or 2 minutes, depending on the ripeness of the peaches. Move them around a bit and quickly lift them out with a slotted spoon. The skins should peel off easily, with just a little coaxing. If the peaches aren't perfectly ripe, the skin will be a bit more difficult to remove. You may have to use a vegetable peeler.

Remove the peach pits and puree the peaches in a food processor until smooth. Place 1 cup of the puree in a large bowl and set aside. Any leftover puree can be drizzled over the finished dessert. Place the cake cubes in a small bowl and sprinkle with the Grand Marnier. Set aside.

With a handheld mixer, whisk the egg yolk with 1 tablespoon of the sugar in a small bowl until very thick and light in color. In another small bowl, whisk the egg whites and lemon juice until foamy and just beginning to hold a shape. Gradually add the remaining 1 tablespoon sugar, beating until the whites form stiff, glossy peaks.

Fold the yolk mixture into the reserved 1 cup peach puree, then fold in the cake cubes. Gently fold in the beaten whites until just blended.

FILL THE SHELLS. Divide the soufflé mixture evenly among the tartlet shells. Bake for 8 to 10 minutes, or until puffy and browned.

MAKE THE ICE CREAM. Place the milk, cream, and ¼ cup of the sugar in a heavy medium saucepan. Bring to a boil over medium-high heat.

Meanwhile, beat the egg yolks and remaining ½ cup plus 1 teaspoon sugar on high speed in the bowl of an electric mixer fitted with the whisk attachment until very thick and pale. The mixture will triple in volume and form a ribbon when dropped from the whisk. This will take 3 to 4 minutes. When the milk has boiled, remove from the heat.

Bring the bowl over to the stove and gradually whisk about 1 cup of the hot cream mixture into the yolk mixture to temper it, then return the tempered mixture to the saucepan and stir well to cook the yolks thoroughly with the hot cream mixture. Pour the custard through a fine-mesh stainless-steel strainer or China cap into a bowl and chill in an ice bath, stirring occasionally. If possible, it is best to make the ice-cream base a day ahead so it has plenty of time to chill thoroughly.

Transfer the mixture to an ice-cream maker and freeze according to manufacturer's instructions. Then, when the ice cream has finished churning and has been removed from the machine, fold in the chopped peaches and ginger.

Waiting until the very end to fold add-ins into ice cream is important for any ice cream that contains chunky ingredients. Here, the pieces of peach cannot be satisfactorily extruded from the machine after churning if using a commercial machine. Also, the peaches will exude too much liquid if added into the churning ice cream.

SERVE THE TARTLETS. Place each tartlet on a plate, drizzle the extra peach puree around, and end with scoops of ginger peach ice cream. Serve at once.

GINGER PEACH ICE CREAM

YIELD: 1 QUART

2 cups milk

2 cups heavy cream

¾ cup plus 1 teaspoon sugar

11 to 12 large egg yolks
   (225 grams or 1 cup)

6 firm-ripe peaches, peeled and
   chopped

½ cup candied ginger, chopped

ASSEMBLY

8 Filled Tartlet Shells

Reserved peach puree

Ginger Peach Ice Cream

POACHED CHEESE DUMPLINGS

In 1991, I had the good fortune to travel around Eastern and Western Europe and their environs for about seven weeks. One stop was Budapest, Hungary, where I ate the most glorious poached cheese dumplings, called *topfenknödel*. They were jumbo-size and so light and delicious, it was unbelievable. When I was little, I used to pass by a dairy store on my way home from school. (That's right, a small specialty store that sold only butter, cheese, eggs, creamed cheese . . . and bars of Lindt Chocolate!) They had the most gorgeous large-curd dry cottage cheese that was sold by the pound and packed in cardboard cartons with little wire handles. My mother would buy a pound or two at a time, which she used for her blintzes. If I got to the carton first, I could make a real dent in the cheese! The curds just burst with flavor. The dumplings in Budapest had that same flavor intensity. I've tried to replicate the recipe here, but I can't say that these dumplings are as light as the ones in Budapest; or perhaps the memory lightens them. Or maybe they just remind me of those walks home from school with the stopover at the dairy store.

DUMPLING DOUGH

YIELD: ENOUGH FOR ABOUT 16
DUMPLINGS

12 ounces farmer cheese

8 ounces small-curd cottage cheese

4 large egg yolks (80 grams or ⅓ cup)

4 tablespoons sugar

4 tablespoons unsalted butter, at room
temperature

½ cup (70 grams) all-purpose flour

4 large egg whites (120 grams or
½ cup)

MAKE THE DUMPLING DOUGH. Rub the farmer and cottage cheeses through a fine-mesh sieve into the bowl of an electric mixer fitted with the paddle attachment. On medium speed, beat in the egg yolks one at a time, then add 3 tablespoons of the sugar, and the butter until well mixed. Sift the flour over the cheese mixture and stir vigorously with a wooden spoon until the flour is completely incorporated.

Place the egg whites in the bowl of an electric mixer fitted with the whisk attachment and beat on medium-high speed until light. Add the remaining 1 tablespoon sugar and continue beating until stiff peaks form. Scoop the egg whites over the cheese mixture and fold them together gently but thoroughly. Cover with plastic wrap and refrigerate the mixture overnight.

The Following Day

POACH THE DUMPLINGS. Bring the water and salt to a boil in a large saucepan over high heat.

Meanwhile, divide the dumpling dough in half and divide each portion into 8 equal pieces. On a lightly floured surface, roll each piece of dough into a ball approximately 1½ inches in diameter. Lower about 6 dumplings at a time into the boiling water, gently moving them around so they don't stick to the pan. Reduce the heat to low and poach the dumplings until they feel firm to the touch, about 6 to 8 minutes. Transfer the dumplings with a slotted spoon to a warm platter and keep warm while poaching the remaining dumplings.

SERVE THE DUMPLINGS. In the winter, serve these dumplings, 2 per serving, warm with warm poached dried fruit compote. And in the summer—with fresh berries. This is just one of those homey, satisfying tastes that doesn't need a lot of extras served with it.

DUMPLINGS

YIELD: 16 DUMPLINGS

8 cups water

½ teaspoon salt

Dumpling Dough

ASSEMBLY

16 Dumplings

Poached dry fruit compote or
    fresh berries

POTATO PUFFS
WITH APRICOT PUREE

SERVES 6 TO 8

This is another one of those dumpling-like desserts that I just can't seem to get enough of! I don't know where my obsession with warm dough and fruity sauces comes from, but these dumplings are just the most comforting winter dessert I can imagine. Once again, my extended trip back in 1991 took me to Germany. In Munich on one dark, cold, and rainy day, I ate potato dumplings. I don't remember the fruit filling as much as the warmth and softness of the dumpling itself and how satisfying it was. I wondered why I didn't see more of this kind of dessert in the United States. So I really wanted to create a dessert just like it to enjoy back home. I love apricots, as they're such a fragrant fruit, but dried apricots hold their flavor so well that they seemed like the perfect complement to the warm puffs.

SPECIAL EQUIPMENT: SILPAT BAKING MAT (SEE PAGE 201) • PIZZA WHEEL CUTTER

APRICOT FILLING

YIELD: ¾ CUP

½ cup dried apricots

1 tablespoon sugar

3 tablespoons kirsch

MAKE THE APRICOT FILLING. Soak the apricots in enough hot water to cover in a small saucepan for 2 hours. Cook over medium heat until soft, about 5 minutes. Puree the mixture in a food processor until smooth.

Return the apricot mixture to the saucepan and add the sugar and 2 tablespoons of the kirsch. Cook until very thick and syrupy, about 5 minutes. Remove from the heat, add the remaining 1 tablespoon kirsch and set aside to cool while making the puffs.

POTATO PUFF DOUGH

YIELD: ENOUGH FOR 15 PUFFS

2 pounds boiling potatoes, scrubbed

½ cup (70 grams) all-purpose flour, sifted

2 large egg yolks (40 grams or ⅛ cup)

1 tablespoon farina (Cream of Wheat)

1 teaspoon salt

⅛ teaspoon ground nutmeg

MAKE THE POTATO PUFF DOUGH. Place the potatoes in a large saucepan with enough lightly salted water to cover and cook until completely tender, for at least 20 minutes. Drain, cool, and peel the potatoes. Put the potatoes through a food mill set over a bowl. Stir in the flour, egg yolks, farina, salt, and nutmeg and mix to a smooth paste. Cover and refrigerate for 1 hour.

MAKE THE POTATO PUFFS. Roll out the dough on a lightly floured surface to a 15 X 9–inch rectangle. Cut into 3-inch squares with a pizza wheel cutter. Place a teaspoon of apricot puree in the center of each square and brush the edges with the egg wash. Fold in half on the diagonal and pinch the edges together to form a triangle. These can be chilled up to 24 hours ahead of time.

POACH THE POTATO PUFFS. Lower 4 or 5 puffs at a time into the boiling water and poach until they rise to the surface, 3 to 4 minutes. Transfer the puffs with a slotted spoon to a heated platter and keep warm until all the dumplings are cooked.

MAKE THE NECTARINE SAUCE. Place the nectarines in a medium saucepan with enough water to cover and bring to a boil. Cook over low heat until the fruit is very soft, about 20 minutes. Cool the fruit, then puree with the poaching liquid and orange juice in a food processor or blender until smooth, in batches if necessary. If you like, add more orange juice to taste. Press the puree through a fine-mesh stainless-steel strainer or China cap into a bowl. Reserve the pulp for the Nectarine Leather.

◆ I SOMETIMES FILL A SQUEEZE BOTTLE WITH A DIFFERENT-COLOR FRUIT PUREE (IN THIS CASE RASPBERRY) AND DRAW SQUIGGLES THROUGH THE ORANGE-COLORED PUREE. I USUALLY USE A FROZEN PUREE SUCH AS BOIRON OR PERFECT PUREE BRAND. BUT YOU CAN ALSO THAW A 10-OUNCE PACKAGE OF FROZEN RASPBERRIES, PRESS THEM THROUGH A SIEVE TO REMOVE THE SEEDS, AND COOK OVER MEDIUM-LOW HEAT WITH ¼ CUP SUGAR UNTIL SLIGHTLY THICKENED WITH NO LIQUID EVIDENT, ABOUT 2 MINUTES OR LESS. COOL THE PUREE BEFORE PUTTING INTO A SQUEEZE BOTTLE.

POTATO PUFFS

YIELD: 15 PUFFS

Potato Puff Dough

¾ cup Apricot Filling

1 large egg, lightly beaten, for egg wash

PREPARATION. Meanwhile, bring 4 quarts water and 2 teaspoons salt to a boil in a large pot. Heat a serving platter.

NECTARINE SAUCE

YIELD: 4 CUPS

½ pound dried nectarines

2 to 3 cups freshly squeezed orange juice, or to taste

NECTARINE LEATHER

YIELD: TWO 16 X 12-INCH SHEETS

8 ounces dried nectarines or reserved
pulp from the Nectarine Sauce

¼ cup sugar

PREPARATION. Line an 18 X 13–inch half-sheet or jelly-roll pan with a Silpat baking mat. You will probably have enough for 2 pans. Preheat the oven to 200°F.

MAKE THE NECTARINE LEATHER. If using the dried nectarines, place them with enough water to cover in a medium saucepan and bring to a boil over medium heat. Cook until very soft, about 10 minutes. Cool them, then drain and puree in a food processor until smooth.

Return the puree to the saucepan or put the reserved Nectarine Sauce pulp into a saucepan, add the sugar, and cook, stirring frequently, until very thick and no moisture exudes from the mixture, about 2 minutes. Spread the puree very thinly onto the Silpat with an offset spatula.

Bake for about 30 minutes, or until dry. Cool, then carefully remove the leather from the Silpat. Cut out various shapes with scissors and layer the nectarine leather pieces between sheets of parchment paper in an airtight container. The leather will remain fresh for up to several weeks.

ASSEMBLY

15 Potato Puffs

4 cups Nectarine Sauce

Nectarine Leather cutouts

SERVE THE POTATO PUFFS. Place 1 or 2 warm puffs on each plate and spoon some of the nectarine sauce around. Garnish with nectarine leather cutouts rolled up into a tube or another fanciful twist and place on the plate.

SCHNECKEN WITH
VANILLA ICE CREAM
AND GINGER CARAMEL SAUCE

Growing up in Baltimore, I ate schnecken at every kind of early-morning get-together. As I recall, the schnecken were small, rather dry yeast rolls studded with raisins, bearing little resemblance to the snail-shaped, buttery, brown sugar–glazed rolls made by the best bakeries. This recipe is an adaptation of an adaptation. It first appeared in Joan Nathan's book *Jewish Holiday Baking,* as William Greenberg Jr.'s Schnecken, written with the help of Michael London, from Greenberg's Bakery in New York City. I love this version of those warm-from-the-oven schnecken almost more than anything else. It's one of those sweets that really tests my willpower. Serving it hot with ice cream almost gilds the lily, but do it anyway!

SPECIAL EQUIPMENT: CANDY THERMOMETER • PASTRY BAG FITTED WITH A ½-INCH
PLAIN TIP (ATECO #26) • ICE-CREAM MAKER

MAKE THE SCHNECKEN DOUGH. Add 1 tablespoon sugar and ¼ cup tepid water to the yeast and stir into a smooth paste. Set aside until doubled and foamy.

Place the flour, salt, and remaining sugar in the bowl of an electric mixer fitted with the paddle attachment. Mix on low speed until thoroughly combined. Pour the yeast mixture into the flour mixture, then all at once add the egg yolks, sour cream, vinegar, and vanilla. Continue to mix on low speed until thoroughly combined, using a spatula to scrape the bowl. If the dough is dry, add enough of the 2 tablespoons water to bring it together. Beat in the butter several tablespoons at a time, until all of it is incorporated into the dough. The dough will be loose and sticky at this point. Beat on medium speed for about 1 minute to bring the dough together and ensure that all the ingredients are thoroughly mixed.

SCHNECKEN DOUGH

YIELD: ENOUGH FOR 12 SCHNECKEN

¼ cup sugar

¼ cup tepid water plus 2 tablespoons

3 tablespoons active dry yeast or ¾
　　ounce fresh yeast (1½ cakes)

2½ cups (350 grams) all-purpose flour,
　　sifted

¾ teaspoon salt

2 large egg yolks (40 grams or ⅛ cup)

½ cup sour cream

1 teaspoon white vinegar

½ teaspoon vanilla extract

6 ounces (1½ sticks) unsalted butter,
　　at room temperature

CONTINUED

Transfer the dough to a clean large bowl. Cover with plastic wrap and let rise at room temperature until doubled in size. Punch down the dough and remove from the bowl. Wrap tightly in plastic wrap and refrigerate for at least 3 hours but preferably overnight. The longer the dough is chilled, the less sticky and easier it will be to work with.

⬥ I LIKE TO MAKE THE DOUGH, THEN REFRIGERATE IT IMMEDIATELY FOR ABOUT 5 HOURS. I THEN ROLL IT OUT, FILL IT, CUT IT, PLACE IT IN THE MUFFIN CUPS WITH THE FILLING, AND REFRIGERATE OVERNIGHT. I BAKE IT THE NEXT MORNING, AND IT'S READY TO SERVE AS A TEMPTING TREAT FOR BREAKFAST OR BRUNCH.

SCHNECKEN FILLING

YIELD: ENOUGH TO FILL 12 SCHNECKEN

4 ounces (1 stick) unsalted butter,
    at room temperature

1¼ cups packed light brown sugar

½ teaspoon ground cinnamon

¾ teaspoon salt

1 teaspoon vanilla extract

MAKE THE FILLING. Place all the ingredients in the bowl of an electric mixer fitted with the paddle attachment. Mix on low speed until all the ingredients are incorporated and it forms a smooth paste. Set aside. If not using the filling the same day, cover with plastic wrap and refrigerate.

I make a large quantity of this filling to have on hand to make schnecken and cinnamon rolls with ease. To bring the filling back to a spreadable consistency after refrigeration, place in the microwave and heat at medium power for 20-second intervals, stirring after each interval, until smooth and spreadable.

Several Hours Later or the Following Day

FILLED SCHNECKEN

YIELD: 12 SCHNECKEN

Schnecken Filling

Schnecken Dough

1 cup dark raisins

1 cup pecans, finely chopped

See Preparation at the top of the next page

ASSEMBLE THE SCHNECKEN. If the filling has been refrigerated, bring it to room temperature by gently warming it in the microwave. Fill a pastry bag fitted with a ½-inch plain tip (Ateco #26) two-thirds full with filling. Pipe a teaspoon of filling in the bottom of each prepared muffin cup.

Roll out the chilled dough on a lightly floured surface to a rectangle that measures 18 inches long, 8 inches wide, and ¼ inch thick, with a long side near you.

Spread a thin layer of filling on top of the dough using an offset metal spatula. Sprinkle with the raisins and pecans. Starting with the edge closest to you, roll up the dough jelly-roll fashion into a tight log. When finished, use your hands to shape the dough at each end into a smooth end. Use a knife to score the dough into 1½-inch portions. Slice the dough into individual pieces using a thin-bladed knife and place 1 piece in each muffin cup cut side down. Push the dough down firmly into the tins, if needed. Cover with plastic wrap and let rise until the dough feels light (but not until it has spread and feels spongy, which means it has overproofed), about 45 minutes to 1 hour, no longer.

BAKE THE SCHNECKEN. Place the muffin pan on the rack. Bake for 20 minutes, rotate the pan from front to back, turn oven to 325°F, then bake for 15 minutes longer, or until the tops are very deep golden brown and firm. (The pan will catch any drippings.) When the schnecken are done, immediately remove from the oven and invert onto the other prepared half-sheet or jelly-roll pan, leaving the muffin pan on the schnecken for about 40 seconds before lifting it off so the caramel filling has a chance to release from the pan. Any filling that remains in the pan can be spooned out and deposited on the schnecken.

MAKE THE VANILLA ICE CREAM. Place the milk and cream in a heavy nonreactive medium saucepan. With the back of a knife, scrape the seeds from the bean and place the seeds and pod in the saucepan. Bring to a rolling boil over medium-high heat. Let the mixture rise up the side of the pan, then immediately remove from the heat.

Meanwhile, beat the egg yolks and sugar on high speed in the bowl of an electric mixer fitted with the whisk attachment until very thick and pale. The mixture will

PREPARATION. Generously butter twelve 2¾-inch muffin cups.

PREPARATION. Meanwhile, position a rack in the lower third of the oven so that the brown sugar at the bottom of the tin is closest to the heat, and preheat the oven to 325°F. Line 2 half-sheet or jelly-roll pans with parchment paper and place 1 half-sheet or jelly-roll pan on the oven floor to catch any drippings from the schnecken. (If the oven has a heating element on the oven floor, this can't be done, so place the half-sheet or jelly-roll pan directly under the muffin pan to collect any drippings.)

VANILLA ICE CREAM
YIELD: 1 QUART

2 cups milk

2 cups heavy cream

1 vanilla bean, split lengthwise

11 to 12 large egg yolks
   (225 grams or 1 cup)

1 cup sugar

2 teaspoons vanilla extract

triple in volume and hold its shape when dropped from the whisk, about 5 minutes. It should be very stiff.

Bring the bowl over to the saucepan. Gradually whisk about 1 cup of the hot cream mixture into the yolk mixture to temper it, then return the tempered mixture to the saucepan and whisk until combined. You want the mixture to be thick enough to coat a wooden spoon. (Run your finger through the custard on the back of the spoon. The custard is thick enough if the line remains.) Pour the mixture through a fine-mesh strainer or China cap into a large bowl. Place in an ice bath or refrigerate, uncovered, until chilled, stirring occasionally. Add the vanilla extract, then transfer the mixture to an ice-cream maker and freeze according to manufacturer's instructions.

GINGER CARAMEL SAUCE*

YIELD: ABOUT 2 CUPS

2 tablespoons finely chopped peeled fresh ginger

2⅓ cups packed brown sugar

1 generous cup light corn syrup

4 ounces (1 stick) unsalted butter

¾ cup heavy cream

1 teaspoon vanilla extract

This recipe can be made a few days ahead.

MAKE THE GINGER CARAMEL SAUCE. Puree the ginger in a mini food processor until smooth. Set aside. Place the brown sugar, corn syrup, and butter in a heavy-bottomed small saucepan and stir until the sugar dissolves and the butter has melted. Bring to a boil over high heat. When a candy thermometer reaches 230°F, remove the pan from the heat and add the pureed ginger, the cream, and vanilla, stirring until the mixture is smooth. Pour into an airtight container, cool to room temperature, then cover and refrigerate until ready to use.

ASSEMBLY

12 Filled Schnecken

Vanilla Ice Cream

12 tablespoons Ginger Caramel Sauce

SERVE THE DESSERT. Serve the schnecken by sitting it next to a quenelle (scoop) of vanilla ice cream that has a spoonful of ginger caramel sauce on top.

SOUR CREAM WAFFLES WITH AVOCADO ICE CREAM

You will need a waffle iron for this dessert, but it's worth it. This is a rich, full-bodied Scandinavian waffle with the classic tang of good sour cream. These sour cream waffles are good alone, dusted with confectioners' sugar, or laced with fruit coulis. But I like to serve them with homemade avocado ice cream. For a change of pace, make miniature-size waffles and stack them up like a club sandwich.

SPECIAL EQUIPMENT: ICE-CREAM MAKER • WAFFLE IRON

MAKE THE ICE CREAM. Place the milk and sugar in a small saucepan and heat over medium heat, stirring occasionally, just until the sugar has dissolved. Pour into a large bowl, add the cream, and refrigerate until cold, at least 1 hour.

Peel and pit the avocados. Puree with 1 tablespoon of the lime juice in a food processor until smooth. When the cream mixture is cold, add the remaining 3 tablespoons lime juice and the avocado puree and mix well. Taste and add extra sugar if needed. Transfer to an ice-cream maker and freeze according to manufacturer's instructions.

AVOCADO ICE CREAM

YIELD: 1½ QUARTS

2 cups milk

1¼ cups sugar

2 cups heavy cream

4 ripe avocados

4 tablespoons freshly squeezed
   lime juice

1 cup sugar

MAKE THE WAFFLES. Place the eggs and sugar in the bowl of an electric mixer fitted with the whisk attachment and beat on high until the eggs are thick, pale, and form a ribbon when dropped from the whisk.

Whisk the flour and ginger in a bowl. Fold half of the flour mixture into the egg mixture, fold in the sour cream, then fold in the remaining flour mixture. Gently stir in the melted butter and let the batter rest for 10 minutes.

Meanwhile, heat a waffle iron as the manufacturer directs. When the waffle iron is ready, ladle ¾ cup of the

WAFFLES

YIELD: 8 STANDARD WAFFLES

5 large eggs (250 grams or 1⅛ cups)

½ cup sugar

1 cup (120 grams) cake flour, sifted

1 teaspoon ground ginger

1 cup sour cream

4 ounces (1 stick) unsalted butter,
   melted

batter per waffle. Cover and bake as the manufacturer directs.

ASSEMBLY

8 Waffles

Avocado Ice Cream

SERVE THE DESSERT. Serve the waffles warm with the avocado ice cream. Cut the waffles into quarters for more servings, if you like. Or stack 2 waffles with ice cream in between, or form a tent with the waffles and have the ice cream centered inside.

NECTARINE AND ORANGE–FILLED STEAMED BUNS

MAKES 22 BUNS

I love dim sum, those varied small hors d'oeuvres and desserts served at Asian restaurants for brunch. This is a simple steamed bun filled with a thickened nectarine-orange fruit paste instead of the classic sweetened red-bean paste. I find that the nectarine filling is a great foil for the chewy white dough. These take a bit of time to steam, as it has to be done in batches. But you can also bake them all at once, if you prefer.

MAKE THE FILLING. Combine all the ingredients in a medium saucepan and cook over low heat, stirring constantly, until thick, about 5 minutes. Cool to room temperature. Puree in a food processor until smooth, then refrigerate.

NECTARINE FILLING

YIELD: ABOUT 2 CUPS

12 ounces dried nectarines, chopped

½ cup orange marmalade

½ cup sliced blanched almonds, finely chopped

3 tablespoons freshly squeezed lemon juice

1 teaspoon finely grated orange zest

½ teaspoon ground cinnamon

MAKE THE BUNS. Crumble the fresh yeast into a small bowl and sprinkle with the sugar. Stir the mixture for a minute or two until it forms a thin syrup. Add the water and stir to combine. (If using dry yeast, add sugar and tepid water to the yeast, and stir into a smooth paste. Set aside until doubled and foamy.)

Place the flour in the bowl of an electric mixer fitted with the paddle attachment and mix in the yeast mixture and milk. Knead the dough until smooth and elastic, about 10 minutes. Transfer to a large bowl, cover with plastic wrap, and let rise until doubled in size, about 1½ hours. Punch down the dough and let it rise again for another 30 minutes.

Turn the dough out onto a lightly floured work surface and form into a roll about 22 inches long. Slice the roll into

STEAMED BUNS

YIELD: 22 BUNS

1 cake (0.6 ounce) fresh yeast or 1 package active dry yeast

1 tablespoon sugar

¼ cup warm water (90°F to 110°F)

4 cups (560 grams) all-purpose flour, sifted

1¼ cups milk, scalded and cooled

2 cups Nectarine Filling

PREPARATION. Cut out twenty-two 2-inch squares of parchment paper.

1-inch rounds. Flatten each round and roll into a 4-inch round. Place 1 heaping tablespoon of filling in the center of a round and bring the dough up and around the filling, drawing the outer edge to the center a little at a time until the filling is completely enclosed in loose folds that join in the center and the dumpling has a round shape. Twist the folded dough in the center so it's firmly sealed. Place the dumpling, folded side down, on a 2-inch square of parchment paper and place on an 18 X 13–inch half-sheet or jelly-roll pan. Repeat with remaining dough and filling. Cover the buns with plastic wrap and let rise for 30 minutes, if baking immediately; or wrap and freeze the dough for up to 1 week. When ready to bake, thaw the dough and, when at room temperature, let it rise for 30 minutes.

STEAM THE BUNS. Bring water to a boil in a rice steamer fitted with a rack with holes. Or use a pot fitted with a collapsible steamer rack or a colander. Steam about 5 buns at a time, for about 1 hour. (If removed too soon, they deflate.) The buns will be puffed but will not color. Transfer the buns to a warm platter and keep soft by covering them with a slightly damp warm kitchen towel. (Or bake the buns in a 350°F oven for 15 to 18 minutes, rotating the pan after about 10 minutes.)

◆ I KEEP THE STEAMED BUNS WARM BY WRAPPING THEM IN FOIL AND LEAVING THEM NEAR A WARM OVEN.

NECTARINE ORANGE SAUCE

YIELD: ABOUT 3½ CUPS

½ pound dried nectarines

2 to 3 cups freshly squeezed orange juice (from about 10 oranges)

MAKE THE SAUCE. Place the nectarines in a medium saucepan in enough boiling water to cover and bring to a boil. Cook over low heat until very soft, about 20 minutes. Cool and puree the nectarines and liquid with the orange juice in a food processor until smooth, in batches if necessary. Press the mixture through a fine-mesh stainless-steel strainer or China cap.

ASSEMBLY

22 Steamed Buns

3½ cups Nectarine Orange Sauce

SERVE THE DESSERT. Serve the buns, 2 per person, as soon as they are ready. If the finished buns have cooled, microwave on medium-high for 15 seconds. Drizzle with warm nectarine orange sauce—the perfect accompaniment.

SWEET CORN BRÛLÉE

This is a succulent, creamy corn custard; a brûlée filling without the "burnt" sugar crust and, for me, as good as anything I've ever eaten. It is a rich, warm custard so imbued with the flavor of sweet white corn that it's perfect on its own. I originally made this to serve as a vegetable side dish, but it turned out to be fabulous for dessert. It still makes a great vegetable accompaniment, topped with some medium-sharp Cheddar cheese.

MAKE THE CORN BRÛLÉE. Puree the corn in a food processor until smooth, then drain in a fine-mesh strainer set over a bowl for 30 minutes. Place the eggs in a large bowl and lightly stir with a whisk just enough to break them up and combine. Add the cream, sugar, flour, baking powder, salt, and melted butter to the eggs and stir until smooth. Add the drained corn and mix well. Pour the mixture into the baking dish and set in the water bath. Bake for 45 minutes, or until lightly golden and a knife inserted in the center comes out clean. Serve warm from the pan or chilled and cut into squares.

VARIATION. *To serve the pudding as a vegetable accompaniment, reduce the sugar to 2 tablespoons.*

◆ YOU CAN USE FROZEN CORN. JUST THAW, THEN PUREE AND DRAIN AS DIRECTED IN THE RECIPE.

CORN BRÛLÉE

3 cups white Silver Queen corn kernels (from about 6 ears)

6 large eggs (300 grams or 1⅓ cups)

3 cups heavy cream

½ cup sugar

1 teaspoon (3 grams) all-purpose flour, sifted

½ teaspoon baking powder

½ teaspoon salt

2 teaspoons unsalted butter, melted

PREPARATION. Position a rack in the middle of the oven and preheat the oven to 325°F. Place a shallow roasting pan large enough to hold a 13 X 9–inch glass baking dish in the oven and fill one-third full with water.

"THE ONE" SWEET ROLLS WITH CRANBERRY PEAR MARMALADE AND BUTTERSCOTCH ICE CREAM

SERVES 12

These sweet rolls are a favorite of mine and similar to a roll developed by Mal Krinn, a world-class bread baker at the Wheaton bakery in Maryland. I wanted to come up with my own version of his rolls, but it was quite a challenge, as I wanted them to be like schnecken but lighter and with less filling. After coming up with a recipe that I really liked, I burst out with "That's it. That's the one!" And that's how these rolls came to be called "The One."

SPECIAL EQUIPMENT: ICE-CREAM MAKER

"THE ONE" SWEET ROLL DOUGH

YIELD: ENOUGH FOR 12 ROLLS

2 cakes (0.6 ounce each) fresh yeast or
  1 tablespoon and 2 teaspoons active
  dry yeast
(¼ cup tepid water [90°F to 110°F]
  if using dry yeast)
½ cup plus 1 tablespoon sugar
3½ cups (490 grams) all-purpose flour,
  sifted
½ teaspoon salt
3 large eggs (150 grams or ⅔ cup)
⅔ cup sour cream
2 tablespoons vegetable oil
2 ounces (½ stick) unsalted butter,
  at room temperature

MAKE THE DOUGH. Crumble the fresh yeast with your fingertips into a small bowl. Add 1 tablespoon of the sugar and mix together. As you stir the mixture, the sugar and yeast will dissolve. The mixture will first become a thick paste, then a thin syrup. Set aside. (If using dry yeast, add the 1 tablespoon sugar and tepid water to the yeast and stir into a smooth paste.)

Place the flour, salt, and the remaining ½ cup sugar in the bowl of an electric mixer fitted with the paddle attachment. Mix on low speed to combine. Add the yeast mixture, eggs, sour cream, and oil all at once, being sure to scrape all the yeast into the bowl. Mix on low speed until combined. Add the butter several tablespoons at a time and continue to beat until thoroughly incorporated. The dough will be loose and sticky at this point. Beat on medium speed for about 1 minute to bring the dough together and ensure all ingredients are thoroughly mixed. The dough will feel damp and slightly sticky to the touch.

Transfer the dough to a large bowl. Cover with plastic wrap and let rise at room temperature until doubled in size. Punch down the dough. Cover with plastic wrap and refrigerate for at least 2 hours or up to 5 hours. The longer the dough is chilled, the less sticky and easier it will be to work with.

MAKE THE FILLING. Place all the ingredients in the bowl of an electric mixer fitted with the paddle attachment. Mix on low speed until all the ingredients are incorporated and form a smooth paste. Set aside. If not using the filling the same day, cover with plastic wrap and refrigerate. To bring the filling back to a spreadable consistency after refrigeration, place in the microwave and heat on high power at 20-second intervals, stirring until smooth.

FILL THE SWEET ROLLS. Roll out the dough on a lightly floured surface to a rectangle approximately 18 inches long, 8 inches wide, and ¼ inch thick. Spread a thin layer of filling on top of the dough using an offset metal spatula, leaving a ½-inch border all around.

With a long side near you, roll the dough up jelly-roll fashion into a tight log. When finished, use your hands to shape the dough into a uniform log. Score the top of the dough with a thin-bladed knife into twelve 1½-inch portions, then slice the dough into individual rolls. Place 6 rolls, cut side down, in each prepared round pan, spacing them evenly so that there is enough space for each roll to rise. Cover loosely with plastic wrap and let rise at room temperature until doubled in size, about 45 minutes to 1 hour, if using immediately; otherwise, refrigerate the rolls overnight, then let them rise at room temperature, about 1½ hours. When proofed, the dough should feel light and springy to the touch.

Meanwhile, position a rack on the lowest level of the oven and preheat the oven to 350°F.

FILLING

YIELD: ENOUGH TO FILL 12 ROLLS

4 ounces (1 stick) unsalted butter, at room temperature

1¼ cups packed light brown sugar

1 teaspoon ground cinnamon

¾ teaspoon salt

1 teaspoon vanilla extract

FILLED SWEET ROLLS

YIELD: 12 ROLLS

"The One" Sweet Roll Dough
Filling

PREPARATION. Generously butter two 9 x 2–inch round cake pans, line the bottoms with parchment paper, and butter the paper. If the filling has been refrigerated, bring it to room temperature. Have ready 2 half-sheet or jelly-roll pans lined with parchment paper to place the baked rolls upon.

◆ I RAISE (PROOF) DOUGH IN A PROOFING BOX. IT IS A CLOSED ENVIRONMENT SET AT A TEMPERATURE OPTIMAL FOR THE RISING. LETTING DOUGH RISE IN A GAS OVEN WITH ONLY THE PILOT LIGHT ON WILL GIVE YOU A SIMILAR EFFECT.

BAKE THE ROLLS. Bake the rolls for 20 minutes, rotate the pans from front to back, and bake for another 10 minutes, or until the rolls are dark golden. Remove the rolls from the oven, immediately invert onto the prepared half-sheet or jelly-roll pans, and lift the round pan off the rolls and remove the parchment. These rolls are best eaten warm out of the oven. They do not freeze or keep as well as the schnecken.

CRANBERRY PEAR MARMALADE

YIELD: 2 CUPS

1 (12-ounce) bag fresh or frozen cranberries

1 tablespoon finely grated orange zest (from 1 large orange)

1 cup sugar

1 cup water

2 ripe Bartlett pears, peeled, cored, and diced to ¼-inch pieces

MAKE THE MARMALADE. Place the cranberries, orange zest, sugar, and water in a medium saucepan. Bring to a boil, stirring often. When the cranberries begin to pop, reduce the heat to low and cook, stirring frequently, until the sauce thickens, about 7 minutes. Remove from the heat; let cool. Stir in the pears. Refrigerated, the marmalade will remain fresh for up to 1 week. To use, gently reheat in a saucepan over medium-low heat.

ICE-CREAM BASE

YIELD: ENOUGH FOR 1 QUART OF ICE CREAM

2 cups milk

2 cups heavy cream

1 vanilla bean, split lengthwise

11 to 12 large egg yolks (225 grams or 1 liquid cup)

½ cup sugar

MAKE THE ICE-CREAM BASE. Place the milk and cream in a heavy, nonreactive or stainless-steel medium saucepan. Use the back of a knife to scrape the seeds from the vanilla bean and place the seeds and pod in the saucepan. Bring to a rolling boil over medium-high heat. Let the mixture rise up the side of the pan, then immediately remove from the heat.

Meanwhile, beat the egg yolks and sugar on high speed in the bowl of an electric mixer fitted with the whisk attachment until very thick and pale. The mixture will triple in volume and hold its shape when dropped from the whisk. It should be very stiff. This will take about 5 minutes.

Bring the bowl over to the saucepan. Gradually whisk about 1 cup of the hot cream mixture into the yolk mixture to temper it, then pour the tempered mixture into the saucepan and whisk until combined. The mixture should be thick enough to coat a wooden spoon. (Run your finger through the custard on the back of the spoon. The custard is thick enough if the line remains.) Pour the custard through a fine-mesh stainless-steel strainer or China cap into a large bowl. Set aside.

MAKE THE ICE CREAM. Melt the butter in a heavy-bottomed small saucepan over low heat. Add the brown sugar and cook, stirring often, until the sugar becomes a deep brown syrup, about 10 minutes. Stir into the warm ice-cream base. Add the vanilla and stir to combine. Place in the refrigerator until well chilled, at least 2 hours. Transfer the mixture to an ice-cream maker and freeze according to the manufacturer's instructions.

BUTTERSCOTCH ICE CREAM
YIELD: 1 QUART
4 ounces (1 stick) unsalted butter
⅔ cup packed light brown sugar
Warm ice-cream base
1 tablespoon vanilla extract

SERVE THE DESSERT. Serve "The One" warm in large shallow bowls accompanied by scoops of butterscotch ice cream and some cranberry pear marmalade.

ASSEMBLY
12 Filled Sweet Rolls
Butterscotch Ice Cream
2 cups Cranberry Pear Marmalade

TOASTED COCONUT PECAN SOUFFLÉ TARTLETS

MAKES 8 TARTLETS

When I worked at The Big Cheese restaurant in Georgetown, we had a toasted coconut pecan pie on the menu, and it was one of the most popular desserts. I thought that lightening it up a bit would make it more modern and that placing the filling in individual tartlet shells would turn it into a more interesting dessert. Easy to prepare at the last moment, this dessert is really an old-fashioned pie turned soufflé.

SPECIAL EQUIPMENT: 4-INCH ROUND PASTRY CUTTER • TWELVE 4-INCH TARTLET PANS

TARTLET SHELLS

YIELD: TWELVE 4-INCH TARTLET SHELLS (THIS GIVES YOU A FEW EXTRA IN CASE OF BREAKAGE)

10 ounces (2½ sticks) unsalted butter, at room temperature

1 cup confectioners' sugar, sifted

1 large egg (50 grams or ¼ cup)

1 large egg yolk (20 grams or 1 tablespoon)

1½ teaspoons vanilla extract

4 cups (480 grams) cake flour, sifted

PREPARATION. Position a rack in the middle of the oven and preheat the oven to 275°F. Have ready an 18 X 13–inch half-sheet or jelly-roll pan.

MAKE THE SWEET DOUGH. Place the butter and confectioners' sugar in the bowl of an electric mixer fitted with the paddle attachment and beat on low speed until well combined. Beat in the egg, egg yolk, and vanilla until just combined. Gradually add the cake flour in three additions, mixing until the flour is barely incorporated into the mixture. Finish by removing the bowl from the mixer and mixing by hand with a rubber spatula until well blended, being sure to scrap the bottom of the bowl. Wrap the dough in plastic wrap and refrigerate for at least 1 hour or up to 24 hours.

MAKE THE TARTLET SHELLS. Remove the dough from the refrigerator and divide into three equal pieces. Work with 1 piece of dough at a time, keeping the other pieces refrigerated. Cut the dough into small pieces and work them with the heel of your hand against the work surface to make the dough more malleable and easier to work with. Shape the dough into a disk and repeat with the remaining pieces. Each piece yields about 4 tartlet shells.

Roll each disk of dough out on a lightly floured surface to ⅛-inch thickness. Cut out a total of 12 rounds with a 4-inch round pastry cutter. Use a metal spatula to lift and transfer them to twelve 4-inch tartlet pans. Use your fingertips to firmly press the dough onto the bottom and sides of the pans, pushing the excess up over the edges of the pans. Use the back of a knife to trim off any excess from around the edges. Prick the dough all over with a fork, cover with plastic wrap, and refrigerate at least 1 hour, until well chilled and firm, or up to 24 hours.

Place the tartlet shells on an 18 X 13–inch half-sheet or jelly-roll pan. Bake for 7 minutes, rotate the pan from front to back, and bake for 7 minutes more, or until the shells are light golden and set. Cool the shells in their pans for 10 minutes, then invert the pans to remove the shells. The shells made with sweet dough must be removed from the tartlet pans within 10 minutes after baking or they will crack.

Wrap in plastic wrap and refrigerate immediately if not using right away.

MAKE THE SOUFFLÉ. Place the coconut on a half-sheet or jelly-roll pan and toast for 4 to 6 minutes, or until lightly colored. Remove from the oven and set aside. Increase the oven temperature to 400°F.

With a metal whisk, beat the egg yolks with 1 tablespoon of the sugar in a medium bowl until very thick and pale. Place the egg whites with the lemon juice in another bowl and whip with a handheld mixer until foamy and just beginning to hold a shape. Gradually add the remaining 1 tablespoon sugar, beating until the whites form stiff, glossy peaks. Stir the toasted coconut, the pecans, and vanilla into the yolk mixture, then gradually fold into the whites until just blended.

ASSEMBLE THE TARTLETS. Spoon the soufflé mixture into the tartlet shells and bake for 8 to 10 minutes, or until puffed and browned on top. This soufflé really needs no accompaniment, but it pairs well with a scoop of Coconut Sorbet (page 292).

PECAN PIE SOUFFLÉ

YIELD: ENOUGH TO FILL 8 TARTLET SHELLS

⅓ cup unsweetened shredded or grated coconut (preferably unsulphured)

2 large egg yolks (40 grams or 2 tablespoons)

2 tablespoons sugar

3 large egg whites (90 grams or ⅓ cup)

1 teaspoon freshly squeezed lemon juice

¼ cup pecans, chopped

1 teaspoon vanilla extract

ASSEMBLY

YIELD: 8 TARTLET SHELLS

Pecan Pie Soufflé

8 Tartlet Shells

PREPARATION. Preheat the oven to 325°F.

TRUFFLED BROWNIE SOUFFLÉ

When we were going over this recipe, Lydia Schlosser, our resident tester, remarked that it was the best chocolate soufflé she had ever eaten, simply because it was so choco-latey. Though most chocolate soufflés are very light, they lack deep chocolate flavor. Here, bittersweet chocolate and unsweetened cocoa are used, which really intensifies the chocolate flavor. I like to serve this soufflé with just a fluff of lightly sweetened whipped cream.

SPECIAL EQUIPMENT: SIX 6-OUNCE SOUFFLÉ DISHES

PASTRY CREAM

YIELD: 1 CUP

¼ cup sugar

2 tablespoons (16 grams) cake flour

1 cup milk

4 large egg yolks (80 grams or ⅓ cup)

1 tablespoon unsalted butter

MAKE THE PASTRY CREAM. Sift the sugar and flour in a bowl, whisking to remove any lumps. This will ensure the pastry cream is smooth.

Bring the milk to a boil in a medium saucepan.

Meanwhile, place the egg yolks in a bowl and mix with a handheld mixer on high speed for about 2 minutes. Add the flour mixture and continue to beat on high until the egg mixture is thick, heavy, and pale. Remove the bowl from the mixer and bring it over to the stove.

When the milk comes to a rolling boil, rising up the side of the pan, reduce the heat to low. Gradually whisk several spoonfuls of the hot milk into the egg mixture to temper it, then return the tempered mixture to the saucepan and continue to cook, stirring constantly, until the pastry cream begins to bubble or "burp." Cook it for 2 additional minutes to prevent a floury aftertaste.

Remove the pan from the heat and whisk in the butter until combined. Pour the cream into a bowl and tightly press a piece of plastic wrap directly onto the surface, leaving only a small area uncovered for the heat to escape. This will prevent a skin from forming on the surface. If you are planning to make the soufflé immediately, you do not need to chill the pastry cream before using it.

Otherwise, refrigerate until chilled, then cover completely with plastic wrap. The pastry cream may be made up to 4 days in advance and kept refrigerated until you are ready to use it.

MAKE THE SOUFFLÉ. Combine the pastry cream, melted chocolate, egg yolks, 2½ tablespoons of the sugar, and the cocoa in a nonstick medium skillet and whisk over low heat until smooth and creamy. The mixture should be smooth and loose enough so the egg whites mix in easily. The chocolate mixture will be rather firm if allowed to cool, so keep it off the heat but near the stove while the egg whites are beating

Beat the egg whites with the lemon juice on high speed in the bowl of an electric mixer fitted with the whisk attachment until foamy and just beginning to hold a shape. Gradually beat in the remaining 2½ tablespoons sugar and continue to beat until the whites form stiff, glossy peaks.

Gently stir in about one-quarter of the beaten egg whites into the chocolate mixture to lighten the mixture. Fold in the remaining egg whites until just blended. Divide evenly among the prepared dishes and bake for 8 to 10 minutes, or until puffed and browned. Serve the soufflés immediately.

◆ SOMETIMES I FIND IT NECESSARY TO KEEP THE WHITES BEATING ON VERY LOW SPEED WHILE I PLACE THE CREAMED CHOCOLATE MIXTURE BACK ON THE HEAT TO WARM AND LOOSEN IT UP ENOUGH SO THAT THE EGG WHITES WILL MIX IN EASILY AND NOT BREAK DOWN.

SOUFFLÉ

YIELD: SIX 6-OUNCE SOUFFLÉ DISHES

3 tablespoons Pastry Cream

4 ounces bittersweet chocolate, melted

3 large egg yolks (60 grams or ¼ cup)

5 tablespoons sugar

1 tablespoon natural or Dutch-processed cocoa

3 egg whites (90 grams or ⅓ cup)

1 teaspoon freshly squeezed lemon juice

PREPARATION. Preheat the oven to 400°F. Butter and sugar six 6-ounce soufflé dishes and refrigerate until ready to fill.

TWO-TONE THAI STICKY RICE

SERVES 8 TO 10

I just love sticky rice with mangos. Here, I took two different types of rice, steamed them, layered them in a rice mold, and paired it with fresh mango. Years ago, when I worked for Chanterelle Caterers in Washington, D.C., a wonderful Thai cook named Chin invited me to her annual New Year's Day party, where she always served Thai sticky rice with mangos. The rice was so fragrant with coconut that it was incredibly addictive. There are many varieties of rice at the Asian market where I shop, including white sweet (sticky) rice and black sweet (sticky) rice. When cooked, the white rice becomes soft and the black rice retains a slight crunch, making this a different and interesting dessert.

I bought some beautiful rice molds at Takashimaya in New York City. I first saw the rice molds used when Ellen Greaves, former executive chef at Takashimaya, made her Bento Box demonstration. She used the molds to form her rice salad.

SPECIAL EQUIPMENT: RICE MOLD OR 3-INCH ROUND PASTRY CUTTER

BLACK RICE

YIELD: 3 CUPS

1 cup black sweet (sticky) rice

5 cups water

¼ cup packed brown sugar

¾ cup frozen unsweetened coconut
   milk, thawed

MAKE THE BLACK RICE. Wash the rice and let it soak in enough water to cover in a bowl for 4 hours but preferably overnight. Drain, then rinse and drain again.

Place the rice and water in a microwave-safe bowl and cook on high power for 15 minutes, stirring every 3 to 4 minutes. Continue cooking until all the water has been absorbed and the rice is cooked but still firm. Mix in the brown sugar and coconut milk. Set aside.

WHITE RICE

YIELD: 3 CUPS

1 cup sweet (sticky) rice

1 cup water

½ cup frozen unsweetened coconut
   milk, thawed

3 tablespoons granulated sugar

MAKE THE WHITE RICE. Wash the rice and let it soak in enough water to cover in a bowl for 4 hours but preferably overnight. Drain, then rinse and drain again.

Place the rice and water in a microwave-safe bowl and cook on high power for 3 minutes. Stir and cook for an additional 3 minutes, then test for doneness. If rice still has a crunch to it (a hard kernel in the center), then microwave for an additional 2 minutes. While the rice is hot, mix in the coconut milk and sugar.

◆ FROZEN COCONUT MILK IS THE BEST KIND OF
COCONUT MILK TO BUY. SOURCED FROM ASIAN MARKETS,
THE FROZEN MILK'S FLAVOR IS MORE PURE AND NATURAL
THAN CANNED. LOOK FOR A COCONUT MILK WITHOUT
SUGAR OR OTHER ADDITIVES. FROZEN MILK USUALLY
DOES NOT CONTAIN THEM. IF COCONUT MILK IS NOT
AVAILABLE, YOU CAN USE FRESH FROZEN SHREDDED
COCONUT. ADD ENOUGH MILK TO GET THE QUANTITY
YOU NEED, AND PUREE IT IN THE BLENDER.

ASSEMBLE THE DESSERT. Fill a rice mold or 3-inch pastry
cutter halfway with black rice, pressing down firmly. Top
with white rice and tamp it down. Lift off the mold and
repeat with remaining rice. Serve immediately with sliced
mangos.

◆ IF YOU HAVE A RICE STEAMER, THEN BY ALL MEANS USE
IT, FOLLOWING THE MANUFACTURER'S INSTRUCTIONS.

ASSEMBLY

3 cups Black rice

3 cups White rice

3 sliced mangos

YEASTY DUMPLINGS
WITH MIXED-BERRY SOUP

Here, light and yeasty milk-poached dumplings float atop a fresh-tasting mixed-berry soup. Serve in the summer, when lighter desserts are preferable and berries are plentiful. I have added this dumpling to my dumpling repertoire as the one with yeast in it, which gives it a nice rise.

DUMPLINGS

YIELD: 24 DUMPLINGS

2 tablespoons sugar

1½ teaspoons active dry yeast

¼ cup tepid water (90°F to 110°F)

¾ cup tepid milk

2 tablespoons unsalted butter, melted

¼ teaspoon salt

2¼ cups (315 grams) all-purpose flour, sifted

POACHING LIQUID

YIELD: MAKES ENOUGH LIQUID FOR 2 BATCHES OF DUMPLINGS

3 cups milk

4 tablespoons unsalted butter

2 tablespoons sugar

MAKE THE DUMPLINGS. Stir 1 tablespoon of the sugar and the yeast, into the water. Set the yeast aside until doubled and foamy.

Place the milk, melted butter, remaining 1 tablespoon sugar, and the salt in the bowl of an electric mixer fitted with the paddle attachment and combine well on low speed. Add the yeast mixture, then the flour and mix until a smooth, elastic dough forms, about 15 minutes.

Remove the dough from the bowl and place in a clean large bowl. Cover with plastic wrap and let rise until doubled in size, about 1 hour. Punch down the dough, divide into 24 pieces, and shape into balls. Loosely cover with a clean kitchen towel and let rise until doubled in size, 15 to 20 minutes.

POACH THE DUMPLINGS. Combine ½ cup of the milk, 2 tablespoons of the butter, and 1 tablespoon of the sugar in a large deep skillet and bring to a boil. Arrange 12 dumplings in the pan in a single layer and cover tightly. Reduce the heat to low and simmer until all the liquid has been absorbed, about 15 minutes. Remove from the heat and keep warm until ready to serve. Repeat with the remainder of the milk, butter, and sugar, and poach the second batch of 12 dumplings.

As an alternative to poaching the dumplings, brush them with egg wash, sprinkle with sugar, and bake at 350°F for 6 to 8 minutes, or until puffed and golden.

MAKE THE BERRY SOUP. Puree the berries in a food processor until smooth. Press through a fine-mesh stainless-steel strainer or China cap into a large bowl. Add the wine and orange juice. Add sugar to taste and mix well.

SERVE THE DESSERT. Serve the warm dumplings in large shallow bowls, three dumplings per serving, surrounded by the mixed-berry soup.

MIXED-BERRY SOUP

YIELD: ABOUT 8 CUPS

2 pints strawberries

2 pints raspberries

2 pints blackberries

1 cup Moscato d'Asti or Moscato Rosa

2 cups freshly squeezed orange juice

Sugar to taste

ASSEMBLY

24 Dumplings

8 cups Mixed-Berry Soup, at room temperature

DESSERT SANDWICHES

ere, in dessert sandwiches, I have let whimsy take over. I just love the idea of sandwiches for dessert. And, really, the idea is as old as desserts themselves. After all, isn't a layer cake really just a cake "sandwich"? And so, with that in mind, I have used Danish dough, croissants, puff pastry, short-bread, sweet dough, yeast breads, nutted meringue, and even custards to create a varied array of sweet sandwiches, many of which are accompanied by silky sauces, smooth sorbets, or flavorful ice creams. These offerings are not only delicious and a little different, but they are also easy to prepare, since many of the components can be made ahead, frozen, and put together at the last moment. In some recipes, the "breads" are reheated so they are nice and warm when served. I have also included French classics such as the dacquoise and the succès, which are old-fashioned desserts that have come full circle in this chapter. By adding cashews to the dacquoise filling and espresso powder to the meringue in the succès, the two have been given a lift and become enticingly current.

APPLE MARMALADE SANDWICHES

SERVES 8

This is a perfect fall dessert! A sweet, aromatic marmalade made from tart apples and cranberries is sandwiched between crisp, buttery cookies and topped off with a refreshingly tangy cranberry coulis. Served in a pool of cranberry-spiked warm caramel sauce with a quenelle of vanilla caramel ice cream off to its side, this dessert is simply lovely. I served this at a James Beard Foundation dinner at Walley Joe's Restaurant and even shipped all the components, including the ice cream, to Mississippi with great success.

SPECIAL EQUIPMENT: 2¾-INCH SQUARE PASTRY CUTTER • ICE-CREAM MAKER

◆ THE 2¾-INCH SQUARE METAL CUTTER IS USUALLY PART OF A NESTED SET OF SQUARE CUTTERS AVAILABLE FROM J. B. PRINCE COMPANY. ATECO MAKES A SET AS WELL.

DOUGH SQUARES

YIELD: MAKES 16 DOUGH SQUARES

5 ounces (1 stick plus 2 tablespoons) unsalted butter, at room temperature

½ cup confectioners' sugar, sifted

½ large egg (25 grams or ⅛ cup or 2 tablespoons)

½ large egg yolk (10 grams or 1½ teaspoons)

¾ teaspoon vanilla extract

1⅞ cups (225 grams) cake flour, sifted

PREPARATION. Line two 18 X 13–inch half-sheet or jelly-roll pans or cookie sheets with parchment paper.

MAKE THE DOUGH. Place the butter and confectioners' sugar in the bowl of an electric mixer fitted with the paddle attachment and beat on low speed until well combined. Beat in the egg, egg yolk, and vanilla until just combined, then gradually add the flour in three additions, mixing until it is barely incorporated. Finish the mixing with a rubber spatula until well blended. Wrap the dough in plastic wrap and refrigerate for at least 1 hour or up to 24 hours.

Divide the dough into 2 equal pieces. Work with 1 piece at a time, keeping the other piece chilled. Roll out the piece of dough on a lightly floured surface to ⅛-inch thickness and cut into 8 squares with a 2¾-inch square pastry cutter. Repeat with the second piece of dough, using the scraps from the first mixed in.

Place the squares on the prepared pans, 1 inch apart, prick the dough in a few places with a fork, and cover with plastic wrap. Refrigerate for at least 1 hour or up to 24 hours.

BAKE THE DOUGH SQUARES. Bake the cookies for 6 minutes, rotate the pans from front to back, and bake for 6 more minutes, or until medium brown. (The slower baking allows the squares to develop a more even color.) Transfer the squares to racks to cool completely.

PREPARATION. Position racks in the middle and lower third of the oven and preheat the oven to 275°F.

◆ I USUALLY BAKE ONE TRAY AT A TIME, SO THAT EACH TRAY GETS MORE EVEN HEAT.

MAKE THE MARMALADE. Peel, core, and chop the apples into medium chunks. Place the apple chunks, sugar, and cranberries in a heavy large saucepan. Cover and cook over low heat, stirring often, until the apples have softened and can be broken up with a spoon, 2 to 3 minutes. Stir in the apricot jam. Cook uncovered over medium-high heat, stirring constantly, about 1 minute. The apples should still have their shape. Remove from the heat and stir in the orange zest and vanilla. Set aside.

VARIATION. *You can vary the flavor by adding 2 tablespoons of Calvados or dark rum. Use only 1 teaspoon vanilla.*

APPLE MARMALADE
YIELD: APPROXIMATELY 4 CUPS

8 McIntosh apples (approximately 2½ pounds)

½ cup sugar

½ cup dried cranberries

½ cup apricot jam

1 tablespoon finely grated orange zest (from 1 large orange)

2 teaspoons vanilla extract

MAKE THE COULIS. Place the cranberries, sugar, ½ cup of the sherry, and the water in a medium saucepan. Cook over medium heat, stirring occasionally, until the berries begin to pop, about 5 minutes. Remove from the heat and cool until tepid. Transfer the mixture to a blender or food processor and puree until smooth. Press through a fine-mesh strainer or China cap set over a bowl to remove the skins and tiny seeds. Thin the coulis with the orange juice

CRANBERRY COULIS
YIELD: 3¼ CUPS

1 (12-ounce) bag fresh or frozen cranberries

1 cup sugar

¾ cup cream sherry, preferably Harvey's Bristol Cream

½ cup water

½ cup freshly squeezed orange juice

and the remaining ¼ cup sherry. Cover with plastic wrap and set aside. Refrigerated in an airtight container, the coulis will remain fresh for 1 week.

CARAMEL SAUCE

YIELD: 1⅔ CUP

1½ cups sugar

½ cup water

1 cup heavy cream

◆ I AM ALWAYS WELL PROTECTED WHEN MAKING CARAMEL SAUCE. I RECOMMEND WEARING A LONG-SLEEVED SHIRT AND HEAVY-DUTY OVEN MITTS SO EVERY PART OF YOUR ARM IS COVERED TO PROTECT YOURSELF FROM THE STEAM OR ANY SPATTERING CARAMEL.

PREPARATION. Have ready a pastry brush and long-handled wire whisk.

MAKE THE CARAMEL SAUCE. Place the sugar and water in a heavy-bottomed medium saucepan over medium heat and bring to a boil. Stir the mixture with a wooden spoon just until it comes to a boil. Stirring the sugar-water mixture helps the sugar dissolve completely, preventing the mixture from crystallizing, which can happen when just one sugar crystal remains undissolved.

Dip a pastry brush in water and run it around the inside of the saucepan just above the level of the sugar to wash away any undissolved sugar. Move the pan gently back and forth over the burner to ensure even heat distribution. The sugar will first turn golden, then nut-colored. When it smells like caramel, is dark amber, and gives off little wisps of smoke, immediately remove from the heat. The caramel can burn very quickly at this point. Wearing oven mitts, stand back a bit and quickly add the heavy cream, whisking rapidly as you pour. The sugar will bubble up and may spatter, but continue to stir until all the cream has been absorbed and the caramel is smooth. Cool the caramel and set aside.

VANILLA CARAMEL ICE CREAM

YIELD: 1 QUART

2 cups heavy cream

2 cups milk

1 vanilla bean, split lengthwise

11 to 12 large egg yolks (225 grams or 1 cup)

¾ cup plus 1 tablespoon sugar

1 teaspoon vanilla extract

1 cup Caramel Sauce

MAKE THE ICE CREAM. Place the cream and milk in a medium saucepan. With the back of a knife, scrape out the seeds from the vanilla bean and add the seeds and pod to the pan. Heat the cream and milk over medium-high heat until it rises up the side of the pot and comes to a boil. Immediately remove from the heat.

Meanwhile, beat the egg yolks and sugar on high speed in the bowl of an electric mixer fitted with the whisk attachment until thick, pale, and the sugar has dissolved.

Bring the bowl over to the saucepan. Gradually add about 1 cup of the hot cream mixture to the yolk mixture to temper it, then pour the tempered mixture back into the saucepan and continue to whisk off the heat until the mixture coats the back of a spoon, 2 to 3 minutes. (Run your finger through the custard on the back of the spoon. The custard is thick enough if the line remains.)

After I temper the eggs with the milk and cream, I do not give the mixture any more heat. The cream mixture is hot enough to cook the eggs. This technique prevents the ice-cream base from overcooking and curdling.

Pour the ice-cream base through a fine-mesh strainer or China cap set over a bowl. Refrigerate, uncovered, or place in an ice bath, stirring occasionally until cold. Add the vanilla. Transfer to an ice-cream maker and freeze according to the manufacturer's instructions. When well chilled but still soft, swirl the caramel sauce through the ice cream.

ASSEMBLE THE SANDWICHES. On a plate, draw a circle of the caramel cranberry sauce mixture using a plastic squeeze bottle. Place one of the sweet dough squares in the center. Gently place a 2¾-inch square metal cutter on top of the square in the middle. Spoon the apple marmalade into the cutter, filling it to the top, then smooth it with the back of a spoon, being sure to gently tamp it down to compact it. Carefully lift off the cutter, taking care not to break the square. Spoon 2 tablespoons of cranberry coulis over the apple marmalade filling, letting it run down the sides, then place a second square of sweet dough on top. Off to the side and directly over a portion of the caramel sauce, place a quenelle (scoop) of vanilla caramel ice cream. Repeat to make 7 more sandwiches. Serve at once.

ASSEMBLY

⅔ cup Caramel Sauce mixed
    with 1¼ cups Cranberry Coulis
16 Dough Squares
4 cups Apple Marmalade, at room
    temperature
2 cups Cranberry Coulis
Vanilla Caramel Ice Cream

VARIATION. *I sometimes add 2 or 3 paper-thin slices of Maryland Strudel (page 114) fanned out to help anchor the ice cream and keep it from sliding.*

APRICOT AND CUSTARD
DANISH SANDWICHES

MAKES 8 SANDWICHES

Danish dough is similar to croissant dough, but with the addition of eggs. The dough is flaky, buttery, and tender. Danish pastry was one of the first pastries I made at the beginning of my career, one of the first desserts that I was ever written up for. Here, orange zest enhances the flavor and takes the Danish to another level. After all these years, I still love the flavor of this Danish and think it stands up well to any I have tasted. I have transformed the dough into stacked sandwiches that are filled with sweet pastry cream and fragrant apricot puree. I love the idea of serving these sandwiches warm after a soup-and-salad supper, especially in the winter.

SPECIAL EQUIPMENT: CHEESE SLICER, TRUFFLE SLICER, MANDOLINE, OR ADJUSTABLE VEGETABLE SLICER

DANISH SANDWICHES

YIELD: ENOUGH FOR 8 SANDWICHES

½ pound (2 sticks) cold unsalted butter
   plus 1 tablespoon diced

2 cups plus 2 tablespoons (300 grams)
   all-purpose flour, sifted

½ cup (60 grams) cake flour, sifted

⅛ teaspoon salt

1 (0.6-ounce) cake fresh yeast or
   1 envelope active dry yeast

¼ cup sugar

1 large egg (50 grams or ¼ cup)

¼ cup cold milk

½ cup chilled water

1 teaspoon vanilla extract

¼ cup water

1 large egg lightly beaten with
   1 tablespoon water, for egg wash

1 cup granulated sugar

PREPARE THE BUTTER. Dust each stick of butter with a little all-purpose flour. Use a cheese slicer, truffle slicer, mandoline, or adjustable vegetable slicer to thinly slice each stick of butter into 7 lengthwise slices. You should end up with 14 thin 5 X 1–inch slices of butter in all. Divide them into 3 groups (2 groups will have an additional slice). Place each group on parchment paper, long sides slightly overlapping, and press them together to form three 5 X 4–inch "sheets" of butter. Refrigerate until ready to use.

MAKE THE DANISH DOUGH. Place the all-purpose and cake flours, salt, and the 1 tablespoon diced butter in the bowl of an electric mixer fitted with the paddle attachment and mix on low speed. Crumble the yeast with your fingertips into a small bowl. Add 1 tablespoon of sugar to the yeast and stir until it forms a thin syrup. Quickly add the yeast mixture, egg, milk, chilled water, vanilla, and the remaining sugar to the mixer and mix until the dough comes together around the paddle attachment, about 2 minutes. It should feel damp and slightly sticky to the touch. If the dough is at all dry, add the extra ¼ cup water a little at a time. (If using dry yeast, place the dough into a small bowl, add two tablespoons of sugar and ¼ cup warm water, 90°F to 110°F, and proof for 5 minutes. Extra water may not be needed.)

Remove the dough from the bowl and with your hands, pat and stretch it into a square; the size is not important. Wrap the dough in plastic wrap and refrigerate for 15 minutes.

Remove the dough and the sheets of butter from the refrigerator and let them warm up until the dough and the butter are of the same consistency and temperature. They should not feel cold to the touch.

ADD THE BUTTER. Roll out the chilled dough on a lightly floured work surface to a rectangle about 16 inches long and 5 inches wide. See the diagram at right. Use a ruler as a guide to mark the dough crosswise into fourths without cutting all the way through the dough (1). Place one 5 X 4–inch sheet of room-temperature butter on the section of dough immediately left of center. Place the butter so it covers that entire section of dough (2). Fold over the flap of dough to its left, bringing it toward the center of the dough, enclosing the butter in the dough. The dough should now be in 3 sections (3). Place a second sheet of butter in the middle section (4) and fold the right section of dough over the butter. You now have 2 sections of dough visible (5). Place the remaining sheet of butter on top of the left section (6) and fold the other half of the dough over it (7). The dough should be roughly 6 X 4 inches.

Rolling forward with a rolling pin, roll out the dough to a rectangle approximately 14 inches long and 6 inches wide. Fold the rectangle into thirds to create a rectangle roughly 6 X 4 inches. Use a pastry brush to brush off any

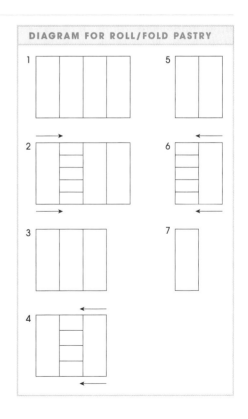

DIAGRAM FOR ROLL/FOLD PASTRY

excess flour. Place the dough on an 18 X 13–inch half-sheet or jelly-roll pan, cover with plastic wrap, and refrigerate for 15 minutes. Or, if the room is cool, leave out for 15 minutes. The first turn (which is made up of 4 turns), has now been completed. Repeat the rolling, folding, turning, and chilling of the dough 2 more times, beginning with rolling the pastry to form a rectangle 14 X 6 inches and ending after folding it into roughly a 6-inch square. The dimensions are not as important as the smoothness and homogenization of the butter throughout the dough. The dough should be uniform in color with no patches of butter showing through.

Place the dough on the half-sheet or jelly-roll pan lined with parchment paper. Wrap tightly in plastic wrap. Place the second pan upside down on top of the dough and wrap the pans together in plastic wrap. This will help keep the dough contained in the plastic wrap, and therefore moist, while rising overnight. Weight the pans with a heavy bowl or skillet and refrigerate for at least 3 hours or, even better, overnight.

PREPARATION. Have ready 2 parchment-lined 18 X 13–inch half-sheet or jelly-roll pans.

◆ SAVE ANY REMAINING DOUGH SCRAPS BY GATHERING THEM NEATLY INTO A MASS. EITHER FREEZE THEM TO USE LATER OR SIMPLY ROLL THEM OUT, BRUSH WITH EGG WASH, AND SPRINKLE WITH SUGAR. ALLOW TO RISE FOR 30 MINUTES AND BAKE.

MAKE THE DANISH SQUARES. Remove the chilled dough and cut it into 4 equal pieces. Return the other pieces to the refrigerator. Roll out the dough into a strip about 10 inches long, fold it into thirds (this is another turn, and the secret to getting a great even rise), and roll again to a strip about 10 inches long. Fold into thirds again. Then roll the dough into a strip about 12 inches long, 4½ inches wide, and ⅓ inch thick. Trim all edges, then cut into 4-inch squares using a trowel, pizza cutter, or knife. Repeat with the remaining 3 pieces of dough, giving each the 2 final turns before cutting into squares. You will get 12 squares. Roll together the larger scraps from the short edges, trim them, and cut 4 more squares, making 16 total.

Let the squares rise until light, about 30 minutes. If you press a finger into the dough and the indentation remains, it has risen enough.

BAKE THE SANDWICHES. Brush each square with egg wash and a sprinkle of granulated sugar. Bake for 15 minutes, reduce the heat to 325°F, and bake for 10 minutes longer, or until light golden and light but firm to the touch. In cases where the dough has risen very high, split one square in half horizontally and use those two pieces to make a sandwich.

◆ I USE RECTANGULAR TROWELS WITH HANDLES AS TEMPLATES WHEN I CUT DOUGH. THEY MAKE IT EASY TO GET AN EXACT AND CONSISTENT CUT AND ARE AVAILABLE IN HARDWARE STORES. IN THIS INSTANCE, I USED A TROWEL THAT IS 4 INCHES WIDE TO GET 4-INCH SQUARES. WHEN I ROLL OUT THE DOUGH, I PLACE THE TROWEL LENGTHWISE ACROSS THE STRIP AND USE A PIZZA CUTTER TO TRIM THE TOP AND BOTTOM EDGES EVEN TO MAKE THE STRIP EXACTLY 4 INCHES WIDE. I THEN PLACE THE TROWEL ACROSS THE STRIP AND CUT 4-INCH SQUARES.

PREPARATION. Preheat the oven to 350°F.

◆ AT ROOM TEMPERATURE, THE SANDWICHES WILL STAY FRESH FOR 1 DAY IF WRAPPED TIGHTLY IN PLASTIC WRAP. FROZEN IN AN AIRTIGHT CONTAINER, THEY WILL REMAIN FRESH FOR UP TO 2 WEEKS. TO REHEAT THE SQUARES, BRING THEM TO ROOM TEMPERATURE, WRAP IN FOIL, AND BAKE AT 350°F FOR APPROXIMATELY 5 MINUTES. WRAPPING THEM IN FOIL WILL ENSURE THAT THEY HEAT THROUGH BUT REMAIN SOFT LIKE SANDWICH BREAD.

MAKE THE PUREE. Place the apricots in a small saucepan with enough water to cover and soak until softened, about 2 hours. Bring to a boil over medium heat and cook, stirring occasionally, until the apricots are soft enough to puree, 5 minutes. Drain the apricots and place them in a food processor or blender. Add the sugar, orange juice, and lemon juice and puree until smooth. Pour the puree back into the saucepan, add the sherry, and cook over medium heat, stirring constantly, until some of the moisture has evaporated and the mixture mounds on a spoon with no residual liquid, about 5 minutes. Transfer to a small bowl and refrigerate.

APRICOT PUREE

YIELD: 1½ CUP

1 cup dried apricots (8 ounces)

½ cup sugar

½ cup freshly squeezed orange juice

2 tablespoons freshly squeezed
   lemon juice

4 tablespoons Harvey's Bristol
   Cream sherry

PASTRY CREAM

YIELD: 3½ CUPS

½ cup sugar

¼ cup (30 grams) cake flour, sifted

2½ cups milk

10 large egg yolks (200 grams or ⅞ cup)

¼ cup heavy cream

2 tablespoons unsalted butter

MAKE THE PASTRY CREAM. Combine the sugar and flour in a bowl, whisking to remove any lumps, which will ensure the pastry cream is smooth. Bring the milk to a boil in a large saucepan.

Meanwhile, place the egg yolks in the bowl of an electric mixer fitted with the whisk attachment and whip on high speed for about 2 minutes. Add the sugar mixture and continue to beat on high until the egg mixture is thick, heavy, and pale. Remove the bowl from the mixer and bring it over to the stove.

When the milk comes to a rolling boil and rises up the side of the pan, reduce the heat to low. Gradually whisk several large spoonfuls of the hot milk into the egg mixture to temper it, then pour the tempered mixture back into the saucepan and continue to cook on medium heat, stirring constantly with the whisk, until the pastry cream begins to bubble or "burp." Continue to cook for 2 more minutes in order to take away any uncooked floury aftertaste.

Remove the pan from the heat and whisk in the heavy cream and butter until the butter melts and the pastry cream is well blended. Pour the pastry cream into a bowl and tightly press a piece of plastic wrap directly onto the surface, leaving only a small area uncovered for the heat to escape. This will prevent a skin from forming on the surface. Refrigerate until chilled, then cover completely with plastic wrap. The pastry cream may be made up to 4 days in advance and kept refrigerated until ready for use.

ASSEMBLE THE SANDWICHES. Fold the whipped cream into the pastry cream until smooth and well combined. Spread a layer of pastry cream over the ¾-inch-thick unglazed side (bottom) of a Danish square. Take a second square and spread a slightly thinner layer of apricot puree over the unglazed side (bottom). Make a sandwich by pressing the 2 squares together, fillings facing in. (This technique is easier than trying to spread the apricot puree onto the pastry cream or vice versa.) Repeat with the remaining Danish squares, pastry cream, and apricot puree to make 8 sandwiches in all.

Served as a stacked sandwich, this Danish treat is so warm and buttery and its flavor so good that it doesn't need other elements to enhance it. Serve with a knife and fork.

◆ I SOMETIMES CUT THE SANDWICHES INTO TRIANGLES. I FIND IT EASIER TO DO THIS BY CUTTING THE DANISH BEFORE FILLING, FOR A CLEANER CUT.

I like to plate the sandwiches while warm and float them in a pool of apricot coulis enriched with fresh orange juice and a touch of Grand Marnier.

MAKE THE APRICOT COULIS. Place the dried apricots with enough water to cover in a medium saucepan. Bring to a boil over medium heat and cook until soft enough to puree, about 5 minutes. Place the apricots with the cooking liquid in a food processor or blender, add the orange juice, and puree until smooth. Add the Grand Marnier. Add a little more orange juice if necessary to make the sauce thin enough to run along the plate.

You can even add some sweet white wine, such as Beaume-des-Venises, instead of orange juice, to thin the coulis, if you like.

APRICOT COULIS
YIELD: 2 CUPS

1 cup dried apricots (4 ounces)
1 cup freshly squeezed orange juice, or more if needed
2 tablespoons Grand Marnier

BLACK-AND-WHITE COCONUT SURPRISES

These sandwiches are a takeoff on a chocolate and cream cheese marble brownie that I love. Here I take the brownie to another level by combining it with coconut, which evokes a certain tropical feeling, while fresh mango contributes a fruity tartness that is a perfect contrast to the rich brownie. Sandwiching the cheesecake brownie between two disk-shaped coconut macaroons is both whimsical and delicious.

SPECIAL EQUIPMENT: ICE-CREAM SCOOP (SPRING-HANDLED, STANDARD 2-OUNCE SCOOP SIZE) •
ICE-CREAM MAKER

COCONUT SLICES

YIELD: 24 TO 26 3½-INCH COOKIES

5 large egg whites (150 grams or ⅔ cup)

⅞ cup sugar

1 teaspoon vanilla extract

3½ cups unsweetened shredded coconut (preferably unsulphured)

PREPARATION. Preheat the oven to 325°F. Line two 18 X 13–inch half-sheet or jelly-roll pans with parchment paper.

◆ I FIND THAT THE EASIEST WAY TO GET UNIFORM-SIZE COCONUT SLICES IS TO USE A 2-OUNCE SPRING-HANDLED ICE-CREAM SCOOP TO MEASURE OUT THE COCONUT MIXTURE.

MAKE THE COCONUT SLICES. Whisk the egg whites, sugar, and vanilla by hand in the bowl of an electric mixer until combined. Place the bowl in a larger bowl filled with hot, not boiling, water and whisk until the sugar has dissolved and the mixture is warm to the touch. Place the bowl in the electric mixer fitted with the whisk attachment. Whip the warm egg white mixture on high speed until it forms stiff and glossy peaks, about 5 minutes. Fold in the coconut. Using the ice-cream scoop, place rounded scoops of the batter 2 inches apart on the prepared pans. Press each cookie lightly with the back of a spoon dipped in cold water to flatten until 2½ to 3 inches in diameter and ½ inch thick.

Bake for 5 minutes, rotate the pan from front to back, and bake for another 3 minutes, or until the slices are very lightly toasted. Let the slices cool in their pans and slide off with a spatula after they have cooled. Store in an airtight container in single layers with parchment between each layer until ready to use. Refrigerated, the slices will remain fresh for up to 1 week, frozen for up to 3 weeks.

MAKE THE WHITE FILLING. Beat the cream cheese, butter, and sugar on medium speed in the bowl of an electric mixer fitted with the paddle attachment until smooth and creamy. Add the egg and vanilla and mix well. Remove the bowl from the mixer and fold in the flour until well combined. Set aside.

MAKE THE BLACK FILLING. Sift the flour and baking powder into a bowl. Set aside. Place the butter and bittersweet and unsweetened chocolates in a small bowl and set over a bowl of hot, not boiling, water, stirring frequently until melted and smooth. Remove the bowl of chocolate from the hot water and cool slightly. Alternatively, place the butter and chocolates in a microwave-safe bowl and heat on medium power at 10-second intervals, stirring after each interval, until melted.

Combine the eggs, sugar, and vanilla in the bowl of an electric mixer fitted with the whisk attachment and beat on medium speed until thick and pale.

◆ IT IS THE AMOUNT OF FLOUR ADDED THAT DETERMINES WHETHER A BROWNIE WILL BE CAKEY OR FUDGEY. THE MORE FLOUR, THE MORE CAKEY THE BROWNIE, AND VICE VERSA, THE LESS FLOUR, THE MORE FUDGE-LIKE THE BROWNIE.

Fold the cooled chocolate mixture into the egg mixture, then fold in the flour mixture until no streaks remain. (The batter will be thick.)

WHITE FILLING

YIELD: ENOUGH FOR 9 BROWNIES

4 ounces, or ½ of an 8-ounce package, cream cheese, at room temperature

2 tablespoons (1 ounce) unsalted butter, at room temperature

¼ cup sugar

1 large egg (50 grams or ¼ cup)

½ teaspoon vanilla extract

1 tablespoon (8 grams) cake flour, sifted

BLACK FILLING

YIELD: ENOUGH FOR 9 BROWNIES

⅓ cup (40 grams) cake flour, sifted

¼ teaspoon baking powder

2 ounces (½ stick) unsalted butter, diced

1 ounce bittersweet chocolate, chopped

3 ounces unsweetened chocolate, chopped

1½ large eggs (75 grams or ⅓ cup)

½ cup sugar

½ teaspoon vanilla extract

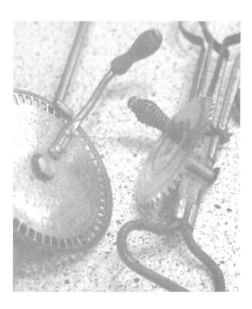

CREAM CHEESE BROWNIES

YIELD: 9 BROWNIES

White Filling

Black Filling

PREPARATION. Preheat the oven to 350°F. Butter an 8-inch-square, 3-inch-deep baking pan. Line the bottom with parchment paper and butter the paper.

◆ THE STRAIGHT EDGE OF A PASTRY SCRAPER IS HELPFUL FOR SPREADING THE BATTER EVENLY IN THE PAN.

◆ I ALWAYS INVERT THE PAN OF COOLED BROWNIES ONTO A CUTTING BOARD, THEN FLIP THEM OVER, RIGHT SIDE UP. I REFRIGERATE THEM UNTIL VERY COLD, THEN SCORE THEM WITH A KNIFE BEFORE CUTTING THEM.

MAKE THE BROWNIES. Pour half of the white filling into a prepared pan. Pour half of the black filling over the white filling, then cover with the remaining white filling, and top with the rest of the black filling. Swirl fillings with a knife to create a marbled effect.

Bake for 15 minutes, rotate the pan from front to back, and bake again for 15 minutes. Cover the pan with aluminum foil and bake for another 15 minutes, or until a cake tester inserted in the center comes out evenly coated with chocolate crumbs. Place the brownies in their pan on a cooling rack and cool completely. Cut into 2-inch squares.

Place the brownies in an airtight container and refrigerate until ready to use. Refrigerated, they will remain fresh for up to 1 week, frozen for up to 1 month.

◆ I TRIM ALL THE EDGES, THEN USE A 2-INCH METAL SPATULA AS A GUIDE AND A 10-INCH OR LONGER KNIFE TO CUT THE BROWNIES INTO 2-INCH SQUARES. BETWEEN CUTS, I DIP THE KNIFE INTO A TALL CONTAINER FILLED WITH HOT WATER, WIPE IT CLEAN, AND MAKE ANOTHER CUT. THIS WAY I ALWAYS GET NICE, CLEAN, PROFESSIONAL-LOOKING CUTS.

COCONUT SORBET

YIELD: 1 QUART

4 cups frozen coconut puree made with 10% sugar, thawed

½ cup water

⅔ cup sugar

1 tablespoon dark rum, such as Myers's, or 1 teaspoon vanilla extract

MAKE THE COCONUT SORBET. Mix all the ingredients in a large bowl. Transfer to an ice-cream maker and freeze according to the manufacturer's instructions. This sorbet needs very little churning time. Remove it when you see it begin to thicken and come together. The sorbet should be very loose and soft. Spoon the sorbet into an airtight container and freeze until ready to use.

◆ MAKE SURE TO USE BOTTLED WATER, SINCE THE IMPURITIES IN TAP WATER CAN LEAVE AN AFTERTASTE IN THIS UNCOOKED SORBET.

◆ I always try to use only fresh fruit for my sorbets. One exception is frozen coconut puree. It is such a superior product and has a greater intensity of flavor than fresh coconut milk. The brand I like is Boiron Frozen Puree, from American Gourmet Foods in Washington, d.c. It is also possible to find frozen coconut milk in Asian markets. If you use frozen coconut milk without added sugar, you may need to stir in some extra sugar. Taste it and add enough sugar to slightly oversweeten the coconut milk, as the sorbet will taste less sweet when frozen.

MAKE THE COULIS. Place the mango puree and orange juice in a bowl and stir well to combine. Slowly add the sugar, stirring and tasting as you go to adjust the sweetness as needed. Add enough water to thin the coulis so it will coat a plate nicely.

MANGO COULIS

YIELD: 3 CUPS

2 cups fresh or thawed frozen
    mango puree

½ cup freshly squeezed orange juice

½ cup sugar, or to taste

About ½ cup water

ASSEMBLE THE DESSERT. Toast the shredded coconut for 5 minutes at 325°F, scatter it in the pan with a spatula, and continue toasting for another 5 minutes, until light brown. Set aside. Slice each brownie square in half horizontally. Place a coconut slice in the center of each plate. Cover the coconut slice with a brownie slice, then a scoop of sorbet, a second brownie slice, and then place a second coconut slice on top. Swirl some mango coulis around the plate and scatter the toasted coconut over it.

◆ To get optimal flavor from the brownies, I microwave them for about 10 seconds before plating them.

ASSEMBLY

1 cup unsweetened shredded coconut
    (preferably unsulphured)

18 Coconut Slices

9 Cream Cheese Brownies

Coconut Sorbet

3 cups Mango Coulis

PREPARATION. Preheat the oven
to 325°F.

BRITTANY CAKE WITH BLACKBERRY FOOL FILLING

SERVES 12 (LARGE PORTIONS)

This Brittany cake dough is actually croissant dough that is rolled and then sprinkled with sugar just before baking. The buttery taste of the dough is a wonderful contrast to the tartness of the blackberry fool. You can also use rhubarb (when in season) or blueberries mixed with raspberries. The baked squares can also be cut diagonally in half and the triangles stacked so the dessert can be served sandwich-style.

SPECIAL EQUIPMENT: CHEESE SLICER, TRUFFLE SLICER, MANDOLINE, OR ADJUSTABLE VEGETABLE SLICER

BRITTANY CAKE DOUGH

YIELD: ENOUGH FOR TWELVE 4-INCH SQUARES

1½ cakes (1 ounce) fresh yeast, or 3¾ teaspoons (a little over 1½ envelopes) active dry yeast

1 tablespoon plus 1 teaspoon sugar

¼ cup cold water

3 cups (420 grams) high-gluten flour

1 teaspoon salt

½ cup milk

½ cup heavy cream

½ pound (2 sticks) cold unsalted butter, chilled

Granulated sugar for sprinkling

MAKE THE CAKE DOUGH. Crumble the fresh yeast into a small bowl with the 1 teaspoon sugar and add the water. Stir to form a thin syrup.

Sift the flour, salt, and remaining 1 tablespoon sugar into the bowl of an electric mixer fitted with the paddle attachment. Add the yeast mixture, milk, and cream and mix on low speed to combine well. Still on low speed, mix the dough until just combined, about 2 minutes; the dough will look rough. It should feel damp but not sticky; if necessary, add a few more drops of water. Remove the dough from the bowl and with the palm of your hand and your fingertips, pat and stretch it into a square; the size is not important. Wrap the dough in plastic wrap and refrigerate for 15 minutes.

PREPARE THE BUTTER. Dust each stick of butter with a little flour. Use a cheese slicer, truffle slicer, mandoline, or adjustable vegetable slicer to slice each cold stick of butter into 7 lengthwise slices. In all, you will end up with 14 thin 5 X 1–inch lengthwise slices. Divide them into three groups (2 groups will have 1 additional slice). Place each group on parchment paper, long sides slightly overlapping.

Press the slices together to form three 4 X 4–inch "sheets" of butter. Refrigerate until ready to use.

ADD THE BUTTER. Add the butter. Roll out the chilled dough on a lightly floured work surface to a rectangle about 16 inches long and 5 inches wide. See the diagram at right. Use a ruler as a guide to mark the dough crosswise into fourths without cutting all the way through the dough (1). Place one 4 X 4–inch sheet of room-temperature butter on the section of dough immediately left of center. Place the butter so it covers the entire section of dough (2) and sprinkle with the granulated sugar. Fold over the flap of dough to its left, bringing it toward the center of the dough, enclosing the butter in the dough. The dough should now be in 3 sections (3). Place a second sheet of butter in the middle section (4), sprinkle with the granulated sugar, and fold the right sections of dough over the butter. You now have 2 sections of dough visible (5). Place the remaining sheet of butter on top of the left section (6), sprinkle with sugar, and fold the other half of the dough over it (7). The dough should measure roughly 6 X 4 inches.

Rolling forward with a rolling pin, roll out the dough to a rectangle approximately 15 inches long and 5 inches wide. Fold the rectangle into thirds to create a square roughly 5 X 5 inches. Use a pastry brush to brush off any excess flour. Place the dough on an 18 X 13–inch half-sheet or jelly-roll pan, cover with plastic wrap, and refrigerate for 15 minutes. Or, if the room is cool, leave out for 15 minutes. The first turn (which is made up of 4 turns) has now been completed. Repeat the rolling, folding, turning, and chilling of the dough 2 more times, beginning with rolling the pastry to form a rectangle 15 X 5 inches and ending after folding it roughly into a 5-inch square. The dimensions are not as important as the

CONTINUED

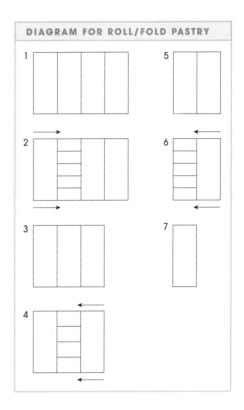

DIAGRAM FOR ROLL/FOLD PASTRY

smoothness and homogenization of the butter throughout the dough. The dough should be uniform in color with no patches of butter showing through.

Place the dough on a half-sheet or jelly-roll pan lined with parchment paper. Wrap tightly in plastic wrap. Place the second pan upside down on top of the dough and wrap the pans together in plastic wrap. This will help keep the dough contained in the plastic wrap, and therefore moist, while rising overnight. Weight the pans with a heavy bowl or skillet and refrigerate for at least 3 hours or, even better, overnight.

BRITTANY CAKE SQUARES

YIELD: TWELVE 4-INCH SQUARES

1 large egg lightly beaten with

    1 tablespoon water, for egg wash

½ cup sugar

PREPARATION. Preheat the oven to 350°F. Have ready 2 parchment-lined 18 X 13–inch half-sheet or jelly-roll pans.

◆ SCRAPS CAN BE ROLLED OUT AGAIN AND CUT INTO STRIPS AND BAKED OR USED TO FORM MORE SQUARES.

MAKE THE CAKE SQUARES. Remove the chilled dough and cut it into 4 equal pieces. Return the other pieces to the refrigerator and work with one piece of dough at a time. Roll out the dough into a strip about 10 inches in length. The width and thickness are not important at this point. Fold into thirds (this is another turn, and the secret to getting a great even rise) and roll again to a strip about 10 inches long. Fold into thirds again, then roll the dough into a strip about 12 inches long, 4½ inches wide, and ⅓ inch thick. Trim all edges, then cut 4-inch squares using a trowel, pizza wheel cutter, or knife. Repeat with the remaining 3 pieces of dough, giving each the 2 final turns before cutting into squares. You will get 12 squares. Brush the squares with egg wash and sprinkle with sugar. Let the squares rise, loosely covered with plastic wrap, about 30 minutes. Bake for 15 minutes, then reduce the heat to 325°F and bake for another 15 to 20 minutes, until firm and golden brown.

MAKE THE BLACKBERRY FOOL. Place the cream and confectioners' sugar in the bowl of an electric mixer fitted with the whisk attachment and beat on high speed until stiff peaks form. Remove the bowl from the mixer and fold in the pureed blackberries.

To substitute rhubarb for the blackberries, cut 4 stalks of rhubarb into small pieces. Place in a saucepan with 1 cup of sugar and stew over medium-high heat until softened, about 8 minutes. Add more sugar to taste if needed, then puree. Refrigerate until chilled before adding to the whipped cream.

ASSEMBLE THE DESSERT. Split the squares horizontally and place 1 square of warm Brittany Cake on a plate. Place a scooped mound of blackberry fool on top. Place the other half of the square of cake over the fruit fool, tilted at an angle. A little pool of Crème Anglaise and some fresh berries scattered around the plate finish the dessert.

◆ IF THE SQUARES HAVE BEEN BAKED EARLIER, SPLIT THEM HORIZONTALLY AND PLACE ON A HALF-SHEET OR JELLY-ROLL PAN LINED WITH PARCHMENT PAPER, COVER WITH FOIL, AND HEAT FOR 10 MINUTES AT 325°F.

BLACKBERRY FOOL

YIELD: 3 TO 3½ CUPS

2 cups heavy cream

3 tablespoons confectioners' sugar, or more to taste

2 cups blackberries, pureed

◆ I EVEN LIKE TO ADD SMALL WHOLE BERRIES TO THE FOOL MIXTURE FOR APPEALING TEXTURE AND APPEARANCE.

ASSEMBLY

12 Brittany Cake Squares

3½ cups Blackberry Fool

1 cup Crème Anglaise (page 29)

Seasonal berries

CASHEW DACQUOISE
WITH KUMQUAT CONFIT
AND CHOCOLATE SORBET

SERVES 12

My friend Patrick Musel, a stellar yet largely unsung pastry chef, is responsible for opening up the doors of learning for me. He taught me the technique of making a nutted meringue known as succès or dacquoise. Sometimes the dessert is one large round, and at other times it is made up of a long strip that is cut into pieces for serving. I like to make small meringue rounds, fill them with a hazelnut and almond buttercream and toasted chopped cashews, and serve them with kumquat confit and deep chocolate sorbet. Organic food stores usually carry almond butter (it's similar in texture to peanut butter), which is called for in the buttercream. This evolution takes the dacquoise out of the realm of just pastry and elevates it to an elegant plated dessert. I have included it in this chapter because it is in essence a meringue sandwich.

SPECIAL EQUIPMENT: PASTRY BAG FITTED WITH A ½-INCH PLAIN TIP (ATECO #26) •
CANDY THERMOMETER • PASTRY BAG FITTED WITH AN ¹¹⁄₁₆-INCH PLAIN TIP (ATECO #29) •
ICE-CREAM MAKER

◆ IT IS IMPORTANT TO USE EQUAL AMOUNTS OF SUGAR AND FINELY GROUND ALMONDS IN THE DAQUOISE, SO I HAVE INCLUDED THE GRAM WEIGHT FOR EACH IN PARENTHESES. IN FRENCH, THE TERM FOR EQUAL AMOUNTS OF GRANULATED SUGAR AND GROUND ALMONDS OR ALMOND FLOUR IS *TANT POUR TANT* (TPT).

◆ YOU CAN GRIND THE ALMONDS WITH THE MEAT GRINDER ATTACHMENT OF YOUR ELECTRIC MIXER OR IN A HAND-CRANKED GRINDER. OR USE ALMOND FLOUR (8½ OUNCES OR 250 GRAMS), WHICH IS AVAILABLE IN SPECIALTY FOOD STORES.

◆ I HAVE FOUND IT IMPERATIVE TO USE ONLY FRESHLY BROKEN EGG WHITES FOR THE MERINGUE IN THIS RECIPE. I USED TO USE EGG WHITES THAT HAD BEEN SEPARATED A COUPLE OF DAYS AHEAD, BUT NOTICED THAT THEY DIDN'T PERFORM AS WELL. THE MERINGUE JUST DIDN'T RISE TO ITS USUAL HEIGHT. SO DON'T BE TEMPTED TO USE WHITES THAT YOU HAVE STORED IN YOUR REFRIGERATOR FOR EVEN A DAY. YOU'LL BE HAPPIER WITH THE FIRMER, MORE DEFINED MERINGUE YOU GET WITH FRESHLY BROKEN EGG WHITES.

MAKE THE MERINGUE ROUNDS. Place ½ cup plus 1 tablespoon plus ½ teaspoon (125 grams) of the sugar, the ground almonds (125 grams), and cornstarch in a large bowl. Mix well with your hands, rubbing the mixture through the palms of your hands to break up any small lumps. It will look like coarse almond meal. Set aside.

Place the egg whites and vanilla in the bowl of an electric mixer fitted with the whisk attachment and beat on high speed until foamy and beginning to hold a shape. Gradually add the remaining ½ cup plus 1 tablespoon plus ½ teaspoon (125 grams) of the sugar in a slow, continuous stream, 1 teaspoon at a time over the course of 1 to 2 minutes, then beat until the whites form stiff peaks that are glossy, about 1 minute more. Do not overbeat.

Fold one-fourth of the meringue into the almond mixture to lighten it. Quickly but thoroughly fold in the remaining meringue until the whites are no longer visible. Fill a pastry bag fitted with a ½-inch plain tip (Ateco #26) two-thirds full with meringue. Holding the tip about 1 inch from the prepared pan and letting the meringue drop from the bag, pipe the outline of a circle, then continue to pipe in a spiral until the entire circle is filled in.

Pipe the meringue in a slow, continuous stream as if you were writing, being careful not to let the tip drag on the surface of the parchment. Pipe the remaining meringue to make more rounds.

Bake the meringue rounds for 15 minutes, rotate the pans from front to back, and continue to bake for 15 to 25 minutes longer, or until the meringue rounds are barely colored, very dry, and easy to release from the parchment. The meringue rounds will grow to about 3 inches. If some meringue remains on the parchment when you lift up a round, bake for 5 more minutes. Let the meringue rounds cool on the pans on racks. If not ready to use, layer between waxed paper or parchment paper and store in an airtight container. Refrigerated, the meringue rounds will remain fresh for up to 1 week, frozen for up to 1 month.

MERINGUE ROUNDS

YIELD: ABOUT TWENTY-FOUR
3-INCH ROUNDS

1 cup plus 2 tablespoons plus
   1 teaspoon sugar (250 grams)
1⅓ cups (125 grams) finely ground
   blanched almonds (grind
   1¾ cups whole)
1 tablespoon cornstarch
4 large egg whites (120 grams or
   ½ cup), at room temperature
1 teaspoon vanilla extract

PREPARATION. Position racks in the middle and lower third of the oven and preheat the oven to 225°F. Line two 18 X 13–inch half-sheet or jelly-roll pans with parchment paper. Trace twenty-four 2½-inch circles about 2 inches apart on the parchment with a dark pencil, using a pastry cutter as a guide. Turn the parchment over so you don't pipe directly onto the pencil lines.

These are somewhat fragile, so you don't want to stack more than 3 layers before starting a new container.

BUTTERCREAM

YIELD: 4 CUPS

1½ cups hazelnuts (about 12 ounces), skinned

1½ cups sliced blanched almonds

1 cup sugar

2 tablespoons water

6 large egg whites (180 grams or ¾ cup), at room temperature

¾ pound (3 sticks) unsalted butter, at room temperature

1 cup almond butter

1 tablespoon dark rum, such as Myers's

PREPARATION. Have ready a pastry brush and a cup of cold water.

◆ IT MAY SEEM LIKE THERE IS A VERY LARGE QUANTITY OF NUTS FOR THE BUTTERCREAM, BUT I'M GOING FOR FLAVOR HERE. THIS BUTTERCREAM IS FABULOUSLY STIFF AND CHUNKY WITH NUTS. IT REALLY IS MORE LIKE A LOT OF NUTS BOUND WITH BUTTERCREAM.

◆ I RECOMMEND BUYING SKINNED HAZELNUTS FOR THE BEST RESULTS, SINCE IT CAN BE DIFFICULT TO REMOVE THE SKIN OF ALL THE HAZELNUTS BY TOASTING THEM.

MAKE THE BUTTERCREAM. Place the hazelnuts and almonds together on a half-sheet or jelly-roll pan and bake at 325°F for 10 to 12 minutes, or until lightly toasted, stirring often so they brown evenly. Set aside to cool. When cool, put them in a food processor and pulse until finely ground.

Combine the sugar and water in a small saucepan and stir to mix well. Place the saucepan over high heat and bring to a boil, stirring to dissolve the sugar. Wash away any sugar from the side of the pan with a pastry brush dipped in water. Do not stir the syrup after it boils.

Meanwhile, place the egg whites in the bowl of an electric mixer fitted with the whisk attachment and beat on low speed until opaque and foamy. When the sugar syrup reaches the firm-ball stage (242°F on a candy thermometer), the bubbles will appear almost plastic-looking. Remove the pan from the heat and immediately pour the syrup into the egg whites, pouring it down the side of the bowl to prevent it from spattering. Increase the mixer speed to medium-high and continue to beat the whites until they are at room temperature, about 15 minutes. If the bowl is cool to the touch, the beating is complete. (I have rapidly hastened the cooling by directing a small electric fan at the bowl of the mixer.)

Reduce the mixer speed to low and add the butter several tablespoons at a time, beating until all the butter has been incorporated and scraping down the side of the bowl if necessary. The buttercream will be somewhat deflated but look very smooth and homogenized.

CONTINUED

Remove the bowl from the mixer and fold in the ground hazelnuts and almonds, almond butter, and rum. The buttercream should taste very intensely of the ground nuts and not be too sweet.

DACQUOISE

YIELD: 12 SANDWICHES

4 cups unsalted raw cashews
   (about 1¾ pounds)
4 cups Buttercream
24 perfect Meringue Rounds

PREPARATION. Preheat the oven to 325°F.

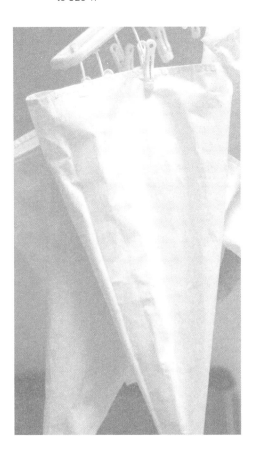

ASSEMBLE THE DACQUOISE. Place the cashews on a half-sheet or jelly-roll pan and bake for 10 to 12 minutes, or until lightly toasted, stirring often so they brown evenly. Set aside to cool.

When cool, put the cashews in a food processor and pulse to get large pieces, remove half, then pulse the rest to get a finer grind. Use the larger pieces for the filling and the finer grind for the sides.

Fill a pastry bag fitted with an ¹¹⁄₁₆-inch plain tip (Ateco #29) two-thirds full with buttercream. (This larger tip will make it easy for the chunky buttercream to squeeze through.) Place a meringue round, smooth side down, on a half-sheet or jelly-roll pan. Pipe a ½-inch layer of buttercream in a continuous circle on top of the meringue round. Pile a ½-inch layer of chopped cashews on top of the buttercream, pressing them down. Pipe a ring of buttercream along the edge on the smooth side (bottom) of another meringue round and place, buttercream side down, on top of the cashews, pressing down gently. Holding the sandwich in the palm of your hand, being careful not to press down on top, pat the finer-ground cashews all around the side of the sandwich. Repeat with remaining meringue rounds, buttercream, and cashews. If not using immediately, layer the sandwiches between waxed or parchment paper and store in an airtight container. Refrigerated, they will remain fresh for up to 1 week.

MAKE THE CONFIT. Place the sugar and water in a medium saucepan and bring to a boil over medium-high heat, stirring to dissolve the sugar. Wash down the side of the pot with a pastry brush dipped in water to wash away any undissolved sugar. When a full boil is reached, add the kumquats and return to a boil. Reduce the heat and simmer until thick and very clear, about 1 hour, watching carefully to prevent burning. Remove from the heat. Transfer to a container, cool, and set aside.

MAKE THE CHOCOLATE SORBET. Have ready a pastry brush and cup of cold water. Place the sugar and water in a medium saucepan and bring to a boil over medium-high heat. Wash down the side of the pan with a pastry brush dipped in water to wash away any undissolved sugar. When a boil is reached, remove from the heat and add the bittersweet and unsweetened chocolates and cocoa, stirring with a whisk until the chocolate melts and the mixture is perfectly smooth. Transfer to a container and refrigerate until chilled, stirring frequently. When cold, stir in the orange juice and Grand Marnier. Transfer the mixture to an ice-cream maker and freeze according to manufacturer's instructions.

SERVE THE DACQUOISE. Place a dacquoise at the top (12 o'clock position) of each plate. Place a spoonful of kumquat confit and a quenelle (scoop) of chocolate sorbet in the center of each plate.

KUMQUAT CONFIT

YIELD: 4 CUPS

2½ cups sugar

1 cup water

1½ pounds kumquats, skins left on, quartered and seeded

PREPARATION. Have ready a pastry brush and cup of cold water.

CHOCOLATE SORBET

YIELD: 1 QUART

1 cup plus 1 tablespoon plus 1½ teaspoons sugar

2 cups water

4 ounces bittersweet chocolate, preferably Callebaut 60/40, chopped

2 ounces unsweetened chocolate, preferably Callebaut, chopped

¾ cup cocoa (preferably Valrhona)

¾ cup freshly squeezed orange juice

¼ cup Grand Marnier

PREPARATION. Have ready a pastry brush and cup of cold water.

ASSEMBLY

12 Dacquoise

4 cups Kumquat Confit

Chocolate Sorbet

CELIA'S ROLLS
WITH CHEESECAKE STICKS

Celia Denton, a pastry chef and friend I worked with at Chanterelle Caterers in Washington, D.C., made fabulous old-fashioned Parker House rolls that everybody loved. They were soft and warm and buttery, which reminded us of rolls we had eaten as children, served alongside a salad and soup, hot from the oven, pulled apart, and slathered with butter. Celia graciously shared her recipe with me. I thought it would be a fun twist to sweeten the rolls just a little and sandwich them with slices of fluffy lemon cheesecake. The texture of the rolls is light and tender but without the back-of-the-mouth taste of preservatives that so many soft white rolls seem to have these days. By cutting back on the quantity of flour, the rolls acquired a lighter-than-air texture, which is what makes them so tempting, especially hot out of the oven. My favorite way to serve the filled rolls is with fresh seasonal fruit on each plate.

SPECIAL EQUIPMENT: 8-INCH SQUARE BAKING PAN • 10-INCH SQUARE BAKING PAN

CHEESECAKE

YIELD: ENOUGH FOR ABOUT 20 ROLLS
(USE ON PLATE TO GARNISH OR FREEZE
EXTRA FOR ANOTHER USE)

3 (8-ounce) packages cream cheese,
    at room temperature

1 cup sugar, or to taste

¼ cup (30 grams) cake flour, sifted

1 cup sour cream or crème fraîche

2 large egg yolks (40 grams or ⅛ cup
    or 2 tablespoons)

2 teaspoons finely grated lemon zest

2 teaspoons freshly squeezed lemon
    juice

2 large egg whites (60 grams or ¼ cup)

¼ cup sugar

See Preparation at the top of the next page.

MAKE THE CHEESECAKE. Place the cream cheese and sugar in the bowl of an electric mixer fitted with the paddle attachment and blend on medium speed until very smooth and creamy. Add the flour and beat until smooth, about 1 minute. Add the sour cream, egg yolks, and lemon zest and juice, beating until completely smooth, scraping down the side of the bowl. Beat the egg whites with the ¼ cup sugar until firm glossy peaks form. Fold the egg whites into the cream cheese mixture and blend gently until no egg white is visible.

Scrape the cream-cheese filling into the prepared pan and place on the middle oven rack. Bake for 20 minutes, then reduce the temperature to 250°F and bake for 1 hour longer, or until set, puffy, and golden. Place the cheesecake on a cooling rack and cool to room temperature, then cover with plastic wrap and refrigerate overnight.

◆ ALWAYS GRATE THE ZEST FIRST, THEN JUICE THE LEMONS.

The Following Day

MAKE THE CHEESECAKE STICKS. Loosen the plastic wrap from the sides of the pan and gently lift it to loosen the plastic from the pan. Place a piece of parchment paper and a cutting board on top of the cheesecake and invert. Lift off the pan and remove the plastic wrap. Use a thin-bladed knife dipped in hot water to slice the cheesecake into approximately 1½ X 2¾–inch "sticks." Cover them with plastic wrap and set aside.

MAKE THE ROLLS. Crumble the yeast with your fingertips into a small bowl and sprinkle with about 2 tablespoons of the sugar. Mix with a spoon until the yeast mixture becomes a thin syrup. Set aside. (If using dry yeast, place in a small bowl, add 2 tablespoons of sugar and ¼ cup warm water, 90°F to 110°F, and set aside.)

Place 3½ cups of the flour in the bowl of an electric mixer fitted with the paddle attachment. Add the yeast mixture, the milk, 4 ounces (1 stick) of the melted butter, the eggs, the remaining sugar, and the salt. Mix the dough on low speed until smooth, elastic, and shiny, about 10 minutes. If the dough feels very sticky, add just enough of the remaining ¼ cup flour to keep the dough from sticking and leaving a residue on your hands. Otherwise, just use the lesser amount of flour, as this will keep the dough light and delicate. Transfer the dough to a clean large bowl, cover with plastic wrap, and let rise until doubled in size, 1 to 1½ hours. Punch down the dough and let it rise for another 30 minutes.

PREPARATION. Position racks in the middle and lower third of the oven and preheat the oven to 350°F. Place a large shallow pan of water on lower rack. Line an 8-inch square baking pan with a double thickness of plastic wrap, letting the wrap extend up the sides to the top but not over the edges of the pan.

◆ THIS CHEESECAKE WILL NOT CUT PERFECTLY CLEAN, BUT THE TEXTURE IS WONDERFUL.

CELIA'S ROLLS

YIELD: 15 ROLLS

1 (0.6-ounce) cake fresh yeast or 1 envelope active dry yeast

¼ cup sugar

3½ to 3¾ cups (about 490 to 525 grams) all-purpose flour, sifted

1 cup milk

8 ounces (2 sticks) unsalted butter, melted (melt each stick or each 4 ounces in separate containers)

3 large eggs (150 grams or ⅔ cup)

¾ teaspoon salt

PREPARATION. Butter a 10-inch square baking pan.

BAKE THE ROLLS. Roll out the dough on a very lightly floured surface into a rough square about ½ inch thick. Cut the dough with a sharp, thin-bladed knife or pizza cutter into strips about 3 inches long and 2 inches wide. Brush each strip with some of the remaining melted butter and fold crosswise in half. When folding the dough over, press down firmly (use pressure) to get the dough to stick to its other half. Place the rolls right next to each other, filling the prepared pan. Cover loosely with plastic wrap and let rise for 30 minutes.

Meanwhile, preheat the oven to 350°F. Brush the rolls with the remainder of the melted butter. Bake for 20 to 25 minutes, or until golden brown. Transfer the rolls to a cooling rack. After 10 minutes, turn the rolls out of the pan and immediately wrap them in foil to keep them soft.

If you bake the rolls ahead, just rewarm them wrapped in foil in a 350°F oven for 5 to 6 minutes. This is a more convenient way to serve this dessert.

ASSEMBLY

15 Cheesecake sticks

15 Celia's Rolls

SERVE THE DESSERT. While still warm, split each roll in half and fill with a "stick" of cheesecake.

CHOCOLATE SPRITS COOKIES
WITH CHOCOLATE ROYALE

These chocolate sprits cookies started out as chocolate jimmy cookies back in the mid-1980s. The cookies had the same form but were a bit sweeter and the tops were dipped in whipped ganache and then in very fine chocolate vermicelli, commonly known as jimmies. I turned them into Chocolate Truffle Cookies in my book *Special Desserts*; then, with a little less sugar and minus the ganache and jimmies, they became Chocolate Butter Cookies. Here, in their latest incarnation, the cookies have been turned into Chocolate Sprits—deeply chocolate, lightly sweet, fragile butter cookies like no other. For special occasions, such as for a New Year's dessert, I like to make a larger cookie and sandwich it with the Chocolate Royale mousse mixture.

SPECIAL EQUIPMENT: TWO PASTRY BAGS FITTED WITH AN $^{11}/_{16}$-INCH STAR TIP (ATECO #27) (YOU CAN USE THE SAME TIP FOR EACH BAG)

MAKE THE CHOCOLATE SPRITS. Sift the flour, cocoa, and baking powder into a bowl. Set aside. Place the unsweetened and bittersweet chocolates in a small microwave-safe bowl and microwave on medium power for 10 seconds, stir, then microwave for another 10 seconds. If the chocolate is not fully melted, microwave for a few 5-second intervals. Set aside.

Place the butter and sugar in the bowl of an electric mixer fitted with the paddle attachment and cream on low speed until just combined. Add the beaten egg, egg yolk, and vanilla and continue to mix until well combined, 1 to 2 minutes more. Remove the bowl from the mixer. Add the melted chocolate and stir in by hand. Add the flour mixture to the butter-sugar mixture in four additions, blending well with a rubber spatula after each addition. The batter will be thick and dark.

Fill a pastry bag fitted with an $^{11}/_{16}$-inch star tip (Ateco #27) one-half to two-thirds full with batter. (The fuller

CHOCOLATE SPRITS

YIELD: 16 ULTRA-LARGE COOKIES

1½ cups (210 grams) all-purpose flour

¼ cup Dutch-processed cocoa

1 teaspoon baking powder

2 ounces unsweetened chocolate, chopped

1 ounce bittersweet chocolate, chopped

8 ounces (2 sticks) unsalted butter, at room temperature

¾ cup sugar

1 lightly beaten egg (50 grams or ¼ cup)

1 egg yolk (20 grams or 1 tablespoon)

1 teaspoon vanilla extract

See Preparation at the top of the next page.

PREPARATION. Position racks in the middle and lower third of the oven and preheat the oven to 275°F. Line two 18 X 13–inch half-sheet or jelly-roll pans or large cookie sheets with parchment paper.

◆ SOMETIMES THE BATTER IS STIFF AND DIFFICULT TO PIPE. IF THAT HAPPENS, GENTLY SQUEEZE THE PASTRY BAG SEVERAL TIMES TO LET THE WARMTH OF YOUR HANDS SOFTEN THE BATTER A BIT.

the bag, the harder it is to pipe.) Pipe out thirty-two 4-inch strips of batter 2 inches apart onto the prepared pans.

Bake the cookies for 15 minutes, rotate the pans from front to back, and bake for at least another 10 minutes, or until the cookies feel firm to the touch, rotating the pan after the second 10 minutes if the cookies need more time in the oven.

Transfer the cookies to racks to cool completely. Use right away or place the cookies in an airtight container and freeze for up to 1 month.

CHOCOLATE ROYALE

YIELD: ABOUT 4 CUPS

6½ ounces bittersweet chocolate, preferably Valrhona Caraibe or Scharffen Berger 70%, chopped

6½ ounces semisweet chocolate, preferably Valrhona Caraque, chopped

3¾ cups heavy cream

MAKE THE CHOCOLATE ROYALE. Combine the bittersweet and semisweet chocolates in a medium bowl and set over a saucepan of barely simmering water, stirring until melted and smooth. Turn off the heat but leave the melted chocolate over the hot water off the heat to keep it very warm.

Whip the cream at medium speed in the bowl of an electric mixer fitted with the whisk attachment for 1 minute, or until the whisk leaves tracks in the cream. The cream should be very lightly whipped (still very loose and liquid). Reserve about one-third of the whipped cream in a small bowl. Quickly pour the remaining cream into the melted chocolate, beating vigorously and constantly by hand with a whisk. This is very important in order to keep the chocolate from forming tiny lumps when it is mixed with the cold cream. When the cream and chocolate are smoothly combined, fold the reserved whipped cream into the chocolate mixture.

ASSEMBLE THE SANDWICHES. Place the flat side of the cookies down on a parchment-lined half-sheet or jelly-roll pan. (This keeps the sandwiches from wobbling.) Using a pastry bag fitted with an $^{11}\!/_{16}$-inch star tip (Ateco #27), pipe a curly circular strip of chocolate royale on the rounded side of one of the sprits, using enough pressure to cover the entire surface. Place a second cookie on top and lightly press down. Repeat with remaining cookies and filling, placing them in a single layer on the half-sheet or jelly-roll pan. Cover and refrigerate. Refrigerated, the cookies will stay fresh for up to 1 week; frozen, for 1 month. Keep in mind that as the cookies sit, they lose their crispness.

ASSEMBLY

32 Chocolate Sprits

4 cups Chocolate Royale

For special occasions, I plate the cookies with fresh raspberry coulis.

MAKE THE COULIS. Place the raspberries in the bowl of a food processor and puree until smooth. Use a rubber spatula to press the raspberries through a fine-mesh sieve set over a small bowl to remove the seeds. Add the framboise, lemon juice, and sugar to taste, stirring until the sugar has dissolved. Refrigerate until ready to serve.

RASPBERRY COULIS

YIELD: 1½ CUPS

2 pints fresh raspberries or

    1 (10-ounce) box frozen, thawed

1 tablespoon framboise (clear raspberry

    brandy)

1 teaspoon freshly squeezed

    lemon juice

Sugar to taste

CREAM CHEESE PUFF

This recipe is based on the classic Greek dessert *bougatsa*, which consists of a custard filling sandwiched between buttery layers of phyllo in a round baking pan. As I find making puff pastry truly satisfying because it really is a culinary feat, I decided to create my own rendition of the dessert using a custard filling laced with citrus zest and a bit of mild goat cheese and my basic puff, to which I have incorporated cream cheese. By turning the puff into squares, I was able to create a kind of cheese sandwich, albeit a very sophisticated one. Serve it, if you feel you need something else, with a quenelle (scoop) of cranberry or other tart-sweet sorbet.

SPECIAL EQUIPMENT: CHEESE SLICER, TRUFFLE SLICER, MANDOLINE, OR
ADJUSTABLE VEGETABLE SLICER • ICE-CREAM MAKER

CUSTARD

YIELD: 4½ CUPS

3 cups heavy cream

¾ cup milk

1 cup plus 1 tablespoon sugar

11 to 12 large egg yolks (225 grams
  or 1 cup)

½ cup plus 2 tablespoons (4 ounces)
  very mild goat cheese, at room
  temperature

2 teaspoons finely grated orange zest

1 teaspoon vanilla extract

PREPARATION. Preheat the oven to
  220°F. Line a 12 X 9 X 1–inch quarter-
  sheet pan with parchment paper.

MAKE THE CUSTARD. Heat the cream and milk with 1 tablespoon sugar until just hot.

Meanwhile, with a whisk beat the egg yolks and ½ cup sugar in a bowl. Bring the egg mixture over to the stove. Gradually whisk several spoonfuls of the hot milk into the egg mixture to temper it, then pour the mixture back into the saucepan and whisk to combine. Remove from the heat and add the goat cheese, the remaining ½ cup sugar, the orange zest, and vanilla. Chill the mixture until luke-warm.

Place the prepared quarter-sheet pan on the upper shelf of the oven. Pour the cream mixture into the pan and bake for about 33 minutes, then turn and bake about 4 more minutes, until the custard is set and doesn't jiggle when shaken. Cool, then chill in the refrigerator until cold, at least 4 hours or up to 24 hours.

MAKE THE PUFF PASTRY. Place the all-purpose and cake flours, salt, and the cubed cream cheese in the bowl of an electric mixer fitted with the paddle attachment. Mix on low speed until well combined, about 3 minutes. Add the water in a slow, continuous stream and mix until the dough is slightly damp, pliable, and gathers into a ball around the paddle attachment. If it looks too dry, use a spoon and slowly add more water, drop by drop. Check the dough with your fingertips. It should be damp but not sticky.

Remove the dough from the bowl and place it on a work surface. With the palm of your hand and your fingertips, pat and stretch the dough into a square; the size is not important. Wrap the dough in plastic wrap and refrigerate until well chilled, about 15 minutes.

PREPARE THE BUTTER. Dust each stick of butter with a little all-purpose flour. Use a cheese slicer, truffle slicer, mandoline, or adjustable vegetable slicer to thinly slice each stick of butter lengthwise into 7 slices. You should end up with 28 thin 5 X 1–inch slices of butter in all. Divide them into 3 groups (1 group will have an additional slice). Place each group on parchment paper, long sides slightly overlapping, and press them together to form three 7¾ X 5–inch "sheets" of butter. Refrigerate for just 15 minutes. It is important for the dough and butter to be at the same consistency or firmness, and most important, the same temperature.

ROLL OUT THE DOUGH. Roll out the chilled dough on a lightly floured work surface to a rectangle about 20 inches long and 8 inches wide. If necessary, sprinkle a little more flour on the work surface to prevent the dough from sticking. Place the dough so a long side is near you. See the diagram on page 312. Using a ruler as a guide, mark the

CREAM CHEESE PUFF PASTRY

YIELD: ENOUGH FOR 12 PUFF SQUARES

3 cups (420 grams) all-purpose flour, sifted

1 cup (120 grams) cake flour, sifted

1 teaspoon salt

2 (3-ounce) packages cream cheese, cut into small cubes and chilled

About ¾ cup chilled water plus ¼ cup to be added as needed

1 pound (4 sticks) butter

1 large egg lightly beaten (on the day you are baking the pastry) with 1 tablespoon water, for egg wash

PREPARATION. Line an 18 X 13–inch half-sheet or jelly-roll pan with parchment paper.

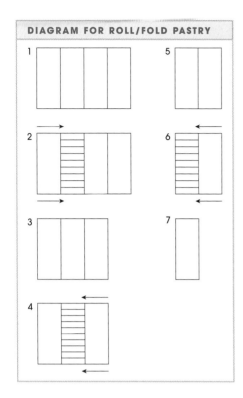

DIAGRAM FOR ROLL/FOLD PASTRY

dough crosswise into fourths without cutting through it (1). Use a pastry brush to brush off any excess flour.

Place one sheet of butter on the section of dough immediately left of center (2). Fold over the section of dough to its left, bringing it toward the center, enclosing the butter in the dough. The dough should now have 3 sections (3). Place the second portion of butter in the middle section (4) and fold the right section of dough over the butter, leaving 2 sections (5). Place the remaining portion of butter on top of the left section of dough (6) and fold the other half over, enclosing all the butter in the dough (7).

With the folded side facing you, roll out the puff with a rolling pin to form a rectangle 18 inches long and 7 inches wide. Brush off any excess flour. Fold the rectangle into thirds to create a rectangle approximately 7 inches long and 6 inches wide. Rotate the dough 90° (a quarter turn).

Place the dough on the prepared pan, wrap it in plastic wrap, and refrigerate for 15 minutes. Repeat the rolling, folding, and chilling of the puff 3 more times.

◆ BE SURE TO BRUSH OFF ANY EXCESS FLOUR WHEN INCORPORATING THE BUTTER INTO THE PUFF AND ALSO WHEN FOLDING THE PUFF. IF ANY EXCESS FLOUR IS LEFT ON THE DOUGH, IT WILL TURN THE DOUGH GRAY AND PREVENT IT FROM STICKING TOGETHER WHEN BAKING. THE END RESULT WILL BE AN UNEVEN RISE BECAUSE THE LAYERS WILL HAVE SEPARATED.

PREPARATION. Preheat the oven to 375°F. Line two 18 X 13–inch half-sheet or jelly-roll pans with parchment paper.

The Following Day

CUT THE DOUGH. Remove the chilled dough from the refrigerator and cut it into 4 equal pieces. Return 3 pieces to the refrigerator. Roll out the dough into a strip about 14 inches in length. The width and thickness are not important at this point. Fold into thirds (this is another turn, and the secret to getting a great even rise) and roll again to a strip about 14 inches long. Fold into thirds again, then roll the dough into a strip about 12 inches long, 4½ inches wide, and ⅓ inch thick. Trim all the edges of the strip and set aside, then cut 3½-inch squares using a trowel, pizza cutter, or knife. Repeat with the remaining 3 pieces, giving each two final turns before cutting into squares. Place the squares on parchment-lined 18 X 13½–inch half-sheet or jelly-roll pans, cover with plastic wrap, and chill for 1 hour. When ready to bake, brush with egg wash and bake for 15 minutes. Rotate the pans, bake for 5 more minutes, then decrease the oven temperature to 325°F and bake for 15 minutes more. Cool on rack.

♦ YOU WILL HAVE ABOUT 15 SQUARES (YIELDING 30 PIECES OF PUFF AFTER CUTTING IN HALF), WHICH IS MORE THAN YOU WILL NEED FOR THIS DESSERT. I LIKE TO HAVE MORE THAN I NEED SO THAT I CAN PICK OUT THE MOST PERFECT SQUARES TO USE. THE EXTRA PUFF SQUARES WILL FREEZE BEAUTIFULLY FOR USE AT ANOTHER TIME, PERHAPS SANDWICHED WITH A COOKED APPLE OR PEAR COMPOTE OR PILED UP WITH FRESH BERRIES.

MAKE THE SORBET. Place the cranberries, 2 cups of the sugar, and 2 cups of the water in a large saucepan and cook over medium heat, stirring occasionally, until the cranberries pop. Transfer to a food processor, add ¾ cup sugar, and puree until smooth. Press the puree through a fine-mesh sieve into a medium bowl. Stir in the remaining 1 cup water, the sherry, and lemon juice. Stir in the remaining ¾ cup sugar, taste, and sweeten more if needed, keeping in mind that the sorbet will lose some of its sweetness when frozen. Cover the bowl and refrigerate until the mixture is cold. Transfer the sorbet mixture to an ice-cream maker and freeze according to the manufacturer's instructions.

CRANBERRY SORBET

YIELD: 1 QUART

2 (12-ounce) bags fresh or frozen
    cranberries
3½ cups sugar
3 cups water
½ cup sherry
1 teaspoon freshly squeezed
    lemon juice

ASSEMBLE THE SANDWICHES. Split each puff square horizontally in half to make 24 pieces of puff. Cut out twenty 2½-inch squares from the chilled custard. (Each sandwich is made up of 3 puff pieces and 2 custard squares.) Place a puff piece on each dessert plate, cut side up, and place 1 custard square on the puff. Cover with a second puff piece, 1 more custard square, then a third puff piece. Dust the top with confectioners' sugar. Serve with a quenelle (scoop) of cranberry sorbet alongside.

ASSEMBLY

12 Cream Cheese Puff Pastry squares
16 Custard squares
Confectioners' sugar
Cranberry Sorbet

♦ YOU CAN USE A 2½-INCH-WIDE SPATULA AS A GUIDE WHEN CUTTING, AND FOR LIFTING UP THE CUSTARD SQUARES AFTER CUTTING.

♦ USE A SMALL KNIFE TO GENTLY SLIDE THE CUSTARD ONTO THE PUFFS.

CREAM-FILLED DUTCH RAISIN ROLLS

MAKES 12 ROLLS

This was a little raisin roll that Mr. Van Tol, the wonderful Dutch chef and pastry cook, made in his Wheaton, Maryland, bakery. Even though it doesn't technically fall under the heading of a sandwich, it just seemed to gravitate to this chapter. I adjusted the recipe ever so slightly by adding just a touch of butter and egg and using dark and golden raisins instead of currants. What I find so fascinating about this bread is that it is a yeast dough that you literally can have ready in about half an hour, due to an unusually large quantity of yeast. These rolls are meant to be eaten right away. And they will be!

RAISIN ROLL DOUGH

YIELD: 12 ROLLS

3½ cups (490 grams) bread flour, sifted

¼ cup whole milk powder

1 teaspoon salt

1 tablespoon sugar

2 tablespoons unsalted butter, at
    room temperature

3 (0.6-ounce) cakes fresh yeast or
    7½ teaspoons active dry yeast
    (a little over 3 envelopes)

1 cup plus 2 tablespoons warm water
    (90°F to 110°F)

1 large egg plus 2 tablespoons
    (50 grams or ¼ cup)

1½ cups mixed golden and dark raisins
    (or currants if you prefer)

PREPARATION. Preheat the oven to
    350°F. Line an 18 X 13–inch half-sheet
    or jelly-roll pan with parchment paper.

MAKE THE DOUGH. Place the bread flour, milk powder, salt, sugar, and butter in the bowl of an electric mixer fitted with the paddle attachment. Place the 3 whole cakes of yeast in the bowl with the flour, making sure the salt doesn't touch the yeast while it sits in the bowl. Add the 1 cup water and the egg and mix on low speed until you have a smooth, elastic dough, about 3 minutes. You may need to add the extra 2 tablespoons of water. (If using dry yeast, add the tablespoon of sugar to the yeast, then add the 1 cup warm water, and stir to dissolve. Let proof for 5 to 10 minutes.)

Add the raisins all at once and increase the mixer speed just a little. You may need to add a few drops of warm water to help mix in the raisins. Be careful not to overmix the dough once the raisins have been added.

◆ WHENEVER YOU MIX YEAST WITH DRY INGREDIENTS THAT INCLUDE SALT, KEEP THE SALT AND YEAST AWAY FROM ONE ANOTHER IN THE BOWL WHILE WAITING TO ADD THE WET INGREDIENTS. THE SALT WILL KILL THE ABILITY OF THE YEAST TO WORK PROPERLY. ONCE THE MIXING BEGINS, THE WARM WATER ACTIVATES THE YEAST, AND THE SALT IS NOT A PROBLEM.

MAKE THE FILLING. Combine all ingredients and stir with a wooden spoon until smooth. Set aside.

◆ I USE A FABULOUS SOFT GOAT CURD THAT IS PRODUCED BY PIPE DREAM FARMS IN PENNSYLVANIA. IT IS SO MILD AND DELICATE THAT WITH JUST A TOUCH OF SUGAR, IT BECOMES THE MOST REFINED OF FILLINGS.

MAKE THE ROLLS. Divide the dough into 12 equal pieces and form each piece into a small ball. Roll out each ball on a lightly floured work surface to a round about 4 inches in diameter and place a tablespoon of the filling in the center. Gather the edges of the dough and, working all around the roll, fold it over slightly in the center to enclose the filling. Pinch all the edges together in the center, then twist the edges closed and press flat. Place, seam side down, on the prepared pan. Cover with plastic wrap and let rise until doubled in size, 20 to 30 minutes. Brush the rolls with the egg wash. Bake for 12 minutes, rotate the pan from front to back, and bake for about 4 more minutes, or until golden brown. These are best eaten warm from the oven.

VARIATION. *Another way to make the rolls is simply to form them into balls by cupping your hand over the dough and rolling them around on a flat surface until smooth and rounded. Bake as before, but when slightly cooled, split and fill with whipped cream, the pastry cream from the Brioche Dome with Fruit (page 224), or with the cheese filling from the Cheese Danish Sucrée (page 100).*

FILLING

YIELD: ENOUGH TO FILL 12 ROLLS

1 (8-ounce) package cream cheese,
    at room temperature

1 cup very mild fresh goat cheese,
    at room temperature

⅓ cup sugar

FILLED RAISIN ROLLS

Raisin Roll Dough
Filling
1 large egg lightly beaten with 1
    tablespoon water, for egg wash

VARIATION. *For Lent, make these rolls as balls and then pipe an X on the top with a simple icing made with confectioners' sugar and milk or water.*

ESPRESSO SUCCÈS
WITH ESPRESSO ICE CREAM

MAKES 12 SANDWICHES

This is a great ice-cream sandwich dessert: a crunchy nutted meringue flavored with powdered espresso sandwiches an intensely flavored coffee ice cream. You can really make this wicked by introducing another flavor of ice cream and a third meringue round to make it a triple-decker. Think about it!

SPECIAL EQUIPMENT: PASTRY BAG FITTED WITH A ½-INCH PLAIN TIP (ATECO #26) •
ICE-CREAM MAKER

ESPRESSO SUCCÈS

YIELD: TWENTY-FOUR 2½-INCH
ROUNDS

1 cup plus 2 tablespoons plus
  1 teaspoon (250 grams) sugar

1⅓ cups (125 grams) finely ground
  almonds (grind 1¾ cups sliced
  almonds)

1½ tablespoons instant espresso
  powder

1 tablespoon cornstarch

4 large egg whites (120 grams or
  ½ cup), at room temperature

PREPARATION. Preheat the oven to
225°F. Line two 18 X 13–inch half-sheet
or jelly-roll pans or two large cookie
sheets with parchment paper. Trace
twenty-four 2½-inch circles about
2 inches apart on the parchment with
a dark pencil, using a pastry cutter as
a guide. Turn the parchment over so
you don't pipe on top of the pencil
lines.

◆ IT IS IMPORTANT TO USE EQUAL AMOUNTS OF SUGAR
AND FINELY GROUND ALMONDS IN THE MERINGUE, SO
I HAVE INCLUDED THE GRAM WEIGHT OF EACH IN PAREN-
THESES. IN FRENCH, THE TERM FOR EQUAL AMOUNTS OF
GRANULATED SUGAR AND GROUND ALMONDS OR ALMOND
FLOUR IS *TANT POUR TANT* (TPT).

MAKE THE SUCCÈS. Place only half of the sugar (½ cup
plus 1 tablespoon plus ½ teaspoon, or 125 grams), the
almonds, espresso powder, and cornstarch in a large bowl.
Mix well with your hands, rubbing the mixture through
the palms of your hands to break up any small lumps. It
will look like coarse almond meal. Set aside.

Place the egg whites in the bowl of an electric mixer
fitted with the whisk attachment and beat on high speed
until foamy and beginning to hold a shape. Gradually add
the remaining sugar (½ cup plus 1 tablespoon plus ½ teaspoon, or 125 grams) in a slow, continuous stream over the
course of 1 or 2 minutes, then beat just until the whites
form stiff, glossy peaks, about 1 minute more. (Do not
overbeat.)

Fold one-quarter of the whites into the almond mixture
to lighten it. Quickly but thoroughly fold in the remaining whites until no traces of whites remain. Fill a pastry

◆ IF YOU LIKE, YOU CAN SUBSTITUTE
ALMOND FLOUR, AVAILABLE IN
SPECIALTY FOOD STORES, FOR
THE FINELY GROUND ALMONDS.

bag fitted with a ½-inch plain tip (Ateco #26) two-thirds full with meringue. Holding the tip about 1 inch from the prepared pan, and letting the meringue drop from the bag, pipe the outline of a circle, then continue to pipe in a spiral until the entire circle is filled in. Pipe the meringue in a slow, continuous stream as if you were writing, being careful not to let the tip drag on the surface of the parchment. Pipe the remaining meringue to make more rounds.

Bake for 15 minutes, rotate the pans front to back, and bake for 15 minutes more. If some meringue remains on the parchment when you lift up a round, bake for 5 more minutes. The meringue rounds should be somewhat colored, firm to the touch, and release easily from the parchment. Let the rounds cool on the pans on cooling racks. If not ready to use, layer between waxed paper or parchment (stacking no more than 2 layers) and store in an airtight container. In the refrigerator, the meringues will remain fresh for up to 1 week, frozen for up to 1 month.

ESPRESSO ICE CREAM

YIELD: 1 QUART

¼ cup instant espresso powder

2 tablespoons dark rum, such as
    Myers's

2 cups heavy cream

2 cups milk

1 cup sugar

1 vanilla bean, split lengthwise

11 to 12 large egg yolks
    (225 grams or 1 liquid cup)

MAKE THE ICE CREAM. Dissolve the espresso powder in the rum in a cup and stir until well combined. If the espresso powder doesn't dissolve easily, stir in a teaspoon or so of hot water. Set aside.

Place the cream, milk, and 2 tablespoons of the sugar in a medium saucepan. Use the back of a knife to scrape out the seeds from the vanilla bean and add the seeds and pod to the pan. Heat the cream mixture over medium-high heat until it rises up the side of the pot and comes to a boil. Immediately remove from the heat.

Meanwhile, beat the egg yolks and the remaining sugar on high speed in the bowl of an electric mixer fitted with the whisk attachment until thick, pale, and the sugar has dissolved.

Bring the bowl with the beaten egg mixture over to the saucepan and gradually whisk about 1 cup of the hot cream mixture into the yolk mixture to temper it, then

PUMPKIN CUSTARD NAPOLEONS WITH PUMPKIN CRÈME ANGLAISE

When you think about it, a Napoleon is nothing more than a fancy pastry sandwich. Here, I've paired a luscious pumpkin custard with puff pastry and sandwiched it high with three pieces of puff and two double layers of custard. It's perfect as is, but it is especially delectable surrounded by a pool of crème anglaise flavored with some cinnamon-scented pumpkin puree.

SPECIAL EQUIPMENT: CHEESE SLICER, TRUFFLE SLICER, MANDOLINE, OR ADJUSTABLE VEGETABLE SLICER

MAKE THE PUFF PASTRY. Place the all-purpose and cake flours, the salt, and the 4 tablespoons of diced butter in the bowl of an electric mixer fitted with the paddle attachment. Mix on low speed until the butter-and-flour mixture is well combined, about 3 minutes. The mixture will look coarse and crumbly. Add the water in a slow, continuous stream and mix until the dough is slightly damp, pliable, and gathers into a ball around the paddle attachment. If it looks too dry, use a spoon and slowly add more water, drop by drop. Touch the dough with your fingertips. It should be damp but not sticky.

With the palm of your hands and your fingertips, pat and stretch the dough on a lightly floured surface into a square; the exact size is not important. Wrap the dough in plastic wrap and refrigerate for 15 minutes. Or skip this step if the room is cool.

PREPARE THE BUTTER. Dust each stick of butter with a little all-purpose flour. Use a cheese slicer, truffle slicer, mandoline, or adjustable vegetable slicer to thinly slice each stick of butter into 7 lengthwise slices. You should end up with 28 thin 5 X 1–inch slices of butter in all. Divide them into 3 groups (1 group will have an additional slice). Place each group on parchment paper, long

PUFF PASTRY

YIELD: 16 SQUARES AND SCRAPS
(2 POUNDS)

3 cups (420 grams) all-purpose flour, sifted

1 cup (120 grams) cake flour, sifted

¼ teaspoon salt

1 pound (4 sticks) cold unsalted butter, chilled plus 4 tablespoons diced and chilled

About ¾ cup chilled water

1 large egg lightly beaten with 1 tablespoon water, for egg wash

1 cup granulated sugar

PREPARATION. Line an 18 X 13–inch half-sheet or jelly-roll pan with parchment paper.

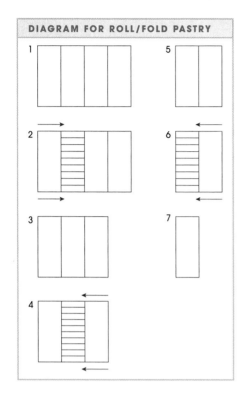

DIAGRAM FOR ROLL/FOLD PASTRY

sides slightly overlapping, and press them together to form three 7¾ X 5–inch "sheets" of butter. Refrigerate for 15 minutes. If the room is cool (below 65°F), no need to refrigerate. It is important for the dough and butter to be at the same consistency or firmness and, most important, the same temperature.

Roll out the chilled dough on a lightly floured surface to a rectangle about 20 inches long and 8 inches wide. See the diagram at left. Use a ruler as a guide to mark the dough crosswise into fourths without cutting all the way through (1). Place one 7¾ X 5–inch sheet of room-temperature butter on the section of dough left of center. Place the butter so it covers that entire section of dough (2). Fold over the section of dough to its left, enclosing the butter in the dough. The dough should now have 3 sections (3). Place a second sheet of butter in the middle section (4) and fold the right section of dough over the butter. You now have 2 sections of dough visible (5). Place the remaining sheet of butter on top of the left section of dough (6) and fold the other half of the dough over (7). The dough should be roughly 9 X 6 inches.

Gently press along the dough at 1-inch intervals to distribute the butter, then rolling forward with a rolling pin, roll out the dough to a rectangle approximately 18 inches long and 7 inches wide. Fold the rectangle into thirds to create a rectangle roughly 7 X 6 inches and rotate it 90°. Use a pastry brush to brush off any excess flour. Place the dough on an 18 X 13–inch half-sheet or jelly-roll pan, cover with plastic wrap, and refrigerate for 15 minutes. The first turn (which is made up of 4 turns) has now been completed. Repeat the rolling, folding, turning, and chilling of the dough 3 more times. The dimensions of the dough are not as important as the smoothness and homogenization of the butter into the dough. The dough should be uniform in color, with no patches of butter showing through.

Place it on the prepared pan and wrap tightly in plastic wrap. Refrigerate for at least 5 hours or overnight.

BAKE THE PUFF PASTRY. Remove the chilled dough and cut it into 4 equal pieces. Return the other pieces of dough to the refrigerator. Roll out the dough into a strip about 14 inches in length. The width and thickness are not important at this point. Fold into thirds (this is another turn, and the secret to getting a great even rise) and roll again to a strip about 14 inches long. Fold into thirds again, then roll the dough into a strip about 14 inches long, 4 inches wide, and ³⁄₁₆ inch thick. Trim all the edges of the strip and set aside, then cut 3½-inch squares using a trowel, pizza cutter, or knife, and place carefully on a parchment-lined pan. Repeat with the remaining 3 pieces, giving each two final turns before cutting into squares. Place the squares on parchment-lined pans, cover with plastic wrap, and chill for 1 hour. When ready to bake, brush the squares with egg wash and sprinkle with sugar. Bake for 15 minutes at 375°F. Rotate pans, bake for 5 more minutes, turn the oven down to 325°F, and bake for 15 minutes longer.

PREPARATION. Position racks in the middle and lower third of the oven. Preheat the oven to 400°F. Line two 18 X 13–inch half-sheet or jelly-roll pans with parchment paper.

MAKE PUMPKIN CUSTARD. Place the pumpkin and eggs in the bowl of an electric mixer fitted with the paddle attachment and mix on low speed until combined. Add all the remaining ingredients and mix until smooth. Place a 12 X 9 X 1–inch quarter-sheet pan on the oven rack and slowly pour the custard into the pan. Bake for 30 minutes, rotate the pan from front to back, and bake for 10 more minutes, or until a cake tester inserted into the center of the custard comes out clean and the custard feels firm to the touch. Cool to room temperature on a rack, then refrigerate for 24 hours.

PUMPKIN CUSTARD

YIELD: ENOUGH FOR 20 SQUARES

1½ (14-ounce) cans (21 ounces) solid-pack pumpkin

4½ large eggs (225 grams or 1 cup)

1⅞ cups heavy cream

⅓ cup plus 1 tablespoon maple syrup

½ cup packed brown sugar

1 tablespoon dark rum, such as Myers's

½ teaspoon vanilla extract

2 teaspoons ground cinnamon

⅛ teaspoon nutmeg

½ teaspoon ground ginger

PREPARATION. Position a rack in the middle of the oven and preheat the oven to 325°F.

CRÈME ANGLAISE

YIELD: 1¾ CUPS

2 cups milk

½ vanilla bean, split lengthwise

5 large egg yolks (100 grams or
  ½ cup)

½ cup sugar

MAKE THE CRÈME ANGLAISE. Place the milk in a heavy medium saucepan. Scrape the vanilla bean in (discard the pod). Bring the milk to a boil over medium-high heat.

Meanwhile, combine the egg yolks and sugar in the bowl of an electric mixer fitted with the whisk attachment. Beat on high speed until very thick and pale, 3 to 4 minutes. The mixture will triple in volume and form a ribbon when dropped from the whisk.

Bring the bowl over to the stove and gradually whisk about 1 cup of the hot milk into the yolk mixture to temper it, then pour the tempered mixture back into the saucepan and stir until it is thick enough to coat a wooden spoon. (Run your finger through the custard on the back of the spoon. The custard is thick enough if the line remains.) Immediately pour the custard through a fine-mesh strainer or China cap into a bowl and whisk to cool. Refrigerate. Refrigerated, the crème anglaise will remain fresh for up to 3 days.

PUMPKIN CRÈME ANGLAISE

YIELD: 2 CUPS

1¾ cups Crème Anglaise

½ cup solid-pack pumpkin

1 tablespoon maple syrup

½ teaspoon ground cinnamon

MAKE THE PUMPKIN CRÈME ANGLAISE. Combine all the ingredients in a bowl and whisk until mixed well.

ASSEMBLY

YIELD: 10 SANDWICHES

Pumpkin Custard

16 Puff Pastry squares

Confectioners' sugar

2 cups Pumpkin Crème Anglaise

ASSEMBLE THE NAPOLEONS. Cut the custard into 2½-inch squares using a 2½-inch-wide spatula as your guide. If your puff has risen high enough, you could slice it horizontally into 3 pieces, but usually it is sliced horizontally in half (to yield 32 pieces; you'll need 30 and will have 2 extra). Place a puff square in the center of each plate. Place a piece of pumpkin custard on the center of the square. Place another square of puff over the pumpkin custard.

Strudel
Dough, 114
Maryland, with Manchego
Cheese and Champagne
Grapes, 114–115
Succès
Dacquoise, Cashew, with
Kumquat Confit and
Chocolate Sorbet,
298–303
Espresso, with Espresso Ice
Cream, 316, 318–319
Sugar
Cinnamon, 231
conversions, 331
Fondant, 168
puff pastry strips, 162, 223
Rum, 154
Sweet Rolls, "The One," with
Cranberry Pear Marm-
alade and Butterscotch
Ice Cream, 266–269
Syrup
crystallization, to prevent,
38
Kirsch, 36
Oranges in, 165
Pear William, 173
Rum, 36, 43

T
Tart(s)
to blind bake, 18
Galette Bretonne, 105
Orange Frangipane,
119–121
oven temperature, 7

Shell, Sweet Pastry Dough,
119–120
Tartlets. *See also* Cups
Candy, 95–97
Cheesecake Soufflé,
233–235
Cheese Danish Sucrée,
98–100
Chess Cakes, 101–104
Coconut Pecan, Toasted,
270–271
Lemon Caramel, 106–108
Lemon Soufflé, 242–244
Lime, 109–113
Mont Blanc, 116–118
Peach Soufflé, with Ginger
Peach Ice Cream,
247–251
Tartlet Shells
Pâte Brisée, 95–96, 101,
103, 233–234, 242–243,
247–248
Sweet Pastry Dough,
98–99, 106–107,
109–110, 116–117,
270–271
Tart or tartlet pans, 18
Terrine, Chocolate, Triple,
210–211
Thai Sticky Rice, Two-Tone,
274–275
That Cookie Plate, 138–143
"The One" Sweet Rolls with
Cranberry Pear
Marmalade and
Butterscotch Ice Cream,
266–269
Thermometers, 19

Timer, kitchen, 8, 18
Toffee
in Candy Tartlet Filling, 97
Chocolate Torte, 57–60
English, 58
Topfendknödel, 252
Torch, butane-heated, 19
Torte(s)
Apricot Orange, 22–26
Chocolate Raspberry, 53–56
Chocolate Toffee, 57–60
Lemon Buttercream, 75–78
Lemon Cream, Meringue
Baskets Filled with a,
189–194
Macaroon Meringue, 79–81
Trifle
Caramel, 155–158
Nesselrode, Rum Raisin,
205, 207
Trowels, for cutting dough,
15, 287
Truffled Brownie Soufflé,
272–273
Truffles, Peanut Butter
Cream, with Shortbread
and Raspberry Gelée,
135–137
Tulip Cups
Amaretto Nougat, 147–148
Grapefruit Soufflé–Filled,
Frozen, 182, 184
Turkish Rice and Rose-Water
Pudding, 212
Turnovers
Fig, with Frozen Armagnac
Sabayon (variation),
122–123